Radical Affections

Essays on the Poetics of O

Miriam Nichols

The University of Alabama Press
Tuscaloosa

Typeface: Minion

∞
The paper on which this book is printed meets the minimum requirements of American National Standard for Information Sciences-Permanence of Paper for Printed Library Materials, ANSI Z39.48-1984.

Library of Congress Cataloging-in-Publication Data

Nichols, Miriam.
Radical affections : essays on the poetics of outside / Miriam Nichols.
p. cm. — (Modern and contemporary poetics)
Includes bibliographical references and index.
ISBN 978-0-8173-1711-9 (cloth : alk. paper) — ISBN 978-0-8173-5621-7 (pbk. : alk. paper) — ISBN 978-0-8173-8441-8 (electronic) 1. American poetry—20th century—History and criticism—Theory, etc. 2. American poetry—21st century—History and criticism—Theory, etc. 3. Experimental poetry—20th century—History and criticism—Theory, etc. 4. Experimental poetry—21st century—History and criticism—Theory, etc. 5. Poetics. 6. Versification. I. Title.
PS325.N53 2010
811′.540932—dc22

2010017170

Radical Affections

In grateful memory of Ellen and Richard Nichols

Contents

Acknowledgments

I am grateful for the hard work of my research assistant, Leif Einarson, who gathered and collated much of the material for this collection of essays, and to the University of the Fraser Valley for providing course releases, without which the project could not have been completed. Peter and Meredith Quartermain were first readers of the Olson essay and I thank them for their comments. I also wish to thank Charles Bernstein and Hank Lazer for encouragements, Stephen Fredman for crucial advice and support, the anonymous readers of this manuscript for their close attention and very helpful suggestions, Chris Dikeakos for the cover image, Dawn Hall for copyediting, and the staff of The University of Alabama Press for seeing the manuscript through the production process.

Abbreviations

Robin Blaser

Fire	*The Fire: Collected Essays*
HF	*The Holy Forest: Collected Poems*
LS	*The Last Supper*

Robert Creeley

CE	*The Collected Essays of Robert Creeley*
CP1	*The Collected Poems of Robert Creeley, 1945–1975*
CP2	*The Collected Poems of Robert Creeley, 1975–2005*
CPr	*The Collected Prose of Robert Creeley*
DB	*A Day Book*
FL	*For Love*
P	*Pieces*
RP	*Was That a Real Poem and Other Essays*
Tales	*Tales Out of School: Selected Interviews*

Robert Duncan

BB	*Bending the Bow*
CG	*Caesar's Gate*
FC	*Fictive Certainties*
GW	*Ground Work: Before the War*
GWII	*Ground Work II: In the Dark*
OF	*Opening of the Field*
RB	*Roots and Branches*
VP	"The Venice Poem"
YAC	*Years as Catches*

Susan Howe

BM	*The Birth-mark*
ET	*Europe of Trusts*
FS	*Frame Structures*
M	*The Midnight*
MED	*My Emily Dickinson*
NM	*Nonconformist's Memorial*
PA	*Pierce-Arrow*
S	*Singularities*
SLT	*Souls of the Labadie Tract*

Charles Olson

CMI	*Call Me Ishmael*
CO and EP	*Charles Olson and Ezra Pound: An Encounter at St. Elizabeths*
CP	*Collected Poems*
CPr	*Collected Prose*
ML	*The Mayan Letters*
MP	*The Maximus Poems*
SV	*The Special View of History*

Jack Spicer

CB	*The Collected Books of Jack Spicer*
House	*The House That Jack Built: The Collected Lectures of Jack Spicer*
MV	*My Vocabulary Did This to Me: The Collected Poetry of Jack Spicer*
ONS	*One Night Stand and Other Poems*

1

Introduction

How to Walk on the Slippery Earth

The six essays gathered here are meant to suggest a contemporary reframing of the New American poetry and its recent cognates. There are many fine readings of the individual poets I mean to engage—Charles Olson, Robert Creeley, Robert Duncan, Jack Spicer, Robin Blaser, and Susan Howe—but the New American line as part of a living countertradition has been colored in its reception not only by generational polemics but also by the theoretical models that academic critics have used to read it. These two frames, the first coming out of poetics essays and the second from academic literary criticism, have coincided to suggest breaks and ruptures where, from another point of view, there is an evolving discourse. The poets themselves have contributed to the argument for rupture, Charles Olson famously in his sweeping claims to break with Western metaphysics, Plato to Melville, his announcement of a paradigm shift post-the-modern, and his critiques of Pound and Williams, his immediate predecessors.[1] In a parallel gesture, language writers distinguished themselves in the 1970s and '80s from their New American predecessors. Marjorie Perloff summarizes the generational gear shifting in her "Language Poetry and the Lyric Subject," where she suggests that the "dismissal of 'voice'" (405) was a key distinguishing mark of language poetry, voice here understood as signaling "self-presence, and authenticity" (406). On the revision of the humanist subject and the rejection of realist epistemology, poets and poststructuralist philosophers converged in the late 1960s and '70s (407). These strategically posed differences—"why should we not also have an original relationship with nature?" Emerson once asked—have the advantage of announcing important shifts in attention and social circumstance, but they can also render certain kinds of poetry unreadable for a time. Poetics essays are expectably polemical: set Wyndham Lewis's *BLAST* ("CURSE the flabby sky that . . . can only drop the season as in a drizzle like a poem by Mr. Robert Bridges" [12]) or Filippo Marinetti's futurist manifestos against Olson's "Human Universe" or Charles Bernstein's finely balanced "Undone Business" and the latter seem positively dainty. Yet in the context of New American studies, the coincidence of generation-next and the popularity of continental theory in North American academies, just as projective verse had begun to attract serious critical attention, had the general effect of cramping the propositional content and methodological potential of it rather than opening it up, and I think for the wrong reasons.

Before I address the wrong reasons, I want to acknowledge some right ones. The 1970s brought a global economic downturn with stagflation opening the door for neoliberal policies that would result in the dismantling of social programs, the accelerated globalization of capital and the intensification of "financialization"—the trade in derivative money products facilitated by the U.S. decision in 1971 to float the dollar.[2] At the same time, the rights movements of the 1960s (civil rights, black power, red power, gay rights, women's rights) had suffered the assassinations of Malcolm X (d. 1965) and Martin Luther King (d. 1968). The Black Panther Party was under internal stress as well as external scrutiny by the FBI, and some of its key members (Eldridge Cleaver, Huey Newton) were either in jail or exile, later to be removed from the Party. The AIM (American Indian Movement) occupation of Wounded Knee in 1973 resulted in a seventy-one-day standoff against U.S. Marshals and FBI agents over which popular support for AIM began to dwindle, although both sides have since claimed victories.[3] Women made some gains, notably with the right to abortion following the Supreme Court case, Roe v. Wade, in 1973, but the women's movement would soon be challenged as narrowly middle class by working women of color who felt that the professional and personal freedoms won by well-educated white women were not meaningful to them.[4] In Harvey Milk, the gay community in San Francisco had the first openly gay politician to hold a civic office (he was appointed city supervisor in San Francisco in 1976), but Milk was assassinated in 1978 and his murderer lightly sentenced. What these few signposts point to is not only an ongoing culture war between progressive and conservative constituencies in the United States but also a deepening divide between the popular will and executive power. The social movements of the 1960s were faltering while the globalizing of national economies exacerbated the perennial gap between the aspirations of progressives and the decision-making process. For serious young poets of the period, the visionary cosmicity and politics of the New Americans seemed too utopian, too out of touch with the social realities of the times.[5] As Adorno warns, art that celebrates creative agency where the real potential for such is limited becomes a travesty. What was needed at the end of the 1960s, it seemed, were poetries oriented to emerging globalization and to the ideology critique of social relations that were increasingly occulted by a changing economy—the elephant in the room.

I do not contest the significance of historical context in shaping poets' perspectives and strategies, but what I hope to show over the course of these six essays is that projective verse offers an adaptable, pragmatic poetic methodology and articulates a range of experience of ongoing significance. I believe it has been too quickly dispatched to the far side of "over" for theoretical reasons—the wrong reasons, in my view. Olson famously appealed to perceptual experience as a means of renewing poetic language and restoring the "familiar"—intimacy with nature and the body—to the human species. In the 1970s and '80s, however, it was precisely perception that fell under Jacques Derrida's poststructuralist critique of phenomenology, a critique that many academics and writers took to be definitive. Over the same period, Jacques Lacan's neo-Freudian psychoanalysis became important in the literary world, and this was another kind of discourse that consigned experience to the imaginary realm of *méconnaisance,* a space to be exposed by the analyst and deconstructed by the aware critic as "always already" mediated by the unconscious and the symbolic order. These philosophies focus on the production of experience through the socialization process: whatever counts for reality at a given moment is to be regarded as a heavily mediated sociolinguistic construct rather than a spontaneous experience. From this perspective, there is no specifiable "outside" to consciousness except the psyche's own internal scission—the "cut" that occurs when infants acquire language and thereby lose to reflexivity and the unconscious their unreflecting, preverbal participation in the flow of physical sensation.[6] In contrast, Olson and others of his company were interested not in how experience is produced, but in how the human species might be redefined and repositioned in relation to planetary life. In the theory decades, however, the vocabulary of projective poetics, steeped as it is in *mythopoesis,* seemed naive in its situating of humanity in a cosmos "outside" the mind when psychology and postmodern philosophies had so firmly moved everything in.

Yet even those theoretical schools less focused on epistemology and more on affect or praxis were dismissive of projective verse. Feminism, although more inclined in its Anglo-American versions to a phenomenology of female consciousness, was quick to pass over work by Old White Men, especially the estrogen-challenged types: from this perspective, a poet like Olson drops off the agenda.[7] The postcolonial turn, prominent in the 1980s and '90s, theorized imperialism and the subaltern positions it produces, and it gave needed voice to muted identities and traditions, but a collateral effect of it was the sidelining of experiences that were not perceived as politically urgent. Homi Bhabha, for example, in *The Location of Culture* (1994), offers the paradigm of agonistic, incompatible cultural worlds that places in permanent question the matter of whose experience is at issue and what exclusions or privileges it entails. This line of questioning can be directed against *anyone's* perspective on the world, and it therefore pushes writers and readers into assuming an ironic position as the only one safe from reproach. The Marxist point of view is equally ungenerous with what Robert Duncan calls the "felt world" because it tends to devalue experience as symptomatic of social relations. Commenting on American literature in his *In Theory* (1992), Aijaz Ahmad argues that the Emersonian line to Pound, Eliot, and Stevens is a conservative one, based on a bourgeois vision of American society as one of petty producers. This vision is blind to a large underclass of slaves, ex-slaves, and indentured laborers not to mention disenfranchised immigrants and aboriginal populations. American romanticism, in Ahmad's view, settles for the oracular and transcendental rather than rooting down in real social relations (51); its radicalism is consequently limited to the idealist tradition that seeks change through the transformation of consciousness rather than by changing the material conditions of life (41).

These various ways of reading cultural works and framing the world offer needed critiques of unsustainable claims to universality and correctives to the blindnesses experience can give rise to because it *is* situated, but none of them offer access to the world as it must be *undergone* as opposed to the world as it can be *known,* and none of them are respectful of particularized experience, especially if it is perceived as occupying ethical low ground. In this context, I find useful a distinction between *undergoing* and *knowing,* which has been made in a number of unrelated philosophical texts such as Eric Havelock's *Preface to Plato* and Giorgio Agamben's *Infancy and History,* the former an important source for Olson.[8] Robin Blaser also calls upon a similar distinction among the various disciplinary discourses in his "Recovery of the Public World," and his polemical essay against positivisms in "Poetry and Positivisms."[9] I have found it again in this description of the Aztec worldview: "Nahua epistemology does *not* pursue goals such as truth for truth's sake, correct description, and accurate representation; nor is it motivated by the question 'What is the (semantic) truth about reality?' Knowing (*tlamatiliztli*) is performative, creative, and participatory, not discursive, passive or theoretical. It is concrete, not abstract; a knowing how, not a knowing that." The principle question of Aztec philosophy is, "How can humans maintain their balance upon the slippery earth?"[10] I quote this description for the striking image and for the succinct distinction between *knowing how* and *know-*

ing that. The difference is the site of a very old methodological quarrel between poetry and philosophy, which I think is reproduced in the theoretical schools I have named above.

In the *Ion,* Socrates predictably humiliates his interlocutor, the rhapsode Ion, by cornering the latter into admitting that his beloved Homer is incompetent to discuss cow herding or making war or charioteering and therefore has no expertise in the matters of which he speaks in *The Iliad.* Ion defends himself unsuccessfully by replying that Homer shows his readers how everybody is doing everything.[11] This exchange between philosopher and rhapsode is stagy and unconvincing both as drama and argument, but it illustrates an essential difference in method between the poet and philosopher. Typically, the Platonic dialogues show that the sophists err in universalizing their partial, interested knowledge of things. The criticism is exactly right, but not in the way that the Socratic intervention implies: it is the inflation of the claim, not the quality of being situated that renders the sophists suspect. *Knowing that* can always reveal exclusions and blindnesses in *knowing how,* but such a critique applies one set of criteria (truth in all possible worlds) to another (how to walk on the slippery earth). Taken alone, each of these methods has limits that result either in the skeptical *disallowing* of perceptual experience—the familiar, Olson would say—or in dangerously inflated claims for local ways of doing things. I am suggesting that contemporary critical theory and its literary critical cognates have for a long time engaged in such disallowings. Given the aim of *knowing that,* theory cannot do otherwise. If I am a relativist, for instance, I *know that* all renderings of reality are perspectival, or if I am a Lacanian, I *know that* my sense of self is structured through misrecognition of my mirror image, or if I am a Marxist I *know that* the field of social relations is fundamentally organized through class. Most importantly, I may very well know these things despite, rather than because of, the way I experience the world. From these critical perspectives, and in an era that has no widely accepted metaphysics, there is no uncontestable ground of which I am aware other than negation (negative dialectics) for which one may still claim the "power to oblige."[12] The issue is not whether theory is needed or not as a corrective to fallibilism. A stick does, after all, look bent in water.[13] Rather, the problem is that during the theory decades, the realm of perceptual experience was effectively eliminated as an element in the intellectual landscape—which is not to say that it ever went away, but rather that it was quietly ceded to agencies like the popular media and the religious right.

In contrast, the poetries I am tracking here give themselves over to *allowings.* Each poet suggests a *Tao,* created through personal traversal of his or her chosen field. By *Tao* I mean nothing more esoteric than "way," "path," "manner," "method," or "unfolding of a life"; a *Tao* suggests a focus on *knowing how* rather than *knowing that*. Olson's "*'istorin*," for instance, is a *method* and it means "finding out for oneself" (*Special View of History* 20). Duncan's "grand collage" of all cultures and all times is his *way* of unfolding a life in poetry. Creeley's autobiographical tracking of himself, Spicer's dictation, and Blaser's "practice of outside" are all particular *modes* of traversing their respective fields of attention. The trail of poems Howe leaves behind as she reads her way through American colonial history records her chosen *path* through time and space. Poetry capitalized, as Duncan has it, is that discourse that accommodates the "felt world," whether or not it is the "correct" one according to the wisdom of the moment. What, then, distinguishes such wanton poetic practice from self-indulgent expression? In my view, it is the poet's ability to present an art precise to his or her earned perspective on the world. A *Tao* is neither true nor false; it is simply more or less efficacious, more or less inspirational, more or less worthy of imitation. Aboriginal cultures retain this idea in the personage of the Elder; earlier European societies had it in the figure of the wise man. Olson champions Hesiodic mapmaking that depends on painstaking attention to a given territory the maker has come to know personally. The heroes of *The Maximus Poems* include such cartographers as Juan de la Cosa, before whom, Olson writes, "nobody / could have / a mappemunde" (*MP* 81). So mapped, a world image is achieved with strenuous effort, "until the sweat / stood out in my eyes," Olson writes (*MP* 202). Spicer's wager is that a world intensely and idiosyncratically articulated will correspond affectively to that of others. Lorca's lemon is Spicer's seaweed, but the two objects evoke parallel emotions. A *Tao* opens certain ranges of experience, as an explorer opens a territory, and these then become available to others who might traverse them differently. As Blaser and Spicer say, the map is not the territory.[14]

My counter to the epistemological reading of projective verse is thus a double one. First, a *Tao* has to be read as a discourse of *knowing how*. It is a category mistake to measure a *Tao* for truth or falsehood as opposed to measuring it for, say, sincerity and rigor. And second, projective verse suggests a strategic, not an essential, division of inside and outside, or as I will call it, figure and ground. This is to say that such polarities are mutually constitutive: there is no priority of one over the other, the perceiver over the perceived. In the context of Olson's work, this point can be made through Alfred North Whitehead and, I think, brought forward into the contemporary through Gilles Deleuze. Blaser makes a parallel argument through Maurice Merleau-Ponty's concept of the chiasm—the idea that perceptual experience comes out of a dynamic interchange between a self and a world that take on specific shape in that event. And Susan Howe brings in another version of the argument in her use of Charles Sanders Peirce in the later work.

A counterreading to the epistemological one, however, is only half the job. The other half has to do with why projective poetics might be worth revisiting now. I have been moved to this project not only out of fondness for the poetries I have selected but also out of a sense of the present need for vocabularies capable of holding onto the "felt world." In *Touching Feeling* (2003), Eve Kosofsky Sedgwick talks about "reparative practices" as opposed to the "paranoia" of critical theories devoted to "demystifying exposure" (144). Her complaint, which I share, is that "reparative motives, once they become explicit, are inadmissible in paranoid theory both because they are about pleasure ('merely aesthetic') and because they are frankly ameliorative ('merely reformist')" (144). As Sedgwick asks, "What makes pleasure and amelioration so 'mere'?" (144). The question resonates with newer theoretical practices now coming to prominence. Over the last decade, much significant work on the affects has been produced by psychologists, philosophers, and literary critics, in the light of which my remark about the need for *more* languages of the "felt" might seem a little Rip Van Winkle-ish. I will distinguish my project from this growing body of newer theory in a moment, but before I do, I need to acknowledge at least two important works in the field that make literature central to their arguments: Martha Nussbaum's magnificent and monumental *Upheavals of Thought: The Intelligence of Emotions* (2001) and Charles Altieri's *Particulars of Rapture: An Aesthetics of the Affects* (2003). Nussbaum combines neo-Stoic philosophy and developmental psychology to argue a eudaimonistic theory of the emotions focused on the individual's efforts to "flourish" (Nussbaum's word) in a world that is largely indifferent to personal needs and wants. Some of the most salient features of her argument for my purposes (I will not pretend to summarize this 714-page work) are her emphasis on the vulnerable, embodied consciousness and her reading of the Western philosophical tradition as in part an effort to escape this vulnerability through pursuit of the transcendental (the ladder of love, ascending from the particular to the general in Plato's *Symposium*, is paradigmatic here). Nussbaum's account of the emotions as rooted in the infantile experience of helplessness (see chapter 4) emphasizes development and hence educability. People and perhaps even whole societies may be persuaded out of self-destructive or antisocial behaviors if they can be educated past beliefs and emotions deriving from infantile fantasies of omnipotence: the impossible desire of the infant to control the world on which he or she so utterly depends. "Flourishing," in other words, implies a quest for the considered life, and Nussbaum ties it to a normative vision of what might constitute individual fulfillment and the good of the social whole in a liberal democracy. In a somewhat better republic, the role of the arts would be to teach and delight.

But teach what, exactly? Altieri's expressivist theory of affect in the arts is directed against the *normative* component in cognitive views of the emotions. Referring to Nussbaum directly, Altieri suggests that she, like other cognitivists, maims the complexity of the arts because she moves too quickly to recruit the play of the affects there for practical reason. By failing to distinguish among sensations, moods, feelings, and emotions, she misses the nuances art can offer, and by linking the emotions to belief, she misses those affects that may have little to do with what agents actually hold to be true about themselves or the world. Alternatively, an expressivist theory directed toward attention to *manner* in the arts can bring out "richer terms than contemporary philosophy seems to possess for clarifying how our enacting of attitudes engages us in gorgeously intricate possibilities for developing and modifying identifications" (111). Identities must be allowed to emerge from such play, even though what emerges might not be desirable if acted out socially. Drawing on Baruch Spinoza's concept of *conatus*,[15] Altieri argues the value of rich, inner dramas in which judgment is immanent to the "conative effects" (143) rather than imposed from without as (moral) law. Intensity (moments of extreme engagement), involvedness (encounters with particularized others), and plasticity (the mental ability to sustain diverse and/or incommensurate affects) are the capacities that Altieri proposes might enable us to "treat what history imposes as if it were a challenge rather than a sentence" (192).

I have stopped a moment over Nussbaum and Altieri because they indicate ways of reading that, were I to venture into the field of psycho-philosophy, might relate to my project as inside to outside. However, I make no professional claims in this area, nor is my primary purpose to mine the poets I have gathered here for exemplary instances of affective play. My focus instead is on the way that poetry may catch and hold our experience of the world as larger than ourselves, and in this my project addresses a territory traditionally held by religion rather than psychology. Psychology's answer to the scandalous historical practice of the world's religions as a means to power or an expression of that "anxiousness to remain personally alive," as Georges Bataille puts it (51), is to find the Other in the depths of the psyche. Freud famously locates religious feeling in the preverbal sensations of infancy, before the child has distinguished itself from the not-me (*Civilization* 15–16). Fast-forward to Nussbaum, and it is to these same infantile archaisms that she attributes our longings for a golden age or environment of "blissful totality" (185) as well as all the subsequent disappointments and efforts after a transcendental return to this impossible state. Alternatively, contemporary philosophy, when it has taken up religion, labors to unname the Other in order to wrest it away from anthropomorphic projection. Consider Derrida's meditation on the *tout autre* (83) in works like *The Gift of Death* (1995) or Emmanuel Lévinas's long effort to establish an Other that cannot be appropriated as an object of knowledge or in any way named: *Totality and Infinity* (1969) is "an essay in *exteriority*" (my emphasis). These treatments of religion as infantile fantasy or wild alterity are necessary correctives to superstition and its horrors, but they do not offer a language for the splendors and terrors of what we *cannot not* experience as outside. What happens to religious *feeling*, in other words, when religion sinks under the weight of our contemporary wisdoms?

Let me illustrate with some snippets from a forum hosted by the Modern Language Association in 2006, in which a number of international scholars were invited to think about the role of the intellectual in the twenty-first century. Their essays point to the difficulty of talking about religious feeling without intellectual embarrassment. Ratna Kapur, commenting on politicized religious fundamentalism (Islam from the perspective of the Euro-American media), says that the "liberal intellectual tradition has produced, justified, and sustained these responses" (26). She also accuses Euro-American intellectuals of disengagement with the politicized religious fundamentalism in their own backyards. Because they fear "a compromise over their agnostic, rational, and universal credentials or the destruction of secularism," she says, "the terrain [of religious discourse] has been completely ceded to the 'God Squad'" (27). Writing for the same forum, Ngugi Wa Thiong'o speaks of free-market ideology as a kind of religious fundamentalism. After World War II, he says, "The market and profit became literally god the father and the son, a religious tendency best captured by Thatcher's TINAism ('There is no alternative'). The World Bank and the International Monetary Fund became temples that decided on the admission and excommunication of members and the World Trade Organization took on the role of economic policeman" (37). On one side of this economic fundamentalism, Thiong'o says, is the Christian Right, on the other, the so-called Islamic terrorists (37). These are the funhouse mirror images that neoliberal leaders have generated of themselves. Julia Kristeva's contribution to the forum centers on the Paris riots of 2005. In this context, she asks if humanism still has a place in a "world caught in the grips of religious wars and technology" (15). As a psychoanalyst she sees the disaffection of French society among disadvantaged youths as a "malady of ideality" (18). This malady "is a matter of needing an ideal that contributes to the construction of the psychic life but that, because it is an absolute exigency, can easily turn itself into its opposite: disappointment, boredom, depression, or even destructive rage, vandalism, and all the imaginable variants of nihilism that are but appeals to the ideal" (18). Unlike earlier European societies or some premodern cultures, Kristeva says, "modern society is entirely incapable of understanding the structuring need of ideality. This incapacity is even more blatant in France's current crisis, which involves adolescents of North and West African descent who are victims of social misery, discrimination, and broken families in which authority is no longer valued" (19). Kristeva calls on parents, teachers, and intellectuals to address the "prereligious need to believe, constitutive of the psychic life with and for that other" (20)—and do this without ceding territory to religionists.

These excerpts are only a few among others that analyze politicized religious fundamentalisms and neoliberal agendas as having triumphed at least partly by an appeal to feelings and emotions that have been traditionally channeled by religion. The ongoing strength of the Christian Right in the United States and Islamic fundamentalism in the Middle East suggest that religious feeling cannot be dismissed as merely false consciousness. What is at issue is more durable, and I suggest it does not yield to skepticism because this latter, however *right* it may be, cannot dislodge the human need for perceptual, value-laded relationships with earth and sky, plants and animals, fire and water, as well as kin and strangers of its own species. What seems to me of ongoing significance for the humanities is everyone's need for affective relations with the world as larger-than-me. Richard Wollheim, in his book *On the Emotions* (1999), defines belief in a way that is relevant to my argument. The function of belief, he says, is to provide the creature with a picture of the world it inhabits that can stand up to available evidence (13). Desire supplies objectives, and the emotions orientation. Belief maps, desire targets, and the emotions color the world (15).

Lest the word *belief* in the context of my comments on religion seem too fraught a term, I would like to bring in Kwame Anthony Appiah's comparison of cultural practices in his *Cosmopolitanism* (2006). The concept "*akyiwadee,*" from his native Asante, Appiah explains, pertains to how one should act given a certain clan membership:

> The *akyiwadee* is . . . thickly enmeshed in all sorts of customs and factual beliefs (not the least the existence of irascible ancestors and shrine gods), and one response to such alien values is just to dismiss them as

> primitive and irrational. But if that is what they are, then the primitive and the irrational are pervasive here, too. Indeed, the affect, the sense of repugnance, that underlies *akyiwadee* is surely universal: that's one reason it's not difficult to grasp. Many Americans eat pigs but won't eat cats. It would be hard to make the case that cats are, say, dirtier or more intelligent than pigs. [...]
>
> Psychologists . . . think that this capacity for disgust is a fundamental human trait, one that evolved in us because distinguishing between what you will and will not eat is an important cognitive task for an omnivorous species like our own. . . . But that capacity for disgust, like all our natural capacities, can be built on by culture. (53–54)

What seems *merely* belief from one cultural angle is reasonable behavior from another—and belief, understood not as superstition but as a world map made up of cultural position plus the best empirical information available is a traditional territory of poetry. In *The Special View of History,* Olson writes that "belief . . . is the same thing as methodology" (42); it pertains to *how* everyone is doing everything, as Ion once tried to tell Socrates. In his arguments contra relativism and positivism in *Cosmopolitanism,* Appiah suggests that the human dramas unfolded by "folktales, drama, opera, novels, short stories; biographies, histories, ethnographies; fiction or nonfiction; painting, music, sculpture, and dance" (30) offer a way into a more generous kind of reason than that required for logical consistency. My disgust over eating cat may not match yours over pig, but we share the capacity for understanding the feeling of disgust and we can therefore converse. In a world of colliding cultures, conflicting interests, and great need, poetries that insist on our *emplacedness* on this planet and the potential shareability of our experiences offer the possibility of conversation. Poetry by itself cannot solve social problems, nor should it be asked to, but it can generate imaginative alternatives to narrow ways of being in the world that promote exploitation over exploration or blind convention over creativity.

I have not yet addressed the question of why these poets and not others that might as easily be read into the projective constellation. Apart from personal preference, the complementarity and mutual influence among the six poets I have chosen make it easy to pursue the story of an evolving poetics. Through long association and voluminous correspondence, Olson and Creeley have emerged as the two major architects of Black Mountain postmodernism. Duncan, Spicer, and Blaser are similarly situated in relation to the Berkeley Renaissance. Students at the University of California, Berkeley, in the late

1940s, they grew up together as poets and contributed significantly to a West Coast postmodernism then in the making. Susan Howe acknowledges Olson, Creeley, and Duncan as significant predecessors, and her work is intimately related to theirs as a radicalization of field poetics. However, my selection of writers is also pointedly calculated to bring forward poetries that deal specifically with cosmicity, including problems raised by working in this area. I am going to make an unsupportable generalization: the 1950s and '60s represent the last moment in recent cultural history when a serious poet could write the word *cosmos* without irony or quotation marks and expect serious intellectual attention. Already I can imagine libraries of nature-themed poetry stacked up in protest, but nonetheless I think my claim useful if taken as I intend it—as a rough distinction between practices of the outside versus those of the inside. I do not mean to imply that spiritual venturing has ever disappeared from poetry. Hank Lazer's *Lyric and Spirit* (2008) for instance, brings forward a wide range of post-1960s experimental poetries that explore the sacred in ways that are neither sentimental nor allegorical (see Lazer's readings of John Taggart, Norman Fischer, Paul Naylor, Jake Berry, Nathaniel Mackey, George Oppen, and Harryette Mullen, among others). In a poem Lazer quotes, Harryette Mullen speaks of "the other side of far" (65), and Lazer makes a good case for "far" as an enduring locus for poetry. But spiritual questing does not have the outward turn of cosmicity—it sits more comfortably as inside work—while it is the cartography of the outside that I wish to track.

The six essays that make up this book are interrelated, but they can be read independently, too. Sometimes this means some overlapping of material for which I ask the reader's indulgence. Olson I take to be the architect of a new kind of landscape and the ground-maker of his generation. A significant extension of Pound's culture-scapes, Olson's *polis* is much more complex than the dirt beneath his feet in Gloucester, Massachusetts; it is rather a matrix of many geohistorical layers or regions of being that endlessly unfurl throughout *The Maximus Poems.*[16] This *field*—Olson calls it "kosmos," I will call it chaosmicity after Gilles Deleuze—includes the interior "scapes"[17] of dream, myth, meditation, and emotion, folded into the outer world in Möbius fashion. Humanity, Olson contends, has lost sight of its place on this cosmic ground. Like Ahab in Herman Melville's *Moby-Dick,* the latter a seminal text for Olson, modern humanity rages against the fact that it is one species among many, that it does not own itself from the ground up, and that it is situated among othernesses that it does not master. As an alternative to Ahab's world, Olson brings forward a version of the "human universe" that is alive, resistant to appropriation and yet imaged. His special care is to re-situate humanity in a richly complex environment that can be related *to,* as figure to ground. In the Olson essay that opens this study, I argue that the figure-ground relationship is religious in the deep sense of the term, not as dogma or supernaturalism, but as the experience of being placed in something larger than the self.

Complementing Olson's work on space is Creeley's on time. In an interview with William Spanos (1978), he defines the "occasion" in Mallarméan terms, as a *coup de dès,* suggesting that a throw of the dice is "that which resolves all other possibilities" (Creeley, *Tales* 129). Yet each *coup* not only decides the past and future but frees them as well, because it is *only* the moment that is so decided. Hence the Mallarméan wisdom, that a throw of the dice will never abolish chance. This is Creeley's *amor fati:* limit becomes the ground of possibility. Creeley's effort to stay in the moment parallels Olson's resituating of humanity in space and for similar reasons. The temporal equivalent to losing a relationship with the familiar is to lose the moment one occupies to atemporal ways of thinking that appropriate the past and future to present will and wish. Ahabian man inhabits time as he inhabits space: by attempting to foreclose possibilities other than those immediately his own. Creeley's alternative is to situate an act in its occasion, thus to enact a temporal *Tao* that minimizes the overdetermination of the future. Creeley would revoke the *mortgaging* of the future to present interests.

Robert Duncan is often associated with *mythopoesis* and the religious imagery of the occult, but in my view he is the most thoroughly secular of these six poets and hence an essential contrast to the others. What he brings to field poetics is a cultural archive that includes the possible as well as the actual, the irreal, and phantasmatic; the camp, the trivial, and the wicked as well as the profound. Locating himself in the realm of Poetry capitalized, Duncan focuses on the range and quality of the feeling that can be brought into the poem—the permission Poetry gives to the "felt world" rather than the actual undergoing of an event or the authenticity of the emotion. Duncan's art is essentially theatrical and inner oriented. Self-described as a derivative poet, Duncan "impersonates" the voices he brings into the poem or the styles of other poets, and this has created a stumbling block for some of his peers and readers because he is willing to stage events and emotions that he has not undergone or that do not belong to current beliefs about the world. Hence Olson's admonition in "Against Wisdom as Such," an essay against the detached mind. As well there is the Blaser-Duncan controversy over the translation of Gérard de Nerval's *Les chimères,* the Duncan-Levertov quarrel, and more recently, Nathaniel Mackey's readings of the Vietnam poems, all centered on Duncan's apparent detachment from actuality. Yet Duncan is able to bring forward emotions and behaviors that challenge the predictability of human affairs, and this is an important solicitation of what counts for real. Anarchic and inconvenient, his poetry knocks at the boundaries of what it means to be human.

On the matter of authenticity, Spicer is symmetrically opposed to Duncan, and the two can usefully be read in juxtaposition, as can Olson and Creeley—for the dimensionality each gives the other. Fiercely lyrical and demanding of emotional intensity, Spicer aims to write the "absolutely temporary" and singular. But how to make language index the outsideness of, say, the body? Spicer's games—magic, mysticism, surrealism, dictation—are strategies in his effort to make poems that can house the singularity of experience as it must be lived. Trained in the same linguistics that would later support poststructuralist and Lacanian analysis (Ferdinand Saussure, Edward Sapir), Spicer offers an *affective* treatment of a linguist's version of language that is entirely contrary in purpose to the theoretical one as well as to Duncan's view of language as the living Word. He is not primarily concerned with showing how perception can be reduced to *méconnaissance* but rather in finding ways to make words point to the flesh that suffers their imprint. Feeling is something specific to living creatures: words do not experience things; bodies do. So Spicer reproaches Duncan with crass facility: "Get those words out of your mouth and into your heart. If there isn't / A God don't believe in Him" (*CB* 253). This lyric intensity contrasts with Duncan's expansive, archival vision. It is not the *imago mundi* or "grand collage" that engages Spicer, but private passion. Above all, he is a poet of undergoings. More so than the others, he dramatizes the nonidentity between knowing how and knowing that, between the body that experiences and the sociolinguistic systems that give it articulation. His emphasis on the *aloneness* of the "felt world" as it must be personally undergone is an admonition to Duncan and a qualification of Olson's large public voice.

Robin Blaser is the dark horse in this group. A late bloomer in relation to the others, he studied Olson, Creeley, Duncan, and Spicer while developing his own poetics, and he pulls his readings of them through his studies in postmodern philosophies, offering a vigorous defense of perceptual experience in essays and poems written over the 1970s and '80s. This head-on confrontation with skepticism through readings in Maurice Merleau-Ponty and Michel Foucault is a major contribution to a contemporary reprise of field poetics because it responds to that challenge where Blaser's peers could not or did not. Spicer died in 1965; Olson in 1970; Duncan in 1987. However, Blaser's major contribution to projective poetics is his lifelong meditation on the sacred. His fascination with prereligious experience before it has congealed into myth or ritual and his searching out of the perceptual content of concepts like "soul" or "God" or "sacred language" is a radicalization of Olson's treatment of myth. Unlike Olson who retains the mythic names and narratives in *The Maximus Poems,* Blaser unnames the sacred back to an imagined beginning in primordial astonishment at the eventfulness of life. His secularized sacred is living relational thought, the core of which is Blaser's recognition that "form is alive" (*Fire* 36). With the hardening of experience into dogma and dogma into institutionalized religion, Blaser suggests, the sacred disappears into anthropomorphisms that do not honor the world as form, but rather express it as an extension of the human will.

Blaser's early serials begin with a strong sense of "cultural orphanhood"—the bereavement of a lapsed-Catholic boy over the loss of a beloved world image and its providing homeliness—but as *The Holy Forest* unfolds, the orphan and exile morphs into the nomad poet. It remains for Susan Howe to work out a poetics that includes the problems as well as the liberations of a contemporary nomadology. As Olson extended Pound's Mediterranean and Chinese territories to include the history of the earth as well as that of the human species back to the Pleistocene, so Howe, like Blaser, expands Olson's field to include diverging perspectives and trajectories. It is Howe, though, who confronts the problem of negotiating worlds in collision. Famously, she has said that she seeks peace as a poet, that she would rescue the forgotten voices of history from obscurity, but the implications of a world with no transcendental realm in which contradiction might be resolved is that lions will *either* go hungry *or* lambs will die. In other words, there is no way that the potentiality of all things to persist in themselves and unfold to their utmost can be actualized and there is no innocent position in the field. In the weeping women and exiles that wander through her poems, and in her treatment of Melville's Bartleby and Billy Budd, Howe confronts the *cannibal* cosmos—the cruelty of becoming, or world-as-process—for which there is no remedy. American exceptionalism, from John Winthrop's "City on a Hill" ("Modell" 19) to Olson's *polis,* finds its logical end in the city of irrational dimensions of Howe's *Pythagorean Silence,* the only kind of impossible space in which peace is imaginable. But Howe's introduction of Charles Sanders Peirce in the later poems suggests a possible response to this aporia—not a solution, but a way to go on. For Peirce, cosmic complexity and evolutionary potential trump individual satisfaction. What he calls evolutionary love or "agapism" invites the individual to embrace a slowly evolving human universe through cooperative action. (In Spicer and Howe, then, the two faces of love: eros and agape.) From Peirce comes a directive toward the *disciplined* imagination—the imagination in tension with a resisting world—and a pragmaticist *Tao.*

There are several through-lines in the six essays. The most important of these is the thought of the "outside," although it will come in various forms with the different poets. I have taken the term from Robin Blaser's essay on Jack Spicer, "The Practice of Outside," where Blaser uses it to describe Spicer's claim to a dictated poetry. Spicer, he says, presents us with a "*re-opened language* [that] lets the unknown, the Other, the outside in again as a voice in the language" (*Fire* 117–18, original emphasis). Spicerian dictation "pushes us into a polarity and experienced dialectic with something other than ourselves" (117). If I read Blaser rightly, the "outside" is not about unmediated experience but about the recognition that life and language exceed us. Individual speakers, poets among them, enter language as one enters the wide world. On this point, Blaser might seem to be in accord with Jacques Lacan, whom he quotes in "The Stadium of the Mirror," an essay predating "The Practice of Outside." But unlike Lacan or poststructuralist theorists, Blaser focuses on an "*experienced* dialectic" (my emphasis), not on the ways that experience is produced through the acquisition of language and the socialization process. From Blaser's perspective, individuals *cannot not* experience the world as polar, just as poets *cannot not* experience their medium as exceeding their intentions. As Blaser argues in his later essays, the erasure of this experienced polarity through an overly strenuous insistence on the mechanisms that mediate it (the determinations of the unconscious, the structure of language as it manifests in every individual utterance) is a kind of positivism.[18] In other words, Blaser is more interested in *knowing how* than in *knowing that,* in what can be thought and accomplished in a poetic discourse rather than in submitting that discourse to a skepticism that might better be quietly assumed as a place from which to move on rather than turned into the main event. In the essays that follow, I generalize Blaser's "practice of outside" to describe the "experienced dialectic" between the human *actor* and his or her *ground* in the world. It is the polarity of the relationship that establishes the *Tao,* because it is that polarizing that does the work of situating humanity in a relation of nonidentity to the larger empirico-transcendental continuum.

To flesh out this concept of the "outside," I have turned to philosophies that are alternative to the poststructuralist. In transcendental empiricism I have found a vocabulary that seems to me promising for field poetics, and I have borrowed from this philosophical line, particularly in setting up this study in the Olson essay. In that essay, where I lay out my theoretical frame, I identify transcendental empiricism as derivative of a group of related philosophies that include the writings of Alfred North Whitehead and Gilles Deleuze. Whitehead was a seminal philosopher for Olson and hence for this gathering of poets. I draw on Whitehead, Deleuze, and their cognates for a description of an ontology that also serves as a poetic method and an ethos in the work of the poets I am tracking. As the name suggests, transcendental empiricism borrows elements both from classical empiricism and its contrary, Immanuel Kant's transcendental philosophy. Classical empiricism locates the source of human knowing in sense perception, but it does not offer a very satisfactory account of how general categories derive from perceptual experience. Kant's transcendental philosophy challenges the primacy of perception by locating the structuring mechanisms of it in certain a priori categories of the mind. Yet Kant does not say how specific minds acquire their specificity, given that the categories are common to all. Transcendental empiricism combines elements from these two contrasting philosophies in order to address this question of the particular. It is a philosophy that acknowledges an a priori field in the role that genetic and social determinations play in the potential for form of all organisms (human and nonhuman), but it also emphasizes the formative effects of the ways in which individual organisms respond to their givens. As an ontology, transcendental empiricism suggests that the major factors contributing to the particularity of organisms are genetic and social structure, the contingencies of an environment and the affect-laden, individual responses an organism makes to these givens. As an ethos, this philosophy emphasizes the interdependence of different life forms and the situatedness of humanity in the continuum of life. As poetic method, it suggests that creative agency lies in the poet's ability to work with what he or she has inherited (personal ability, social history, cultural environment) as well as to respond to immediate circumstances and contingencies. Between figure and ground, in other words, is an "experienced dialectic," and that liminal zone is the site of creativity.

As may be obvious by now, another through-line in these essays is my formalist focus on method and strategy. I read this constellation of poets as laying methodological groundwork and proposing broadly existential *conditions* rather than directly addressing the sociality of their times or thematizing nature. (I here give notice that I am not heading toward theme-based nature poetry, although if the poetics of deep ecology mean attention to the living othernesses of the planet, I may get there by other means.) Sociality is always embedded in a work, and the resisting reader can certainly return the poetry to its historical moment (read it as symptom). My focus, however, is on the prospective possibilities: what might these poetries enable us to think and feel rather than what of their times they failed to account for. And finally, I suggest that these poetries present the world modalized through love—that love is another way of understanding and describing a practice of outside. By this I mean something more precise than the softness of the word might suggest. In an essay on the Vancouver artist Christos Dikeakos, Robin Blaser turns to Octavio Paz's writings on technology to distinguish between the world constructed by technology as an obstacle to be overcome and that constructed by the artist as a shape to be articulated. Blaser adds that "there is nothing wrong with technology *per se*, as long as we know that it is merely an extension of the 'blind self'—the human will without intelligence of its own violence" ("Mind Canaries," *Fire* 236). An important Olson image of the world as shape is Venus rising ("The Ring of"); the Creeley parallel may well be the rooms of detritus created by the artist Dieter Rot.[19] Rot would live in a room until it became uninhabitable, seal it off, and move on to the next. As wildly different as are these images, they both hold the world as shape. Hence my title, "Radical Affections." The root or radical of the "felt world" is Eros. Love is that mode of seeing that evokes the world in its "beautifuls and uglies" (Blaser's phrase), and it is the deep ground of religious feeling. I have chosen the term *affection* to accommodate love as I describe it here, but also because it is a general term I want for this study of the *conditions* that allow for affectability rather than a taxonomy of the affects. Love, cosmicity, the practice of outside—these are abject words that I would tenderly lift from the dark side of theory. How they sit in the work of these six poets and why they should matter is the subject of this book.

2

Charles Olson

Architect of Place

Introduction

On 4 January 1946, Charles Olson began a series of visits to Ezra Pound at St. Elizabeths Hospital for the criminally insane in Washington. Pound was friendless and in disgrace after his pro-Fascist radio broadcasts from Rapallo, Italy. Olson had resigned from government service on 18 May 1944 (Charters 9) and was on the threshold of a new life in poetry. "The K," written in February 1945, announces his decision to leave public life and declares a shift in cultural exigencies from "romans, hippocrats and christians" to the beginnings of a geopoetics in the "salts and minerals of the earth" (*CP* 14). Yet Pound was still the master maker, and the record of their meeting, now collected and edited by Catherine Seelye in *Charles Olson and Ezra Pound: An Encounter at St. Elizabeths* (Olson 1975), shows both the respect Olson had for Pound's work and his repulsion at the older poet's unrepentant anti-Semitism. Because I wish to present Olson's poetics as a particular response to the modern problematizing of representation and the search for value terms, I open my study of Olson with this encounter to recall the particular conditions under which this problematic came to seem exigent after the war. The notes Seelye has published reveal two related differences between the postwar world that was just beginning and the *avant guerre* of Pound.

The first of these comes from a change in perception of global populations. The populace of nation states has always been diverse, but growth in numbers, combined with the trauma of the holocaust as it drove home the effects of ethnic hatred, brought the new heterogeneous "masses" onto the world stage. Hence in Olson's view, Pound suffered a "200 year *political lag*" in his wish to retrieve "a small nation of farmers and city-state politicians, all

Boston Brahmin and Philadelphia brick" (*CO and EP* 53, original emphasis). "It comes to this," Olson says,

> a rejection of the single most important fact of the last 100 years, the most important human fact between Newton and the Atomic Bomb—the sudden multiple increase of the earth's population, the coming into existence of the MASSES. Pound and his kind want to ignore them. They try to lock them out. But they swarm at the windows in such numbers they black out the light and the air. And in their little place Pound and his kind suffocate, their fear turns to hate. And their hate breeds death. They want to kill. And, organized by Hitler and Mussolini, they do kill—millions. But the breeding goes on. And with it such social and political change as they shall not understand. (53)

Here, the *close* world—what Olson would later call the "familiar"—means not just a return to the material ground of personhood but also the crowding of the earth and a destruction of the social commons Pound called the "tribe," "Boston Brahmin and Philadelphia brick," the arbiters of shareable reality and of the national *vertu.* When the heterogeneous masses make their way into public view, it is no longer possible to represent them without facing up to the repressive homogeneity representation implies, whether it be paternal as in Pound's Confucian cantos, or openly aggressive as in the Nazi example. Pound and Eliot had responded to this social and political state of affairs by retreating respectively to political and religious conservativism. But the war had made the former position untenable and philosophical skepticism had made the latter an unlikely choice for a forward poet like Olson, bent on a big poetry capable of facing up to history.

Skepticism, in fact, was a modernist behest, and it reinforced postwar social change. In 1944, Carl Jung published in German the first edition of *Psychology and Alchemy,* a book that would later play a significant role in the second and third volumes of Olson's *Maximus Poems.* In his introduction, Jung argues that the urgent task of psychology is to relocate the affective territory of the world's religions in the psyche (*Psychology and Alchemy* 17) rather than in the sky. But whether one follows Jung in this move or not, the old metaphysics had lost its legitimizing efficacy. In her essay, "Thinking in Dark Times" (2006), Julia Kristeva phrases it this way: "Nietzsche and Heidegger warned us: modern man has undergone 'the absence of a sensible and supersensible world with the *power to oblige*'" (16, my emphasis). From the contemporary side of the postmodern, it is possible to read the unfolding of the period between the postwar and the millennium as a series of ongoing challenges to that power—to the vestiges of the old metaphysics, to discriminations of gender, race, class, and sex, and to new mutations of economic imperialism under technological revolution.

The second condition that was of immediate interest to Olson concerns the place of the poet. It follows from the loss of metaphysical certitude and clear social identity that the poet cannot tell the tale of the tribe. Without recourse to metaphysical or political authority and without an identifiable audience, "der weg stirbt" (the way dies) as Olson would write in "Human Universe" (*CPr* 160). Certainly the epistolary form of *Maximus* and Olson's rhetorical address to his "fellow citizens" in poems as well as in letters to the Gloucester newspaper reach for a broad readership of "citizens" who "care / for what kind of world / they [choose] to / live in" (*MP* 408). Olson also tried out the voice of the rhapsode ("I sd, 'Rhapsodia . . ." [*MP* 72]) and the bard (the "stopping / of the battle" in "Maximus to Gloucester, Letter 27 [withheld]." Yet as "Letter 5," addressed to Vincent Ferrini suggests, finding a meeting point with even one other differently minded interlocutor is not so easy: "It is no use," Olson writes finally, "There is no place we can meet. / You have left Gloucester" (*MP* 29). The question of representation that Olson recognized as problematic in Pound and that became an initiating impetus for his own project as well as those of his peers is exemplified in this confrontation with Ferrini. The two poets continue to occupy the same physical space, but they do so in ways that exclude each other to the point where Olson can say that Ferrini has "left Gloucester." So the problem becomes one of method: how to create value terms; how to argue measure without a rigid yardstick; how to create common places where a couple of poets might meet.

Olson's response to this problematic of the early postmodern has been discussed now for four decades. Briefly, Olson combines a polemic against the Western metaphysical tradition (the "universe of discourse" from Plato to Melville) with an insistence on the necessity of reimagining humanity in its relationships with nature and its own sociality. *The Special View of History* (1956), coming after "Projective Verse" (1950) and "Human Universe" (1951) is a mature presentation of poetics and one of Olson's most schematic; it will be a primary focus of this study. In *The Special View,* Olson elaborates on the trios that are to replace the "three drags" of Chaos, Man, and Void, which he says "[hang] over the present from the old cosmology" (48).

The new vocabulary, announced in the "Letter to Elaine Feinstein," will be topos, typos, tropos, homologous, as Don Byrd explicates over the course of his *Charles Olson's Maximus,* to space, fact, stance; genetics, morphology, world; and mother, father, son. Before I turn to these triads and Olson's new "human universe," I need to digress to set up the critical context in which I wish to position them. In his own terms, Olson proposed an alternative to the "universe of discourse" in a poetics of perception that resituates the human species inside a cosmos that is not entirely human. But perception, as many critical theorists and philosophers of the later twentieth century understood it (see my introduction), is mediated by a host of linguistic and social determinations, and Olson thus seems to open himself to the reproach of misplaced concreteness or epistemological naïveté. If I am to propose an alternative to this skeptical reading of Olson's work, an approach I believe cramps the real possibilities of projective verse and maims Olson's project as well as that of other New Americans, I will need to address this question of the concrete. I will begin this chapter, then, with a brief review of the extant criticism followed by a sketch of a theoretical frame I think serves Olson's poetry better than do those I have named above. Once I have this frame in place, I will use it to re-read Olson's triad: topos, typos, and tropos.

So, to the criticism. From the mid-1970s to the early 1980s a number of extended studies of Olson have explored the terms of the major essays and poems. Apart from George Butterick's marvels of editorial attention are the readings that have explication as their aim. I have in mind Paul Christensen (*Call Him Ishmael,* 1975), Sherman Paul (*Olson's Push,* 1978), Robert Von Hallberg (*Charles Olson: The Scholar's Art,* 1978), and Don Byrd (*Charles Olson's Maximus,* 1980). Other works take up specific elements of Olson's poetry or his affinities with other writers: Ann Charters (*Olson/Melville: A Study in Affinity,* 1968) offers a study of Olson and Melville through a reading of *Call Me Ishmael;* Charles Stein (*The Secret of the Black Chrysanthemum,* 1978; rpt. 1987) explores Olson's use of Carl Jung. Paul Bové (*Destructive Poetics,* 1980) and Judith Halden-Sullivan (*The Topology of Being: The Poetics of Charles Olson,* 1991) offer Heideggerian readings of Olson's poetics, as does William Spanos in "Charles Olson and Negative Capability: A Phenomenological Interpretation," an important essay in *Contemporary Literature* (1980). Ralph Maud has published a number of scholarly works and editions: *Charles Olson's Reading: A Biography* (1996); *Charles Olson and Frances Boldereff: A Modern Correspondence* (1999), edited with Sharon Thesen; and *Selected Letters* (2000). Maud is also the author of a detailed exegesis of "The Kingfishers" (*What Does Not Change,* 1997) and a biography, *Charles Olson at the Harbour* (2007). Stephen Fredman (*The Grounding of American Poetry,* 1993), in his study of Olson and Thoreau, explicates the relationship between Olson's projective poetics and American transcendentalism.

The purpose of this partial list is to identify a certain pattern in Olson criticism. As Bové shows, Olson was mostly ignored by the New Critics because his poems do not fit the model of the well-wrought urn (217–34). Then, around the end of the 1970s, there is a flurry of extended interpretations that presumably would have been initiated shortly after Olson's death in 1970. Insofar as these are favorable, they reflect the perceived viability of phenomenology and structuralism at that point.[1] Alongside and after this initial effort, there are studies of various particularized aspects of Olson's work that do not depend on literary critical currents, and there is an ongoing trickle of essays, including important noticings by the language writers who followed Olson generationally. Charles Bernstein's "Undone Business" (*Content's Dream* 1986) is a carefully balanced assessment of *The Maximus Poems*, and Barrett Watten has usefully historicized New American and language poetry in pieces like "The Turn to Language and the 1960s" (*Critical Inquiry* 2002), "Radical Particularity, Critical Regionalism, and the Resistance to Globalization" (Web) and his paper, "Late Capitalism and Language Writing" (2008). There are also postings on various Olson Web sites.[2] Nonetheless, contemporary interest is modest, particularly among academic readers, and, more importantly, the method and stance Olson labored to articulate—that which in his work he presented as prospective—has been largely consigned to literary history. Von Hallberg's *Charles Olson: The Scholar's Art* and Andrew Ross's assessment of Olson in *The Failure of Modernism* (1986) suggest why. These not-so-sanguine readers are disturbed by what seems to be naive epistemology in Olson's insistence on lived experience as the necessary foundation for a new symbolization of value. Von Hallberg, despite many engaged readings of the poems and essays, sees in Olson's method the same weakness that Olson identified in Pound: if a poet cannot access cultural representation as a given, and if he or she rejects tradition as vigorously as did Olson, then that poet needs a means by which to select his or her material and to make value judgments. Olson accuses Pound of holding the cantos together with the "beak of his ego" (*ML* 27), and Von Hallberg sees the same problem in Olson. Olson, he suggests, presents the universe of Maximus as exemplary, but in fact it is merely a personal perspective on historical materials arbitrarily selected. Moreover, Olson inverts Whitehead when he asserts that man is the image of order in *The Special View:* "Order for Whitehead is process, and process begins with the atom, not with man," Von Hallberg says (115).

Andrew Ross is another resisting reader. As the date of his book might suggest, his thesis is theoretically oriented to the poststructuralism of the 1980s. To follow his argument, the "failure" to which his title refers consists of a modernist misunderstanding of the difference between subjectivity and subjectivism. Attempting to rid his poetry of subjectivity, Olson, like other moderns, naively assumes that a vocabulary and syntax oriented to speech and sense perception rather than the rhetorical tradition can yield a world that is more authentic and less mediated than that of the tradition he rejects. Whitehead is also to be faulted for simply standing Kant on his head (106): he supposes a world of objective entities without accounting for the relations between them. Ann Charters had made a similar observation much earlier. She writes in *Olson/Melville: A Study in Affinity* that "the difficulty with Olson's philosophy is not with the basic comprehensiveness of topography as a realization of what *is;* the difficulty lies with the limitation of topology as a philosophy in itself. Although the universe is discernible to human beings through their sense receptors, human perception is more complex than a series of sensory reactions to a collection of things" (19, original emphasis). And Charles Stein, one of Olson's most sympathetic and sensitive readers, wonders at the end of his study on Olson and Jung whether "what we have been calling 'the concrete' should come under suspicion" (162).

This critical picture is beginning to change. Shahar Bram has published a favorable study of Olson and Whitehead in *Charles Olson and Alfred North Whitehead* (2004), and Henry Ferrini's bio-documentary film, *Polis Is This* (ca. 2007) has achieved wide circulation in educational institutions and public broadcasting venues. Anne Dewey's *Beyond Maximus* (2007)[3] takes up the social dimension of Black Mountain field theory and new studies are on the way, notably from Rachel Blau DuPlessis' series with Palgrave, Modern and Contemporary Poetry and Poetics. As I write this, Carla Billitteri's *Language and the Renewal of Society in Whitman, Laura (Riding) Jackson, and Charles Olson* (2009) has just been released from Palgrave, and Andrew Mossin's *Male, Subjectivity and Poetic Form,* another treatment of Black Mountain poetics, is announced for 2010. In these new studies, the question of Olson's concrecity has dropped out of urgency not because of effective counterargument but because the critical discourse has moved on. However, my focus is specifically on the outside and the cosmic, and for this reason it is specifically that concrecity I need to address. In the remainder of this introductory section, I will sketch out a theoretical frame that I hope may render more artful the construction of Olson's empiricism. To do this, I will need the help of Olson's philosophical cognates.

Before and after Whitehead

Classically defined, empiricism is "the theory according to which knowledge not only begins with experience but is derived from it" (Deleuze, *Empiricism and Subjectivity* 107). This seems to parallel what Olson's earlier critics have in mind when they reproach him with misplaced concreteness. The perception of an array of objects, as Charters suggests, does not well account for the mechanisms of perception that mediate the way we perceive the relations between those objects. This critique of empiricism ultimately derives from Immanuel Kant. In the Kantian tradition, the things of perception are organized by a priori categories of understanding. These are categories that are innate to the human mind and are not derived from experience. In Kant's account of the transcendental field, the categories are quantity (unity, plurality, totality); quality (reality, negation, limitation); relation (substance, cause, community); and modality (possibility, existence, necessity). Modern philosophies or psychologies that emphasize the mediating role of language or sexuality on perception are indebted to Kant, however much they revise Kant's arguments.

In a discussion of Gilles Deleuze's revisionary empiricism, Levi Bryant (*Difference and Givenness* 2008) argues the limitations of both Kantian transcendentalism and the classical-empirical traditions. If empiricism cannot well explain how perception might move from the particular (an array of objects) to the general (categories, relations, abstractions), Kant's transcendental idealism does not offer a very satisfying account of how general a priori categories common to everyone might produce very particularized individuals.[4] Transcendental empiricism is a philosophical practice that addresses the question of how the *particular* givens we perceive come to be given so particularly. It is thus a practice that must account not just for perception in general but also for the unique perceptions of actual persons. In other words, it has to account for the new. It is "transcendental" because it takes perception as deriving from a preconscious field of syntheses; it is "empirical" because it grounds the development of individuals in actual events that take place in particular topographies (I will have more to say of topography in the next section of this essay).

The term *transcendental empiricism* is associated with the philosophy of Deleuze, but I want to emphasize that it derives from a family of philosophies, notably for my purposes those of Baruch Spinoza (1632–1677), Gottfried Wilhelm Leibniz (1646–1716), and Alfred North Whitehead (1861–1947). What these philosophers share (I am speaking at a high level of generality) is the view that the world we perceive as an array of disparate things is actually a Whole, variously inflected by the entities that compose it. Subjects and objects are local *modes* of the universe rather than essentially discrete entities, and as such they are tied to the cosmic totality as figures on a ground to which they are neither separate nor identical. So for example, Spinoza, rejecting René Descartes' dualistic account of spirit and matter, proposes a monistic cosmos in which individual entities are modes of a single universal substance for which God and Nature are simply two synonymous names. Responding to what he saw as certain problems in Spinoza's worldview, Leibniz altered the picture in his *Monadology:* his cosmos is composed of atom-like metaphysical units ("monads") that constitute the irreducible building blocks of the Whole. The monads are eternal, indecomposable, individual, un-interacting and, unlike Spinoza's modes, discrete. But each reflects, like a mirror, the entire universe, and through a principle of preestablished harmony they add up to a single, unified world. Leibniz directly informs Whitehead, and Whitehead, of course, was Olson's philosopher of choice. Deleuze I take to be the primary contemporary practitioner from this kinship group of philosophers, and he is important to my study because he offers concepts and tropes that help to clarify tendencies in Olson's work and that of other New Americans that are not so easy to discuss in Whiteheadian language.[5] Deleuze brings forward the implications of transcendental empiricism for contemporary thought.

So what are the features of this philosophical practice as it might bear on Olson's work? I will sketch out Whitehead's account of the genesis of organisms first before turning to Deleuze because these are the two philosophers I will call on most frequently in my reading of Olson. Whitehead calls the minims or building blocks of his cosmos "actual entities." These are monad-like units (Whitehead here acknowledges his debt to Leibniz[6]) that Whitehead describes as "drops of experience, complex and interdependent" rather than discrete entities (*Process and Reality* 28, I.II.I). Despite the terminology, process, rather than substance, is primary and unending. Like atoms that combine to form molecules and finally organisms, the actual entities serve as data for one another in an ongoing creative process of recombination. Whitehead terms the manner in which the actual entities relate to one another "prehension": entities select or reject others to create aggregates or communities that manifest as the organisms we perceive. "Concrescence" is Whitehead's name for the process by which entities form communities and take on perceivable shape. This process involves "rules" for combination that represent the *real* potential for the formation of organisms as opposed to the pure potential of, say, time and space as the abstract coordinates of all existents. Whitehead introduces the "eternal objects" of his cosmology as the virtual, genetic components of creation that "ingress" (his term) into groups of entities as these prehend one another. Again, the word "object" is misleading: "eternal objects" might better be compared to DNA than to thinglike substances.

If we step back a bit from Whitehead's very specialized language, what we have is an account of creativity—Whitehead would say the creative advance of the world—that is *genetic* and *affective.* Another way to think about transcendental empiricism is as a kind of genetic structuralism that can be used to describe both the physical and social-psychological components of an organism. The genetic component limits the possibilities for combination as DNA limits the biological potential for the form of living organisms; the affective component leaves room for novelty because organisms partly shape themselves by responding to their circumstances. Whitehead maintains that every actual entity in the universe has a determinate relationship with every other one, but the relationship with the remote is likely to be that of negative prehension—that is, the remote would not be selected as a component of the entity's becoming. Actual entities take on specific form through their *encounters* (this is the empirical element) as well as their genetic heritages. The resulting organism is (1) the product of chance (the contingencies of circumstance); (2) genetic determination (physiological and social evolution); and (3) affection (predilection, response to circumstance). Agency lies in the capacity to respond—and notice that the further the entity can extend its prehensive range the greater the chances for complex interaction and hence development. Olson takes this Whiteheadian account of creativity as a model for his poetic method.

I turn now to Deleuze's ontology. It is complex and still very much under debate so I have to qualify my sketch of it as a simplification, oriented toward my discussion of Olson. Deleuze writes of two planes: the plane of consistence is one of relatively unstructured matter moving at different velocities; "molecules or particles borne away by fluxes" or "hecceities" ("thisnesses"), which he glosses as "an hour, a day, a season, a climate, one or several years—a degree of heat, an intensity, very difference intensities which combine" (qtd. in Bryant, *Difference and Givenness* 177). The other plane is one of genetic order: it is "a plane of transcendence, a kind of design, in the mind of man or in the mind of a god, even when it is accorded a maximum of immanence by plunging it into the depths of Nature, or of the Unconscious" (qtd. in Bryant, *Difference and Givenness* 176). Deleuze, like Whitehead, accounts for the derivation of more structure from less structure through a series of passive, unconscious syntheses. These syntheses produce all entities, including the human. Habit is one such series and it derives from the development of organisms through repetition and difference; from moment to moment as entities react to their environments, they repeat themselves, but always with a difference because they must carry along their past, each moment is different because it has to include the moment that just was. As Deleuze writes in *Difference and Repetition,* "What organism is not made of elements and cases of repetition, of contemplated and contracted water, nitrogen, carbon, chlorides and sulphates, thereby intertwining all the habits of which it is composed?" (75). Organisms are *historic routes* (Deleuze and Whitehead converge on this point); they behave more like verbs than nouns and they carry their history with them. At the cellular level, as well as at that of consciousness, habit produces nature, and for Deleuze it is the "paradox of habit" that also accounts for novelty. Ian Buchanan (*Deleuzism: A Metacommentary* 2000) helps me summarize: habit, he writes, "is formed by degrees (therefore it is constituted not constitutive), and, at the same time, it is a principle of nature (therefore it is constitutive not constituted)" (86). Or as Deleuze says in *Difference and Repetition,* "difference lies between two repetitions" (76). This account of generation parallels that of Whitehead; the organisms we perceive as well as the perceptual apparatus with which we perceive them are the products of many syntheses. Some of these go back to the origin of the species, some to the social history of the organism (its group context), and some take place from moment to moment. As Levi Bryant writes, the organism "creates its own form of being in unfolding. The adult oak is a unique actualization of the seed that cannot be comprehended without comprehending the history of the oak tree. In actualizing itself, the seed as potentiality finds itself in a problematic field defined by its relation to other elements in its environment as well as its genetic history. The uniqueness of the oak is the manner in which the oak tree lives as a solution to other elements in its environment" (105). The acorn derives from a transcendental field—"the idea of time independent of subjects and objects and out of which subjects and objects are generated," as Bryant glosses it (181)—and this field, on the one hand, is a priori to any given acorn. On the other hand, the oak develops a posteriori as a unique response to contingent circumstances; it develops through its encounters and this is its empirical dimension.

Deleuze's empiricism is thus "transcendental" in that the relations that order sense experience are external to immediate sense events, but these relations evolve from temporal syntheses across the "horizontal" physical plane rather than "vertically," from an ideal dimension—or better, what we experience dualistically as the physical and mental orders of the real arise out of the same processes. Unlike Kant, Deleuze does not argue a difference in kind between intuition (sense perception) and cognition (conceptual understanding); rather, these functions differ in degree. And unlike Kant, he does not make primary the cogito (the categories of the understanding) because the cogito is produced through repetition and difference. A self generated temporally as continuous becoming is always already divided into a past that is not fully retrievable and a future that is to come. "I" is already an Other and its apparent identity is an effect of suturing over the differences between repetitions. Bryant spells out the implications of this ontology.

Kant, he says, proposed a Copernican revolution in philosophy by suggesting that "we cease trying to determine how mind conforms to objects, and instead seek to determine how objects conform to mind" (181). Deleuze proposes a second revolution[7] when he asserts the primacy of difference over the identity of the mind, thus displacing the mind from the center of the world in its becomings. Deleuze's emphasis on becoming over being implies that dualisms of matter and mind, content and form, the sensible and the intelligible, the finite and infinite are better understood as zones of varying intensity in an ever-evolving, heterogeneous continuum stretching from a grain of sand to the depths of space—what Bryant terms the "Open Whole" (198) and Deleuze the "chaosmos"—rather than discrete orders of the real. Set in motion and open to diverging series of becomings, cosmos becomes chaosmos.

To summarize: the elements of transcendental empiricism that I want to bring forward as my theoretical frame in this reading of Olson are as follows. First, genetic history (physiological and social evolution), plus chance and circumstance, plus individual, affect-driven decisions and responses are the principle elements of the process through which unique entities come to be. As a historic route of occasions, the organism includes not only a personal past but also a genetic past (its entire evolutionary history) and the pure past (the structure of time as such) as its transcendental ground. It follows that the new and the particular come about through the way the organism selects and redeploys the past it inherits as it responds to the contingencies of its environment; it is a route, a path—a *Tao*—rather than a static substance. Second, it follows that the organism, as an inflection of, or processive differentiation from its empirico-transcendental ground, is neither separate from nor reducible to its temporal histories and spatial coordinates. For Olson, and I think for other New Americans as well, the individual is similarly conceivable as a figure on a ground. Third, traditional dualisms are better treated as polarities in a dynamic field of becomings. Subjects and objects are not primary but rather synthetic derivatives of this field; in Whitehead's terms, they are positions that actual entities occupy in relation to one another rather than ontologically distinct categories. (An actual entity may be a subject for itself, but it is a datum for other actual entities—a "superject" in Whitehead's language.) Robin Blaser's phrase, "the practice of outside," resonates with this philosophy of becoming; the human subject is chiasmatically entangled in and open to a dynamic "outside" that it cannot gather up as an object of knowledge. Like the Möbius twist, the inside turns into the outside and outside to the inside.

Now back to poetry. What I am claiming for Olson is not a systematic philosophical argument, nor do I intend to treat his poetry and poetics as mere instantiations of Whitehead's "philosophy of organism" or anticipations of Deleuze's thought. Poetry cannot be so simply translated into other kinds of discourse. Olson's orientation is not toward the detailed working out of a philosophical practice or an account of how perception is produced, but rather toward the possibilities of the Whiteheadian chaosmos as a model for poetic creativity and a new way to imagine the human way of being in the world. Whitman thought that it was the poet's task to find a pathway between reality and the soul ("Preface," *Leaves* 11, in *Whitman: Selected by Robert Creeley*); Olson translates this task as a search for a worldview and stance that might issue in a new ethos. In the terms I have suggested in my introduction, he is interested in *knowing how* rather than in *knowing that.* In the sections of this essay that follow, I will argue that Olson *assumed* a more complex view of perception than that with which he has been credited. But *assume* is the operative term; it was not to his purpose to produce a full account of sense experience any more than it was to practice the kind of nuclear physics that he also used as a source and inspiration for his poetry. Rather, as a scholar-poet, he adapted the most promising materials he could lay hands on in order to construct an *imago mundi.* From Whitehead he took the basic contours of transcendental empiricism as I have summarized them: an account of creation that emphasizes chance and circumstance, genetic determination, and individual agency through creative response to these givens. This account of creativity then serves him as ontology, ethos, and poetic method: it becomes a *Tao.* As early as "The Kingfishers," Olson writes: "not accumulation but change, the feed-back proves, the feed-back is the law" ("Kingfishers," *CP* 89). "Feed-back," the redeployment of what has been received, is the source of novelty and agency.[8] The question of concretism with which I began this digression leads to questions of how the relations between things are to be conceptualized and how creative agency is to be plucked from chance and circumstance as well as skepticism. Olson explicates the question more particularly through topos, typos, and tropos. I turn to this triad now.

Topos: "the geography of it"

> The basic trio wld seem to be: topos/typos/tropos, 3 in 1. The blow hits here, and me, "bent" as born and of sd one's own decisions for better or worse (allowing clearly, by Jesus Christ, that you do love or go down). *CPr* 252

This comment from the "Letter to Elaine Feinstein" is typical Olson—elliptical and breathless—but in this case, a dead-on description of the structure of his oeuvre. Over the next three sections of this essay, I will take the triad one term at a time, beginning now with topos. The Greek word is *place* but it combines suggestively with other suffixes. Topography, for instance, is literally the writing of place (*topos* + *graphia*). Topology, from the Greek *topologia* means the "study of place," or more literally, the *logos* (words, reasonings) of place. Topology is now a branch of mathematics, which has as its object the study of the properties of space as these are preserved under deformation. Homeomorphisms, or functions that stretch space, are of particular interest. Notably, the Möbius strip is an object of topological interest, and it is a superb metaphor for the relationship between the inner, psychic life and outer reality as Olson conceives it.[9] In the chapter titled "Topology" in *The Special View of History,* Olson associates topology with cosmology. The chapter explicates cosmic becoming as Whiteheadian process—a process that does indeed suggest the Möbius twisting of the inner and outer surfaces of things through mutual prehension. By leaving topos untranslated, Olson can allow the various possibilities of the term to accumulate and resonate. Certainly *The Maximus Poems* include topographies of Olson's homeplace in Gloucester, Massachusetts, but the writing of place is a more complex matter than geographical description. As it unfolds through the poems and essays, the human universe turns out to be layered and dynamic, a series of moving *scapes*[10] or regions of attention that are geological, historical, and mythical as much as they are landscapes.

Call Me Ishmael (1947), Olson's innovative reading of Herman Melville's *Moby-Dick,* is a first major statement and an important step in the construction of topos as human universe. "SPACE [is] the central fact to man born in America, from Folsom cave to now" (*CMI* 17), Olson says by way of an opening. Writ large in this book, it is "what lies under" (16). At the deep physical level, as Albert Einstein demonstrated to Olson's generation, all things do flow and no thing is discrete. But like the sea that ultimately engulfs Melville's Ishmael, the universe of the atom is not entirely human. The prologue of *Ishmael,* titled "First Fact," tells the story of the wreck of the *Essex* at sea in 1819 (the year of Melville's birth), and of the extremity of the sailors as they resorted to cannibalism. Olson recounts this grim tale as dry reportage, concluding with remarks about some of the survivors who lived to old age and went on to other adventures at sea. "First Fact" descends to the bottom physical nature of things where the human being becomes meat before it returns to the dance of the atoms. I pair this story of the *Essex* with Olson's later essay, "The Resistance" (1953), which refers to the reduction of persons in fascist concentration camps "to so much fat for soap, superphosphate for soil, fillings and shoes for sale" (*CPr* 174). It is an implication of early twentieth-century physics that morphological difference does not mean ontological privilege: soap, shoes, and persons all reduce to material flows. When "what lies under" rises up, personhood is overwhelmed; as in "The Resistance," this is "the way of the beast, of man and the Beast" (*CPr* 174).

I am suggesting that "SPACE," as Olson begins to conceive of it in *Ishmael,* is his plane of consistence. In "Equal, that is, to the Real Itself," an essay adjunctive to *Call Me Ishmael,* Olson associates the "inertial structure of the world" (*CPr* 125) with Einsteinian relativity and what he calls the "metrical" with Riemannian geometry. The German mathematician Bernhard Riemann, he says in this essay, "distinguished two kinds of manifold, the discrete (which would be the old system, and it includes discourse, language as it had been since Socrates) and, what he took to be more true, the continuous" (*CPr* 120). Riemannian topology is "smooth" space, in Deleuze and Félix Guattari's more recent and ample description of it. This is space that is "infinite, open, and unlimited in every direction; it has neither top nor bottom nor center; it does not assign fixed and mobile elements but rather distributes a continuous variation" (*Thousand Plateaus* 475–76). In *Ishmael,* Olson gives image to this kind of space in his description of the sea, the American plains (*CMI* 114), and the descent of the body to its physical quanta. As he comments in "Equal, that is," "the structures of the real are flexible, quanta do dissolve into vibrations, all does flow, and yet is there, to be made permanent, if the means are equal" (*CPr* 125).

The human longing for permanence—for relief from the terrible insecurity of being in the world, to recall Nussbaum's *Upheavals of Thought*—is part of the emotional content of the old metaphysics for which Olson seeks new form. The story of the *Pequod,* Melville's famous whaling ship, complements that of the *Essex:* if the *Essex* points to "what lies under" the human universe, the *Pequod* draws attention to what rides over it. A microcosm of American diversity as Melville writes of it in *Moby-Dick,* the crew of the *Pequod* is nevertheless brought under the yoke of a single will. As the bodies of the *Essex* men become meat and so sink back into the flow of life, in a symmetrically opposite event, the very different minds of the *Pequod*'s crew are brought to serve one megalomaniacal Idea: Ahab's obsession with the conquest of the white whale. These two stories reveal the outer limits, or switch points of the human universe where humanity becomes something else, either by returning to matter-energy or projecting itself as God. At this latter pole of topos is Ahabian man. Ahab is the last representative of the old metaphysics in Olson's view, and this is because Ahab, like the traditional, anthropomorphic Christian deity, acknowledges no ground other than his own will. The contrast here is Ishmael as he bobs on the sea, clutching a coffin. In this image, Ishmael is a small figure, a temporary hang-up, on a vast flowing ground. ("I set out now / in a box upon the sea," Olson would write in the second volume of *Maximus* [*MP* 373].) Ahab, however, acknowledges no such ground because he cannot see past his own projected image. As Olson narrates it, "Ahab's rage and hate is scaled like Satan's, the largest enemy of the Father man has imagined" (*CMI* 34–35). This rage against the Father says in mythical terms that Ahab would deny his own origin in something other than himself, his own *placement* in the continuum of life. In condensed form, this is Olson's critique of traditional humanism: humanity loses the familiar—itself and its ground—by projecting itself so large that it obscures the ground it stands on with its own shadow. Hence Olson's effort to repossess humanity of "the *lost* dimension of space" (*CMI* 85, my emphasis) will later be rewritten in *The Special View of History* as a recovery of the familiar.

Between these two poles of topos (dance of the atoms and fixed Idea), as topos is threaded through Ahabian man, is the Pacific as sweatshop. Olson writes: "Consider whaling as FRONTIER, and INDUSTRY. A product wanted, men got it: big business" (*CMI* 23). In this section of *Ishmael,* Olson inserts "document" to describe the extreme conditions of the whaling industry: "lowest wages and miserable working conditions" resulting in massive desertions (21). Whaling, he writes, was exemplary of the development of America: "The first men in it, the leaders, explorers, were WORKERS. The money and the glory came later, on top with the exploiters. And the force went down, stayed where it always does, at the underpaid bottom" (21). This section of *Ishmael* suggests that the instrumentalization of nature and of human lives is of a piece with Ahab's appropriation of space, his ground of origin. The seizing of the unbound and infinite for the purposes of the finite mind is another aspect of Ahab's Satanism, his evil.[11] The sweatshop is its manifestation in the *ordinary* world of human affairs. Ahab's seizure of the physical bodies of the crew—his commanding of them—is parallel to his binding of their wildly diverse minds into the unity of one, obsessive Thought. In the *extraordinary* realm of survival, cannibalism is the extreme of instrumentalization, although the *Essex* story is not about evil but about the loss of personhood in survival behaviors that lead to the switch point where Hunger returns the person to the unstable plane of consistence—to indifference and death. Cannibalism may be a metaphor for Ahab's megalomania, but megalomania is not a valid descriptor of cannibalism at the border of the human.

These extremes of topos haunt the poems and essays as Olson works toward the articulation of a human universe *between* these poles that might stand as an alternative to Ahab's world. In the last two volumes of *Maximus,* the myth of Tyr and Fenrir, the wolf of Norse mythology, recurs in various forms. As the myth goes, the people complain to the god Tyr of Fenrir's ravagings. Tyr tricks the wolf into letting himself be bound with a magical thread made of imaginary things, but he has to place his hand in the wolf's mouth as surety before Fenrir will submit. The wolf is restrained, but Tyr loses his hand. In this myth, Dog and God appear together in the image—the Dog tied to the God by a thread, the God caught by the Dog who bites his hand. I suggest that this image figures the bottom and top of topos respectively—the borders of the human universe. The Dog, of which Fenrir is one manifestation, recurs throughout volumes 2 and 3 of *Maximus,* where he becomes a key trope in Olson's elaboration of process. The "salavarating" Dog (*MP* 206) is a figure of appetition, the flow of becomings. He is thus both destructive from the perspective of human individuals who wish to persist in their being and yet he is generative as well—a creator-destroyer figure in Olson's *mythopoesis.* In its bottom nature, appetition is "Mouth-Without-The-World-To-Eat" or simply χάος, the flow of energy and matter (*MP* 547). Yet the saliva in the mouth of the Dog suggesting anticipation—what Whitehead would call the "'intuition of probability' for the origin of novelity"[12]—is already a marker of the temporal syntheses that govern the generation of living forms (anticipation implies retention of the past as memory and expectation of a future). Olson recognized very early that temporal process, if it is taken as primary, implies the destruction of stable identities and problematizes agency. In a notebook entry dated September 1946, he writes:

> So that reality is never allowed to keep its own form & ease, either the reality of people or of things, but distends, until the strain is beyond yourself, things, or other people. . . . The static, therefore, becomes a condition of things you crave, to stop the draining out of everyone & everything into infinite. . . . Mortality is. If you once admit it, then life is the matter, and all you can do with it is, together, to make certain things out of it with one another. I am a landscape, and not a man. What you have so far had are the seasons, as a landscape does. It changes, is acted on, does not itself act. The lack of act is the upshot of the strain between the static and infinity, which wipes out the mortal. Your sense of space, and generalized emotion . . . is the only fruit which one can pluck from such a sense of the world and the race. . . . And you will not express that satisfactorily until you see it as a pain, and no glory. Glory is also a generalization. (Olson, "Enniscorthy")

In this passage in which Olson talks to himself, the "static" is a longed-for condition the poet is beginning to see as unsustainable. But rather than rejoice at the release from the old Ahabian metaphysics ("reality is never allowed to keep its own form & ease"), Olson registers the pain of lost identity ("a pain, and no glory"). The poet *is* landscape; that "fact" seems first to have registered as a devastating loss of self, a flattening out of vertical man into horizontal space that Olson then had to "ride" through his studies in Whitehead and comparative mythology back into active agency. In the mythopoeic language of *The Maximus Poems,* Hunger is first, before the world. Earth follows, and then Tartaros "*within* her." Typhon is born of Earth and Tartaros through the mediation of Love (547). The difference between Typhon, who is a figure of desire, and Hunger, a figure of raw becoming, is that Typhon has the Earth for mother. When Mouth *has* a world, it can become creative energy, grounded on "the 'mother' / rock." The switch point between Mouth and Typhon is the appearance of the world, and with it, the possibility of love. I will come back to this point.

Between the extreme poles of topos, between God and Dog, are the many layers or scapes of a chaosmos that can be actualized and experienced, and these are what Olson goes on to develop in his mature essays and *The Maximus Poems.* In a letter to Frances Boldereff dated Friday, 14 July 1950, Olson urges the idea that the human universe is composed of *planes* that include nature and the archaic. "Another fallacy of history," he writes is "to assume that, because on the plane of sociology, conditions change, that therefore nature's forces in man and woman, on man and woman, change. What I am getting at is, that, because there was nomadism, then agriculture, then the urban, now the machine, that, therefore all previous formularies are old-hat, no use. What is missed in this is, that there are other planes, conspicuously, the persistence of identical and common intimate conditions which do not so change. And the marks of sociology stay permanent" (420). This passage presages the manner in which Olson develops his account of the human universe in *The Special View of History.*

I turn now to *The Special View,* where Olson offers one of his most detailed and schematic accounts of how space becomes place so that it neither swallows the human figure in the nonhuman world of sheer becoming nor causes the Otherness of the world to disappear into the shadow of a humanity that has made itself God. The purpose of this section of my commentary is to show that Olson understood the world of perceivable phenomena to be organized through a series of evolutionary, passive syntheses, parallel to the creative process as both Whitehead and Deleuze understand it. The empirico-transcendental ground of life is both other to consciousness (because consciousness is produced through an irreversible, evolutionary biosocial route) and continuous with it (because the human creature, like all other organisms, dies into the becoming of the world without ontological privilege). Olson proposes the human species as a figure held in an irreducible relationship of nonidentity with its sustaining ground: we are figures-on-a-ground, neither separate from nor identical to the chaosmos in which we find ourselves.

The Special View is a dense, elliptical series of lectures, and I have to emphasize again that the arguments are not systematic. However, they sketch out a view of perception resonant with transcendental empiricism and considerably more complex than the realism Olson is sometimes thought to hold. The content of these lectures divides into two intimately related facets of the real as we can come by it: the *process* by which it is produced and the nature of the *determinations* that bear on it. The process can be summarized fairly quickly. Olson presents it in three different ways: through Whitehead's account of concrescence; through *mythopoesis;* and through the Hegelian dialectic, modified by Keats's negative capability. He summarizes Whiteheadian process as follows: "I return now to the three stages of feeling. The first is that in which the multiples of anything crowd in on the individual; the second is that most individual stage when he or she seeks to impose his or her own order of order on the multiples; and the third is the stage called satisfaction, in which the true order is seen to be the confrontation of two interchanging forces which can be called God and the World" (*SV* 50). This passage reveals the contours of Whitehead's description of concrescence as well as Olson's adaptation of it. Through prehension, actual entities combine themselves into communities that become organisms: the "multiples" crowd in. As the organism develops, the multiples take on coherence as an "individual" that finds its "satisfaction" through the full actualization of its potential for form. In Whitehead's cosmology, the *primordial* God is the principle of relevance whereby actual entities and eternal objects can combine to yield something rather than nothing and he is the "lure for feeling" by which an actual entity intuits its possibilities for form. In his *consequent* nature (Whitehead's term), God is the sum of past actualities (superjects[13]) as well as present processes: he is the world in its actuality. The primordial God represents the potential for future becomings; the consequent God the sum of past actuality. God and the World, as Olson names them in the above passage, are the virtual and actual components of the creative process, the DNA in the acorn and the actual life story of the oak. "Satisfaction" (Whitehead's term) is that stage in concrescence when the organism has fully unfolded its potential. At this point, it passes into God's consequent nature as a datum for future prehensions (it becomes "history"), although Whitehead emphasizes that every becoming is a datum for every other at all times.

The above passage also suggests the use Olson has made of Whitehead. The "individuals" Olson references seem to be persons rather than monadic "actual entities," and the chapter in which this passage occurs in *The Special View,* the chapter Olson titles "The Topological," appears to confirm this reading. Olson writes: "If order is not the world—and the world hasn't been the most interesting image of order since 1903, when Einstein showed the beauty of the Kosmos and one then does pass on, looking for more—then *order is man.* And one can define the present (it does need to be noticed that the present is *post* the Modern) as the search for order as man himself is the image of same. Whitehead, then, makes sense in proposing a philosophy of organism, exactly how he defines his own system" (47, original emphasis). What allows Olson to make the leap from Whitehead's "philosophy of organism," which begins with the minims of life, to the idea that "order is man" (Von Hallberg's question)? I have already suggested that Olson extrapolates an ontology, a poetic method and an ethos from Whitehead. But how does this make humanity the arbiter of order? If I read Olson rightly in the above passage, it is because Einstein and other scientists brought forward the Otherness of the material universe, that the parameters of the human world can be rearticulated. The "order is man" specifically because the human universe is *not* equivalent to the Open Whole—because it has a ground in becomings that are not strictly human. This is an important difference between Olson's new humanism and the older kind. The human universe is a construct that has a top and bottom. The older humanism simply took the human view of things to be the only one, the Whole as such. Einstein, however, showed that the universe is beyond our space-time perceptions. Whitehead, the psychoanalysts (Jung for Olson), and the life scientists argued that our bodies and minds are also largely beyond our will and ken. The "order is man" when the world as we can come by it is identifiably other than the matter-energy continuum: the human universe is the view from here, the human perspective, on that continuum.

Olson glosses the Whiteheadian account of genesis in the above-cited passage with a second, mythopoeic rendering, and myth catches the partiality of the human universe precisely. It speaks in anthropomorphisms, certainly, because there is no getting around the human point of view, but it nonetheless gives independent agency to nature. It does nature that courtesy of respecting its Otherness. As Olson tells it, Chaos and Spirit combine to create Desire, and all three generate "Mot," or mud, from which comes the world egg (*SV* 51). Olson interprets Chaos as multiplicity (unstructured matter) and Spirit as genetics (matter condensed and ordered through a historic route of syntheses); hence, "life genetically occurs as autoclytic multiplicity" (*SV* 51).

Topos (Mot, mud, world) is crucial to this account of creativity because active agency depends on the organism's response to its environment, and response requires an alertness to whatever lies proximate. So in more abstract language, Olson writes that "*coincidence* and *proximity*... become the determinants of *chance* and *accident* and make possible *creative success*" (*SV* 49, original emphasis).

In yet another telling of the creative process, Olson turns to the Hegelian dialectic, modified through Keats's negative capability. The "three sides" of the "Logical doctrine" are stages: "the Abstract side, or that of Understanding; second, the Dialectical, or 'that of negative reason'; and third, the Speculative, or that of 'positive reason'" (*SV* 43). Olson approves of the first two stages of the dialectic that present "the dynamic which lies at the root of every natural process, and, as it were, *forces nature out of itself*" (*SV* 43, original emphasis), but he objects to the third stage as a falsification of process. "The need for the finite is overwhelming," he writes. "Man cannot do without it. He is philosophical. He is himself dialectical. He is the dynamic. He falls to the status of Understanding—what Hegel defines as '*nothing allowed to remain vague and indefinite*'" (*SV* 44, original emphasis). In Olson's view, Hegel takes "what is condition as result, instead of leaving it, as Keats does, *penetralium*" (*SV* 43, original emphasis). The negative capability is a corrective to the "irritable reaching" of the mind after certainty or completed understanding. It follows that the third moment of Whitehead's process ("satisfaction") is not one that organisms can possess, in Olson's view. Satisfaction is the point at which "the enjoyment and the desire are one" (*SV* 52), but this is also the moment of death. Satisfaction "is never possibly the trope Man. [. . .] the trope Man is only the creature at the second stage of feeling" (*SV* 52). Reaching satisfaction, "any man or woman recedes as God does from his creation" to become a datum for the new (*SV* 52).

What has to be noticed about this description of the dialectical relationship between figure and ground (actual entity and multitude, individual and environ) is that Olson does not slight the role of understanding (fact, reason, discourse). Rather, he positions it as "condition," inside the process, rather than as end or outcome. Olson's image for the process is the double cone (*SV* 54): "You will recall that, in drawing the cone of creation, I suggested that the movement from the elementary principle *Chaos* via Spirit to Desire, and from all three, Order of Kosmos is a succession of events moving from the widest and to the narrowest, and so back, in fact, the circuit, or double movement, makes a double cone" (54, original emphasis). The cone holds in an image all three tellings of the creative process: the philosophy of organism, mythic cosmogony, and the Hegelian dialectic.[14] The wide end of the cone suggests the early stages of the process as form emerges from combinative activity. As the process advances and the creature emerges into its form, the cone narrows; when the creature reaches maturity and begins to return to the flow of things, the cone widens. Consider the human embryo in its progressive differentiation, its journey to personhood and its return to a more dispersed existence in death, or the genesis of an artwork and its afterlife as it is disseminated and absorbed among viewers and other artists. In terms of the unending dialectic Olson references in the Hegel passage, figure differentiates itself from ground, returns to it, and differentiates again, in some other form.

This is the *process* of creation as Olson sketches it in *The Special View;* the second major theme of the *View* is Olson's account of the *determinants* of the process. What limits the potential for combination and sets the terms of relationship? Olson proposes four categories: "THE PROCESSES," "THE FACTORS," "THE QUALITIES," and "THE LAWS." This schema is crucial to the measure of Olson's concretism, because it is here that he gives his most elaborate account of the syntheses that mediate experience and condition agency. The first category, "THE PROCESSES," also referred to in the body of the lectures rather confusingly as "THE OBJECTS," deals with the evolution of human and nonhuman nature as anthropology and earth science. Included in this category are nature, civilization, and culture. Olson glosses nature as "cosmic processes" and "mountains and mammals" (*SV* 60). Man emerges in the Miocene period along with "trees/brain/single child." Civilization comes with tools and stereoscopic vision. In the Pleistocene period, physical "evolution [is] exchanged for culture" with the development of speech (*SV* 60). Olson offers little amplification of this outline in the lectures, but in "Enantiodromia," the final chapter of *The Special View,* he writes: "On either side of what I am saying here about methodology the real stuff lies. That is, previously, I would have talked about man's history, how he was after mountains and mammals in Tertiary time, how he wasn't any fixed physical equation until he did get stereoscopic vision and speech—at which two points he became first 'civilized' (because he could see round, he could use tools) and then 'cultured' (with speech he was able [. . .] to substitute precept for example), and with that—with society—he exchanged culture for evolution. He no longer had to physically change" (*SV* 57–58). Here the evolutionary history of the earth and of the human species suggests the genetic determinants of the human universe. Labor and language (civilization and culture, tools and speech) are the key processes in the development of humanity. Olson provides the barest of sketches, but it nonetheless suggests that he understands human nature as emerging out of evolutionary syntheses that were both physical and social.

Olson's second category consists of four "FACTORS": the unitary, the plural-binary, the majority-multiple, and the actual-singular. This rather difficult category of the "FACTORS" summarizes abstractly the *kinds* of relations that govern the creative process. "THE PROCESSES" emphasize space-in-time; "THE FACTORS," time-in-space. Olson says that the latter "pitch us into the mystery of time-space not as it is substantive but as it is operative: you are a unit as ego and also things happen to you in units because of what I called the binary problem, that at any moment of essential experience you are making a choice, and thus have to choose between one of two. Thus experience is single, at its core, no matter how multiple it may seem in its coming at you" (37). The FACTORS can be itemized, so I will take them one by one.

1. The unitary: In Whiteheadian language, the actual entity is the "unit," but as Whitehead insists, the entity is not a thing, but a process. As Olson adapts Whitehead, the unit comes to suggest the conscious individual, but the unity of Olson's "I" is not just a mistaking of the specular image for the self (Lacan); it is instead a matter of the individual's *Tao.* It is consistent with Whitehead and with Olson's comments in the *Special View* that the individual is an ongoing synthesis and modalizing of his or her environs (the "multiple . . . in its coming at you").

2. The second factor, the plural-binary, as Olson explains above, pertains to the process of prehension, or the selection of data from the "multiples" of the environment that "crowd in." Whiteheadian selection is both plural and binary because each actual entity has a relationship with every other in the universe, but *either* through positive *or* negative prehension. Those actual entities that are *not* proximate (actual entities that are "unaware" of one another) nonetheless negatively prehend one another.[15] In the chapter on "THE FACTORS," Olson expands on this point with reference to "The Human Universe": "I tried to state in what way and at what place the traffic of out and in can be said to be located and to happen in such a way that the imperative of the familiar is abided to. I emphasized there the skin . . . as both the boundary and the door, both in and out" (*SV* 32). This traffic in and out, he says, "tremendously modifies the old static of one (the unitary)"; it means that "a man is at once subject and object, is at once and always going in two directions" (*SV* 32). This account of "the traffic of out and in" is one of those moments in "The Human Universe" and *Special View* that might seem to propose perception as the gateway to authenticity or unmediated access to things. But perception, derivative of "THE PROCESSES," is already a complex of past and present syntheses.

3. Olson adds the third factor of the "majority" to this ongoing series of

syntheses. This factor suggests various collectivities. The species is one such, society another. Olson comments that "the majority factor . . . has done away with a lot of species of nature's own creation by failure of majority decisions to cope adequately with environment" (*SV* 38). Decisions at the species level and/or those at the level of smaller social groups mediate the outcome of the creative process for individuals.

4. This outcome is the actual, the fourth factor. The actual emerges through the historical interaction of figure and ground—the particularized past of the organism, its route—and its potential to further unfold itself. In summary, human individuals, like other organisms, receive and synthesize data, most vividly from whatever is proximate to them. As they absorb data, they also serve as such for other organisms, *but* their choices are mediated by their evolutionary and personal histories as well as their circumstances.

Olson's first two series outline the conditions under which the human universe generates itself. The third category, "THE QUALITIES," pertains to the affective state of the individual facing his or her environment and hence the quality and range of the individual's creative agency. "THE QUALITIES or Basic Conditions" are love (Eros), beauty, and idea as these modify the will. The challenge is to make them "as solid as the other two sets, and not any longer to be left floating in the vaporousness of their apparent words" (*SV* 38). Because these four are so entangled in Olson's thinking of them, I will take them up together rather than singly. In "THE OBJECTS," Olson says that *will* and beauty "go together, and are either disparate twins that produce death and culture, or they are what mythologically they once were, Venus and Adonis, love and desire" (30). If I read Olson rightly, the myth holds his meaning more firmly than the abstract terms. Adonis is the idealized image of his own "shadow," which was "a wild hog," and it is to be recalled from the myth that Adonis is *lost* to Venus when he is gored by a boar. Olson comments that "his will corrupteth his desire." The image suggests that the will on its own behaves like a wild boar; it is another trope in the series Hunger, Mouth, Dog. Carried to its limit, the desire to possess the Other implies the merging of two into one to the destruction of both. The Freudian twins, Eros and Thanatos, here make a guest appearance. And as Adonis relates to Venus, so humanity relates to nature through culture. When culture loses touch with Beauty capitalized (nature as independent Other) it begins to speak death, either as dissolution of the figure or appropriation of the ground: "And it got so bad Rimbaud had to toss Beauty off his knees, she was so sour" he says (*SV* 31). The old metaphysics—the worldview of Ahabian man—makes the beauty of the chaosmos disappear into the mirror image of humanity. Beauty goes sour when it turns out to be only the stale reflection of ourselves. The logical end of such megalomania or "Mouth-Without-The-World-To-Eat" is a narcissism so intense that it would willfully devour the ground of its own being.

Alternatively, there is beauty as "a permanent of creation whether man is in the picture or not" (*SV* 39). This is a good place to recall from my introduction Robin Blaser's use of Octavio Paz to distinguish, on one hand, the world constructed through technology as an object of the will and, on the other, the world as it appears in its "beautifuls-uglies" (*HF* 89); the former is obstacle, the latter is shape (*Fire* 236). Paz does not inform Olson, but I find the distinction a useful gloss to the QUALITIES. Through the Venus and Adonis story, love is evoked by beauty (shape); in the chapter on the "QUALITIES," Olson also connects it to ethos. The chapter titled "MUTHOS" shows how he makes the connection. Here *Eros* is one of an "interlocking trio" (*SV* 54) that includes *Economos* ("to preside over, direct, rule, your own house") and *Ethos* ("custom use habit fashion manner usage practice a rite ceremony institution ordinance") (*SV* 55). Eros tempered by *Economos* and *Ethos* becomes Love and *Tao* (54, original emphasis), a path toward the considered life. One stays in one's house (*Economos*) while recognizing the Otherness of one's ground as Beauty (*Eros*) to which one relates through ceremony (*Ethos,* formal recognition of one's belonging to the chaosmos as participant). Or as Olson writes in *Maximus,* "he who walks with his house on / his head is heaven" (*MP* 311).

From these comments scattered throughout *The Special View,* the picture that emerges of love and beauty is that of a way of seeing the world as form rather than an obstacle to be overcome or a projection of the human will. "One loves only form" (*MP* 7), Olson writes, and love of form leads the poet to reach for a world image. This revisionary aestheticism says that "what used to be aesthetic in the old cosmology—secondary, because purpose was and had to be primary, is seen to be the nature of the stain of form across all reality" (SV 49). The effort after form is also the "good" in Whitehead.[16] This is the "lure for feeling" that God represents for the actual entities. In mythological language, the world rises like Venus ("*apophainesthai*" [*MP* 240]), and there are those who also "rise, they do who / are born of like / elements" ("The Ring of" [*CP* 243]).

Let me sharpen the implications of this visionary ethos by juxtaposing it to Deleuze's reading of Spinoza. In Spinoza's *Ethics,* good and bad are relative terms. If two-legged food is good for the saber-toothed tiger, it may not be so considered by the *Homo erectus* being eaten. But these terms also have a secondary meaning that is "subjective and modal." The "good individual" is one who

> [s]trives, insofar as he is capable, to organize his encounters, to join with whatever agrees with his nature, to combine his relation with relations that are compatible with his, and thereby to increase his power. . . . That individual will be called bad . . . who lives haphazardly, who is content to undergo the effects of his encounters, but wails and accuses every time the effect undergone does not agree with him and reveals his own impotence. For, by lending himself in this way to whatever encounter in whatever circumstance, believing that with a lot of violence or a little guile, one will always extricate oneself, how can one fail to have more bad encounters than good? How can one keep from destroying oneself through guilt, and others through resentment, spreading one's own powerlessness and enslavement everywhere, one's own sickness, indigestions and poisons? (*Spinoza* 23)

I read Olson's argument for love as an argument for the good life in the Deleuze-Spinozist sense, where "good" connotes maximum complexity rather than moral normativity. "One finds no object of love if one does not believe in love," Olson writes, adding that "belief . . . is the same thing as methodology" (*SV* 42). Love is not essential to life—at least not in the short term—but as Olson says in the "Letter to Elaine Feinstein" with which I began this section, "you do love or go down" (*CPr* 252), literally to the limits of topos beyond which the human becomes something else. A "good" life, in contrast, is one that most expands the agent's image of the world—the "clear zone" (Deleuze's phrase), the zone of affectability and hence the potential for complexity of form. Applied to Ahab, for instance, this ethos shows how megalomania narrows his range of affectability to just those experiences and relations that pertain to his one obsession. In the end, he loses even Pip. Ishmael, in contrast, finds the capacity to respond to the diversity of the *Pequod*'s crew and the ineffable mystery of the whale. And in the end, he floats.

The other two QUALITIES, idea and will, take definition from Olson's description of the creative process and Keats's negative capability. Truth and idea are interchangeable terms that Olson renders dynamically as the act of "taking thought" (SV 39). The whole of *The Special View of History,* not to mention the prosody of *The Maximus Poems,* supposes the dynamism of thought, and this is an important underpinning of Olson's concretism. In the chapter on "STANCE," Olson says of history that there are two alternatives inherited from the split between science and fiction: "make it up; or try to find out. Both are necessary" (*SV* 20). And in his lecture "Poetry and

Truth," he remarks that "truth is specific," "*veritas efficaciae*" (45), and rises out of "The Dogmatic Nature of Experience" (*Muthologos* II, 44); it is that which stands up (*knowing how,* rather than *knowing that*). The evidence of *The Special View,* as I hope I have shown, is against the interpretation of such comments (the "dogmatic nature of experience") as classical empiricism, first because Olson locates the origins of experience in the bio-social codes inherited by the organism, and second because he argues the act of the moment as dialectical interaction with chance and circumstance. Olson's polemic is directed against "wisdom *as such*" (my emphasis) because this kind of knowing removes knowledge from its context in *events:* "What Socrates did was to isolate the value and thus raise and isolate the man-time from space-time. What he performed, however, was a removal from the particular, which, as Whitehead, in calling any occasion the actual, is the absolute, because it is in fact the way the absolute energy asserts itself" (*SV* 27). Ian Buchanan (*Deleuzism*) gives me a helpful comparison.

> One does not need to recollect the long process by which the arm evolved from a foreleg, and the foreleg from a fin, and so on, in order to be able to throw a curve ball: that data is nevertheless stored in the deepest recesses of our being, our DNA, and we draw on it to our very depths in throwing curve balls, but never give it a second's thought. However, having said that, it cannot be said that all we need to throw a blistering curve ball is the recently acquired memory of technique, for without the recessed memory of what an arm can do, all the coaching in the world would be useless. Our very flexibility (torsion versus tension) is a sign to be interpreted by our skill. "In other words, the active syntheses of memory and understanding are superimposed upon and supported by the passive synthesis of the imagination." For coaching to be effective, then, it has to induce a resonance between the two levels of retention and anticipation; it does this by foregrounding (extracting) the difference between them—*what one can do, and what one is doing,* making the former the measure of the latter. And this we come to understand is what Deleuze means when he says everything happens in between. (65, my emphasis)

To take thought as a dynamic practice is to see the difference between "what one can do, and what one is doing." Hence the aim of *The Maximus Poems:* to present an image of human possibility that will serve as measure.

The last of the QUALITIES is the will and I will pass over it quickly because Olson defines it most fully in the chapter on "ETHICS" in the discussion of Hegelian dialectic I have outlined above. In that chapter, he polarizes the man of power and the man of achievement. The will is rectified—Fenrir bound and Ahab put in his place—by giving the will something to which it can relate other than itself, and this something other is the chaosmos. When the familiar is restored, the will can be directed through love (*Tao*) toward beauty (shape). It then becomes the driving force in a creative process through which the organism seeks to enlarge its "clear zone" and thereby maximize its potential for form.

Olson's last category consists of "THE LAWS," "Enantiodromia" or "Universe of Opposites." The term *enantiodromia* (Greek, *enantios*, "opposite," and *dromos*, "running course") as Jung used it means that one libidinal tendency produces its compensatory opposite. The same principle is operative in Heraclitus. As Olson employs them, the "LAWS" formalize the dialectic of *The Special View*. The pairs of opposites are space-time and human-time; the primordial and consequent natures of God; form as structure (the phylogenic given) and form as creation (ontogenesis); the morphological and genetical; the metrical and topological; place and name; subject and object (*SV* 61). Each term of each binary has its own potential and actual poles that play out internally and in dialectical interaction with the poles of the other term. So space-time manifest as nature, for example, is continuously involved in the actualization of its biological, geographical, or geological potentials. The same applies to history or human time, its contrary, which is also in the process of self-actualization. And each becoming is intimately involved in the becoming of the other. Olson summarizes the whole schema in the phrase "actual willful man." The actual is parsed by the FACTORS (unitary, plural, majority); the will is modulated by the QUALITIES (beauty, love, idea); and man is defined by the PROCESSES (nature, civilization, culture). In yet another gloss, Olson writes that "the objects are nature, the numbers are God, the qualities are man" (*SV* 46), which is to say that the species is nature's own child and a mode of the Mother Rock, although it creates its own fate there. The result of recognizing oneself through the PROCESSES, FACTORS, and QUALITIES is STANCE, which I take as literally having one's feet on a ground that has suddenly sprung to life.

The Special View lays out the processes by which space becomes place. That the field is polarized as figure-ground suggests a form of "nonreductive materialism":[17] the figure evolves through a long, evolutionary series of syntheses but it is not ontologically different in kind from the dance of the atoms. To reflexive consciousness, however, the chaosmos cannot not appear in binary form. The evolutionary process is irreversible; development of consciousness is irreversible. There is no unmediated access to the fluidity of "smooth" space as figured in the sea or the American plains in *Call Me Ishmael*—the plane of consistence or flow of the real. For humanity, there is only topos. In the next section I will follow Olson as he further unfolds his topography through typos. If topos is about the becoming of space into place, typos emphasizes the durable, genetic elements of the process. This means a synthesis of Whitehead's "eternal objects" and Jung's archetypes.

Typos: " 'bent' as born"

Olson's typos is close to its etymology. The Greek word means "dent, impression, mark, figure, original form," from the root "*typtein,*" "to strike, beat." There is, perhaps, a resonance with Puritan typology, the practice of explicating the figures of the Old Testament of the Bible as foreshadowing those of the New Testament. Jonah is a type of Christ, for example, and his three-day sojourn in the whale's belly an anticipation of Christ's three days in the tomb. Perhaps as well we are to think of the typewriter and the use Olson makes of it in "Projective Verse," where he argues that with this device it is possible to score the lines of the poem as if one were scoring music. With typos, Olson addresses the durables of the human universe—the pattern, the musical score that binds the dancing atoms into shapes. He does it by conflating Whitehead's "eternal objects" with Jung's archetypes.

On "eternal objects" I cannot do better than Donald Sherburne in his *Key* to Whitehead's *Process and Reality:*

> Any given actual entity does not make its decisions with utter freedom. "An actual entity arises from decisions *for* it and by its very existence provides decisions *for* other actual entities which supersede it" [PR 68]. The past, from which it inherits, presents it with certain forms of definiteness that it is compelled to reiterate. "Some conformation is necessary as a basis of vector transition, whereby the past is synthesized with the present." (*Key* 221, original emphasis)

A few pages later, Sherburne offers this example: "in terms of pure possibility it is possible that a five-foot, fortyish, fat man could high jump seven feet, but this is not a real possibility. Real potentiality is the limitations, the restrictions upon pure potentiality, that the conditions of a given, factual world impose upon any particular actual entity arising out of that world" (*Key* 224). Typos is analogous to genetic information that organisms carry forward from the past even as they instantiate it uniquely.

Like the eternal objects, the Jungian archetypes can also be read as channeling relatively unstructured energy into certain real potentialities for form. Introducing his terminology in *Psychology and Alchemy,* Jung describes the archetype in language that Olson later takes up: "The word 'type' is, as we know, derived from τύπος, 'blow' or 'imprint': thus an archetype presupposed an imprinter" (14). And Olson, in the "Letter to Elaine Feinstein": "The 'blow' hits here, and me, 'bent' as born" (*CPr* 252), or in a late *Maximus* poem, "the Blow is Creation" (*MP* 634). Affinities between Jung and Olson include Olson's dialectical treatment of the creative process, which bears some resemblance to Jung's description of individuation as the unfolding of the Self through the interaction of opposing psychic energies like the anima and animus. As well, the idea of the progress and regress of the Jungian Self is congenial to the philosophy of organism as Olson takes it up. As the libido differentiates, it becomes capable of more varied attachments; if the psyche regresses, however, it moves toward dissolution in infantile union with the mother. Charles Stein, in his Jungian reading of Olson (*The Secret of the Black Chrysanthemum,* 1979) notes the importance of this process to Olson. Regression occurs when the psyche is blocked in its unfolding. To progress further, it has to regress to confront its repressions at the archetypal level. The infantile stage to which regression leads consists of nutritive (sucking) and rhythmic behaviors ("rubbing, picking, boring, stamping, clapping"). Rhythmic activities such as poetry have the power to take the ego back to the archetypal realm (Stein 57). This description of psychic becoming is not difficult to assimilate to the double cone of creation as presented in *The Special View.* Individuation unfolds in a series of narrowings and widenings of libidinal energy.

But Olson does more than borrow from Jung in constructing the archetypal figures of *Maximus.* First, there is no lived reconciliation of opposites in Olson, no possibility of completed individuation as there is in Jung: satisfaction is death. Second, Olson concretizes the archetypes. Discussing this move, Stein notes that Jung suggests an analogy between organs and archetypes in his *Psychological Types* and in *The Archetypes and the Collective Unconscious* (42, 43), but the analogy is *merely* such.[18] Olson, in contrast, seems to actually place the archetypes in the body as organs. Stein calls on Olson's marginal notes in a copy of Jolande Jacobi's book, *The Psychology of Jung,* to show that Olson aligned the heart with mother, the brain with father, the liver and kidneys with brother and sister (Stein 42). "Proprioception" offers further evidence:

Physiology: the surface (senses—the "skin": of "Human Universe") the body itself—proper—one's own "corpus": PROPRIOCEPTION the cavity of the body, in which the organs are slung: the viscera, or interoceptive, the old "psychology" of feeling, the heart; of desire, the liver of sympathy, the "bowels"; of courage—the kidney etc—gall (Stasis—or as in Chaucer only, spoofed)

And a few verse paragraphs later:

The "cavity"/cave probably the "Unconscious"? That is, the interior empty place filled with "organs"? for "functions"?

THE "PLACE" OF THE "UNCONSCIOUS"

The advantage is to "place" the thing, instead of it wallowing around sort of outside, in the universe, like, when the experience of it is interoceptive: it is inside us/& at the same time does not feel literally identical with our own physical or mortal self (the part that can die). In this sense likewise the heart, etc. the small intestine etc, are or can be felt as—and literally they can be—transferred. Or substituted for. Etc. The organs.—Probably also why the old psychology was chiefly visceral: neither dream, nor the unconscious, was then known as such. Or allowably inside, like. (*CPr* 181–82)

I have quoted at length to get at the *oddity* of these speculations. Olson's concretism in this context seems just the kind of fanciful speculation that usually gets dismissed as poetic license. But the comment in "Proprioception" that "process in reality redeems all idealism fr theocracy or mobocracy, whether it is rational or superstitious" (*CPr* 190) is revealing in this context; the archetype cannot stand apart from the process. Stein usefully reads Olson's locating of the archetypes in the organs as evidence that he may have understood them as analogous to the genetic code and was thus able to reconcile the atemporality of the archetype with the mutability of an actual physical organ (48). This would mean that the archetypes could be repositioned in the creative advance, as the product of evolution, but at a *velocity* much slower than that of the individual human life.

This reading is supported by attending to the apparent error Stein notices (48) in Olson's references to eternal objects in *Maximus* where he repeatedly uses the term "eternal event" rather than "object." In the poem "for Robert Duncan, / who understands," Olson writes, "I walk you paths of lives I'd share with / you simply to make evident the world / is an eternal event" (*MP* 208). In "Later Tyrian Business," "Eternal Events" drop from the tongue of "the Salivarating / Dog" (*MP* 206). Again, in the opening poem of *Maximus V*, "A Later Note on Letter #15," "the objective . . . // is a lie / as against what we know went on, the dream: the dream being / self-action with Whitehead's important corollary: that no event // is not penetrated, an intersection or collision with, an eternal / event" (*MP* 249). An event, in Whitehead's terminology, is "a nexus of actual occasions interrelated in some determinate fashion in some extensive quantum. . . . For example, a molecule is a historic route of actual occasions; and such a route is an 'event' " (Sherburne 222–23).

Olson's events, I suggest, are composed of spatiotemporal strata of varying velocities. For instance, the universe is a fluid continuum of matter and energy at the atomic level, but it appears discrete when the atoms combine into organisms. The earth is "quick" and molten in the center and striated at its crust. Human cells live and die at a greater velocity than do the organs. One of the most distinctive features of *Maximus* is the different temporalities that Olson plays simultaneously. Geological time, as represented by the westward drift of continents, is slow compared with the shifting features of surface landscapes. The history of the human species reveals a longer evolutionary trajectory than the rise and fall of civilizations, or the living memory of individuals. Hence the psychic "organs" of the species—its archetypes—may suggest the glacial speed of genetic drift, but they are nonetheless in motion, subject to evolution and even disruptive mutation (analogous to volcanic eruption). Olson's poem beginning "Astride / the Cabot / fault" has the poet straddling the major temporalities: westward "continental drift," human migration as instantiated by the explorer John Cabot, the "history // of the nation," and "the wall / of a city" that the poet evokes in the present tense as his own labor—that is, the creative work of the moment (*MP* 404). I will take up the sudden disruptive kind of change in the next section on tropos, but here I wish to emphasize Olson's comment that process saves idealism. In *The*

Special View, Olson says of myth that it is a reenactment that "does enlarge in that it celebrates what men have selected from what their ancestors did which seemed to them useful. It's what we call tradition. They [Trobriands] call it rites" (57). The repetition and consequent "enlargement" of an event might suggest (I speculate) a description of the evolutionary history of an archetype. As Olson writes in "Letter 22," "What weeds / as an explanation / leaves out, is / that chaos / is not our condition" (*MP* 100). Human nature includes some durables by definition. The advantage of reading archetypes or eternal objects back into living process in this way is that we gain a vocabulary for talking about the permanent elements of creation without having to essentialize them.

"MAXIMUS FROM DOGTOWN—I," is one of Olson's most frequently explicated poems, and with good reason. This story of the handsome sailor who dies on Dogtown Commons wrestling a young bull features a number of Olson's favored archetypes, and it further suggests what Olson might mean by "eternal event." In this poem, the *event* of creation as it takes place at different velocities and on different strata of the human universe is what does not change. The plot of "DOGTOWN—I" has been summarized by others and I will pass over it quickly. Butterick identifies Erich Neumann's *The Great Mother* as a key source of the poem, and most readings acknowledge this Jungian component. Stein, for instance, reads Merry's contest with the bull as the male ego's confrontation with its anima: the bull is a representative of the Mother to whom Merry regresses and eventually succumbs. In Jungian analysis, Stein says, the ego faces two perils in the quest for individuation: engulfment and inflation. The ego may be subsumed in the overwhelming presence of the archetype and lose itself there, or it may inflate by identifying with archetypal figures. Merry exemplifies the latter (the Ahab complex) when he tries to wrestle with the Mother in the form of her little bull (Stein 139). This plot can be read on many levels—as enacting topos, typos, and tropos as they explicate one another (Byrd 116); as the primordial struggle of Anthropos with nature (Christensen 148); or even as establishing Olson in a Hesiodic, rhetorical tradition—the poet *asserts* his worldview without justification and substitutes *narration* for explanation (Von Hallberg 135). What I want to add is a summary of the various layers or scapes of this poem in order to show that Olson's field works as a complex matrix combining multiple velocities. I also wish to show that the "eternal event" in this poem is indeed eventful.

This "MAXIMUS" parses topos as cosmogony, geology, and geography. Olson begins with a restatement of Hesiod's account of the birth of Okeanos from the union of Earth and Heaven, "the one which all things are and by which nothing is anything but itself, measured so" (*MP* 172). Earth, Heaven, and Okeanos are the cosmic enactors of the creative process, and Olson writes them large because they set in motion the process as it is repeated at every level of the Whole. He gets the grand scale he wants through repetition of the mythic trio in different guises. Heaven and Earth, for example, are repeated as Geb and Nut, and Earth returns again as the Mexican goddess and terrible Mother, Mayauel. The same (pro)creative event is repeated at the geological stratum of the poem. Here topos is the "watered rock" of Dogtown—literally a moraine of glacial deposits permeable to water (Butterick, *Guide* 242). The action of the glacier as it once tossed the rock that solidified to become Dogtown repeats the cosmic coupling of Heaven and Earth: earth "ploughed" by the glacier yields Dogtown, which becomes in the course of the poem a "park of eternal / events" parallel in generative function to Okeanos, the offspring of Heaven and Earth and a mythic figure of creative becoming (*MP* 175).

The geographical stratum sits under the cosmic and over the geological. Juxtaposed to the first telling of Merry's story is a memory of Dogtown in these lines:

                    . . . the roads
of Dogtown trickling like from underground rock springs
under an early cold March moon

                              or the hot summer and my son
                              we come around a corner
                              where a rill
                              makes Gee Avenue in a thin
                              ford

                                 after we see a black duck
                              walking across a populated
                              corner

                                      life spills out (*MP* 173)

This passage repeats again the cosmic and geological action as well as the historical narrative of Merry (the tropic component). The roads trickle water (Dogtown is "watered rock") and the "hot summer" recalls the procreative heat of the proem. The black duck, foolishly attempting to negotiate a "populated / corner," is a thumbnail sketch of the brazen Merry. Cosmogony, geology, and geography thus mirror each other as the multiple layers of topos in this poem.

This pattern repeats itself from all angles. If we focus on the archetypal reading and begin with typos rather than topos, the poem turns into a mandala. Over the course of the three separate tellings of Merry's story, the "watered rock" of Dogtown appears in two as "soft rock" (*MP* 173). Stein makes the connection with carbon (150). Jung found in the quadratic molecular structure of this "soft rock" a pattern analogous to the mandala, a symbol of the individuated Self. As well, carbon suggests the coincidence of opposites: black coal yields the diamond, a trope of the alchemical "black-gold flower." From this perspective, the poem is about the individuating Self. Merry's contest with the bull is a historical instance (tropos) of individuation that has its archetypal event (typos) in the coupling of Heaven and Earth in the proem and its locus (topos) on the "watered rock" or cosmic mandala that is Dogtown.

From the tropic or historical point of view, the fishermen who used to come to Dogtown to "whore / on Saturday nights / at three girls' houses" (*MP* 173) unwittingly repeat the cosmic act of love in the proem and the (pro)creative glacial action against the rock. This relatively recent history of Gloucester is layered with epochal human history in the line, "Pisces eternally swimming" (173). Stein notes Jung's rendering of the Christian era as Piscean, an era at its end in the twentieth century. Pisces also had historical significance for Olson as an emblem of Gloucester's rise and decline as a fishing port. The triad, then, is Dogtown commons (topos); the amorous fishers, stretching back in history all the way to Christ (typos); and Andrew Merry (tropos).

In numerical terms, "DOGTOWN—I" consists of the pattern, 1 + 3. Stein notes that Jung's mandala is a circle (three) squared (four). The "square symbolizes the innate ordering capacity of the primordial Self . . . [and the] circle represents the Self's holistic, inclusive capacity . . . the square is the material substrate of the psyche, the circle its spiritual fact" (138). The proem (the "one") lays out the creative process on the cosmogonic level, and I suggest it is set off from the body of the poem (three tellings of the event) because the ontogenetic process is not exclusively human: Heaven, Earth, and Okeanos precede the human species as the way in which all things come to be, and this persistence of physical nature before and beyond the human is insisted upon throughout the poem in lines that position the human action between heaven and earth: Geb and Nut are "vault / above and below / watered rock on which / by which Merry / was so many pieces / Sunday morning" (172). To note, here also is the prepositional shift: Merry is "on" the "watered rock," and is also laid in pieces "by" it: heaven and earth are both place and process, or rather place *is* process. This establishing of the priority of nature and the species dimension of human life contributes importantly to the cautionary element of the tale that follows: Merry does *not* respect species limitations when he tempts the bull.

The three repetitions of Merry's story, echoing the triadic structure of the setting and event, illustrate the Whiteheadian principle that the present tropes on the past. Each telling includes a narration of the event and a reiteration of cosmic becoming as a large-scale manifestation of that which Merry undergoes. So in the first telling, for instance, Merry seeks to "manifest / his soul," and the stars also seek to "manifest their souls" (172). All components of the triad are included in each telling, but the details change. The repetitions serve as enlargements in the sense that Olson speaks of them in the passage I have quoted above from *The Special View* ("A reenactment . . . does enlarge in that it celebrates *what men have selected from what their ancestors did which seemed to them useful*" [57, my emphasis]). They do this by adding detail that allows figure and ground to stand more revealed, but they also enlarge by uniting different levels and velocities in one process of becoming. These velocities include the mythic-aeonic, the natural-cyclical, the epochal time of geological and human history, and finally the linear time of historical narrative. The only eternal in the poem is the process itself—process *is* reality—here presented through mythological personae that form the deep ground of all the other becomings. Superimposed on this cosmic ground (Heaven "screwing" Earth) are nature's cycles as represented in the "early cold March moon // or hot summer" (173). These times support the slow stratum of epochal time, which then in turn becomes the spatiotemporal ground of the more recent histories of the species in its evolutionary development, in its western migration as instanced in references to the settlement of Cape Ann (the bullfight takes place near Jeremiah Millet's house, one of the founding settlers of Dogtown [*MP* 173]), and finally in the story of Merry.

I have given the poem a (genetic) structuralist reading in order to demonstrate the density of the layering, the intimate connection between Olson's triads, and the emphasis on the event—the (pro)creative act—as that which remains constant at all the levels and velocities of the poem. The same points could be made at greater length by reading the poem through the schema of *The Special View,* as layerings of the PROCESSES (nature, civilization, culture) as well as the FACTORS and QUALITIES, the whole set in motion by the LAWS. To note particularly, however, is the essential role the qualities play (love, beauty, idea, and will) in this story about a man who seeks to "manifest / his soul" (173), but fails to understand his place in the world as one of nature's creatures. This is a failure of love, and Olson draws attention to it when he opens with the birth of Okeanos through the union of heaven and earth "in whom love lies" (172). Like the will of Adonis as Olson writes of him in *The Special View,* Merry's will infects his desire and because he cannot see the world as form, he must experience it as formless, literally through his own dismemberment unto death. In mythical terms, Merry does not respect the Earth as Venus in the form of her bull (the bull is a mere instrument in self-actualization); he therefore encounters Mayauel, the Mother Rock in her archetypal form, which is overwhelming to the finite mind. Mayauel's four hundred breasts are echoed in the "four hundred gods / of drink," and the "400 pieces [of] / his brain shot" (175).

In "MAXIMUS FROM DOGTOWN—I" the difference-in-repetition of the various levels and velocities of the procreative event suggests that the relationship between archetype and history is not so simply instantiation; the bullfight manifests an "eternal event" (the effort after individuation) that is as old as the earth and common to all things. But the event exists only as it is enacted. Merry does not simply exemplify a preexisting paradigm; he *participates* in a process that only takes on particular form through him, which is to say that his act assembles the event in which he is a participant. From this perspective, Mayauel is the mode of the earth that Merry's act of self-fashioning calls forth. I began this section by discussing Olson's treatment of the archetypes as organs. This apparent oddity, I suggest, is part of a larger strategy through which Olson adapts structuralist synchrony—composition by field—to show mutability of form, thus to position the human universe in the evolutionary stream. To repeat: process saves idealism.

Tropos: "one's own decisions for better or worse"

I turn again to etymology for the sense of Olson's tropos: the Greek word glosses as "turn, direction, turn or figure of speech." In rhetoric, a trope is a figure of speech in which a word or phrase is used in a sense other than the literal. In the context of Olson's work, tropos is the spin one puts on what one is given, as Merry distinctively makes manifest the "eternal event" in which he participates. Tropos is Olson's hot button. It is the site of creative agency and core to Olson's contention that a human life is an allegory. Tropos is a response to the structuralist conundrum Olson inherited from Pound: if the past is immanent in the present, how does one select from it without expressing perspectives that are *merely* egoistic or idiosyncratic? How does one overcome the challenge of solipsism?

Olson offers a two-part response to the problem. First, he expands the

Poundian field into the matrix of the various scapes of the human universe, and second, he sets up a dialectical relationship between the individual and this matrix. In refiguring the field, Olson claims an advance over Pound. As he writes to Robert Creeley in *The Mayan Letters,* "one has to give Ez his due: that he did write KULCH," but he adds that "the materials of history which he [Pound] found useful are not at all of use" (*SV* 84). Or in the same letter, "the Old Deal, Ez as Cento Man, here dates" (*SV* 82). In comparison to Olson's field, *The Cantos* are more narrowly focused on those cultures Pound finds luminous.[19] The cultural and intellectual levels of the human universe are relatively "quick" in the sense that they can change fairly rapidly in relation to, say, geological formations or the genetic code or epochal historical pressures (the history of settlement in North America in relation to indigenous cultures, for example). If the mental realm is taken to be the only significant level of the field, then the long history of syntheses that have produced human nature through physiological and social evolution (life, labor, and language[20])—the slower and more conservative scapes—are missing and with them a truer measure of human possibility. Absent from the picture is the body and its fragilities, the nonhuman species, and the multitudinous orders of the earth.[21] Without these elements, there is only culture and void and because culture can change in relatively short periods and through relatively few agents, it skews the measure of human agency. The cultural-intellectual plane invites Ahabian projection (Man as sole author of his destiny) as well as the sort of change by fiat that is an element of the fascist seduction (culture by decree). From Olson's perspective, Pound lacks an adequate picture of his ground, and because Pound also dismisses the factor of the multiple (the "masses" at the window) he is thrown back on the ego. Olson's reconfiguration of the field draws in as many "antecedent predecessions" (*MP* 184) of the individual as possible, and these give a better picture of humanity's real versus pure potentiality. Real potential then becomes the measure of the actual: this is what one can do; this is what one is doing.

Another element of Olson's account of agency lies in the particular kind of dialectic he sets in motion. This is a kind of dialectical monism that unfurls as the continual infolding of polar elements different in quantity and intensity but not kind. In Deleuzean language, this twisting is similar in function to becoming-other. Olson's polarizing of the field marks the tropic perspective of the human species, not ontological privilege. This dialectic differs from Slavoj Žižek's Lacanian-Marxist version, a theoretical position in competition with the Deleuzean. I will digress here briefly to describe the difference because I think it clarifies the implications of Olson's position through contrast. The key to the distinction is what Žižek calls quilting

(*Sublime Object* 87–88). In Lacanian terms, the individual has no access to the undifferentiated libido (the χάος of the real) because this energy is always already channeled through the phallus (the signifier of signifiers) from the moment of initiation into the symbolic order. The terrain of the psyche is thus "quilted" (organized) through "castration" or foreclosure of the infant's preverbal sensations in and with the mother. The resulting infantile wish to become the object of desire of the (M)other thus to control her ultimately refers to the death drive because literal return to the mother would mean psychosis or death. The *lack* of this ultimate object of desire is constitutive of the subject. Without separation the subject could never individuate, but the price of becoming an "I" is incurable desire that will henceforth be displaced through *méconnaisance* on various objects ("*l'objet petit a*"). However, through negation—the "this-isn't-it" of unsatisfied desire—desire becomes a dynamic and creative force. At the social level, it may become the source of freedom and change. From Žižek's Marxist-Lacanian perspective, the social field is quilted analogously through class antagonism. The effort to actualize empty signifiers like freedom or justice produces particular instantiations that fall short of these empty universals, leaving an excluded other that manifests as the subaltern. This excluded other, made visible by the non-identity of the particular and universal, then becomes the site from which the system can be challenged and the key to its structure.[22] The dialectical process through which every particular determination of desire (the actual) is negated as falling short of the universal (the virtual) derives from Hegel as does Olson's dialectic, but the poles of Žižek's field are determined through the privileging of sexual and social antagonisms. It is crucial to this picture that the Lacanian ground be dualistic in the sense that irreducible Otherness (the real that is foreclosed to the subject) is essential to the formation of the psyche. Hence from Žižek's point of view, Deleuze fails to pinpoint the real source of change in sexual and class antagonism; instead, he offers an array of competing antagonisms on a neutral ground, this latter homologous politically to an idealized democratic space in which antagonism could be resolved—at least in theory. This seems to me the core of the disagreement.

Olson's field is not quilted in Žižek's sense. Even though sex and class may be definitive organizers for human sociality, it is not human sociality that Olson is ultimately after. The figure-ground relationship serves to describe the human species as it is situated in a dialectical relationship within a larger universe that is not strictly human. I therefore propose that Olson's field invites contention not because it suggests direct versus mediated perception (the epistemological argument), but rather because it de-privileges the human place in the Open Whole. Olson's geopoetic does not deny the determining effects of genetics, language, or social structure or the antagonistic polarization of the man of power and the man of achievement, but it does not privilege any one stratum of the human universe, like psychology or politics, as a foundational determination of the whole field. Let me return here to Olson's *mythopoesis.* The switch point between Mouth and Typhon, or Mouth as raw becoming and Mouth as Muthos, capable of love and relationship, is the appearance of earth. The mythology would seem to suggest an obvious analogy with the Lacanian account of the psyche that begins to develop personhood when the infant is initiated into the symbolic order and the flow of the real is foreclosed. Personhood begins with an awareness of the world as "not-me." In this context it is worth recalling that Olson's account of the birth of Venus in "The Ring Of" specifies the castration of Chronus by Saturn as the initiating event—Venus rises out of the "genital / wave" (*CP* 243) as the world rises up for every child initiated into personhood. It is possible to multiply examples. The Cut, for instance, is a geographical feature of Gloucester.

Yet for a number of reasons, Olson does not privilege lack. In Olson's thinking lack (and death) are tucked into Whiteheadian process. Even if we accept that human subjectivity may be oriented by death, the chaosmos knows no individual death at the level of the atom or at that of the stars or of the earth's core or at that of the species level of life, and Olson wants to get these not-strictly-human strata into the field because they unsettle stale anthropomorphisms and defamiliarize the ground so we can see it again. The human universe is not a universe centered on the human; rather, it is a human-nonhuman continuum as perceived (inevitably) from the human point of view. Olson also relies on anthropological accounts of human development, not just language-based theories of the psyche; in his view, language is one factor among other, equally determining factors that bear on the individual, such as the physiology of the body and the rhythms of the earth. Olson's focus is thus directed across the strata, and from this point of view, the psycho-social planes have to be repositioned inside a chaosmos that includes the "salts and minerals of the earth" (*CP* 14). Privileging sex or class structures limits the universe to the human species, and this is just what Olson wants to change; his argument for a *new* humanism is an argument for a human universe in which the Otherness of nature is palpably immanent and the human role is diminished. From this perspective, the Žižekian formation looks like an antidote to Ahabian man that nonetheless enshrines Ahab as an *inevitable* mode of life because humanity cannot avoid itself epistemologically. But it is precisely the Ahabian way of being in the world—humanity as the only reality—that Olson wants to challenge for reasons of ethos rather than epistemology.

If I read him rightly, his polarization of the field into figure and ground, inside and outside is strategic, not essential. Figure and ground rise up together out of the flow of the real as a function of human reflexivity, and for humanity the trope may be definitive ("order is man"). And yet space lurks in place and at bottom, all things do flow. The advantage of writing what lies beyond experience as "outside" rather than "inside" is an ethical one that allows Olson to rethink the human species in its relations with nature: "For a man is himself an object, whatever he may take to be his advantages," he writes ("Projective Verse," *CPr* 247). What should be controversial about Olson is not epistemology, but rather the strategic advantages of a "practice of outside" (cosmicity) as opposed to what has become the more common "practice of inside" (psycho-sociology, psycho-philosophy).

Those readers who suspect something religious in this positing of an outside are not wrong, but cosmicity is "religion" that aims to undo the scandal of its historical, institutional practice. The experience of being inside something larger than oneself is primary to human perception, and this experience, I want to argue, is religion in its deep structure. I will have more to say on this in the Blaser essay, but the point I want to make now is that this affective dimension of perceptual experience is unavoidable. Primary to infancy, as the mind comes to consciousness, is the distinction between a me and not-me. That is where relational thinking begins and it is also where organized religions have traditionally stepped in, at the primal point where human fear and desire begin to project themselves on what is felt to be Other. The path of Ahabian humanity is to seize that experience of the Other for the purposes of the finite mind whether through organized religion or rational demystification of nature, the latter equally an erasure. But what remains alive and pressing in religious thinking is this experience—this meeting with an "out there." And yes, it can be written as a "practice of *inside*" (as lack, as foreclosure of the real), but the social sciences are not imaginatively attuned to living othernesses that resist nomination, nor do they specialize in the finessing of linkages to that wildness there at the skin, as Olson would say. Philosophy, tied to epistemic considerations (*knowing that*) has to leave the Other imageless. Poetic cosmicity, however, can move in on this range of experience. What Olson sees in myth, I think, is a planet that is still alive enough to be felt as a presence and hence there to be related to. Certainly myth humanizes nature—the mind cannot escape its own forms—but in that human shape, nature is allowed the dignity of independent agency and humanity the chance for complex relationship with it. By this I mean the possibility of relations that do not collapse either in self-idolatry (humanity projects itself as God) or instrumentalization (rational humanity demystifies the numinosity of nature as its own projection but then leaves it as meat). Ahab exemplifies both tendencies and shows how they complement each other. Because he admits of no ground other than himself (Ahab is God) he is able to treat the whale *and his crew* as, at best, a threat to be reduced (nature is obstacle or lump; the Pacific is sweatshop; the body is tool). The strategic advantage of Olson's "practice of outside," providing it can be taken away from the epistemological reading, is that it situates the human species in a universe that is larger, older, and other. To recall the creative process, the new comes about through a troping on the givens of life, labor, and language as these arise from genetic determination, chance, and circumstance. Olson's revisionary human universe is a matrix of becomings where everything depends on the "between," and where relational thinking can be developed as a dynamic art rather than degraded in religious hypostasis or dismissed in skepticism.

Now back to tropos. Situating humanity complexly in the world is Olson's way of rethinking measure, and this is where I want to turn now. Measure requires the establishment of a relationship between the actual and virtual (this is what we can do; this is what we are doing). One significant form of this push in Olson's poetics is his attack on syntax. The polemics of "Proprioception," "Projective Verse," "Human Universe," and *The Mayan Letters,* not to mention the syntactic leaps of *The Maximus Poems,* constitute a wager against the permanence of any given syntactic configuration. In "Proprioception," for instance, Olson defines "logography" as "word writing" rather than "idea-writing" (*CPr* 184). The name Neilson he renders ideogrammatically as "kneel" and "sun," "a drawing of knees plus the sun to express the personal name of 'Neilson'" (184). This example of picture writing suggests that the name comes out of an event or act; it locates a verb in the noun. In the following section titled "GRAMMAR—a 'book'" (*CPr* 191), Olson works with the etymologies of "why," "what," "how," "who," "the," and "that" to suggest that these words were once inflections of a stem as opposed to syntactically determined function words. The pattern in his speculations is that the noun can be made flexible, and this mobilizing of the noun-thing renders it capable of more varied syntactic arrangements and nuanced emphases deriving from the context of the usage. Given the aim—to render order mutable, to put form back into the creative process—Olson's interest in picture writing and inflected languages is obvious; these two symbolic systems emphasize inflection of a stem and variable juxtapositions over fixed syntactic relations. Inflecting the stem of a noun to show relation rather than fixing its place in a sentence multiplies the syntactic environments in which the word functions. Metaphorically, it increases the "affectability" of the word, its ability to form linkages in different lexical and grammatical environments. In relation to the kind of agency that tropos implies, syntax is a prime point of intervention for poetic creativity because it is the poet who is most practiced in ungluing the order of words to allow for recombination.

A second crucial function of tropos is to render the individual life allegorical. This is the source of Olson's dogmatic insistence that the poet stay with the process, that he "cannot afford to traffick in any other 'sign' than his one, his self" (*CPr* 261). In *The Special View,* Olson accepts Jung's definition of the Self as "center and circumference" (36). Situated among the various layers of the human universe, the Self is Olson's exit from solipsism. Only if an act makes evident both the actor *and* the ground of the action is it going to be of common interest. This is the message of "Projective Verse": the poet has to transfer energy from where he got it over to the reader (*CPr* 240); the poet must compose by field (*CPr* 240); the poet must attend to the syllable through the ear and to the line through the breath (*CPr* 242); the poet must treat the objects that occur in a composition "exactly as they do occur therein and not by any ideas or preconceptions from outside the poem" (*CPr* 243). Olson's language is not guarded, and it is all too easy to play "gotcha" with such statements on epistemological grounds. But if these dicta from "Projective Verse" are read back into Olson's practice, it is not so difficult to see what he is after. If the poet faithfully records an event as the elements present themselves to him or her, the resulting record will articulate a figure doing something on a ground, and this articulation will be shareable. There is no person who does not inhabit the earth, no person who is not a member of the species, and relatively few who cannot undergo the chronic human emotions. What is essential in the presentation of an event is not the actor, but the actor as he or she brings forward the ground. There is no mistaking that Maximus is a persona constructed from an Anglo-American male perspective situated at mid-twentieth century. Olson's machismo, for instance, seems too obvious to warrant criticism: one may as well set out to chastise Dante for being Catholic. The *figure* is inevitably fallible and historically specific. Indeed Olson's selection of materials for *The Maximus Poems* is contingent, and as his critics have pointed out, he sometimes gets things wrong.[23] But if the poet can make the ground ride along with the figure, he may achieve measure. To go back to "DOGTOWN—I," Merry is hardly exemplary of nice behavior, and as a historical person, he surely did not act in awareness of his allegorical significance. (Who but a poet would get up in the morning in order to become an allegory?) The alchemy of poetry, however, turns this act into a revelation of cosmic context and human possibility. Hence in the third repetition of the story, Olson can write "*We* drink / or break open / our veins solely / to know" (*MP* 175, my emphasis). The "we" calls the reader into the common, elemental space between heaven and earth where living things manifest, there to witness an act that reveals something about human possibility. Here is the poet as "Gold Machine" (*MP* 301), transmuting the lead of the everyday into the gold of a human commons.

It could be argued, of course, that anything a person does, however silly or mundane, is an image of human possibility, but it is obvious that Olson has something sharper in mind. His selection of historical and mythical heroes comes out of a search for defining moments. These heroes are not always good or wise, but like Merry, they appear to us at the limit of an act because it is there that they stand most revealed. The strength of a man is less than the strength of a bull, and since it is strength and speed that Merry wants to test rather than, say, the more Odyssean quality of guile by which he might have won, it is by these qualities that he falls. That is, he takes the terms of the test to the limit in death and thereby reveals not only the banality that a bull is stronger and faster than a man, but that foolish "braggart man" (*MP* 172) is a chronic human possibility. Olson's bet is that the gestures enacted by the personages he selects will resonate emotionally with readers—that Dogtown will, in fact, turn out to be a "park of eternal / events" (*MP* 175)—*if* he can stay close enough to the action to bring along the ground of it. The moment the human actor becomes blind to his situatedness, however, he begins to act as Ahab or figure writ large.

The second creative wager Olson makes concerns the poet's ability to hotwire the system. An unquilted field is a potentially hotter one and less predictable than the quilted because change can be interruptive as well as dialectical. It may come, for instance, from any of the many levels that compose the whole of the field, even the slow, conservative ones. Volcanoes erupt, and for a moment the heat at the earth's core bubbles to the surface and transforms all. What I think of as hotwiring is Olson's reach across the strata to search out various "faults" where the matrix of scapes has shifted in the past or might shift again. At such points, what seems to be the solid rock of reality runs molten. Hence the poet's stance "on Main Street like the Diorite / stone" (*MP* 221) or "astride the Cabot fault." Diorite is formed through a partial melting of mafic rock over a subduction zone (a zone where two tectonic plates converge), and it is usually found in volcanic belts. The splitting of the atom and the general theory of relativity was an analogous hot point in Olson's era and a principle reference for his announcement of a paradigm shift "post the modern." Mao's revolution was another, referred to in "The Kingfishers." By image, *The Maximus Poems* return over and over to these flash points. The "geography / which leans in on me I compel / backwards I compel

Gloucester / to yield, to / change," Olson writes (*MP* 185). Compelling Gloucester backward resituates the community in the plentitude of its own past amid all of its layers, thus enormously expanding the ground of its potential becoming and increasing the number of fault lines ("lines of flight" in Deleuzean language). Or again, Olson records his effort to call up the liquid core of the ground in the poem, "I forced the calm grey waters" (*MP* 202). In this poem the poet stares at the sea "until the sweat / stood out in my eyes" and "what lies under" rises. Here as elsewhere, Typhon is the chthonic principle of desire and the dynamic of Olson's chaosmos, "entwined / throughout / the system" (*MP* 291). Olson made the study of comparative mythologies his particular care, including those of non-European cultures like those of the Maya and Algonquin, because such studies show the variability with which human beings can order their world. Comparison cracks the syntactic rock of a given reality. Through such comparisons—through those seams that allow a glimpse of the otherwise—the poet makes measure. This, in Olson's world, is what poets do.

"you do love or go down"

I want to conclude by returning to the encounters with Pound and Ferrini with which I began. Does Olson's method hold something for a crowded, heterogeneous world? Has Gloucester become large enough to accommodate Olson and Ferrini? By the end of *The Maximus Poems,* Gloucester has expanded to the poles of the earth and the constellations in the sky. Certainly at this cosmic level everyone is included. But this is to beg the question of the social antagonisms I have described at the beginning of this study. I think Olson has to make a trade-off to get past the Scylla of authoritarianism and the Charybdis of relativism: he has to give up the "power to oblige" for *Tao* and allegory. His *Tao* is a means of avoiding foundational claims without ceding everything to relativism. The promise of the *Tao* is that it may lead to a considered life ("good" in the Whiteheadian-Deleuzean sense) through the resituating of Ahabian man. This is no small achievement of methodology, not the least because Olson points to the need for a powerfully affective world image that includes engagement with nature and with the human body. Since Olson's death (1970), some of these engagements have come from the ecology movement, the closest scientific counterpart to his poetic vision. Unlike the social sciences, ecology deals with planetary life as a whole, and unlike the traditional humanities it positions the human species as one among others. Yet the contemporary Ahabian relationship with nature persists however, and it is slicker and more seductive. Power always is. I have in mind not just big energy and communications, but also the pharmaceutical and cosmetic industries as well as medical research that has as its goal the making obsolete of death. There is nothing wrong with the techno-sciences per se, unless they are carried out without regard for diminishments to the overall complexity of the planet. This, I speculate, would be Olson's point.

Another gesture that gets Olson past the evil twins is the making of his life into allegory. This gesture, however, cannot be read from the perspective of the moralist. Olson was no saint, as Tom Clark's biography makes clear, nor was he always brilliant as a poet, right as a scholar, or considerate as a teacher. The point is that he did not always have to be. The allegory does not consist of leading a perfect life or producing unassailable scholarship, but of showing a figure seriously at work on a ground. Without the actions of the figure the ground cannot appear; the figure acts to make manifest the ground. Hence the "good" of the figure consists of expanding its zone of affectability to let more of the ground appear and to enhance its own potential to become through interaction. Again, this is a deceptively simple move. The ability to be affected is foundational to any kind of sustainable world, and it belongs to what I have been calling the deep ground of religion, the encounter with an "outside." Already in Olson's time it was territory ceded to the media; now, with the reemergence of religious fundamentalisms as political theater, it is equally the terrain of political and religious leaders cynical enough to manipulate the hopes and fears of their constituents. War, murder, and torture have become the wallpaper of the evening news and the clichés of documentaries. Homeless people, casualties of decades of neoliberal public policy, line the streets of the world's major cities, and ordinary well-meaning people pass them by because what might have once been perceived as urgent has become commonplace and finally barely perceptible. To these social examples might be added the killing off or brutalization of nonhuman species, environmental degradation, and the prospect of catastrophic climate change. At issue is more than a precept for which a poet is hardly needed; it is the possibility of imagining a different relationship with the planet. Relational thinking is prereligious imaginative ground that needs to be cultivated if we are to even dream of an "actual earth of value." The situated mind, actively engaged with the multiple dimensions of its world, is a mind capable of holding the world as shape. Such engagement is not a panacea—it does not guarantee good behavior or imply an instant solution to social problems—but it does multiply the ways in which it is possible to imagine being in the world. This is what the arts can do better, I think, than the social discourses—they can retie the mind and the will to the world through imagination.

I turn to Deleuze again to help me sharpen this final point. In *Empiricism and Subjectivity,* an essay in which Deleuze channels David Hume, he writes that "One of Hume's simplest but most important ideas is this: human beings are much less egoistic than they are *partial*" (38, original emphasis). In the commentary that follows, Deleuze suggests that everyone is part of a clan or community. The problem of society is how to integrate this multitude of exclusive, sharply angled perspectives. Here, Deleuze says, is the "difference between morality and nature" (40). The moral world is an artificial one that works to integrate partialities and extend our sympathies beyond immediate kith and kin. The significance of Olson's "Kosmos" is similar. The cosmos *is* a fiction, even if I spell it "chaosmos." But the thought of the Open Whole reveals a grain of intractability in religious feeling, a small something that survives skepticism because it is an artifice called for by the partiality of human nature. If knowing and feeling are unavoidably situated, if what we call the Self is an inflection of a region of being, if we are all localized by chance and circumstance, then the Open Whole is a corrective to the conflicts implicit in that situatedness insofar as it calls us to extend ourselves imaginatively, to enlarge our clear zones. This is where Whitehead's definition of God as a "lure for feeling" might take on a certain urgency. In a chapter of his Hume study titled "God and the World," Deleuze writes that "there is no complete system, synthesis, or cosmology that is not imaginary" (83), and the corollary is that all cosmologies will fall before the critical intellect. "The idea of God, as originary agreement," Deleuze writes through Hume, "is the thought of *something in general;* as for knowledge, it can only find content in self-mutilation" (77, my emphasis). The "something in general" is not knowledge (*knowing that*) but a *techne* of the imagination (*knowing how*). By such means, according to myth, the Dog is bound:

> *. . . the noise*
> *of a cat's footstep; the beard of a woman;*
> *the roots of a rock; the sinews of a bear;*
> *the breath of a fish; the spittle of a bird.*[24] (original emphasis)

3

Robert Creeley

Occasional Verse

Like Olson, Robert Creeley began his writing life with a sense of cultural trauma. In his essay "On the Road: Notes on Artists & Poets 1950–1965," he writes that the "chaos" of the war, as well as ongoing industrial change to the "neighborhood" had left the arts in need of a new "*picture of the world*" (*RP* 74, my emphasis): "There was no place, finally, from which to propose an objectively ordered reality," he says, "a world that could be spoken of as *there* in the convenience of expectation or habit" (74, original emphasis). Creeley renders this generational feeling of crisis brutally in "The Dilemma," an essay first published in the *Black Mountain Review* (1954):

> On the one hand, there are too many people—you cannot kill them all, you cannot find a logic quite sufficient to do this. And if they will not die quickly enough with sickness, or tiredness, old age and the like, then at least they can be confined to those places where one will not have to, simply, consider them.
>
> [. . .]
>
> Some people cannot "live" anymore. There is neither reason for them to nor room nor means nor values, nor any of those things by which others, certainly more fortunate, may still claim "significance." And by much the same token, it is a little hysterical to feel our own securities are endangered by the specific reality of something like the hydrogen bomb. (*CE* 475–76)

Here is the same despair of adequate value terms as in Olson's description of concentration camp bodies in "The Resistance." However, the logic Creeley references in "The Dilemma" is more like that of Adolf Eichmann as Hannah Arendt portrays him in her coverage of his postwar trial, *Eichmann in Jeru-*

salem (1963). Responsible for thousands of deaths, Eichmann reduced lives to the logistics of getting rid of them. His life story, as it unfolded during his trial, reveals a man more occupied with career advancement than with the actuality of what he was doing.[1] Olson, in his confrontation with the holocaust, descended to a vision of the human meat; Creeley's comparable moment is a confrontation with the statistical and the subsequent terror of erasure—of lives never receiving "specific witness" and therefore disappearing as if they had never been ("The Creative," *CE* 540). In "Ecce Homo" Creeley writes that the moderns had lost "an *image of man,* some order of and in experience, both collective and singular, that could propose itself as constituting *something,* in whatever dimension or context of practical fact was elsewise the case" (*CE* 403, original emphasis). This is Creeley's project: the articulation of an "*image of man*" that proposes "specific witness" at the mundane level of personhood.

In "Inside Out" (*Was That a Real Poem,* 1979), an important essay on the autobiographical mode, Creeley writes that "what the autobiographic does, primarily, is to specify *person*" (*CE* 559, original emphasis). Autobiography is his particular care, and his counter to the statistical. I find Lyn Hejinian's comments on personhood helpful in this context, although her essay "The Person and Description" (2000) postdates Creeley's development as a poet and does not refer to him. The person, Hejinian says, is not generalizable (*Language of Inquiry* 201), nor is he or she reducible to a given set of social identities. The person *becomes* through his or her actions within a "matrix of possibly infinite contingencies and contextualities" (202). Personhood derives from an individual exercising his or her real possibilities within this matrix, where "real possibilities" include all the limits that make up the determining givens of a person's history and circumstance. Like Olson's layered landscape, "contingencies and contextualities" are the ground and *occasion* of personhood.

In an interview with William Spanos for the *boundary 2* special on him of 1978, Creeley discusses the term *occasional.* Spanos connects the word to *cadere,* to fall, and Creeley picks this up with a reference to Mallarmé's *coup de dès,* remarking that Duncan and other "poets of my dear company" are "given to write poems," as opposed to willing them. The thought here is that the poet who stays in the occasion is ventured, like a die cast. What befalls him or her in the actuality of an event resolves the contingencies of that event into a state of affairs, such that "there can be no appeal from anything other than which is" (*Tales* 129). Quoting the physicist P. W. Bridgman, Creeley says the present is " 'that which resolves all other possibilities.' That is, the present is that which resolves the past and/or the future. The present is where it comes to be" (*Tales* 130). A poetry of occasion is one in which the poet is ventured from moment to moment—in which he himself literally comes to pass. In a famous analogy from "Notes Apropos 'Free Verse,'" Creeley likens poetic receptivity to driving a car where the road "creat[es] itself momently in one's attention to it, there, visibly in front of the car" (*CE* 493–94). As the driving metaphor says, the poet has to be both receptive and participatory if he is to move beyond the orders of habit and assigned identities into active self-fashioning. Like Olson, Creeley mobilizes an ongoing tension between figure and ground. This is the relation crucial to the method and ethos of their shared poiesis. If the poet presents only the figure, he winds up in an older kind of humanism that took the cogito out of time and proposed an unproblematic transparency between representation and world; if he shows only the ground as a welter of determining systems[2]—the person as a social construction—he misses the accumulation of choices that makes the person unique, and he risks a dangerous conflation of individual voice and abstract system. Like Olson's Self that is center and circumference (point and region), the person takes specific form from his or her path; he or she is a "how" rather than a "what."

This *Tao* has been recognized by Creeley's readers in two closely related exegetical lines. Much attention has been paid to Creeley's precise articulation of emotional states and perceptual experience. Warren Tallman's groundbreaking essays of 1973 emphasize the all-importance of perceptual relationships to the persons of the poem. Tallman shrewdly notices that what is significant is not the precise content of the poem or story (Creeley has said this himself on multiple occasions) but that the content be precisely rendered. The receptive act and the poet's ability to render such acts singular and available as acts is significant. The accumulation of these is what makes the form, Tallman says (25). Other examples of this exegetical line—I take these samples out of many of the 1970s and '80s—are Arthur Ford's book *Robert Creeley* (1978) and Harold Mesch's important essay, "Robert Creeley's Epistemopathic Path" (1982). Epistemopathy is Mesch's term for the process of apprehension whereby the poet writes himself in as participant in the occasion of the poem, rather than standing apart. Cynthia Edelberg (1987), writing about *The Day Book,* remarks on the "effect of untampered-with immediacy" (282) she finds there and the "illusion" that a "connection does in fact exist between the one and the many" (295). At shorter remove, Clive Meachem (1999) discusses Creeley's revitalization of the cliché, and Paul Christensen (2000) writes of Creeley's "camera eye" and sharp rendering of the felt world.[3] Common to these readings is an emphasis on the creativity of reception.

A second, related exegetical line, and one that accounts for Creeley's relative currency through the theoretical decades of the 1970s and '80s, focuses on the reflexive play between the conceptual apparatus the poet brings to an occasion and his effort to go beyond it to respond imaginatively to the event at hand in a way that is emotionally satisfying. Creeley is famous for painful, stuttering self-examination, as in the title poem of *For Love:*

If the moon did not . . .
no, if you did not
I wouldn't either, but
what would I not

do, what prevention, what
thing so quickly stopped.
That is love yesterday
or tomorrow, not

now. Can I eat
what you give me. I
have not earned it. Must
I think of everything

as earned. . . . (*FL* 159; *CP1* 257)

Creeley himself speaks of his Puritan heritage as a factor in his practice of "auto-bio-graphy" (*CE* 555), which he defines as "a life tracking itself"—sometimes into labored confessionals as in the above lines (*CE* 562). But what has interested his more philosophical readers is his acute awareness of the reflexivity of consciousness and hence the decentered "I." Where Olson has been taken as epistemologically naive, Creeley is credited with more sophistication because he makes drama of self-reflexivity as opposed to simply assuming it. So, in the interview for the Creeley issue of *boundary 2* (1978), William Spanos links the priority of process over substance in Creeley's projective poetics with Heideggerian temporality (*Tales* 133) and the deconstructive project. In the same collection, Charles Altieri locates Creeley's work as a modification of an objectivist aesthetics to "concrete renderings of complex movements of the self-reflexive psyche" (523). He develops this attention to Creeley's finely tuned equilibrations of form and feeling in the context of his more recent study of the affects in *The Particulars of Rapture* (2003) (133–37). Mesch's article mentioned above (published in *Sagetrieb*, 1982), carefully distinguishes Creeley's effort to overcome habit from naive faith in the immediacy of the sense experience. Jerry McGuire, writing for the same *Sagetrieb* collection, gives Creeley a favorable deconstructive reading, locating his work between the haiku with its disseminative, centrifugal force, and the riddle, which points centripetally toward an answer or a presence. In a later collection, *Robert Creeley's Life and Work,* edited by John Wilson (1987), Robert Haas links Creeley's reflexivity to that of the continental theory then afoot. He writes:

> Poetics, for the last seventy years, has assumed the existence of a dialectical tension between conscious and unconscious thought. The system of analogies derived from Lévi-Strauss and Lacan and Derrida seems to assert that consciousness carries with it its own displaced and completely symbolic unconscious, that is, the structures of language by which consciousness is constituted; and this unconscious is to consciousness what language—"the collective, structural, unconscious system of differential relationships which constitute the possibility of any individual speech act"—is to particular acts of speech. This is what Creeley's mode and the attractiveness of his mode have to do with, at least much of the time; it is a poetics which addresses the tension between speaking and being spoken through language; and he makes a brilliant and unnerving music out of it. (397)

Other readers have suggested that Wittgenstein is Creeley's closest philosophical cognate. Among these are Altieri in the article mentioned above (525), Peter Quartermain in *boundary 2* (330, 331), as well as Linda Wagner (310) and Hugh Kenner (412) in the Wilson collection.

These readings of Creeley are not interchangeable. To hear in Creeley a congeniality with Wittgenstein's argument that meaning derives from language games and social interactions situated in complex contexts is not the same as to read him through deconstructive theory. Yet both kinds of readings acknowledge reflexivity as a major element in Creeley's poems against which the poet struggles to respond freshly to the occasion. This has made Creeley more congenial than Olson to next-generation language writers as well. In "A Packet for Robert Creeley" (*boundary 2*), Robert Grenier picks up "the stuff in *Pieces* . . . where the primary interest is language process/energy released by an intensity of perception given closeup to the elements of language (letters, syllables, words) in the process of their self-formation" (422). Charles Bernstein's essay in the *Sagetrieb* collection emphasizes duration as key to Creeley's sense of place: place is a sequence rather than a geographical immediacy. This is an important noticing because it repositions the local in time rather than space. Creeley's definition of the local is that it is "not a place but a place in a given man" (*CE* 479). Although I think that Creeley is more the transcendental empiricist than language writer, these noticings show how his awareness of language as system makes him congenial to readers sensitized to language-based philosophies. Bernstein, for instance, recognizes in Creeley's variable measure a kinship resemblance to Silliman's constructivism and Robert Grenier's *Sentences* ("Hearing 'Here'" 93).

As these exegeses show, many readers have recognized Creeley's finely drawn inner scapes as well as the reflexivity that always qualifies his attention to perceptual events. In my view, however, reflexivity is not the main event but a tensor in the articulation of personhood. Again, Hejinian helps me with a description:

> But, in fact the sense of being, of selfhood, can only be reached after one is in place and surrounded by possibilities. That comes first: the perceiving of something, not in parts but whole, as a situation and with a projection of possibilities. The recognition of those possibilities follows and constitutes one's first exercise of possibility, and on that depends one's realization that oneself is possible. It is in the exercise of that possibility that one inescapably acknowledges others, which have in fact already been admitted when and as one initially perceived something. And the exercise of possibilities (including that of consciousness) amid conditions and occasions constitutes a person.
>
> It is here that the epistemological nightmare of the solipsistic self breaks down, and the essentialist yearning after truth and origin can be discarded in favor of the experience of experience. (203)

Hejinian's last sentence is particularly important to my reading of Creeley. It is finally the "experience of experience" his poetry points toward as the common place of the species. In a way complementary to that of Olson, Creeley claims the familiar by repossessing the person of his or her temporality, and he does this by establishing a rubric of *knowing how.* He is thus able to treat experience without the irony that has become a ubiquitous defense of writers attuned to the reflexivity of consciousness. My reading of Creeley as a poet of *Tao* is meant to draw attention to an ethos in which sincerity takes precedence over irony and recognition[4] of the familiar over cognitive certitude. Sincerity is a concept I hope will accumulate significance throughout this essay through my readings of Creeley's poems, but for a short definition

I cannot do better than George Oppen who writes that "the image is encountered, not found; it is an account of the poet's perception, of the act of perception; it is an act of sincerity, a test of conviction, the rare poetic quality of truthfulness" (175). I would add to this that sincerity may well involve the expression of feelings and attitudes that are quite ugly. The poet's integrity, in such cases, depends on precise rendition of the occasion at hand, not, as Oppen says, on a display of "right thinking and right sentiment, a dreary waste of lies" (175).

Creeley's *Tao:* The Practice of Time in Space

In the Wagner interview, Creeley describes himself as "very, very edgy those few times when I have tried to gain a larger view" (*Tales* 47). In a later interview with Michael André (1970), however, he is less reticent. Asked by André if the "acceptance of 'process'" constitutes the 'larger view'" he says, "[i]n some ways it is a larger view"; "I don't think it solves everything—simply that one's life goes on" (*Tales* 103). Creeley's rendition of the occasion takes the place of the larger view, although eventually it becomes one. The occasion is a counter to history understood as the master narrative of a tribe or nation-state or ethnic group. It is Creeley's alternative to both the heroic (the great man) and the statistical (rule by bureaucracy and opinion poll). Olson's quarrel with the universe of discourse brought him to dissolve the grand historical narratives and myths back into their smaller components. The effort of his research into the history of Cape Ann and the European settlement of America was directed toward the specificity of who did what when, and it was his democratic impulse to urge a version of reality that might be perennially open to like action. However, he often retains the big names of persons like John Winthrop who were, in their times, in positions of power, or who were by chance, management, or commission in the position to be firsts of some kind. The heroes of *The Maximus Poems* are those persons who pushed the limits of human possibility and who therefore stand as the historical counterparts of mythical heroes. There is epic glory in the giant astride the Cabot fault, or the luminous figure of Merry as an image of "actual willful man," crucified on a bull's horns. In comparison, Creeley's personae are ordinary and minimally competent—the bumbling husband, the bickering couple, the hesitant lyricist are familiar persons of the poem. There is an obvious difference in scale, in other words: Olson writes on an epic scale, Creeley on the lyric.

How then, does the Creeley occasion compare with Olson's special view of history? For both, story is the act of a figure on a ground. As Olson's man of action has to be dwarfed by the ground in which he is positioned (Ishmael at sea), so Creeley's average Joe has to stay in his[5] particular temporal moment. He thus appears to have no history other than personal memory, even though he carries the former with him as genealogy and circumstance. *Having* is the operative verb. The person cannot possess a history she is inside of; she does not own the past, whatever her narrative reach, nor can she project herself into the future. "Le Fou," dedicated to Olson, is among the most important of Creeley's early poetics poems in *For Love* (1962). Characteristically short and extremely dense, the poem is a tribute to Olson and a manifesto for the Creeley occasion at the same time.

who plots, then, the lines
talking, taking, always the beat from
the breath. (*FL* 17; *CP1* 111)

Creeley has said that while a poem cannot be willed, it must be prepared for; a poem may therefore be plotted or planned. But plotting also has a cartographic sense that brings up the Olson-Creeley focus on location. The poet records his place and time, figuring himself in by taking the "beat from / the breath." Once he has a locus, he can then choose the appropriate mode of address. Olson favored the public letter, often in heightened rhetoric. Creeley counters with "talking." Talk is as much an artifice as any other mode of address, intensely so in Creeley's carefully crafted poems, but it serves to position the poems in the intimate conversational zone between an I and a you. The poet moves from the givens of his circumstances that include his body (which has a personal and species-level genealogy), his locus in time and place (geography, history), to his immediate social situation (talking). In very condensed form, these first lines of "Le Fou" reprise the principles of projective verse as they assemble the basic components of an occasion: chance, circumstance, and agency. The aleatoric component of the occasion is hinted at in the verb "taking"; the poet takes the lead from his breath as he also takes the lead from whatever is happening in front of him. But notice that his plotting balances receptivity to the contingent with intentionality. In the "plotting" of lines, intention comes in, but it is directed toward the craft of the poem, rather than toward any effort to control the occasion. In *Pieces,* Creeley would write, "I am tired of purposes, / intent that leads itself / back to its own belief" (78). Paradoxically, purpose limits the poet to what he or she already is and knows, as opposed to what he or she might possibly become. So the poem begins to move *outward* from the initial coordinates of the occasion:

the breath
        (moving slowly at first
the breath
        which is slow—
I mean, graces come slowly,
it is that way.

So slowly (they are waving
we are moving
                away from   (the trees
                             the usual   (go by
which is slower than this, is
                             (we are moving!
goodbye (*FL* 17; *CP*1 111)

The repetitions of "the breath" suggest hesitation and underscore the assertion that what is moving in the poem is slow, hesitant. But in the last stanza there are two speeds. There is the movement of the "we," which seems to be picking up pace, we the makers of the lines in stanza one, perhaps we the projective poets. Then there are the points that let the poet measure his speed, the "they" who wave and the trees he is passing. But notice the unbracketed lines: "we are moving / away from / the usual / which is slower than this, is / goodbye." Slow as the poet moves, the "usual" is slower. The poem suggests first that the matter of speed is relative—hence the principle of variable measure. Second, the poet is moving away from whatever seems to be relatively stationary like the trees, because his attention is more acutely focused on the moment than "usual." In the Wagner interview, Creeley says, "One time, again some years ago, Franz Kline was being questioned . . . and finally he said, 'Well, look, if I paint what you know, then that will simply bore you, the repetition from me to you. If I paint what I know, it will be boring to myself. Therefore I paint what I don't know.' And I write what I don't know, in that sense" (*Tales* 26). "Le Fou" shows the poet moving away from what he already knows.

Thus far, this poem demonstrates projective principles, enacted at the intimate level of personhood. The French title, however, offers further possibilities. "Le Fou" is a poem by Aloysius (Louis) Bertrand (1807–1841),[6] a prose poet and precursor to the symbolists. His "fou" is a gnome who gathers the false coinage of the moon to buy himself a place in the sun. The poem has Scarbo cashing his false ducats and florins in the speaker's cellar, but the implication is that he remains under the influence of the moon—that he cannot take this currency into the day world where fancy does not pass so easily as coin of the realm. Another possible reference is to "le fou de Bassan," a cliff-dwelling bird, awkward on its feet, but graceful in the air. It nests on sea cliffs because it needs to launch itself from them to become airborne. The most obvious reference, however, is to the Fool of the Tarot deck who later comes into *Pieces* as the zero in Creeley's sequence on numbers (33–35). In this later work, Creeley quotes A. E. Waite's description of the Fool in the Tarot deck, a young man "at the brink of a precipice," poised as if about to step over (*Pieces* 34; Waite 152). He is "a prince of the other world on his travels through this one" (Waite 152)—in conventional metaphysics, the soul on its earthly journey. Poised on the edge, the Fool doubles as the bird that has to step off the cliff to fly—and perhaps Bertrand's Fool as well who has stepped off into the night world of imagination and dream.

In my view, the Fool—any one or all three of them—is an image of time in the context of this poem. To move past the "usual" one has to step off the present into the no-place of the future: this is Creeley's version of the "practice of outside," where the "outside" is realized as a dimension of time rather than space. Every *coup de dès* is a toss into the abyss. The earth under the Fool's foot will rise up as the foot comes down, at which moment the future will reopen again and the Fool will again step into the abyss. In *A Day Book* (1972), Creeley would write: "In the boat of it, so to speak, going, but rather in the fact that from here is there, and the past a wake of curious resonance, and forward no more than the body's movement, in walking, the one foot lifting, to find place ahead of itself, else behind" (n. pag.). From the perspective of a consciousness living its time, the future is an aporia like death; it can be conceptualized but not experienced. Like the mathematical zero (the Fool's number in the Tarot), it is an empty set that exists nowhere in nature, but which makes possible speculative operations with real effects, as the mathematician's zero makes possible the realm of negative and imaginary numbers. In the context of Creeley's thinking of the cogito, the zero functions like a blind spot that accompanies consciousness, comparable to Deleuze's "pure" past or Lacan's "real," neither of which can be experienced.[7] As Creeley conceives it, the mind is divided into a mysterious "I" that perceives and a "me" that is the object of the perception. So he writes in his essay, "The Creative": "Speaking now, it must be that this factual person, *me,* is familiar, so like so many, in fact, his hair, teeth, pants, etc. But the *I,* as Wittgenstein put it, is what is 'deeply mysterious.' In a world of objects, *mes,* this is the one manifestation of existence that cannot so see itself as literal *thing.* It is my experience that what I feel to be the creative has location in this place of personal identity" (*CE* 539–40).

In contrast, Olson takes the cosmic perspective, from which vantage there is no zero, no death, no incompleteness, and no lack because the individual is just a temporary particle in the becoming of the cosmos.[8] From the cosmic view, the universe is complete in its becoming from moment to moment. Death, absence, and the aporias of time belong to human consciousness rather than the process of the Open Whole. It is not that Creeley is unaware of such cosmicity, but that he chooses to focus on the *person* for whom death and time are urgencies and ultimates. Consciousness is thus accompanied by its Other—its abyss—and this is where, in the stepping off, Creeley locates creativity. On more than one occasion, he cites these lines of Olson's as inspirational:

He left him naked,
the man said, and
nakedness
is what one means

that all start up
to the eye and soul
as though it had never
happened before. (*Tales* 139; *CE* 482)

For both poets, these lines are about freshness of perception and the effort to move beyond habit—about leaving the "usual"—but again the difference is as space to time. The Olsonian field is a synchrony of various times, variously active, which stretch far beyond the individual's reach or clear zone, so that the figure is of the field and working the field, but in a relationship of nonidentity to it. The Creeley occasion is analogous, but it differs in feel, not only because his personae are drawn from the domestic sphere, but also because they seem to play no part in the grand historical narratives. At issue with these naked characters, however, is not a naive refusal of historical determination. Determination is there in the syntheses that make up the habits of the species, the givens of the person and of his or her circumstances—and no one works harder than Creeley to confront habit and the pressures of memory. Deleuze, in his analysis of repetition, notes that the mind's movement from past to present through a series of memory-making passive syntheses is from the particular to the general: "from the particulars which it envelops by contraction to the general which it develops in the field of its expectation (the difference produced in the mind is generality itself insofar as it forms a living rule for the future)" (*Difference and Repetition* 71). I suggest that the effort of the Creeley occasion is to minimize expectations, at least at the already highly synthetic level of consciousness; by focusing on the actual moment, the poet tries *not* to foreclose the future by projecting it as an extension of the past. This is Creeley's battle with habit, and it parallels Olson's effort to keep the figure in a relationship of nonidentity with its ground. In terms of temporality, imposing the past on the future (reducing the future to predictability) is like writing oneself too large, and it obscures one's own *familiar* ground in the actual unfolding of the moment. The condition of nakedness, like the Blakean innocence of the Fool, speaks again to an ethos of containment, complementary to that of Olson's, and to an effort after poiesis rather than epistemology.

Rhythm and Rhyme: Subjective Time

To arrive further at Creeley's version of ethos and agency I have to follow him through the dimensions of subjective time. Like Olson's space, Creeley's time-scapes are polyvalent. "To And," an early poem from *For Love* (1962), balances rhythmic, seasonal time against direction:

To and
back and forth,
direction
is a third

or simply fourth
of the intention
like it
goes and goes.

No
more snow this
winter?
No more snow.

Then what replaces
all the faces,
wasted,
wasted. (*FL* 126; *CP1* 224)

The "to" that opens the poem indicates direction, as in an address to someone or a route taken toward some place. "To" implies a point of arrival. "And," however, qualifies the movement. If a person moves "to and fro" as the almost-cliché of the first line suggests, or "back and forth" as in line two, he or she defines a space by the back and forth movement. There is direction, but no ultimate arrival. The poem links intention ambiguously with direction as a third or fourth factor, and I think the ambiguity comes from the different ways the poem proposes to deal with direction. Directional movement changes if it becomes traversal, and traversal changes again if it "goes and goes." Going and going might either suggest repetitious traversal or a kind of wandering that goes without doubling back on itself. Intention may be involved in all three kinds of movement, but it is seriously qualified as soon as the movement is no longer about traveling from A to B. Like rhythm in poetry, the traversal of a space has no natural end except the stopping of the breath or the exhaustion of the content. If, by analogy, I shift the attention to cognition, then the linear movement from A to B parallels the mind's desire to arrive at some conclusion, while the back and forth movement or the nomadic "going and going" suggests *recognition* of what has become familiar rather than *knowledge* as the expectable effect of the movement. When a person traverses a space, he or she does not so much arrive at a point as create a place.

Rhythm is what the body shares with other species and with nature's cycles: the body rocks till it stops. For living creatures, however, there is also directional, Heraclitean time (you can't step in the same river twice), counterpointing repetitive rhythms so that each beat ("taking the beat from the breath") is unique and irrevocable. The third stanza about snow makes this point. The snow is gone for *this* winter, even though snow qua snow may return as winter returns. Countering the repetition, the cliché about the uniqueness of every snowflake (itself a kind of repetition) hovers unspoken around this stanza to come home in the last verse in the "faces, / wasted." The repetition of "wasted" intensifies the play between the generic and the particular, and underscores the loss of the latter to the passage of time. The poem ends with the possibility of elegy for all the individuals wasted—a superimposition of the linear time of a life (or a snowflake) on the cyclical time of species life and seasonal rhythms.

"To And" inevitably brings to mind "The Rhythm" of *Words* (1967). Among the best known of Creeley's poems, this one reviews a common literary topos. What era, after all, has not had its poets celebrating human participation in the rhythms of nature.

It is all a rhythm,
from the shutting
door, to the window
opening

the mind in men
personal, recurring
in them again,
thinking the end

is not the end, the
time returning,
themselves dead but
someone else coming. (*Words* 19; *CP1*)

As these lines show, the content of the poem does not tell the reader anything that he or she could not gather from, say, Whitman's "Crossing Brooklyn Ferry." Yet Creeley counterpoints the theme of species continuity and seasonal repetition with the distinctive syncopated rhythms of the poem, each stanza a little different, so what the reader actually hears is difference in repetition. As well, he steers the poem away from the consolation that this trope usually offers. The "force moves on," he says, and it is "not mine" (*Words* 19, 20). The two kinds of rhythm position the "mind in men" in nonidentity with nature's cycles—a figure-ground relationship.

I want to pause here briefly to consider the larger significance of what Creeley is doing. Western idealism has tried to extend the ephemerality of individuals with at least three kinds of imaginary identifications. History and myth, used as foundational narratives, have been the comfort of warrior societies from those of Homer to the author of Beowulf. The exemplary individual achieves a kind of immortality by setting his mark on a group of people who value him as a model or remember him in stories that define group values. (If we think we are beyond this, consider the cults of Hollywood or Bollywood.) Another reach for immortality has come through Christianity, distinctive among religions in specifying the eternality of the individual soul and personal accountability as the ground of faith. The romantic rebellion against Christian orthodoxy—an ongoing countertradition to that of the mainstream enlightenment—centers on pantheistic identification. But romanticism has as its central contradiction an identification of the individual consciousness with the vital force of nature. As Freud notices,[9] the paradox is that mystical oneness, whether with nature or God, implies the absorption into that larger whole of the individual consciousness, "like water in water."[10] As Creeley says in *Pieces,*

In the singular
the many cohere,
but not to know it. (*P* 73; *CP1* 439)

At the social-economic level, as opposed to that of the idealist tradition, the reach for immortality manifests as the cooption of the past (its otherness, its unmanageability) and mortgaging of the future for the extension of present interests. Capital accumulation is enabled through deferral of the moment (the *coup de dès*). The investment or hoarding of wealth and the selling of credit extract tribute from the future for the present well-being of the owning classes. Not only is the future "owned" by the creditor or investor and to that degree determined, but also the present is constructed as lack. Under capital, the worker mortgages her future literally if she is a borrower, and, as a worker, lives a deferral of enjoyment because the present has been taken out of circulation, so to speak, by the owning class, in the form of interest and surplus value and through the production of never-ending desire. Lack is the first, enabling product of capital, and because the market is based on desire, not need, lack can be extended endlessly.[11] The existential given under such a system—the cultural heritage, the resources of the earth—simply flattens into raw material for production dedicated to present interests.[12]

What is problematic about identifying with any of these extensions of the individual is that they invite a serious inflation of the personal voice and will. So in "The Rhythm," Creeley specifically gives away the continuity and the largeness of species life (it is "not mine, / not mine"). Recall the Jungian willfulness of Olson's Merry: he identifies with the archetypes and hence fatally missteps on the ground he can no longer see because he has so overshadowed it by that inflation. Again, I circle back to my premise that Creeley, like Olson, has to show a figure working its ground if he is to avoid the pitfalls of the Ahab complex on one hand and the erasure of personhood on the other. Figure and ground constitute a model specifically cut to the human scale, to a life lived in time. Creeley grapples with articulating this polarity as a temporal relation in "The Rescue":

The man sits in a timelessness
with the horse under him in time
to a movement of legs and hooves
upon a timeless sand. (*FL* 133; *CP1* 231)

Time past and future exist nowhere else but in the mind-body, manifesting in the syntheses that create memory and cellular movement. As Creeley would write in *Hello*, in a little poem called "Time," "Can't live, / mindless, / in present" (*CP2* 53). The man in "Rescue" "sits in timelessness." Yet if the man is *in* time he is inside a structure that is itself timeless. Past, present, and future are dimensions of the present, Deleuze argues, but no one actually lives the simultaneity of the structure of time—this would be to experience timelessness. Instead, the man's body, like that of any other animal, rocks under him according to the (particular) rhythms of (his) nature. And it moves forward, bound to the syntheses of cellular memory that cause time to pass. Under the horse the man rides is "a timeless sand"—timeless again because time and space are the enabling relations of relation and as such are timeless, even though they exist nowhere but in the actual, shifting relations (sands) that instantiate them. The last two stanzas, in which the figures of the poem are burning, draw out the consequences of this condition. The horse "ran / and runs to come in time." The concept of being "in time," in the sense of arriving promptly for some event, follows from the directionality in which the man is caught as an embodied consciousness. The movement around the man—the blowing wind and the burning of man, horse, and wind in the final stanza—show that time and space, mathematically relative, are absolute conditions from the individual's point of view—that is, they cannot not be experienced as movement. In this poem, consciousness does indeed become mysterious, as Creeley says in "The Creative." If nature's time is rhythmic and seasonal, and if the mind sits in an eternal now where all the tenses of time are co-present, then how is it that time comes to pass? The pure past, Deleuze says, the past that causes time to pass, is transcendental. So the man is caught in a temporal outside that contains him and that he cannot master; he burns up with the horse and the house and the wind, as a life burns up from its beginning to end. The title of the poem plays off the double sense of being "in time." Presumably the "rescue" is about saving the man or house or horse from burning up, but the pun on "in time" turns this sense of arriving in time to rescue someone to that of being constituted by time. "Running to arrive," man and horse come into time; the harder they run, the more they feel themselves subjected to time. In the poem "Time" cited above (from *Hello*), Creeley writes: "can't make past, / or future, enough place" (*CP2* 53), which is to say that no one can spatialize time enough to live in timelessness. Past and future can be *conceived* as dimensions of the present but not *experienced* as such—that is the crucial polarity that distinguishes figure and ground. In "The Rescue" it is as if the man were literally being pulled out of his ground in the timelessness structure of time into personhood as his body moves forward with the horse. Creeley registers this polarity again and again in the play between "here" and "there." So in *Pieces*, "No one / there. Everyone / here" (3; *CP1* 349). The poem balances "no one" and "everyone," "there" and "here"; the abstract structure of time against the actual undergoing of it.

The above poems present lived, directional time in a relation of nonidentity to both the structure of time and the rhythms of physical life. In fact these contraries define the outer limits of the occasion, as Olson's topos is bordered by the human meat at one extreme and the Idea at the other. Harold Mesch rightly emphasizes Creeley's distinction between the real and the actual: the former is the world of things as positivism understands them; the latter is "the dialectical interrelation of subject and object, of concept and thing . . . *logos* and *physis*" (58). By staying in the actual, Creeley resists both the temptation of the absolute (the old metaphysics) and the romantic identification with the species life of nature.

If rhythm is the way that persons participate temporally in physical life, rhyme is a poet's way of remarking the *difference* in that repetition, the singularity of persons and moments. "For W. C. W." exemplifies:

The rhyme is after
all the repeated
insistence.

There, you say, and
there, and there,
and *and* becomes

just so. And
what one wants is
what one wants,

yet complexly
as you
say.

Let's
let it go.
I want—

Then there is—
and,
I want. (*Words* 27; *CP1* 273)

The first stanzas of the poem add Heraclitean time to Williams's dictum: "No ideas but in things." Each thing becomes itself as it persists in time, there and there and there. The thing is thus never *simply* there, but complexly so, because in its enduring the living thing also differs from itself. This is what the poem calls insistence.[13] The repeated words in the poem show how repetition folds back on itself to create difference. The three "theres" add temporality to an ostensive spatial gesture: three repetitions, but three different loci and three moments in the becoming of "there." In the tautology—"what one wants is / what one wants"—the repetition of the two phrases emphasizes the particularity of the one wanting and that of what is wanted, so that repetition becomes insistence in both senses of the term. The last three lines condense these temporal relations. "Then there is—" catches the time lag between concept and percept: "there is," as an ostensive gesture, always comes after a "then." In subjective experience, things are never fully present. There is always the zero point of a past that never was and the aporia of a future that by definition is not yet. Hence there is always an "and" to follow the "is," and a desire for presence that is ontological as well as situational ("I want"). "Let it go," Creeley says, let the substantives (the "it," the *things* of Williams's "no ideas but in things") pass into time. In *A Day Book*, Creeley marvels at his friend, the painter John Altoon, who remarked of his tree drawing that it was *sincere*. Creeley interprets the comment as meaning "that's as much tree as was possible to realize, there, that's all of it, all at once, all I see. And it is—i.e., is crazily intensive seeing, and all *at once*. He [Altoon] speaks of fact he does not work comfortably in 'accumulating' the image, has to be 'all at once' " (n. pag., original emphasis). To notice in this comment is that while Creeley admires the intensity, he does not allow that the tree can be apprehended "all at once." In his own work, form emerges through accumulation or difference in repetition rather than simultaneously.

In Creeley's prose works, subjective time "goes and goes," as opposed to the poems in which the moment is anatomized. Charles Bernstein comments: "Place inevitably emerg[es] out of whatever collocation of pieces, always closing, foreclosing perhaps but only in the sense that life in time is always limited by the condition of time. So that this duration of particles, occurrences, particulars is, like Heraclitus' river, always flowing, always another river, always this one" ("Hearing 'Here' " 94–95). The prose of *A Day Book* (1972) is impossible to paraphrase because it is ordered temporally rather than conceptually. Certainly Creeley has his themes—sexuality, personal identity, the act of writing, time and space—but these are not treated in a way that lends itself to summary. At any given moment, the possibilities of the occasion are both more and less than any concept one might try to abstract from them. "The consciousness *thinks* it has experience of this or that. Conceptualizes. Like Alpert's note of the ratio between conceptual units and the content admissible in perception, something like 1 to 20,000 per second. Itself a somewhat unwieldy 'idea' " (*DB*, original emphasis). The concept spirals open with the variousness of the content it collects. Certainly Creeley makes generous use of abstract relations, as these denote mental or emotional states and in this sense his writing can be very abstract, but in Heraclitean time, the concept is under constant centripetal pressure from perceptions that "go and go."

For readers, an autobiography articulated as is *A Day Book* does not deliver up the person as an object of knowledge but the person as a subject of recognition. As we read through the prose, we become slowly acquainted with the speaker, as if we were living with him, and the more acquainted we become, the less able we are to sum him up.[14] Warren Tallman, in his discussion of "Three Fate Tales" makes two crucial points. First, because the self is singular, there is no possibility of representation; instead, there is correspondence—my particularity corresponds with yours. Second, representation gives place to the counting or telling over of perceptions such that these accumulate to make a form. In the stories of *The Gold Diggers,* for instance, Tallman notices rhyme in the recurrences of screams, of chairs and sticks and stones. Consider the notorious little poem in *Words* called "A Piece":

One and
one, two,
three. (115; *CP1* 352)

The poem contrasts two kinds of counting. The first counting by ones takes account of the particularity of each one. The second counting suggests several readings. Peter Quartermain hears in it "the collection of singularities" (333) that cumulatively make form—particles that add up to something, in other words. But cumulative counting also suggests the statistical that abstracts something generic from the specificity of the things counted. These different ways of counting contrast two ways of looking at the world: poetically, in the singular, or statistically, in the categorical. Tallman writes that "nothing that is perceived will have value unless it has some use in human space" (13). Hence the poet's task. The telling over of things by ones draws them into the "human space" as elements that have to be taken into account. Through this process, space becomes place and self acquires its measure through the network of relations created by the counting. Creeley, more than any poet of what he calls the "company"—his peers and compadres—practices the telling over of his world.

In counting by ones, the *Tao* of subjective time *produces* the familiar. In *For Love* and *The Island,* for example, Creeley tracks the affective minutiae of a life. "The Operation" describes the "you" of the poem after an illness, but it is the speaker's compulsion to describe that is the real topic: "Cruel, cruel to describe / what there is no reason to describe" (*For Love* 34). These lines draw the reader toward specific personhood as it emerges in the gesture of telling. Similarly, in *The Island,* John's inner life is the subject of a telling as in this sequence that records the character's neurotic self-hatred through his bedeviling of his children and wife: "Where did you put it. I put it back. Where did you put it after you took it from my table. I put it back. It isn't there. Where did you put if [*sic*] after you took it" (*CPr* 229). *Mabel: A Story* brings this painstaking accounting of things to bear on the occasion of writing itself, so that the speaker is always qualifying and commenting on his own "takes": "I know the condition of those around me, or rather think that I do. One wants to say, *these days.* There is a tacit paranoia I have begun to enter into all such accounting. Again, I do not know if it is an age, my own, biological, or something so patently the case that one moves apart from it" (*CPr* 272, original emphasis). In these examples and many others, counting by ones means the minute inspection of thoughts, feelings, and sense data as these unfold. Out of this unfolding comes recognition and finally familiarity. This, I take it, is what Creeley means when he writes that "the local is not a place but a place in a given man" (*CE* 479). What is local is the unique trajectory of a life rather than geographical location (recall, in this context, that for Olson, too, place is process). Recognition builds incrementally and form emerges from traversal.

This is a point where method twists into ethos. Interviewed by Lewis MacAdams (1967), Creeley comments on *The Island* that it demonstrates "the *horrors* of thinking that thought can possess the world" (*Tales* 97, original emphasis). The point comes up again in the important essay, "Inside Out," where Creeley repeats a Ginsberg story that illustrates the difference between agency as representation and agency as one can come by it in subjective time. "One time, years ago now, Allen Ginsberg was at a party in New York talking with a young woman about the apparent hostility publishers then felt toward the younger American poets, myself in particular. She was, as it happens, a junior editor at Harper's, and listened patiently to his irritation. Then she said, we've been in business for over eighty years and I think we know what we're doing. At which point Ginsberg naturally flipped—You? *You've* been in business for over eighty years? Why you're only twenty-two years old!" (*CE* 560, original emphasis). This story shows how the cogito that reaches beyond its occasion bears with it an inflated claim to authority. The young publishing agent conflates her own experience and voice with what probably would untangle as a number of experiences undergone by a number of people, and then translated into a teachable policy. So congealed, the policy acquires its definite article and royal we: *the* editorial policy; *we* know what *we* are doing. It is to the point that the publishing agent makes this appeal in response to a challenge. Her response is aimed at legitimizing a position that she has not arrived at on her own and that is prior to the interchange with Ginsberg. And notice that the agent not only speaks with an authority not her own, she also misses the occasion Ginsberg's challenge opens for her. In falling back on someone else's ready-made position, she actually narrows her own potentiality for personal growth, even though she seems to be asserting herself.

The ethos implicit in this story is spelled out elsewhere in the essays and interviews. In "A Note," for instance, Creeley writes that "Pound, early in the century, teaches the tradition of 'man-standing-by-his-word,' the problem of *sincerity*" (*CE* 477, original emphasis). Again, that word. In the Wagner interview, he elaborates on this point, arguing that the poet's public task is to take responsibility for his or her words: "You see, we're back again to Williams's sense of the government of the words as our responsibility. What outrages the articulation of feeling in language, what makes language subverted to the meager reality of distorted and finally criminal acts against men such as are evident in this circumstance—what distorts and beguiles and coerces by means of language can only, I think, be confronted by a use of language which makes obvious that criminal distortion on the part of those who make use of it" (*Tales* 35). If this poetics be taken at all seriously, it represents a significant challenge to the statistical way of looking at the world and to all modes of representation that implicitly or otherwise lay claim to a voice larger than the one speaking the words—in other words, to just about all modes of public address currently in use. I have suggested above that the statistical is an aspect of the war trauma from which Creeley pushes out into poetry. Yet in contemporary democracies, statistics and opinion polls have become normalized as key tools of governance. Statistics claim the authority of collective assent but they have no locus in any actual group of persons. In fact, statistics depend on the participant group *not* being recognized. Opinions derived from polls, or studies that yield averages in order to graph trends or predict future situations become a means for legitimating public policies or economic decisions that affect many people who then have to live out those decisions in time and in the singular. And if such decisions cause grief to the many who must abide by them, who is there to stand by the words?[15]

Creeley's alternative is everywhere in the poems, but here it is thematized in "Edges," from the 1994 collection, *Echoes:*

. . . thinking I am not simply a response to this, this light,

not just an agency sees and vaguely adumbrates, adds an opinion.
There is no opinion for life, no word more or less general.
I had begun and returned, again and again, to find you finally,

felt it all gather, as here, to be a place again, and wanted to
shuck the husk of habits, to lift myself to you in this sunlight. (*CP2* 445)

The poem focuses attention on the back and forth movement (traversal) that creates recognition ("I had begun and returned, again and again"), and it registers the poet's effort to respond to the possibilities of the moment ("to lift myself to you in this sunlight"). This is where the agency is: not in opinion, but in the effort to speak the occasion into a place where you and I can recognize each other beyond "the husk of habits." In the Wagner interview (1968), Creeley says that "choice does not exist except as recognition" (*Tales* 47). I will come back to this comment in my final section. For now, the point I wish to emphasize is that the patient counting by ones, the pacing back and forth, the going and going, and the rhythm and rhyme are Creeley's way of practicing the outside and stepping-out place from time-space—perhaps from there to propose "some common places of feeling" ("The Company," *CP* 304).

Common Places: The Quality of the Affection

In "The Creative," Creeley cites Pound's "respect for Confucius, for that 'sound given off by the heart's core'" as the "measure of sincerity" (*CE* 544). Sincerity, I will repeat, is a primary value under the logic of Creeley's *Tao,* rather than rightness or wrongness, truth or falsehood. The poet may well be mistaken or morally "wrong" and still utterly sincere in his presentation of "wrongness," as is often the case with Creeley's fallible personae. Rather, sincerity is about engaging the energies and relations of the occasion as fully as possible. His speakers are notoriously fallible—the philandering husband, the angry father, the obsessive neurotic, the selfish, uncaring man, as well as the ardent lover and the poet of finely tuned attentions. To repeat, the ethical energy lies in the care, honesty, and attention given to the rendition of an event, not the content, as Creeley has said in many different ways. Citing Pound in the interview with Wagner, for example, he says that it is the "quality of the affection" that endures (32), as opposed to "assumptional sentiment" (33). It is for this reason that, in my view, Libbie Rifkin's objection to the projective poets misses the point. Rifkin, in *Career Moves* (2000), argues that Olson and Creeley create authorial selves that exclude others' difference (71). In particular, Creeley's use of women as the defining other of the "I" is at issue (70). I can agree with Rifkin that the women in the poems *do* function in this way, but the point is not to model the right social values. Like Olson, Creeley uses himself for material because his own inner world is the only one available to him, but by locating his personae as actors engaged in some event or relational network he avoids making the poem *about* his own will and wishes. He thus does not attempt to avoid the ego position because that is impossible; rather, he diminishes it by placing it in a situation. Certainly there is gender bias in the poems, and certainly all readers will *not* recognize themselves in Creeley's personae. What is there to be seen, however, is a very specific person literally speaking for himself.

Of course the catch is that the person cannot speak only *to* him or herself if the poem is to attract readers. The corollary of sincerity has to be correspondence. In his introduction to the Penguin *Selected Whitman,* Creeley writes that "the common *is* personal, intensely so. [. . .] it is paradoxically, the personal which makes the common insofar as it recognizes the existence of the many in the one" (*CE* 3, original emphasis). Creeley offers a number of ways to register the correspondence between the situatedness of one person and that of another, given that the perspectives of other minds are not directly communicable. In the Spanos interview, Creeley glosses Olson's "polis / is eyes" as mutual witnessing, such that lookers-on share the sensation of witnessing the same event: "You *saw* it too!" (*Tales* 151, original emphasis). This is an aspect of Creeley's commons that Alice Entwistle picks up in her essay "'For W. C. W.,' 'Yet Complexly': Creeley and Williams": "The shared experience in and witnessing of the moment, being at once individual and common, remains somehow single, bringing coherence which is not proscriptive but which permits possibility" (146). Entwistle's point is that the reader, on the one hand, is both included and excluded; if the poet can only speak from his own perspective, then his voice necessarily excludes that of the reader's. On the other hand, the reader is called to the possibility of bringing his or her own distinctive perspective to the occasion. When the event is mental or emotional, the question will be whether or not the reader has *come to* such an occasion and is therefore capable of recognizing it. If the reader cannot recognize the event so depicted, then he or she may react with alienation and that will be the relationship established. But if the reader can see the relations Creeley is after, as opposed to whatever specific content he uses to articulate them, then the likelihood of alienation may be significantly reduced. I take seriously Creeley's protest that content is not a primary interest—that his poetry has no "subject" ("A Sense of Measure," *RP* 13). What matters is the "experience of experience" (Hejinian).

I have chosen three examples from *For Love* to showcase the variousness of Creeley's strategies in articulating the "experience of experience." I hear "The Paradox" as a poem about the structure of perception:

Looking down at her
long hair,
we saw the position
in which we placed her.

Yet our own
a formula, the street
she walked up
she looked down on. (*FL* 134; *CP1* 232)

The first stanza shifts from present to past tense, from a concrete object of attention ("her / long hair") to a more abstract one ("the position / in which we placed her"), and from *looking* at someone to *seeing* (understanding) one's own role in positioning her. The gaze in this first stanza ricochets from perceived back to perceiver. This is a formula for perception itself; whatever we see, we see through some kind of cognitive frame, yet at the same time, the perceptual act is intimately bound to the particularity of its occasions. And we need to look at something in order to become aware of how we frame our looking. In the second stanza, the attention shifts to the actions of the woman. Object in the first stanza, she is subject in the second, but this shift of positions does nothing to undo the formula. The woman has to look *down* on any street she walks *up*. Perception always has to come from somewhere, but as the poem suggests, the up and down, the present and past, the "we" and "she" are relations with no fixed point of reference. The fact of being situated is nonnegotiable; the meaning of any situation is relative and context-dependent. That is the paradox; perception is both relative with regard to act and fixed with respect to the facticity of its situatedness. The poem is of the same kind as "A Method," from *Words*, where the demonstratives emphasize the context dependency of sense and relativity of position: "This / and that, that / one, this / and that" (*Words* 100; *CP1* 339). In these poems, the relational web created by multiple perspectives is the providing ground of the common, my view corresponding in its specific thereness to yours.

My second example shows how clichés can be made alive again to potential real relationships. This is a point that Meachem has noted: Hank Williams's songs "are great because their 'trite, trivial and hackneyed' disclosures allow us entry to the human condition; we all know what the songs are about and we simultaneously fill up their spaces with our own individual contexts" (143). Meet you at the OK Corral. I would rephrase Meachem to say that what takes place in the revitalized cliché is place itself. Here is "The End of the Day":

Oh who is
so cosy with
despair and
all, they will

not come,
rejuvenated, to
the last spectacle
of the day. Look!

the sun is
sinking, now
it's
gone. Night,

good and sweet
night, good
night, good, good
night, has come. (*FL* 135; *CP1* 233)

The sunset is the occasion for the display of the speaker's singular mood. First, this is one who can be "cosy with / despair," a phrase suggesting someone content to remain miserable, rather like John in *The Island.* Then the poet introduces the idea that a sunset can rouse such a person out of his or her morose state. Notice that not a word is spent on description. There is no plea for the beauty of sunsets or the fineness of some particular sunset or any homily about the salutary effects of nature on a depressed spirit (imagine "Tintern Abbey" for the contrast). The whole effort of the first stanzas is to inhabit, in all particularity, a cliché. The exclamation, "Look!" marks a turn toward the reader. But what is there to be looked at? Instead of description, the poem undergoes another tonal modulation with the repeated emphasis on night, "good and sweet / night." Suddenly the hackneyed phrase ("good night") becomes alive and full of mystery. Has the speaker experienced the necessary renewal and does he now bless the ministers of nature, as does Coleridge in "Dejection: An Ode"? Or is it closing time at the bar in Eliot's *Waste Land* that echoes here in all its tawdriness and cheap gaiety—"Good night ladies, good night." And why celebrate the *end* of the desired sunset, if that is indeed what is happening? What is it that makes the night good and sweet? Has the speaker sunk back into an emotional darkness even deeper than "cosy despair" and does he now welcome the night as the black analogue of his mood?

The focus of the poem is on the nuances of a finely rendered mood—let's say depression mixed with hope, irony, and perhaps a dash of obsession as hinted in the repetitions. So what happens to the reader, summoned to a sunset that she or he never gets to see? The short answer is that the poet cannot say because he cannot see through the reader's eyes. But the cliché on which the poem builds is certainly recognizable across any number of social or cultural differences: the beauty of nature rejuvenates the spirit. But what about this particular spirit, on this particular occasion? Or this one? Or this one? What might have been a meaningless pleasantry—"Look at the beautiful sunset (and you'll feel better)"—suddenly becomes an actual occasion. It is as if someone were to respond to a casual "how's it going?" with as much sincerity and detail as possible. All of a sudden, the greeting turns into the possibility of a genuine relationship that may or may not be transformative but that insists on participation and attention. (Recall, in this context of the drawing out of the "good night," Coleridge's Mariner and that first touch of the skinny hand that detains the wedding guest.) It is not just the sunset or the speaker's mental state that the reader is urged to regard, but his or her own as well. In effect, the poem says stand with me in this place and look at the sunset—and now that you are here, "HOW'S IT GOING?" The sunset and the informing cliché about the beauty of nature twist into an occasion for calling together any number of disparate persons around the big existential questions (despair of what?). In this sense, the cliché is like a well-known landmark, used as a meeting place for whoever accepts the poet's invitation.

Another way of approaching the common is through generic feelings and behaviors. Whatever the mystery of other minds, human behavior suggests empirically that persons share certain physical needs and psychological states. Creeley maps such states as Olson mapped the history of Gloucester. "A Wicker Basket" is a good example because it shows the difference between a cartographic treatment of the inner life and a moral one. Certainly the point of this compellingly unattractive poem is not to evoke sympathy or approval for the speaker. It begins this way:

Comes the time when it's later
and onto your table the headwaiter
puts the bill, and very soon after
rings out the sound of lively laughter—

Picking up change, hands like a walrus,
and a face like a barndoor's
and a head without any apparent size,
nothing but two eyes—

So that's you, man,
or me. (*FL* 65; *CP1* 161)

The first stanza sets the scene. A night out, and plenty to drink. The speaker leaves the restaurant in a sensual blur, in the company of others likewise situated. The "you" ("your table") seems to be male, although the word "man" in the vernacular of the 1960s could apply to either gender. The hip talk, smacking of drunken posturing, continues:

. . . I make it as I can,
I pick up, I go
faster than they know— (*FL* 65; *CP1* 161)

"I make it as I can" holds the double entendre of sexual conquest and inebriated fumbling, while "faster than they know" has something of the braggart in it, as in I can make a sexual conquest faster than they, my friends, realize. Beer hall big talk. Over the next two stanzas, the speaker encounters "old friend Liz" who fortunately seems to have a Cadillac and the wherewithal to "turn [him] on." Look at what happens next:

There are very huge stars, man, in the sky,
and from somewhere very far off someone hands me a slice of
        apple pie,
with a gob of white, white ice cream on top of it,
and I eat it—

Slowly . . . (*FL* 65; *CP1* 161)

This stanza is a wonder of comedy and sense experience. The legendary effects of marijuana—it makes you hungry, distorts your sense of time and space, and dilates your pupils—are amusingly imitated in the speaker's sudden fascination with "huge stars" and his evident relishing of the pie and ice cream, real or imaginary. Everything in this stanza slows down as the sensual effects of the drug kick in—the too-white ice cream and the focus on the sense of taste. Here's the end of the poem:

. . . And while certainly
they are laughing at me, and all around me is racket
of these cats not making it, I make it

in my wicker basket. (*FL* 65; *CP1* 161)

It is not precisely the sexual conquest that makes these lines stand out, but the spectacle of an outrageous enjoyment. In the eating of the ice cream and the conquest of the girl, the speaker positions himself to be spectated and envied—indeed the whole point of the poem is to display the speaker's enjoyment of the woman, the Cadillac, and the free ride all this entails. The "wicker basket" literalizes the mix of beat and hippie slang (the speaker thinks he is a pretty cool cat so the poet gives him a wicker basket), but this is merely clever. What makes the poem powerful is that the basket image draws out the infantile aggression in this scene; it displays the speaker's jouissance as it feeds on the envy of others.

In "A Wicker Basket," Creeley intuitively cuts to the bone of human aggression. What is it that pushes young men to strut and swagger or the same to fight for some vaguely conceived notion of honor (drunken braggadocio in the context of this poem)? Or upping the bets, what compels groups of people to murder each other for relative advantage and power over, as opposed to cooperation with, their supposed enemies, even if cooperation might further the interests of both more than the spoilage and waste of war? What is it that the human creature wants to the point of self-destruction, and where finally does rivalry find its reductio ad absurdum? This poem easily lends itself to a reading through post-Freudian psychoanalysis. If desire, as Lacan argues, is desire of the (M)other (I want the Other to want me), jouissance is the enjoyment of a substitute for the (M)other. Performed as it is in "Wicker Basket," jouissance is aggressive: not only do I want to incite the Other to desire me (because then I can control it/him/her) but also to display my enjoyment in order to incite envy in others. This is the *obscene* face of enjoyment Žižek has searched out.[16] Consider, in this context, "I eat it— // Slowly." Creeley's poem predates this theorizing, but it is not necessary to be schooled in neo-Freudian theory to recognize a psychological state that children act out intuitively when they jostle to position themselves to be envied by their peers. The poem articulates a set of affects that, deducing from human behavior, has very wide applicability. Humanity is a social species, and its sociality includes the desire to attract the attention of others. Whether that desire *must* take the form described by psychoanalysts is a question I cannot answer. But the poem hits a very common nerve, and it is a good example of what can be accomplished with sincerity as opposed to social correctness.

The above examples show that the common is so in several senses. Common to everyone is particularity of perspective as in "The Paradox"; this is the commonality of difference. Common as well is the sharing of the planet and the recognition sometimes enabled by well-frequented places of humanity's inner and outer scapes as in "End of Day" and "Wicker Basket."

A cliché becomes such because many people have used it. Everyone on the planet is positioned to experience the sunset, although the blind will register it differently; everyone feels the weather; and everyone responds emotionally to charged social situations. In many of Creeley's poems, these universal features are positioned on the Möbius twist where the outside becomes inside and vice versa. That twisting point between the physical and mental, the generic and particular, or concept and percept is the site of the experience of experience and the taking place of place. The twist is where the human universe occurs momently. The poet's sincerity in exposing a situation precisely as in "Wicker Basket," without regard for the moral desirability of his persona's acts or for saving face, is what makes the common place truly recognizable.

Basic English

Before I try some conclusions, there is another important instance of the common I want to draw in. This is Creeley's use of language, in particular a "plain" speech close to Basic English. Cid Corman (1987) notes "Creeley's own original desire to write in Basic English, [and the fact that] he very nearly does even now" (111). John Thompson (1987) writes about Creeley's use of the gerund, "as in 'the growing of things,' [as] a way of generalizing action so that what takes place has no particular time" (153). Creeley "likes to compound tenses" and fuse identities, he says, so that the "words are so general, the situation so vague, the personages so ectoplasmic, the action, if any, so small and obscure, that the reader is invited to fill this vacuum by himself in 'projection'" (153–54). Alice Entwistle (2001), in the article cited above, comes to a similar conclusion when she draws attention to Creeley's use of the generic to *summon* the particular. Clichés and plain speech serve a parallel function: the generic or the trite—the easily recognizable—are gathering places for singular perceptions and emotions. The concept of the generic works at a meta-level to gather a number of different Creeley occasions, just as *in* the poems, the generic word or phrase or event assembles particularities.

Basic English is a bare-bones version of the language designed to facilitate learning by nonnative speakers. Basic has an 850-word vocabulary, and a pedagogy emphasizing visual aids and the most concrete meanings of the words. Prepositions, for example, are visually illustrated. In his description of Basic, I. A. Richards (1943) discusses the rationale and methodology that produced it. The aim to improve global and domestic communication came out of the postwar need for reconstruction, a need Richards obviously anticipates, given the date of his publication. New transportation and communication technologies would link the world, and trade would require a common language. Increased migration would mean that heterogeneous populations at home would have to be informed of public matters such as health care. The reading and writing skills of ESL (English as a Second Language) students would have to be addressed. These are the arguments for a simplified world language, and Richards spends a lengthy first chapter in arguing English as the logical choice (it is not inflected, it is easier to learn than, say, Chinese, it is a natural versus invented language and therefore has a rich heritage, it already has a large number of speakers, and so on). As Richards presents it, Basic has a utopian aspect to it as well as being a practical method of teaching English as a second language. A world language, he implies, would facilitate more empathy among different cultures as well as practical communication. The argument that underlies his support of Basic is that the world needs to understand itself better (115), and that improved relations must start with a common language: "To turn a world language into an actuality," he writes, "we must see it as a way of remaking man" (132).

Is there a utopian component in Creeley's use of plain speech as well? In the essay, "The Creative," Creeley distinguishes between two kinds of abstraction:[17] "the ability to make of all the seemingly endless divergency and occasion of thing [*sic*] a general agreement, a *one* in which the *all* of its situation might come to rest and be recognized; but also, the impulse to have the one be a part of the whole, in a way which overrode it, became specific more intensely than all the other 'parts' otherwise equally present, an 'I' that wants so much more than to be merely 'human' or 'people' or, simply, 'like them' " (*CE* 540, original emphasis). The first kind of abstraction holds the most common meaning of the term; the part-whole relationship implies the subordination of the singular to some generic concept. Abstraction of this kind tends to treat particularities as if they could be fully expressed in a concept, and of course this extends enormously the mind's capacity to *grasp* its situation, providing the actuality of the occasion be ignored. In contrast, the first kind of abstraction is a generality that *assembles* particulars: the individual, the "I," is more than its generic group identity (it is not just "like them"). This is the kind of abstraction at work in Creeley's plain speech and his use of cliché. Plain speech is a *u-topos;* it exists nowhere but in the occasions it assembles but is not identical to them. Creeley's repeated assertion that he has *been given* to write of certain things and that he has *come to* certain places in language or thought further holds this sense of voluntary assembly. Basic, in the loose sense of the term as a set of grammatical functions and a few symbols used concretely, is a Creeley strategy for this difficult emptying out of the generic in a way that accommodates many particular "I's." "Juggler's Thought" from *For Love,* exemplifies:

Heads up to the sky
people are walking by

in the land with no heads
tails hanging to trees

where truth is like an apple
reddened by frosts and sun, and the green

fields go out and out
under the sun. (*FL* 55; *CP1* 151)

The images have the quality of a child's drawing—I think of a crayoned sun, tree, and field. The people may be stickmen or ovoids, perhaps, with body parts proportioned to the child's awareness of them. The sun is a yellow circle with lines coming out of it for rays. The trees are fuzzy green balls on brown vertical lines and the blue sky is separated from the ground by a blank space that, every child knows, is just empty. Of what does this picture really consist? A small vocabulary of geometrical symbols, first of all. A circle, straight and wavy lines, perhaps squares, rectangles, and triangles if the picture were to include a house. Then there are the colors, the arrangement of the figures, and the proportions of them that mark the child's affective investment in the scene. In "Juggler's Thought" the heads go up to the sky, suggesting a child's perspective on a world filled with people taller than herself. But this crayon land is headless in another sense as well. Childhood perception combines extreme abstraction with intense specificity of occasion—a polarity that the mind has to juggle. Given the circle, the square, the line, the ovoid, the triangle (think of Cézanne), the child draws his or her view of things as if they were generic. Every item wears the definite article because in the limited experience of childhood, there are a countable number of houses, persons, trees, or apples; hence, "*the* sky," "*the* land," "*the* green / fields." And because the symbols are few and readily learned, and because the singularity of the emotional investment recalls anyone's childhood by correspondence, this very distinctive picture of a headless land with tails hanging in trees that surely no one has ever seen except in this poem and perhaps on somebody's fridge door achieves wide recognizability. The child's drawing shares with

Basic English a limited grammar and vocabulary that can be used in a very wide range of contexts and remain accessible to persons of widely different backgrounds. At the same time it presents an utterly unique perspective (*the* land, *the* green fields, *the* sun).

Creeley's "The Language," from *Words* (1967) shows how this tension between the generic and particular plays out when the big emotions are at issue. Creeley is not far from poststructuralist philosophers who take the linguist's perspective on language as a system of relations (an *écriture* preceding speech). He differs, however, in his interpretation of what this might mean. In "The Language" the speaker tries to locate the words "*I / love you*" (*Words* 37; *CP1* 283, original emphasis). In the first stanzas, he walks the reader through the absurdity of trying to find these emotionally charged words somewhere in the body, perhaps "in // teeth and eyes" (*Words* 37; *CP1* 283). This leads to the thought of love's pains as inflicted by the teeth ("bite / it but // take care not / to hurt" [*Words* 37; *CP1* 283]). But of course the "hurt" that can be inflicted by teeth is nothing like the pain of love. In the second half of the poem, the speaker looks to the words themselves. "Words / say everything" (*Words* 37; *CP1* 283); there is no getting away from them to something underneath, more unique or more authentic. The poet is then faced with a paradox: emotions have to be undergone individually, even though they take form from a shared system of symbols (this is where Jack Spicer's "Homage to Creeley" makes sense and William Burroughs's complaint that language is a virus from outer space begins to sound plausible). The words, "I love you" illustrate the point poignantly. While they usually indicate that the speaker is undergoing a powerful emotion, the words themselves are as common as bathroom graffiti. Beneath the words and absent from them there is someone's beating heart.

One solution to this dilemma of nonidentity between words and affects—what can be said and what must be undergone—is to index the singularity of love by making it present as absence (this would be Spicer's special art). Hence Creeley's "Language" poem offers words "full / of holes" (37). Again, there is nothing here incongruent with a poststructuralism that emphasizes the priority of the linguistic system over speech and hence the impossibility of expressing singular presences. But in the last lines, "Speech / is a mouth" (37). The mouth is now the hole and it is filled with speech. The mouth is also an organ of love, and when the words "I love you" fill someone's mouth, then it is possible to hear the beating heart beneath them. The performative solution to the failure of representation to render experience in the singular is in this intimate locating of the most "basic" of words. Here is another instance of the twist, the undecidable border between the generic and particular, between concept and perception.

Creeley's last published book, *On Earth* (2006), includes a long poem called "Caves" that builds on this twist between the inside and outside of things. The poem resonates with a comment on Plato's cave that Creeley makes much earlier in his career, in the interview with William Spanos:

> In any case, I was suddenly thinking, O.K. you could propose, say, Plato and what derives from his modes of thinking as the process of abstraction and the unity of possible states, the possibility of forms as being unifying and bringing together into a singular condition of experience, the efficacy of forms so proposed and so conceived. And then I said, well, he's a poet, not a poet—He's a thinker therefore primarily of this *inside* state of existence. To me it's instantly interesting that, of course, he does use a cave, though he speaks magnificently of the possibility of getting out of it. It's very interesting to me that he begins with a cave as the imagination of the human place and experience thereof. (*Tales* 130–31, original emphasis)

When he comes to write "Caves" years later, Creeley meditates on the big questions inspired by a visit to these places of the human morning. What makes this species ruthless and stupid enough to destroy its own planet? How could the same bloody-minded creatures make *art* for no apparent advantage, as they did in the cave paintings? Searching the caves of prehistory leads Creeley to the cave of the mind; searching the mind, he is returned to the caves of prehistory. Like an echo chamber or "any old camera" (*CP2* 624) the mind reveals traces of a passage but not the recording apparatus. Similarly, the prehistoric leads only to "an arched dark space, the rock, / and what survives of what's left" (625). So there is no "possibility of getting out of it" as Plato had hoped, and yet the logic of experience requires an elsewhere, there where "I" is not. That polarity resonates with Plato's dualism, and yet "Caves" changes entirely the meaning of transcendence. "This is where it connects," Creeley says in the last stanza, this primordial twist between the caves of the skull and of the earth, but "*not meaning anything one / can know*" (625, my emphasis). So "Caves" affirms the *u-topos* at the heart of this poetry: "One's here / and there is still elsewhere" ("On Earth," *CP2* 627).

Such Measures

As I hope the above section makes clear, Creeley's "field" is, like Olson's, unquilted at the existential level. The string of tropes and associations connected with the common place—the zero, the hole, the cliché, Basic English, the twist—all suggest a space in which place takes place and the experience of experience unfolds. The neutrality of the field is a function of the level at which Creeley has it play out. This metalevel of place is to be distinguished from the corporate. As Creeley has it in *Robert Creeley and the Genius of the American Common Place,* the corporate "is the imagination of a body" (Clark, 90), which implies singularity of purpose; whereas the common is "an insistent presence of diversity, . . . [that] excludes nothing" (89). So oppositional relations take place within the common, but because the field is existential it unfurls at a higher level of generality than does the *socius* in which the antagonisms of the Freudo-Marxian model (sex and class) play out.[18]

In my view, Creeley's poetry works best at the personal and existential levels, rather than the sociopolitical.[19] In a 1997 article, Claudia Keelan raises a number of questions that I think are still common among contemporary readers of poetry. The poetics of witness, she says, fail in a secular, class-divided society because the writer has to assume common ground with his or her readership. They fail as well under circumstances where action in the public sphere is limited to polls and statistical analyses. A change of consciousness means little under circumstances in which the manipulation of government and media by lobby groups is the only version of praxis left (83). It might have been news to Blake's readers that people suffer at the hands of others but it is not news today (83). In short, poetry cannot make a difference in the real world, so whatever cachet it may have had as radical or liberational has gone stale. Worse, it can no longer even console if its potential to liberate has lost credibility. I bring Keelan in here because I think her objections to poetry surface in many different guises in the critical reception of the arts, particularly in the assumption that any kind of cutting-edge art should embed a moral or political position considered desirable by the reader in question.

Creeley's poetry simply disappears under such demands. Let me review what *is* on offer. The principle ongoing dialectical tension in his work is between the person acting and the occasion of the action. At the metalevel, this dialectic *is* open to everyone as the experience of experience. In other words, Creeley establishes a rubric that articulates and validates experience as that which is the case. This is already much to accomplish. But as with Olson, there is an allegorical dimension to this poetry as well. As I said above, the poet has to use himself for material because his inner life is the only one available to him, but the point of the resulting autobiography is to reveal personhood as such. The measure of the efficacy of the poem in this regard is sincerity. Sincerity is what saves the poem from egocentrism because it takes the "centrism" away from the ego. In the careful tracking of an occasion, the poet places the cogito in something larger than itself. Olson does this with space; Creeley with time. What the figure is doing may not at all attract the *sympathy* of readers, nor are its acts meant to elicit moral approval. Yet if it is situated in a common place it may evoke recognition, and Creeley increases the *likelihood* of recognition by having his personae haunt that originating twist between nature and culture. The reader may thus find common ground either at the metalevel (the poem as an experience of experience), through correspondences (one particularity calls to another), or by recognizing some well-worn topos of thought or feeling.

I can now go back to Creeley's comment in the Wagner interview that "choice does not exist except as recognition" (*Tales* 47). If the reader insists on a way back to the world from the poem, then meaningful choice that comes out of recognizing real possibility is the most likely path. The common place that assembles a range of recognizable attitudes, affects, or behaviors becomes a place where human possibility is allowed to appear, even in its eccentric, abject, or reprehensible forms. This ethos (as opposed to ethics) sets poetry up as measure—exactly where Creeley and Olson would have it. Measure does not offer consolation, nor does it necessarily yield political homologues. If Creeley be mined for such homologues, then the reader is not going to get much further than the model of an ideal democracy in which everyone counts—a model that seems quaint in the postdemocracies of the twenty-first century, although it may still work as a lure for feeling. In my view, this is not the most artful way to read the poems. Consider Creeley's comments in "A Sense of Measure":

> I want to give witness not to the thought of myself—that specious concept of identity—but, rather, to what I am as simple agency, a thing evidently alive by virtue of such activity. I want, as Charles Olson says, to come into the world. Measure, then, is my testament. What uses me is what I use and in that complex measure is the issue. I cannot cut down trees with my bare hand, which is measure of both tree and hand. In that way I feel that poetry, in the very subtlety of its relation to image and rhythm, offers an intensely various record of such facts. It is equally one of them. (*CE* 488)

Seeking measure, the poet comes into the world and discovers there what is his or her own. The deep ground of measure, I repeat from the Olson commentary, is the prereligious feeling of being positioned inside something that is larger than oneself and to which one is called to respond. This sense of placedness is more difficult to articulate than perhaps it ever has been because of the history of religious practices as projections of the human will and covers for privilege. Secular intellectuals, eager to be done with superstition and violence, have been wary of any kind of discourse that comes out of experience. It is not simply that experience can be shown to be mediated, although this is enough to make it subject to skepticism but also that it supposes transcendence. Under the rubric of experience, the cogito has to stop before the mystery of other minds and the aporia of its own future and death. It has to stay within its temporal and spatial limits. Transcendence, in this context, is that which does not go away, that which one is absolutely up against. Where Creeley shines is in modeling how to live with the resulting "mysteries, uncertainties and doubts" day by day by day.

4
Robert Duncan
Master of Rime

Introduction

Robert Duncan shares with Olson and Creeley the urgency of response to what he calls "the squalor and stupidity of the American mercantile, industrial and capitalist world" (*H. D. Book,* "Rites of Participation" 28). Like his companions in poetry, Duncan saw the need for reconceiving the human universe, and like them, he recognized that any such visionary effort would have to account for multiplicity and process. The culture of the future, he writes, will be a "symposium of the whole," that includes "the female, the proletariat, the foreign; the animal and vegetative; the unconscious and the unknown; the criminal and failure—all that has been outcast and vagabond must return to be admitted in the creation of what we consider we are" ("Rites of Participation" 7). Duncan here stands beside Olson and Creeley in his effort to extend the attentions of the poet beyond his or her cultural backyard. Before globalization became a buzzword of the millennium, Duncan saw that the "drama of our time is the coming of all men into one fate" ("Rites of Participation" 6). This generational resemblance to his Black Mountain compadres, however, conceals some significant differences.

Unlike Olson, who developed some of his most cogent statements of poetics by way of rejecting the cultural "western box" from Plato forward, Duncan rejects nothing. Instead, he reinvents the meaning of the box. No less contemptuous of positivism than Olson, Duncan is after *deep* convention in his retrieval of world cultures. I'm adapting this concept of convention from T. S. Eliot's "Tradition and the Individual Talent" and Paul Alpers's *What Is Pastoral?* to conjure an assembly of participants gathered over some matter of common concern. A convention in this sense of a *convening* makes a verb of the noun and leaves room for dissent and innovation. Alpers, in his discussion of pastoral, questions the possibility of fixing upon a set of defining criteria for the genre and evokes instead a gathering of "shepherds" who engage one another in singing contests, each one trying to outdo the others in prowess and audacity. So Duncan joins the company of poets, living and dead, who inhabit the "commune of Poetry" (*BB* vi). Capitalized, Poetry is his term for the "grand collage" (*BB* vii), the whole of the human story that unfolds the life of the species. Duncan's poetics are *not* based on a quarrel with the Platonic-Christian tradition as are Olson's, nor is he an empiricist. His is a poetry of radical hermeneutics rather than radical empiricism; a mythologizing of history rather than a historicizing of myth; of Penelope at the loom, weaving, unweaving, reweaving rather than the handsome sailor and the voyage of discovery. Because Duncan is a poet of organic continuities, he has a versatility and breadth not immediately evident in the work of his Black Mountain peers. Like Emerson, he is a poet of the ever-widening circle; strife at the local level becomes order in the larger, cosmic whole, so he can accommodate closed poetic forms as well as open ones; war poetry and anarcho-pacificism.[1] Perhaps for this reason Duncan has attracted a wide range of critical attention. Some readers have found rich ground in his hermeticism, others in his inventive readings of such diverse companions in thought as Freud, Darwin, Dante, Pound, Stein, or Olson.[2] Like Whitman, Duncan can rightly claim to contain multitudes. It is therefore more difficult to summarize trends or exegetical lines in Duncan criticism than it is to gather that which has grown up around the work of Olson and Creeley. What I will do instead is offer a survey of those sources that most inform my own argument.

Michael Davidson's early work on Duncan still seems prime to me. In the Duncan issue of *Ironwood* (1983), Davidson published "Cave of Resemblances, Cave of Rimes: Tradition and Repetition in Robert Duncan," an essay that would later make its way into his book, *The San Francisco Renaissance* (1989). Discussing the conversation between Duncan and Olson triggered by Olson's "Against Wisdom as Such," a conversation Duncan carried on in print, Davidson writes that "the argument between the two men . . . is an argument over two notions of tradition: one as the archaeological (and archetypal) structure of certain dynamic ideas realized throughout history by a few capable imaginations, the other as *the open-ended series of variations on a corrupt and corruptible text*" (*San Francisco Renaissance* 129, my emphasis). I will come back to the differences between Olson and Duncan because these require complex response; in this passage it is Davidson's characterization of Duncan's hermeneutical method that I find concise and compelling. Another related point about tradition I have taken from Davidson and from Michael

André Bernstein, who makes it as well, is that the postmodern poet and Duncan in particular engages in self-fashioning by creating his or her own canon (Davidson, *San Francisco Renaissance* 131; Bernstein, "Robert Duncan: Talent and the Individual Tradition" 180).[3] This comment supports what I have taken from Alpers about convention and convening, suggesting that convention is a moveable feast where masterworks are constantly renewed through the novel configurations proposed by newcomers.

Wendy McIntyre's essays on Duncan's hermeticism in *Maps* (1974) and the *Ironwood* collection are another essential noticing. In the earlier essay, "The Logos of Robert Duncan," McIntyre usefully gathers the Gnostic and Kabbalistic sources that inform Duncan's use of language—"the ineffable articulation generating Cosmos" (84) of hermetic lore like that of the Zohar, which has Yahweh creating the world through the agency of the Hebraic alphabet. Most importantly, she argues that Duncan "invests with the power of the Logos" the ordinary words of "feeble human speech" (83). In the later *Ironwood* essay, "Psyche, Christ, and the Poem," McIntyre draws out the centrality of the Cupid and Psyche story as an enabling myth of Duncan's poetics and shows that in Psyche's suffering and Eros's withdrawal Duncan replays the Christian pathos. In another important reading of the hermetic, George Butterick recognizes the Neoplatonic elements in Duncan's poetic practice. His "Seraphic Predator: A First Reading of Robert Duncan's *Ground Work*" (1985) precisely catches "the interfolding, layers upon layers, the interfering with simplicity" and the "simulation of movement" everywhere in Duncan's poetry since "The Venice Poem" (278).

Davidson, McIntyre, and Butterick draw out prime hermeneutical and hermetic elements in Duncan's poetics; Duncan is unreadable without such groundwork. Peter Michelson and Nathaniel Mackey then ask the necessary ethical questions that come out of a hermeticism that embraces the goods and evils of the world in the name of the greater, cosmic whole. Michelson raises important objections to Duncan's mythopoeic treatment of historical events like the Vietnam War because this deferral to the cosmic level seems to set aside the question of actual historical agency. Mackey's essay of the early 1990s, "Gassire's Lute: Robert Duncan's Vietnam War Poems," now collected in *Paracritical Hinge* (2005), explores this same central problematic of Duncan's politics: "Given Duncan's belief that the cosmos, the totality of What Is, is the prototypical poem, the challenge of his poetics (and the challenge to it as well) is the necessity of acknowledging both the ideals of a poetic conception and the equally poetic perversions of those ideals. The objectionable, anti-'American' actions of the United States take part in the 'greatest poem' the universe ultimately is, so however much Duncan might move to protest those actions the underlying assurance of his poetics is that they too belong to the scheme of things" (*Paracritical* 127). Along the same line, *The Poetry of Politics, the Politics of Poetry* (2006), a collection of commentaries on the Duncan-Levertov correspondence edited by Robert Bertholf and Albert Gelpi, focuses on the implications of Duncan's hermeticism and his anarchist politics as manifest in the quarrel with Levertov over her antiwar poetry of the Vietnam era.

My reading of Duncan will focus on his Neoplatonic version of the figure-ground relationship I have been tracing through Olson and Creeley's work. Neoplatonism blurs the relationship between figure and ground,[4] and this, in my view, is at the root of the ethical questions Michelson and Mackey raise as well as the differences Duncan has had with Olson, Spicer, Blaser, and Levertov. Both Olson and Spicer reproach Duncan in writing for "trafficking" in signs that were not his own. For Olson, figure and ground have to be distinguished if the figure is not to project itself as God (*CPr* 262). Spicer's response to Duncan was pithier: "If you don't believe in a god, don't quote him," he writes in *Language* (*CB* 226; *MV* 383). In many pieces, Duncan seems to offer the same kind of polarized field as Olson and company, but there is a persistent tendency in his treatment of sources literary and cosmic to allow polarity to drift into identification and figure to reverse into ground. I have argued that *knowing that* and *knowing how* propose different rubrics, the former a *mathema* suggesting knowledge acquired by study or by testable means and measurable as truth or falsehood; the latter a *pathema* suggesting the living-through of experience, the impossibility of certitude, and a *Tao* whose efficacy as a life-path is an ongoing experiment, not measurable as true or false. Duncan's Neoplatonism allows for the fusion of these two contrary kinds of knowing, and with considerable consequence.

What I want to establish first through a survey of "The Venice Poem" and "Poem Beginning with a Line by Pindar" is the structural importance of the Neoplatonic Eros to Duncan's cosmology, psychology, and poetic method. Duncan is an eclectic poet, overwhelmingly so in the range of his references. But this variety of content serves to explicate and reinforce rather than change the basic hermetic model of form in back of his work. My second consideration will be the implications of this model as it bears on Duncan's theory of translation and derivation, his selection of materials, and his ethos. In the section on "Order and Strife" I will consider Duncan's differences with Blaser and Levertov as these have been preserved in writings around the translation of Gérard de Nerval's *Les chimères* and in correspondence. My concluding section will consist of a brief reading of Duncan as a poet of the *via imaginaria* and high drama.

Essential Fictions: Eros, Psyche, and the Hermetic Tradition

The myth of Cupid and Psyche comes from Apuleius's *The Golden Ass,* a Latin text many times translated, notably so by Robert Graves in 1951. In a 1968 installment of *The H. D. Book,* "Two Chapters from H. D.," Duncan summarizes: "There was the Palace of Eros. Psyche was to inherit all, on the condition that she not seek to see her Eros in the light. Her mind must not become involved in knowing" ("Two Chapters" 69). According to the myth, Psyche enjoys a luxurious life with Eros, her mysterious lover and spouse, but all is conditional on her not looking at him. Eros comes to Psyche only at night and vanishes at dawn. For a while they are happy in this arrangement. But Psyche cannot contain her doubts and curiosity; she *will* hold the lamp up to Eros, and of course immediately she loses him. Heartbroken, Psyche asks for the help of Venus, Cupid's mother, in recovering her love, and Venus sets her a number of impossible tasks. The story is about paradise lost, purgatorial trial, and redemption. It is about the human species in its coming to reflexive conscious and its subsequent separation from the rest of nature. And it is also a story about the psychological development of every child who must undergo individuation and separation from the mother in order to come into personhood. "Eros and Psyche are personae of a drama or dream that determines, beyond individual consciousness, the configurative image of a species," Duncan says ("Two Chapters" 68). Before her "sin," Psyche is a "dilettante" (69). She is loved without loving, infantile and unreflective as animals are. In order that she may come to maturity as a discrete individual, capable of love, she must first undergo the pain of separation and later the humbling of the intellect.

To Apuleius's story has to be added the Kabbalistic creation stories. Gershom Scholem's account of Isaac Luria's cosmogony is as useful as Apuleius's myth because it includes formal features that have key expository significance for Duncan' poetry. Well-known to Duncan through Scholem and other sources, Luria was a Jewish mystic (1534–1572) whose version of creation begins with *tsimtsum,* a term for the self-limitation of God. The cosmos begins when God withdraws into himself in order to create a space for something other than himself to exist (Scholem, *On the Kabbalah and Its Symbolism* 110). The resulting space, or "pleroma," however, contains elements of God's sternest judgment, concentrated and mixed with divine light, and this is the mixture that is the root of evil. Scholem explains:

> In the pleroma arise the archetypes of all being, the forms, determined by the structure of the *sefiroth,* of *Adam Kadmon,* of the creator God

> who takes a hand in Creation. But the precarious co-existence of the different kinds of divine light produces new crises. Everything that comes into being after the ray of the light from *en-sof* has been sent out into the pleroma is affected by the twofold movement of the perpetually renewed *tsimtsum* and of the outward flowing emanation. Every stage of being is grounded in this tension. From the ears, the mouth, and the nose of the Primordial Man burst forth lights which produce deeply hidden configurations, states of being and inner worlds beyond the penetration of the human mind, even in meditation. But the central plan of Creation originates in the lights which shine in strange refraction from the eyes of *Adam Kadmon.* For the vessels which, themselves consisting of lower mixtures of light, were designed to receive this mighty light of the *sefiroth* from his eyes and so to serve as vessels and instruments of Creation, shattered under its impact. This is the decisive crisis of all divine and created being, the "breaking of the vessels," which Luria identifies with the Zoharic image of the "dying of the primordial kings." (*On the Kabbalah and Its Symbolism* 112, original emphasis)[5]

First there is the ineffable obscurity of the infinite, analogous to the preverbal darkness in which Psyche lives with Cupid before she comes into the light of reflexive consciousness. Then, through internal exile, the infinite explicates itself in finite form, first through the primordial Adam, the creator-god, and then in the manyness of creation. Depending on the interpretation, *tsimtsum* is either an act of purification through which God expels his own evil or an act of love. Clearly, however, Luria's story leaves room for the heresy that God includes both good and evil—a heresy that translates into Duncan's thinking as cosmic "order and strife." Scholem writes that "the lights from the eyes of *Adam Kadmon* return upward, rebounding from the vessels, or break through downward. . . . Nothing remains in its proper place. Everything is somewhere else. But a being that is not in its proper place is in exile. Thus, since that primordial act, all being has been a being in exile, in need of being led back and redeemed" (*On the Kabbalah and Its Symbolism* 112). The plot of the story thus parallels that of Cupid and Psyche: first, there is a fold that appears as a scission; then a purgatorial period of testing; and finally the hope of redemption.

In the Neoplatonic synthesis of Kabbalah, Christianity, and Platonism, the darker elements of Jewish mysticism are muted. Edgar Wind describes the mysticism of the Neoplatonics as a circle of love. Creation flows downward from the Divine One to the Many and upward from the Many who seek to return to their source (*Pagan Mysteries* 43). Citing Marsilio Ficino, an important creator of the Neoplatonic synthesis, Wind writes: "For the supreme maker first creates things, then seizes them, and thirdly perfects them. . . . Thus they first flow from that perennial fountain as they are born, then they flow back to it as they seek to revert to their origin, and finally they are perfected after they have returned to their beginning" (42). In a chapter on the medallion of Pico della Mirandola, Wind traces the circle of love in the image of the three Graces, refigured in the Florentine Academy[6] as Amor, Pulchritudo, and Voluptas. Amor begins with Pulchritudo and ends in Voluptas, as Socrates' ladder of love in *The Symposium* begins with individual beauty and leads upward to absolute beauty (the impersonal Good).[7] The circle, Wind summarizes, consists of "procession, conversion, and return" (44), a paradigm easily adapted to Christ's descent, incarnation, and return. The difference between the Neoplatonic creation narrative and that of Christian orthodoxy, however, is that the Neoplatonics imagine a continuous hierarchy of angels, men, and demons *connecting* God and Man, as Socrates' ladder of love connects secular, earthy love with the philosopher's love of the Good. As Pico della Mirandola says in his oration, *On the Dignity of Man*, the most famous of Neoplatonic meditations, humanity has no fixed position on the chain of being; the human creature may rise to the level of angels or sink to that of demons. Orthodox Christianity, of course, allows no such scope for human agency in the work of redemption. The Neoplatonic ladder follows from an emanationist version of creation as opposed to the ex nihilo version of orthodoxy that emphasizes the distance and difference between the human and divine. Scholem explains that Kabbalistic literature treats creation as an extension or explication of God rather than a separate realm (*Kabbalah* 23–24). And if God is immanent in the human individual, then it follows that the path to redemption lies in the purification of the divine spark within. Hence, the Neoplatonic tendency to invert the usual part-whole relationship. If the whole is in the part, the part begins to assume the dignity and power of the whole. Orthodox Christianity positions humanity within a larger cosmos that is beyond the comprehension of the finite mind; depending on the sect, God may or may not be immanent in the world, but he is always also transcendent. Neoplatonism plays with the idea that humanity can become God. "Play" is the operative word, I think, for Pico and his fellow Florentine, Marsilio Ficino, because they teeter between orthodoxy and radical heresy.

To go back now to Duncan's Eros chapter in *The H. D. Book* ("Two Chapters"), the hermetic lore assembled there coheres around this emanationist model of creation. Of course, Duncan is a poet, not a mystic, and he radicalizes the circle of love by applying the model to Poetry as opposed to religious inquiry. So, for instance, alchemy becomes a metaphor for the ongoing transmutation of sensual experience to the spiritual gold of Poetry ("Two Chapters"). Gnosticism is similarly a search for the sparks of light (glimmerings of human potentiality) scattered throughout the mundane world; like Psyche sorting the seeds, the Poet is to gather these sparks as his contribution to the One Cosmic Poem ("Two Chapters" 74). Texts like the *Sefer Yezirah* and the *Zohar*[8] come into his thinking as particularly apt metaphors for Poetry because in them God creates the world through the letters of the Hebraic alphabet. As he breathes into the letters, they form the sephirot, a mystical tree, each branch of which consists of a letter signifying an attribute of God. The Shekhinah, an important, recurring figure in Duncan's poetry, is the lowest point on the tree and an all-important gateway between the material and spiritual worlds. Originally signifying the presence of God in the world, the Shekhinah was later hypostatized into a separate female figure. She is flanked on the Left and Right sides by two paths, one leading up and the other down.

In "Two Chapters," Duncan pursues this esoteric history of erotic cosmogony backward to the archaic and forward to his modern peers. The Provençal poets, so important to Pound, practiced love cults based on Neoplatonic ideas, and these are discernible in Dante, who follows a personified Amor from hell to heaven in the service of his Lady, Beatrice ("Two Chapters" 78). Then there are the Grail legends, another manifestation of the quest for spiritual redemption. Explicated in Jesse Weston's famous study *From Ritual to Romance* (1920) as a Christianization of archaic fertility symbols (cup and lance), the grail and its stories take Duncan to Pound, Eliot, and Olson, key poet-companions who either drew on Weston or took up some element of the quest as a part of their poetic practice. Duncan also moves behind this history to retrieve the archaic Eros. Before he became a creator-god, Duncan says, Eros was unwrought matter or "herm"—a stone that reason understands as inert but which the imagination seizes as "seed or egg of the universe . . . the primal chaos of matter" ("Two Chapters" 70). This is an important version of Eros, discernible in many poems. Duncan describes him this way:

> In the old rites Eros appeared as an unwrought stone, a herm. And from our childhood, for some of us dim, for some of us vivid, memories remain of the suggestion a stone may have of being alive. The presence or luck of a stone, the protective genius of a stone, even its speech. For the sculptor the stone "speaks" and the form emerges along the lines of a colloquy between the artist or poet and the inspiration of his material.

> Back of the erotic stone there lies, we know, a dumbness or meaninglessness, in which the stone is only chaotic matter. For what we call our common sense, for the mind that is fearful and then contemptuous of being influenced by things, the stone is inert. But for the imagination, for the mind seeking creation, even seemingly inert matter is alive. So, for the Orphic poets, the seed or egg of the universe is created by *Hyle*, the primal chaos of matter. ("Two Chapters" 70, original emphasis)

From the "primal chaos of matter," Eros unfolds in the personages of Osiris, Christ, Dionysus, Orpheus, and the Gnostic Lucifer. The stone rises up into the human universe through the agency of the Logos as the Logos descends to its incarnation in matter; this is the cognitive version of the Neoplatonic circle. So McIntyre writes: "Because [Duncan] so totally identifies the simple word with the Cosmic Utterance, and the poetic composition with the living soul, he can conceive of language as incarnating the spirit of Christ, a fusion of omnipotence and revelation" ("The Logos" 97).

I turn now to a brief survey of "The Venice Poem" (1948) to show the Neoplatonic turn in the use Duncan makes of these cosmogonies. This poem is structured like a sonata of symphonic scale, with an overture, three movements, and a coda.[9] In addition to the complicated layerings of the symphonic form—the images modulate from movement to movement—the poem is simultaneously a cosmogony, a poetic methodology or scene of writing, and a psychology. It thus establishes poetic ground that would serve Duncan throughout his writing life. The first two movements, "A Description of Venice" and "Testimony," are cosmogonic: Venus and Venice rise up from the sea as primordial creation. The poem begins with an overture that establishes the setting in the square of San Marco, Venice. From the facade of the famous San Marco church, Duncan fastens on a bronze boy with "jewel blue eyes," and the crouching stone lions of the frieze (21). The sapphire of the statue's eye is *the* central image of the poem, drawing together sky and sea as well as the hermetic references. Sapphire sounds like Sefirah, and in fact the term *Sefirah* is related to the Hebraic "sappir" or sapphire (Scholem, *Kabbalah* 99). In Talmudic symbolism, the throne room of God is said to be paved with sapphire, and the color blue generally signifies heaven. The stone is thus related to the Shekhinah and through Duncan's syncretism to other female personages. Venus rises out of a blue sea; Mary is often depicted in a blue robe. "Our Lady," as Duncan names her, is a synthesis of these figures and of the archaic Eros in the shape of the Venus of Lespuges who makes her entrance later in the poem. The sapphire thus contains in embryo various female manifestations of Eros and, according to Duncan's notes, the "sapphire of intellect, the passionate intellect, maleness."[10] In the jeweled eye of the bronze boy, the sapphire is "cruel and absolute," "as if . . . all love was frozen there." In this work of art, the stone is "frozen" in an image that is both religious (through the hermetic references), aesthetic (this is high art), and secular (the stony eye of a faithless lover)—all exemplifying gorgeous indifference to human suffering (VP 21). Something is needed to render the stone generative, and Duncan finds it in the "the gold of sound" from the bell tower of the church. So there is a dialectical tension set up in the first few stanzas between the frozen stone and warm, ephemeral sound. Before creation can begin, the stone must be drawn into the realm of sound as sound must incarnate itself in stone to achieve durability. This is what happens at the end of the overture when from the stone there proceeds "as if rays / a melody" (21).

Duncan explicates this first generative polarity throughout the first movement. Shakespeare enters Venice as a person of the poem, accompanied by the "flies of jealousy and rage" (22) and the characters of his *Othello.* Passionate, secular, embodied love thus follows the cold eternality of the sapphire in the overture. Duncan imagines Iago as the Doge of Venice and a cynic, playing him against "Saint Shakespeare" who in faith still lights the "holy tapers" of love. Faith and knowledge, spiritual and carnal love collide as the frozen images of the Basilica spring to life: the crouching lions on the frieze of San Marco and the lines/lions on the page as well—become leaping beasts "among the mosaics, / the jewels and gold" (22). The blue of the sapphire now rhymes with the blue sea on which Venice floats (23). Out of that sea, on a shell that is also the coil of an ear, Venus begins to rise and the dance of creation begins again, through "sight, sound and intellect" (Louis Zukofsky's phrase). "Love's betrayal of love" begins the dance, as Psyche's exile initiates her self-fashioning, and the folding of the infinite on itself initiates creation in the Kabbalah. Carnal love with its jealousies and rages seemingly betrays the spiritual dimension of the sapphire, but the sapphire *requires* this restlessness of the flesh for the work of creation.

In "Testimony," the second movement of the poem, cosmogony morphs into a scene of poetic creativity. From Stravinsky's *Poetics of Music*[11] Duncan takes this citation:

These natural sounds suggest music,
    but are not yet themselves music;
    Pleasing in themselves
    they are but promises of music.
    It takes
a human being to keep them. (27)

Duncan replays the motif of art as the alembic wherein the artist transmutes nature's things. In the lines immediately following, the relationship of ephemeral natural sound to music is as that of lust to love:

To savour lust and to create
        from lust love's
        immortality—
        like Venice
        created out of the waters, or Venus. (27)

The unwrought herm takes on intelligibility and relative permanence through the alchemy of the poet-musician or the creative power of the Logos, "as if it were the mind itself / which descends in the poem / and becomes manifest" (27–28). And as the mind descends, the physical world rushes up to meet it like a fountain ("Where shall my heart feed / but from this fountain" [27]). As Duncan says in the passage I have quoted above from *The H. D. Book*, the stone "speaks" to the sculptor. Neoplatonic creation lore avoids the question of whether language or matter comes first because both the intelligible and the sensible are emanations of the One. In the last stanzas of "Testimony," the sapphire turns into a phonograph needle, "good for 1000 performances," stone and sound fused. As well, the cruelty of art, first referenced in the "cruel absolute" of the overture, here returns in the phonograph *needle* that is also the sting of Jealousy capitalized. From the pangs of love, the poet makes art. So in the "Recorso" section that follows, the "tide of event"—human history, I take it—is like a sea that rises and falls, tossing up sights and sounds. That ephemerality assumes form and stability in Poetry: "the dropd cup reappears from its fragments / springs to the hand as if from nowhere / complete" (38). Similarly, the sea of life congeals in the blue of the intellectual sapphire and then disseminates again in the music of a "1000 performances" as the circle turns.

The psychological register of this creative process, as distinguishable from the cosmogonic or methodological, is most evident in the coda of the poem through a series of images that bring in the famous stone Venus of Lespuges and end with an infant's birth, here also the rebirth of the poet. The coda does much more than just reprise the theme; it focuses on the loss of Eros through jealousy and a consequent failure of the imagination. "Between the sapphire and the sound / unfurls the rose of vision," Duncan writes, but "where there is neither faith nor vision" the rose of the world becomes an "enormity," "more sickening than beautiful" (44). Without the imaginative bridge between the ideal and the real, there is only sterile separation of the two and no creativity. How is the poet to overcome this catastrophe?

There must be a moment when that faith returns.
The artist searches out the deepest roots.
He is violent. He is animal.
Driven by language itself
alive with such forces,
he violates, desiring to move
the deepest sound. (46)

This passage does not explain directly. But originary violence is key to Duncan's imagination of creativity.[12] I have noted that the Kabbalistic version of creation begins with an exile and the breaking of the divine vessels. To go back to the Eros chapter of *The H. D. Book,* Duncan draws on this cosmic violence as mythology and psychology. From his readings in Jane Harrison's *Prolegomena,* he remarks on an archaic image of a woman rising out of the earth, flanked by two men armed with mallets, one of whom strikes the head of the woman ("Two Chapters" 71). Duncan suggests that this violation of the Mother parallels the mythical castration of Uranus by Chronus. The figure of the rising woman and two men (penis and testicles), along with the act of striking her, replay the castration of the god, from which "psychotic act . . . the castration of the Father," Venus rises.[13] From the opening of the Mother comes the Child; from the castration of Uranus, Beauty. In Neoplatonic mythology, the severed genitals of the god "convey to formless matter the seed of ideal forms"(Wind, *Pagan Mysteries* 133). In Freud's hands, primal castration becomes a trope for the development of consciousness. Through repression and displacement of an initial unity with the mother (Freud, *Civilization* 16), the individual comes to understand himself or herself as a separate entity. Analogously Duncan writes the break-up of a love relationship as a breaking-open of the female Eros (the [M]other) and creative rebirth.

In an interview with Jack R. Cohn and Thomas J. O'Donnell, "'The Poetry of Unevenness'" (1985), Duncan discusses the pains of love as he experienced them in youth:

> I suffered in adolescence from extreme and even painful jealousy and passional rages, and I experienced them as something wrong in myself, not in the person I had fallen in love with. And Plato uncovers the possibility that in actually loving we are addressing a figure that is not the person, so we've got another activity that occurs in love that's very different from the passional attachment. The passion is aroused, not only because of sexual passion but because one's got what was often viewed as an ideal figure in Plato or an archetype, as Jung would put it. You are

> practicing immediately a love addressed to one that stands behind love, like language stands behind language. (99)

To notice here is that Duncan handles literal emotional pain by Platonizing it. In "The Venice Poem," he makes the same move. Creatively blocked by jealousy, he responds by going deeper into the archetypal possibilities of Venus, moving at the end of the poem to the archaic figure of the Mother in the Venus of Lespuges and from there to imaginative rebirth. In other words, the poet's pursuit of Eros through its many manifestations is a way of cracking the hard blue stone of the bronze boy's eye and drawing Poetry out of emotional violence like this: "you can hear the bed groan and the adulterous sounds / wound and wound but they do not kill" (VP 46). From an eye of stone and a broken heart, the poet makes art. In the last few stanzas, poem and poet are "flung out from the fat form" of the little stone Mother to be reborn in the square of San Marco. Returning to the opening scene in front of the Basilica, Duncan again juxtaposes sapphire and sound. Now, however, the blue of the jewel corresponds to the blue of a newborn's eye, and the sound of the bell from the church tower becomes the scaffolding on which the child climbs upward from the obscure sensations of infancy toward self-articulation. The gendering of the bell in the phrase "Fatherly towers" reiterates the Freudian drama as well as the hermetic creation stories that form the subtext of the poem. The child reaches up from Mother Matter to Father Logos. The archaic stone Venus, the "obscurity" out of which the birth takes place ("Born. // Out of what obscurity?" [51]), is transformed through language to the divine sapphire (Shekhinah, Venus, Mary) through the alchemy of the Logos; as the primal herm becomes Eros, Christ, or Dionysus, so the Mother is born again from the Father to become a figure of the male intellect. I will come back to this point.

"The Venice Poem" is an important early example of the significance of emanation to Duncan's poetic practice. Later, in *The Opening of the Field* (1960), when Duncan comes to publish "Poem Beginning with a Line by Pindar," the same pattern emerges. "Discovery, dispersion, purgatorial tasks and, finally, re-constitution," Michael Davidson says of the plot ("A Book" 78), and the plot unfurls endlessly in Duncan's work, always different yet always the same. The four movements of the Pindar poem detail Psyche's separation from Eros and her subsequent fall from mythic time into history. They are not in a landscape, Duncan says, but an "obscurity" (*OF* 62). Then Psyche insists on seeing her Love, a gesture that gives image to the human creature's initiation into separate personhood. The resulting possibility of objectifying the primal Other can be read both as the birth of the individual out of the obscurities of infancy and the species development of reflexive thought. Psyche's way back to Eros takes her through the long purgatory of history. The wholeness of the world as sensuous continuum, now shattered into *thingness*, has to be regathered. So Venus sets Psyche the task of sorting piles of seeds. In Apuleius's *Golden Ass*, Psyche accomplishes this impossible task with the help of insects. The rational mind, in its parsing of the world, has to be brought to the point of its incompetence; this is a lesson of Psyche's labors. Forced to depend on the nature from which it had thought to distinguish itself, rational humanity begins to learn its place in the world. Yet Psyche can never return to the obscurity in which she first lives with Eros, no more than the individual can return to the M(other). As Duncan suggests in the third section of the Pindar poem, Love's other face is Death: "Rilke torn by a rose thorn / blackend toward Eros. Cupidinous Death! / that will not take no for an answer" (*OF* 67). The "Poem Beginning with a Line by Pindar" ends with a redemptive image of children dancing in a circle, but it is an image that moves back into mythical time:

In the dawn that is nowhere
  I have seen the willful children

  clockwise and counter-clockwise turning. (*OF* 69)

The circling children are "nowhere," as the reunion of Psyche and Eros must be nowhere. Yet if the circle does not exist in historical time, it nonetheless inspires the quests that constitute the human saga. The myth speaks to the potential of humanity to reconcile its inner and outer worlds in the One Life; in Whitehead's language it is a "lure for feeling." So in the Pindar poem Duncan conflates mythical quest stories like that of Jason and the Golden Fleece ("the hero who struggles east . . . so that the fleecy sun go back from Troy, / Colchis, India" [66]) with the historical westward movement of Europeans across North America in search of a legendary West.

Two related issues come out of these narratives of Eros in *The H. D. Book*, "The Venice Poem," and "Poem Beginning with a Line by Pindar." The first concerns the fortunate fall. A reader of the Pindar poem might be excused for wondering if the actual conquest of the West, for example, did not simply result in the dystopia that Duncan also recognizes in that section where he lists American presidents who have tolerated or perpetuated "great scars of wrong" (*OF* 64). Is justice always to be deferred to the cosmic plane? This is the question raised by Michelson and Mackey. The second issue, through which I will address the first, is that Duncan's account of the distinction between figure and ground differs significantly from the same figuration in Olson and Creeley because he writes it as an initiating act rather than a description of the field as such. The "opening of the field" takes place *after* the wound or break or fall out of mythic time, so that the emerging figure—the Adam or Cosmic Man—is actually the whole of the field because the generating ground simply withdraws. In effect, the (M)other is excluded as an *operative* principle in the field. From Duncan's perspective, this is commonsense psychology; anything humanly thinkable belongs to consciousness, including the unconscious, the physical, or the nonhuman. Yet for Olson and Creeley (Spicer and Blaser as well) the "obscurity" of the (M)other accompanies the embodied consciousness as its Other and outside. To partition it off from historical time clears the way for a resacralization of the human universe.

The alternative, as I have argued in the Olson and Creeley essays, is to leave the obscurity folded into the field of articulated forms as process and aporia, so that the figure acting there can never become coextensive with its ground and the forms themselves never ultimate. This is what Olson does in insisting on the negative capability and Creeley in holding open each moment to the abyss of the future. It is essential to their figure-ground modeling of the field that the mythical origin *not* be sealed off from historical time but disseminated in historical time. Hence Olson's interest in myth as the living possibility of the instant and his Whiteheadian insistence that the primordial is always ahead in new configurations of the field rather than behind as a hypostatized origin. Here as well is Creeley's labyrinth of memory that leads only to the empty cave at the dawn of the species ("Caves"). In other words, humanity cannot access its origin as an object of knowledge because the origin is embedded in the prehistory of the earth, the Mother Rock, and the syntheses of time, and yet this Otherness is everywhere dispersed in the human universe. In contrast, Duncan's mythologizing of the origin as a primal *Logos*, if it is not understood as human projection and therefore historical, is a conventionally religious gesture. The Cosmic Man of Kabbalistic lore absorbs the nonhuman world into the human image and masculinizes it as well. The loss of a ground distinguishable from the human view of things is the consequence. As I have conceded in the Olson essay, nature is always already part of the human universe in the sense that it is always mediated by same, but it does not follow that what has been so articulated is reducible to the human species.

Duncan, however, has a fascination with *naming* the primordial, and this is an impulse that parallels the mystic's reach beyond ordinary human awareness to direct contemplation of the divine. For example, there is *Adam's Way,* a theosophical play on the origins of Man. Here the cosmos, like the primal herm, is unwrought when the play begins—it is a darkness that murmurs semiotically with tree-shadows and daimons, but without the light of reflexive intelligence. Adam is ripped untimely from a pod by the elf-shadows, Pook and Bobbin (*RB* 141), and is immediately flanked by his good and bad angels, Michael and Samael, a trio that echoes the Eros trinity (penis and testicles) in the castration scene of Uranus. It is Samael, the bad one that lives in the "denial of love" (162), who tempts Erda/Eve with the tree of knowledge and brings about the expulsion of Adam from Eden—fortunately so, of course, because this initiation into time is needed for the unfolding of the Adam, literally a pea in the pod in this play. Once the seed is expulsed into the light of day, the historical world can unfold.

For me, Duncan's most astonishing treatment of the primordial creative event occurs in "As in the Old Days, Passages 8" from *Bending the Bow* (1968).

. . . I am
        at the lips   before speech,   at life's
                labia,   Her   crack of a door opening,
her cunt   a wound now
        the gash in His side
from which monthly   blood flows
                so Zinzendorf saw,
        all maidens bear Christ's sign   with them
                at this flowing
                  souls gather
At the babe's birth
        the whole woman
        opens   the flower bleeding,   life-lanced
                the head of the embryo
shoved forth from its red pod,   from the pain she knows,
                        into the Child's place
                            cries

                "To be born again from the wound in His side"
From the horizon   ancestral
                echoes ring
        In the streams of the wound they
        "*want to have little beds, and tables,*
        and everything else." (*BB* 24–25, original emphasis)

This poem gathers much of Duncan's syncretic thinking about creativity and origins. The Maiden deflowered conflates here with Christ and Dionysus, the latter reborn from the male womb as Christians are born again from the wounds of Christ. The child is born once of the (M)other and again of the Logos. In *The H. D. Book,* part 2, "Nights and Days," chapter 9, Duncan draws attention to the practices of Count von Zinzendorf, a patron of the Moravians, an eighteenth-century Christian sect. The count fused sexual and spiritual images, so that the "spear, the wound, the flow of blood from Christ's side were deliberately related to the penis, the vagina and the menstrual flow" (65). Quoting a source, Duncan writes: "'It is said that a niche covered with red cloth was built into the wall of the church, into which children were placed to symbolize their lying in Christ's Side-Wound, and that Christian Renatus, Zinzendorf's son, built a *Side-Wound* through which the congregation marched'—called 'the true Matrix.'" "Zinzendorf, like Freud," he adds, "worked towards a sense of words in which '*venerate*' and '*venereal*' were again restored" (65). The Zinzendorf material informs that truly bizarre image of the poem in which the wound is furnished with "*little beds, and tables, / and everything else.*" That Duncan conceives the wound/womb/door as a threshold between the *languaged* world and the preverbal is evident at the beginning of the passage where the poet is brought to "the lips / before speech."

Like the cosmic pod, or the generative wound, language is also a container to be opened. In a key passage in "Rites of Participation" (*H. D. Book*), Duncan discusses his view of language as the primary ground of human community—the global commons into which all members of the species are called. His quotation of Edward Sapir in this context is significant:

> "*The single experience lodges in an individual consciousness and is, strictly speaking, incommunicable," Sapir writes in Language: "To be communicated it needs to be referred to a class which is tacitly accepted by the community as an identity. Thus, the single impression which I have of a particular house must be identified with all my other impressions of it. Further, my generalized memory or my 'notion' of this house must be merged with the notions that all other individuals who have seen the house have formed of it. The particular experience that we started with has now been widened so as to embrace all possible impressions or images that sentient beings have formed or may form of the house in question. In other words, the speech element 'house' is the symbol, first and foremost, not of a single perception, nor even of the notion of a particular object but of a 'concept,' in other words, of a convenient capsule of thought that embraces*

> *thousands of distant experiences and that is ready to take in thousands more. If the single significant elements of speech are the symbols of concepts, the actual flow of speech may be interpreted as a record of this setting of these concepts into mutual relations.*" (9, original emphasis)

Duncan adds that "there is no isolate experience of anything, then, for to come into 'house' or 'dog,' 'bread' or wine,' is to come into a company" (9). "House" *houses* things. Breaking open the pod of the Concept, the poet finds it furnished like Zinzendorf's Wound. The Concept or Word here stands in the place of origins rather than the obscurity of physical life. This is precisely what Olson saw and feared in the Platonic-Christian tradition. He read that tradition as an entrenched habit of mind that can dispense with actual bodies à la Auschwitz because it has already distanced itself from them by fully identifying with the abstraction language is. When Duncan furnishes the primal wound, he anthropomorphizes the origin as religions do; he projects Man as God. Hence Olson's comments in "Against Wisdom as Such": "I fall back on the difference I am certain the poet at least has to be fierce about: that he is not free to be a part of, or to be any, sect; that there are no symbols to him, there are only his own composed forms, and each one solely the issue of the time of the moment of its creation, not any ultimate except what he in his heart and that instant in its solidity yield. That the poet cannot afford to traffick in any other 'sign' than his one, his self, the man or woman he is. Otherwise God does rush in. And art is washed away, turned into that second force, religion" (*CPr* 261–62). Olson's assumption here is that mythical narratives are historical, not foundational; in the etymology given in *The Special View,* "muthos" means "what is said" (20). Art becomes religion when myth is understood as foundational and prior to history as opposed to a particular historical rendition of cultural potencies or nonhuman nature.

But of course Duncan is no orthodox religionist. In one of his many responses to Olson's challenge, Duncan takes on the role of heretic in relation to what he says are Olson's "analyzable Catholic origins" (Cohn and O'Donnell, "Interview" 516). Heresy he had imbibed with mother's milk. In part 1, chapter 5 of *The H. D. Book* (1968), subtitled "Occult Matters," Duncan describes the theosophical world of his parents.

> And in the inner chamber, the adults, talking on, wove for me in my childish overhearing, Egypt, a land of spells and secret knowledge, a background drift of things close to dreaming—spirit communications, reincarnation memories, clairvoyant journeys into a realm of astral phantasy where all times and places were seen in a new light, of Plato's

> illustrations of the nature of the soul's life, of most real Osiris and Isis, of lost Atlantis and Lemuria, and of the god or teacher my parents had taken as theirs, the Hermetic Christos. The word *teacher,* as I first heard it, before I went to school, meant the same as a god. God was not a god, but from His Being He sent out teachers or gods. True teachers, like Christ, Buddha, Hermes, or Lao-Tse, were Light Beings, messengers of the Sun Itself. (5, original emphasis)

As this passage shows, occult spirituality focuses on the *inner* world of the soul and the possibility of knowing secret things through mystical experience. While Catholicism has recognized certain mystics through canonization, it is based on faith rather than knowledge of the divine, and when faith in the literality of the other world collapses as it does for Olson, that world is no longer available. Reference to it can only be charlatanry. For a heretic of heresies like Duncan, however, the world of divine things corresponds to the "universe / of felt things" (VP 39) in which the poet can roam freely within the zodiac of his own wit. Catholic faith takes on ultimate reality as external to the individual; the (heretical) mystic takes on that ultimacy as internal. Hence Olson, while stepping away from Catholicism, anchors Maximus in an "outside," grounding his persona in history and species life. In Olson's world, the poet, whatever his dreams, is a wayfarer in an actual, physical world that others also inhabit. Duncan's world is very often interior, and of course in that world all the old gods and potencies play their parts in the emotions and fantasies of individuals. Yet Duncan often speaks as if certain mythical forms could precede and determine historical processes, and this is to court the kind of essentialism Olson protests.

Tied to this question of origins is Duncan's handling of figure-ground relationships. Poetry becomes a vast, shifting sea of forms in which figure and ground are coextensive and interchangeable. In the Eros chapter I have discussed above, for example, Duncan writes: "There is no way then but Psyche's search, the creative work of *a union in knowledge and experience*" ("Two Chapters," my emphasis). In *The H. D. Book,* part 1, chapter 2 (1967), Duncan comments on Virginia Woolf and H. D. that they "presented *a correspondence between inner feeling and outer appearance,*" adding that the "*cooperation of fantasy and reality,* the interchange of being, had a counterpart in the old Celtic affinity for interweaving forms, shape-changings, reincarnations, in *an art where figure and ground may be exchanged*" (30–31, my emphasis). Like the mystic, Psyche moves toward experiencing what cannot be experienced—a reunion with Eros—that implies the death of consciousness or its Neoplatonic transmutation into godhead. A figure of the questing mind, she moves toward a merging with the realm of nature she pursues. This is also to fuse knowing and undergoing, because like the mystic, Psyche wants to actually *experience* what can only be known by transcending finitude. Similarly, the correspondence between "inner feeling and outer appearance" fuses the inner life of the emotions with what in external reality can be empirically tested, lending the former the authority of the latter. Most significantly for my argument, Duncan makes figure and ground interchangeable in the above passage. Thus while the field of the poem may be polarized as it is in "The Venice Poem," the poles can morph into each other. The stone of the physical *becomes* the sapphire of the Concept. But if the concept is taken to be adequate to the actual world, then figure and ground are coextensive.[14]

This Neoplatonic tendency to let figure and ground morph into each other suggests two contrary possibilities, both of which are operative in Duncan's poetic practice. On the one hand, Duncan treats historical actualities as the evolution of myth ("variations on a corrupt and corruptible text"); on the other, he writes the historical as an *incarnation* of eternal forms. In these two possibilities are the two kinds of abstraction Creeley discusses—the generic as the empty universal and convening place of the particular (suggesting a generative nonidentity between figure and ground), and contrarily the generic as repression of the particular. So it is with the particular voice of the poet and the Persons of the Poem. On the one hand, Duncan is a servant of the Word and faithful follower of its unfoldings, a wayfarer in the land of Poetry. On the other hand, as he says in "The Structure of Rime I" in his address to the "unyielding Sentence," "I name myself your master, who come to serve" (*OF* 12). Or in a letter to Robin Blaser, "Dec. 19, 1957": "When the poem is most exalted, who is the poet? Mouthpiece for the stars. I am, anyway, not to be a Master but a Servant. Feudal enough in my learning to recognize my need for grandeur there: where the only servant of the Empire is the Emperor" ("Letters" 117). As "mouthpiece," Duncan is simply a participant and witness to the imaginative life of humanity as it has been recorded in the arts. As Emperor, however, Duncan moves into the old sites of power, impersonating them (his term), altering the field from a position that resonates with more than his one voice. The Master of Rime sits in the place of the creator-god. Yet even if this place of the primordial is secularized as psychology, it cannot serve as generic common ground if the poet fills it with his own images. This is the difference between Duncan's treatment of the generic and that of Creeley. It is Creeley's effort to *empty* the generic of particular content so that it can truly become common and open to the reader. In contrast, Duncan *fills* the generic with his own particularized images, rather as Zinzendorf furnishes the wound, while investing those images with the full power of the Logos. In "The Architecture, Passages 9," for instance, the house has "curtains of daffodil-yellow," bookcases with "the glimmering titles arrayd," a staircase linking "the social part of the house and the upper regions," and "ornamental cushions" on which the poet sits listening to "strains of *Mahogonny* on the phonograph" (*BB* 26–27). This is not a generic house; it is Duncan's house. And yet as the poem unfolds, this particular house also presents as the generic "architecture" of Psyche with her upper and lower regions and of Poetry with its words inside other words. Hence the particular house of "Passages 9" accumulates the creative potential and authority of House in general. As in the Neoplatonic cosmos, the part contains the whole. Here is the source of the "permission" in "Often I Am Permitted to Return to a Meadow." The poet has *permission* to reorder the grand collage because his own words shake with the power of the Logos. As in the Christian mystery, the Father (concept) and Son (incarnation) are one. Part three of "A Sequence of poems for H. D.'s Birthday" in *Roots and Branches* underscores this filial relationship. I quote the last stanza:

Father who grows in the plant,
Father who moves the animal,
Father whose anguish is because of our suffering,
Father whose presence means there is joy even in hell,
Father who must find His face in a mirror of me,
Father uncreated, Father evolving,
Father whose signature is in the chemical bond,
          how long you have searcht for me;

          I am your son. (*RB* 12)

What is missing in the closed circle of Father and Son is the Mother Rock, the "obscurity" before the advent of the Logos.

In an argument that informs my own, Giorgio Agamben argues the classical distinction between "experience and science, human knowledge and divine knowledge" (*Infancy and History* 19). As late as Montaigne, he says, "the ultimate goal of experience [is] a nearing to death" (19)—that is, humanity advances to maturity through an anticipation of death; death is the extreme limit of experience. Modern science and Cartesian philosophy, however, have collapsed the impersonal good of the Platonic intellect and the individual subject of experience into a single, knowing subject for whom experience is the pathway to the kind of certitude that used to be reserved for God. "Through this interpolation of experience and science in a single subject (which, being universal and bounded and at the same time an *ego*, unites in itself the properties of the separate intellect and the subject of experience), modern science re-effects that liberation from the *páthei máthos* and that conjunction of human knowledge with divine knowledge which constituted the precise character of the experience of the Mysteries and found their pre-scientific expression in astrology, alchemy and Neoplatonic speculation" (*Infancy and History* 20, original emphasis). Neoplatonic mysticism, Agamben says, was a first move toward the fusion of knowledge and experience in a single subject. "It is only because Neoplatonic Hermetic mysticism had bridged the Aristotelian separation between *nous* and *psyche* and the Platonic difference between the one and the many, with an emanationist system in which a continuous hierarchy of intelligences, angels, demons and souls . . . communicated in a 'Great Chain' which begins and ends with the One, was it possible to establish a single subject as the basis for 'experimental science'" (20). Agamben concludes that the modern cogito "has its roots in a mystical notion" (21). The result, in the terms of my study, is Ahabian man, a creature who has appropriated Plato's impersonal Good and the all-knowing formerly attributed to the Christian God for uses imaginable by the finite mind. Like Kronos, who castrated Uranus in order to usurp the throne of heaven, and like Milton's Satan, who defied God because he would become his own Ruler, "Ahab's rage and hate" (Olson, *CMI* 84) is that of a Son who wishes to murder the Father in order to take his place (82, 83).

Is this Duncan's case? Not exactly. Duncan is more shaman than Ahab, a role he explores early in his writing life in pieces like "Toward the Shaman," and the "Epilogue" of *Caesar's Gate,* which he subtitles "A Hypnagogic Phantasy Induced by Dictation" (*CG* 59). In this latter prose piece, Duncan is the participant, taking instruction from "the leader" in what sounds like a séance with the subconscious. But elsewhere, he is the leader both in poetry and life.[15] The shaman's claim to authority is much weaker than that of modern, scientific man. Like the poetic cartographer, the shaman is there for those who accept his *Tao* and wish to follow, and like a historical explorer, he is only as good as his maps and narratives. The story has to fascinate and the map has to go someplace that others find interesting or the initiates will be few. "You with the dark eyes waiting," Duncan writes in "Toward the Shaman," "your touch uncovers a desire to wander, a geography of migrations" (*YAC* 7). But the interchangeability of figure and ground within the field of the poem brings out the stronger version of authority as well. When Duncan speaks in the voice of the Logos it is the Emperor we hear. In the next section, I will follow this latter tendency in Duncan through his argument with

Robin Blaser over the translation of Nerval's *Les chimères* and his correspondence with Denise Levertov.

Order and Strife

When Robin Blaser completed translations of Gérard de Nerval's *Les chimères* in 1965, Duncan responded by publishing his own version of the poems as a "corrective" to Blaser's. The resulting quarrel between the two poets is partly recorded in a Duncan issue of *Audit/Poetry* (1967). One might expect Duncan to treat translation in a way analogous to derivation, as subversion of, as much as submission to, a source text. But listen to this opening salvo:

> My translations of *Les Chimères* of Gérard de Nerval came about after a questioning of and then a radical disagreement with Robin Blaser's *Les Chimères,* published by Open Space in 1965. . . . Taken as what they are—a serial poem loosely derived from Nerval's sequence, at once asserting an alliance with the Romantic Movement and at the same time using the original as a point of departure, eliminating elements of Nerval that do not serve the translator's design and, further, altering the original to suit his own purposes (as in the garbled opening stanzas of the concluding poem)—Blaser's *Les Chimères* would have their justification, of course. The form of the homage has been well-established in this century. One thinks of Pound's *Homage to Sextus Propertius,* of Stravinsky's *Pulcinella* "after Pergolesi," or of Picasso's Variation on Velazquez' painting *The Maids of Honor,* which are translations, not into a common language but into the uncommon language of a highly personal signature. (*Audit/Poetry* 42–43)

It is impossible to miss the patronizing tone of this passage. And yet given Duncan's free treatment of sources as in, for example, *Writing Writing,* the objection that Blaser "alter[s] the original to suit his own purposes" is puzzling. Is it simply that Duncan distinguishes between a translation and a derivation, requiring greater fidelity to the original in the former? This does not seem a satisfying answer, given a poetics that rests on the creative violation of sources.

In this same issue of *Audit,* Duncan publishes several uncollected imitations of Stein. These pick up Stein's syntax and rhythm, but they are by no means faithful to her use of language to represent the " 'concrete chaos' of immediate perceptual experience" (Walker, "Exercises in Disorder" 26). Here is

"A Little Bit of a Tumbler" from Stein's *Tender Buttons:* "A shining indication of yellow consists in there having been more of the same color than could have been expected when all four were bought. This was the hope which made the six and seven have no use for any more places and this necessarily spread into nothing. Spread into nothing" (472). The yellow of the tumblers is there and possibly the occasion of buying them ("there having been more of the same color"). Then there is something else—six and seven—possibly more matching tumblers than place settings needed at the table? So is it the buying of tumblers that "spreads into nothing"? the breaking of them? or the whole business of tumblers desired and purchased that turns out to be a small affair. The elements of narrative are present in an object (tumblers), an occasion (acquiring them), a feeling (expectation), and an event ("spread into nothing"), but they have been collaged rather than narrated. Yet however opaque the result, "Tumbler" coheres around something physical and some kind of event. The materiality of language here foregrounded is referential in the way that a cubist collage references its sources in a scrap of newspaper or a cutout of something. Here, in contrast, are a few of Duncan's lines in a piece called "Cloudy":

> Passages in time or clouds as in passing. Clouds as in a Tiepolo scene.
> Clouds in tableau, a table-d'hôte pass ring.
> A skirt. A scattered. Magic. In scattering. Scatter, a ring of clouds about a scant, cloud as a scatter. (*Audit/Poetry* 34)

Certainly something happens here. Clouds pass. But the piece is about sound and word association, not a collaged event. The Stein-feel of the piece is superficial in relation to what the words are doing. Is this not a case of "altering the original to suit [one's] own purposes"?

A closer look at the argument in *Audit/Poetry* shows that Duncan's objections center specifically on Blaser's handling of the "architectonics" of the poems:

> I began with El Desdichado, the one poem in which Blaser tells us in his terminal Note to *Les Chimères,* he kept the "Shape" of Nerval's poem, I found the terms which Nerval had taken exactly from his occult studies—constelle, le soleil noir, la Melancolie, la nuit du tombeau, la mer—or, as with El Desdichado, Luisignan and Biron, from his sources in literary romances, in order to form a community of meanings in his poetry, gathering the images and personae he knew as initiate, *mystikos,* as student, as dreamer in the unifying reality he knew as poet—

> these terms which Nerval had insisted upon were imprecisely rendered and even discarded in Blaser's version. Whatever Blaser meant by the "Shape" he felt he had kept, he had treated carelessly indeed key elements in the architectonics of the meaning of the poem—but this architectonics of meaning is itself significant form. What else had Creeley's "Form is never more than an extension of content" meant to convey? (43)

"Shape" is clearly the operative word. Blaser eliminates certain formal features of Nerval's poems because, in his view, they are no longer operative in the culture. Duncan takes particular exception to the first poem in the series, "El Desdichado."[16] He reads Nerval's lines as unfolding a "structure of quarternities." The star, lute, black sun, and Dürer's *Melencolia I* figure the "four elements of the poet's destiny" (*Audit/Poetry* 44). These are balanced by the four stages of an alchemical transformation, symbolized in the Night of the Tomb, the Consoler, the Holy Mountain (Posilipo in the poem), and the sea.[17] The Flower, the arbor, the grape vine, and the rose are Gnostic symbols that "unite the mysteries of Iakchos and the Romance of the Rose" (44).[18] In these hermetic elements, Duncan reads the "emergence of entities—in poetics, personae; in psychology, archetypes—in the process of initiation: Amor and Phoebus as powers in one order, the daimonic, and Lusignan and Biron[19] as two in a second, the heroic—myth and history" (44). My purpose is neither to challenge Duncan's reading nor explicate Nerval's poem along the hermetic lines Duncan indicates. Clearly the sequence of fours opens onto a hermetic world that expands indefinitely under close reading. What is essential to such a reading, however, is that the "quarternities" remain intact because they represent the cosmogonic structure that gives form to an eclectic content.

Blaser is not committed to preserving this structure because for him form rises up in historical rather than mythic time. In a response to Duncan, also published in *Audit/Poetry,* Blaser writes: "I find it impossible to understand how a reading of my translations could be interpreted as 'removing the Hermetic' . . . My note in the back of the book explains that I made decisions about the meaning of the poems, and did my best to make that complete, so long as they were my poems. Not enough attention is being given to the months long effort to keep my language real, so that the tie of the actual and the other is absolutely real. A reality" (45). While Blaser denies taking out the hermetic, he distances his language from the symbolism of *Les chimères* and introduces the actual as measure. This is a serious challenge to Duncan's poetics along the same lines as Olson's "Against Wisdom," and it was doubtless rendered the more intolerable to Duncan because of ongoing personal rivalries and Blaser's more junior status as a poet.[20] "If I attack you for substituting 'that hill for 'Posilipo,' " Duncan writes, "it is because I believe Nerval to be of such an order in Poetry that the Posilipo, El Desdichado out of Scott's *Ivanhoe,* Lusignan and Biron, are not literary or personal references to be let go, but, like Dante's Beatrice, eternal places and persons, revealed places and persons of Poetry" (*Audit/Poetry* 48). And if these revealed forms are not eternal, as Blaser's translations suggest, then it might appear as if the Wizard were simply a little man behind a curtain and the Emerald City a projection. To say this another way, the impersonal intellect (Plato's Good, the Christian God) loses its impersonality as soon as the transcendental foundation of it dissolves in disbelief. In place of that foundation, Duncan substitutes myth, grounding it in the inner life of imagination and feeling. But by insisting on the inner life as transhistorical, universal, and *formally* specific he plays with the notion of a sacred language that *he* can then access as shaman and initiate. Andrew Mossin comments on the *Chimères* episode that "Duncan's move from the outset . . . was toward a contention for the 'originating author'—whose connection to himself and his own mythopoeic imagination allowed Duncan to establish his mastery not only over Blaser but, in a sense, over Nerval as well" ("In the Shadow" 689). This seems to me the affective core of the issue. If Nerval's architecture is not fully there, then Duncan's ability to inherit the house of "Nerval" will be compromised, along with the whole hermetic topology of his oeuvre. The Father must be preserved if the Son is to take his place.

An area of Duncan's poetic practice that is closely related to this dispute over translation is his inclusivity in preserving all the elements that come into a poem, and I want to stop over this conservative, small "c," streak before moving on to the Levertov correspondence. Nothing can be left out of Poetry because everything is meaningful; everything is meaningful, because the whole is in the part. But if this is so, how is it possible to describe the canyon-sized gap between a Duncan poem and, say, the free associations of an apprentice writer? The 1972 preface to *Caesar's Gate* opens with a rebuttal of a critical comment made by M. L. Rosenthal on Duncan's "Dream Data" section of the "Sequence of Poems for H. D.'s Birthday" (1959). Rosenthal had objected to the tonal unevenness of a certain passage and some "sentimental philosophizing" that he heard as "emptily facile" (*CG* i). He takes issue with the *quality* of the passage, in other words. Duncan's reply is instructive:

> It does not seem to have occurred to Rosenthal that just this tone and tenor of each line as he gets it—the shifts from narrative mode (he calls

> it the "literal") to pathetic exclamation to projective sentiment—are to be taken not as some affect of the writer's indisposition in need of expression but as content of the poem itself, as poem data, to be read as dream data and feeling-tone are read as factors in the structure of meanings in the dream. It is the constitution of the field of the poem that determines the line . . . it is not verisimilitude that determines the line-tone but its belonging to the projective feeling of the poetic structure as I work with it in writing. (*CG* i)

So the lines in question have their justification at the level of the whole poem. Duncan has repeatedly described his method of composition as a reading of clues or "omens" that lead him toward form. Consistency of tone is of less importance than the generative potential of these elements to the whole. Acknowledging the "reader's discomfort," Duncan argues for "a field of possible readings . . . [wherein] dream data, poetic fiction, original feeling, even the recognition of cliché and the critical perspectives of sympathies and dis-sympathies, unite in a widening suspicion in which he [the poet] designs" (*CG* iii). The poem as reenactment of life (Olson) gives way to the poem as sign, leading the poet to undiscovered Asias of the imagination (the enabling trope of *Caesar's Gate*). And what applies to the line applies also at the level of the poem, the series, the oeuvre. Duncan's comment on Whitman's line is relevant to his own: "In each individuation there is . . . its intimation of another meaning . . . some meaning of conflict yet to know in the Whole" (*FC* 202). Evaluative judgment, then, has to refer to the whole. If the line seems awkward, the poem is to be consulted; if the poem falls flat, the series or the book or the suite requires just that flatness. The poet has to have an intuition of the fit of the part to the whole as much as he does of the radiant energy of the whole in the part.

What I think of as the "Sally Rand" chapter in *The H. D. Book* provides an example of Duncan's thinking on selectivity. Here the question is about high versus low art. In the context of this chapter, Sally Rand, an early burlesque fan dancer and the butt of vulgar jokes is "incarnate, a creature of the hey-ding-ding touch" (part 2, chapter 5, 72). The latter phrase is H. D.'s, and the context a well-known admonition to William Carlos Williams to delete the trivial or vulgar from his poems. Duncan, of course, would keep the "hey-ding-ding." Sally Rand, he says, is like Georgina's birthmark in Hawthorne's tale, "The Birthmark," or she is a Freudian screen image, a substitute (77) for a memory that has been occluded or made up. Linking Freudian substitution with the alchemical principle (as above so below), Duncan finds that psychoanalysis and alchemy—and Poetry, of course—transmute shit to gold (81); all work in the "muck" of the repressed, the sexual, the hidden, the disallowed. As Duncan works the changes, Sally's fans become the veils to the temple of Isis and a trope for psychoanalysis as well. Like a fan dancer, psychoanalysis in its vulgar form promises to strip away the veils of the psyche. In Duncan's hands, however, every strip show is an addition, not a subtraction. Hence from a marginal figure who he initially rejects as inappropriate subject matter, comes a Figure of the Margin, who leads the poet to consider components of experience usually repressed or rejected. These (Freudian) symptoms turn out to be keys to his identity—marginalized as homosexual—and to the shape of the composition at hand. Joining Duncan in the practice of creative hermeneutics, we follow him outward from a seemingly insignificant image, dream, or Freudian slip toward ever-larger areas of thought and experience. What saves Sally Rand or the sentimental element of the "Sequence of Poems for H. D.'s Birthday" is the immanence of the cosmos in the most insignificant of its parts. In the essay "Man's Fulfillment in Order and Strife," Duncan revisits the question of what gets into the poem, affirming Mae West, despite the vulgarity, and Hitler, despite the Holocaust; reject these two, Duncan says, and "you have to go to battle against the very nature of Man himself, against the truth of things" (*FC* 115). As long as the question is one of human possibility, it is easy to agree, and Duncan's insistence on inclusivity suggests anarchic rebellion against political or ethical correctness. But this is where the contest between Duncan and Levertov is instructive.

To summarize the quarrel recorded in the *Letters,* Duncan objected to what he saw as Denise Levertov's political activism during the Vietnam years when it became a part of her poetry. In the exchange of letters leading up to the end of the friendship, Duncan's are full of poetry news—works completed and ideas about poetry. Levertov's letters more often detail her political activities and her urgent sense that people need to be informed about the effects of the war. "The fact is," she writes, "if one's life is a whole, and not compartmentalized, one cannot speak of one's art, without speaking of one's moral convictions" (Bertholf and Gelpi, *Letters,* 602). Duncan responds to these letters by reading them hermeneutically. In a letter of 30 March 1968, for instance, he attributes to Levertov a "demotic personality" and warns that "the soul is sacrificed to the demotic persona that fires itself from spirit" (607). While Levertov writes to Duncan in her own voice, he responds to the Logos latent in her words, just as he does in his own poems in which he characterizes the actual war in Vietnam as an eternal human possibility. In the 30 March 1968 letter, he writes of the war that it is "a revelation of the truth of the potential evil of 'America' " (608), previously revealed by "Blake,

Hawthorne, Melville, Lawrence—Whitman in his 'Eighteenth Presidency'" (608). In the same letter, he argues an analogy between the "suicidal" impulse of humanity in creating the atomic bomb and in overpopulating the earth. These human actions he compares to cancer, which grows "with no sense of the functions and needs of the total body" (609). The series of analogies are thus war-overpopulation-suicide-disease. But there is a difference in the kind of human agency implied by each term of this string of catastrophes. By reducing them to equivalence, Duncan implies that war is as little a matter of individual responsibility and volition as is disease. Historical agency disappears into the mythical paradigm, and the ethical dimension of the war is elided. In subsequent letters, Duncan vigorously resists the idea of taking a political stand or expressing conviction about an issue as a poet. Rejecting all "thou shalt nots," he writes that he "actively seek[s] to keep alive all volitions" (611). Levertov, he writes, reduces the "content of the world-anger" by moralizing (663), and in this she betrays Poetry. And then comes that much-quoted sentence: "The poet's role is not to oppose evil, but to imagine it" (669).

Support for Duncan's position rests on several arguments. First, there is the defense offered by Robert Bertholf in "Decision at the Apogee: Robert Duncan's Anarchist Critique of Denise Levertov," in which Bertholf argues that the rejection of Levertov's activist poetry is consistent with Duncan's long-held anarchist principles. Duncan saw the collective action of the Vietnam protest movement as an infringement on individual freedom and simply another form of the oppressive bureaucracy that it was meant to oppose. This is to base the disagreement between Levertov and Duncan on an ideological difference. A second line of argument has to do with the role of poetry in relation to public policy. So in "The People's P**K," from the Gelpi-Bertholf collection, *Robert Duncan and Denise Levertov: The Politics of Poetry, the Poetry of Politics,* Aaron Shurin suggests that for Duncan, the purpose of the poem is not to persuade its auditors toward some action but to direct attention to the poem itself as a field of action (72). In the same collection, Brett Miller cites Jean Jacques Lebel to the effect that "if poetry gets down on its knees in front of reality, it is no longer poetry" (96).[21]

Levertov responds to the critique, including Duncan's depiction of her as Kali raging in his "Santa Cruz Propositions" (*GW* 45), with hurt and, finally, silence, but her comments in a letter of October 1971 pinpoint an important issue that goes beyond the question of poetry as reflexive field or social message. "I think you are setting me up as an adversary without due reason," she writes. "Because you *do* have the habit of projection, of setting people up in roles—of mythologizing, as you did for instance when you identified me with

Kali. . . . That leads to the deadly abstract, the inhuman, the false" (Bertholf and Gelpi, *Letters,* 662). Duncan would argue that the "false" is as necessary to the image of Man as the true. But Levertov makes an important point in calling Duncan's attention to the abstraction built into his poetics "deadly" from the ethical perspective because it does not distinguish between what can be thought and what must be undergone. I return here again to the distinction between *knowing that* and *knowing how.* Certainly Duncan honors experience—it is emotional verity that attracts him to poetry as an adolescent (*H. D. Book,* part 1, chapter 1)—but his "felt universe" allows for the detachment of emotion from the actual undergoing of it; feeling can be a strictly poetic performance. Levertov sees the violent potential in this habit of mind. Arguably, Duncan saw it too in "The Venice Poem," when he turned the needle of jealousy into a sapphire phonograph needle—a device for making art out of what had begun as anguish.[22] In a later letter Levertov writes to Duncan that he *willfully* misapprehends her poems (Bertholf and Gelpi, *Letters,* 674)—this after a long letter from Duncan in which he reads certain tropes in Levertov's war poetry in typical Duncanian fashion.[23] Duncan "willfully misapprehends" because the actual context of the Levertov poems is of lesser significance to him than the generating Logos that inheres in the poems qua act of language. This is the similarity between the Blaser and Levertov episodes; both Blaser and Levertov commit crimes against the Logos because they treat it as historically contingent. Levertov reaches for words that will articulate an actual suffering-through of events; Duncan focuses on the power of Language to generate meanings and relations in the conceptual field of the Logos.

I have argued that the Neoplatonic model of form allows for the blurring of the particular and the universal. This is the model, I think, behind the aggression Levertov feels coming from Duncan. "You say you object to coercion," Levertov writes, "yet you relate to people in a coercive way" (Bertholf and Gelpi, *Letters,* 675). What Levertov hears as coercion involves a double move on Duncan's part. First, when he takes historical events as instantiations of mythical paradigms, he banalizes the actual suffering-through of such events. The Vietnam War becomes one of many wars explicating human violence and stupidity. Duncan writes in a letter dated "Oct. 16/1971": "All the history of Asian, Africa, Europe and the 'New World' is written in insane greed, racism and empires and exploitations. Back of 'racism' where white enslaved black, was tribalism where black enslaved black, where Semite swore undying hatred of Semite, where Celt devourd (literally) Celt, and Rome burns Carthage to the ground and salts the earth" (663). In this long parade of human perfidy and misery, the body count gets lost. Second, Duncan's way of lifting source texts out of their time-space context amounts to a kind of appropriation. Duncan decontextualizes Levertov's words in order to reactivate the Logos in them that he feels Levertov has let lie. But in that slide between the particular and generic, it is Duncan's version of the Logos that wakes up and begins to run the show. So in a famous example, Duncan takes issue with lines in Levertov's "Advent": "the obscene sell out, the coprophiliac spasm / that smears the White House walls" (Bertholf and Gelpi, *Letters,* 672). The reproach is that Levertov is not taking responsibility for all levels of the metaphor: "Since I know of no story of Johnson's being a coprophiliac, I can only imagine that your projection alone supplies this as an image of evil," he writes (672). This is to move "Advent" from politics to psychology, where it becomes a Duncan text, readable as projection rather than protest. The question of whether or not poetry has or should have a political dimension is not the immediate point, nor is the quality of Levertov's war poetry at issue. Duncan does not just refuse Levertov her ground; he insists that her poems work on *his* ground, which, it often seems, is *the* ground of the Logos as such.

The whole push of Levertov's Vietnam poems is toward the articulation of suffering that is too great for words, and her integrity in the face of that task is to persist despite inevitable failure because *as a poet* she takes it as her job not to let suffering fall into cliché or useless pity, and *as a poet* she insists that her countrymen face up to their complicity in brutality. This is not to comment on her success or failure in these aims. The poem "Advent 1966" (*To Stay Alive* 1971) lays out the problem with reference to Robert Southwell's "The Burning Babe" (1595), a poem about the poet's aerial vision of the infant Christ on a "hoary" Christmas eve. Southwell's Christ is an allegorical Child, burning with his own redemptive love ("My faultless breast the furnace is, the fuel wounding thorns, / Love is the fire, and sighs the smoke, the ashes shame and scorn"). Levertov's "Advent" begins this way:

Because in Vietnam the vision of a Burning Babe
is multiplied, multiplied,
                                        the flesh on fire
not Christ's, as Southwell saw it, prefiguring
the Passion upon the Eve of Christmas

but wholly human and repeated, repeated,
infant after infant, their names forgotten . . . (*To Stay Alive* 16)

The most unique element of Christianity is individual redemption; each soul is recognized and counted by God, and this is the *passion* of Southwell's Christ Child. In "Advent" Levertov doubles the horror of war by showing the spiritual reduction it imposes on those who must suffer through it—the anonymous bodies to be disposed of, or maimed lives that no longer matter even to those who have to live them. This is humanity as meat. And for Levertov the spectacle so sears her "poet's sight" that the inner eye films over, as with a cataract. In the last verses of the poem, she imagines her sight taken over by an insect, which "will not permit [her] to look elsewhere" (*To Stay Alive* 4). At one level the "monstrous" insect eye conjures the massification of suffering victims of war—individuals become so many ants to be trampled on, while the eyes of the survivors become "dulled and unfocused" with the spectacle of it, as do the emotions when confronted with overmuch. War entails this radical *belittlement.* But Levertov's metaphor may also remind us that insect eyes (bees, ants, crickets, for example) are compounded of thousands of "simple eyes" called ommatidia, each of which has its own lens and visual cells.[24] The insect eye can detect the polarization of light and use it to navigate. Does this eye propose an answer to the vision demanded by the spectacle of suffering: thousands of eyes for thousands of deaths, each one counting?[25]

In his "Seventeenth Century Suite" (*Ground Work*), Duncan gives two renditions of Southwell's poem. The first of these is typical Duncan. The burning babe is an "Infant Joy" (conflated with the "Joy" of Blake's *Songs*) who reopens "Life's wounds." Through this release, the poet comes to reconcile the warring contraries in himself—his inner winter's night, his cold refusals, his jealousy and pain—with the healing fires of joy and desire. "It is no more than an image in Poetry," Duncan writes:

. . . as though
"*his floods should quench his flames,*
 which even with his tears were bred" until

tears breeding flames, flames breeding tears,
I am undone from what I am, and in Imagination's alchemy
 the watery Moon and fiery Sun are wed. (*GW* 74, original emphasis)

In this version, imagination brings about redemptive possibilities because the action is firmly situated in the Logos where "Imagination's alchemy" can do its work.

In the second version of the poem, Duncan begins with a reflection on art and suffering. The redemptive Babe enters the poem in the first stanza as "a Christ of Poetry" who is "Art's epiphany of Art new born" (*GW* 75). This Christ "leaves no shadow, where he dances in the air, / of misery below" (75). Art, "good for 1000 performances," floats above the suffering flesh. But in the second verse, another Christ enters the poem, the Crucified one who has been forsaken by God:

Another Christ, if he be, as we are,
Man, cries out in utter misery;
and every Holy Martyr must have cried
        forsaken in some moment
that from Christ's "Why hast Thou forsaken me?"
        has entered our Eternity
or else is not true to itself. (*GW* 75)

If I read Duncan rightly here, Christ's passion is a type of the human abjection that rises up under unspeakable conditions like those suffered by the victims in Vietnam. During the crucifixion, the Father deserts the Son and the crucified one becomes simply suffering flesh. This is Duncan's introduction to "catastrophe incommensurate / with meaning, beyond hate or loss or / Christian martyrdom, unredeemed" (*GW* 75). What is most horrifying in this vision of the war is the imagination's inability to transcend it—to derive redemption dialectically from suffering. "My heart / caves into a space it seems / to have long feard," Duncan writes. And then,

I cannot imagine, gazing upon photographs
        of these young girls,   the mind
transcending what's been done to them. (*GW* 75)

Duncan's first version of the poem transmutes grief into the larger, mythic life of Poetry. Poetic alchemy rewrites a suffering world on the cosmic plane. At the end of that first poem, "the Language of What Is and I / are one" (*GW* 74–75). The poet can affirm "what is" despite the existence of suffering because he identifies with the redemptive potential of the cosmic whole, here in the form of the incarnate Christ. In the second version, however, the crucified Christ has been forsaken by the Father. In this case, the threat is that there is not going to be any transformation of suffering through Poetry because the horror is so great that the poet-creator cannot imagine things otherwise. Instead there is a travesty of rebirth when the "heretics," here meaning the enemies of America, are "baptized" by napalm. What comes out of this moment are the accusing eyes of those war victims whose lids have been burned away.[26] The two stanzas that present actual images of war parallel the darkness of Christ's crucifixion: "Victor and victim know not what they do / —the deed exceeding what we would know" (76). The phrase "what we would know" suggests that the not-knowing is partly willful, partly a refusal to imagine. In this penultimate stanza, Vietnam adds itself to the bad conscience and unacknowledged crimes of America. The stanza echoes Duncan's "Up Rising," but instead of the high-flying antiwar rhetoric, Duncan asks the important question, "What can I feel of it?" (76).

This is a question that haunts Duncan's war poetry and his correspondence with Levertov. It haunts his critics as well. Writing on "The Burning Babe," Paul Lacey wonders whether Duncan really convinces his readers of a "transcendence caught in Art and Song" ("Vision of the Burning Babe" 179). The rhetoric of poems like "Up Rising" or "The Soldiers" or "The Multiversity" can sound cheap, first because the poet conjures with horrors he himself has never suffered and second because his redemptive vision comes at the further expense of the victims whose personal agony he refers to long line-ups before the cosmic court. Recall in this context Duncan's own "Reflections": "That he wore the god head and did not worship he should have been the first to know, deriving his self from joy and even suffering that was not his" (*CG* 38). The question posed in the second version of "The Burning Babe" thus represents an important moment of self-questioning about the obligations of art in the face of suffering and by extension the political role of poetry.

. . . What can I feel of what was done?
All hatred cringes from the sight of it
and would contract into self-loathing
to ease the knowledge of what no man
can compensate.   I think I could bear it.

I cannot think I could bear it. (*GW* 76)

Duncan's "I think I could bear it" suggests that the poet is prepared to face up to "our nation's store of crimes" (*GW* 76), even if it means self-loathing. But the verb "bear" points precisely to the problem with this impulse. It is impossible to *undergo* someone else's suffering, although the poet may take on the guilt of complicity. The next sentence implies that this is not enough. "I cannot think I could bear it" suggests that bearing (with) the unbearable, especially when one has not been called upon to undergo it, adds insult to horror. The parallelism in the opening words of these two final sentences, "I think" / "I cannot think" implies a limit to thinking that is rarely there in Duncan poems: thought stops at the suffering flesh. This poem hints at the difference and distance between knowing and undergoing that Duncan rarely acknowledges.

Both Levertov and Duncan experience a failure of vision confronted by images of Vietnam, and perhaps this failure is the most fitting and eloquent response possible. In "Poetry's Ethics?" (2006), an essay on Adorno's aesthetics that cites Duncan, Robert Kaufman takes up Adorno's infamous statement that no poetry can be written after Auschwitz (73). Explicating Adorno, Kaufman argues that the ethical dimension of art follows from the autonomy of the aesthetic as an "as if" discourse. Resisting the intractability of reality as it is, art proposes an alternative world that is not free from history, but rather free from prevailing *concepts* of history (105). In challenging extant concepts, art proposes novel configurations of the historical field and hence opens the present moment to a "rich indeterminacy" that holds out new possibilities of agency (108). To be successful, however, art's visionary world has to be credible—it has to suggest a possible world, objectively available (108). When, under conditions of war, life is such that no meaningful choices can be made, the whole question of ethical behavior or the life well lived is moot. Art will either become a travesty, suggesting freedom from determination when in fact freedom is not possible, or it will be driven back into the negative, able to negate what exists or critique phony alternatives but not to propose new worlds.

If I bring this description of art to the Duncan-Levertov exchange, then it becomes clear that both poets risk aestheticization, but in different ways. Kaufman defines this Adornian concept as the fusion of art's world and that of reality. This would mean that art loses its critical distance from reality and indulges in the "sociopolitical or ethical delusion that the artwork or poem itself constitutes not merely a powerful formal spark toward the sensing of agency but an already substantive ethical or sociopolitical action" (Kaufman, "Poetry's Ethics?" 110). So in Duncan's view, Levertov loses the necessary distance between art and life in her political poems because she overwrites poetry's potential to create new meaning by insisting on the urgency of the historical here and now. In an "October 4, 1971" letter, Duncan writes to her: "Revolutions have all been profoundly opposed to the artist, for revolutions have had their power only by the rule that power not be *defined*. And, as workers in words, it is our business to keep alive in the language definitions as well as forces, to create crises in meaning, yes—but this is to create meanings in which we are the more aware of the crisis involved, of what is at issue"

(Bertholf and Gelpi, *Letters,* 661, original emphasis). If the poet can "create crises in meaning," she better challenges the intractability of an ugly reality than by treating the poem as a political tract. But if Levertov tends to collapse the aesthetic and political, Duncan risks incredulity in his visionary alternative to the here and now. The Logos is simply of another order than embodied experience (this is the core of Spicer's resistance to Duncan). The combinative flexibility of language does not translate into actual historical agency, except perhaps indirectly through the evolutionary potential of the species to reinvent itself—and there is something repugnant about urging the big picture on the suffering individual. Perhaps for this reason the second "Burning Babe" poem has to stop after the line "I cannot think I could bear it." Even a hermeneutical imagination as insistent as Duncan's might hesitate to draw vision out of lidless eyes. But of course the purpose of art, Duncan's oeuvre implies, is not to comfort. To recall "The Venice Poem," art *is* cruel in the face of suffering because it hypostatizes emotions that, in the flesh, have to be lived through. "There is no pain / I would not bear for her sake" (VP 50), Duncan writes.

I think Duncan's exchange with Levertov is a cruelty of this order. Asked to support her political commitment, Duncan faults Levertov for mistaking her task as a poet. As soon as poetry is made to serve ends other than its own, it loses what power it has to imagine things differently. This seems to me a valid point. But the affective content of the exchange is that Duncan responds to an emotional appeal with a cold readiness to treat the language of the letters, as well as that of the poems, hermeneutically. If Duncan reproaches Levertov for lack of imagination and *poetic* integrity, her responses suggest that Duncan lacks empathy. Perhaps this is to argue goats for cabbages. Duncan is concerned with the function of poetry as poetry, and from his perspective, poetry is not about taking the right position but about prying open positionalities. So Kaufman puts it, praising Duncan's "A Song from the Structures of Rime Ringing as the Poet Paul Celan Sings," as an example of poetry "that keeps determination and ethical possibility open for exploration, over against the delusion that the poem itself is already an ethical or political act" (Kaufman, "Poetry's Ethics?" 118). But Duncan is guilty at least of a breach of decorum by dodging the personal appeal of a friendship and using his craft to chide a former protégé who has gone her own way. What Duncan cannot allow is a poetics deriving from premises other than his own. In the heat of their argument, Levertov writes to him: "I have always had a strong preference for works of art in which the artist was driven by a need to speak . . . of what deeply stirred him—whether in blame or praise. I'd sooner read *Dubliners* than *Finnegans Wake.* Beckett bores me. Most of Gertrude

Stein bores me" (Bertholf and Gelpi, *Letters*, 679). These comments reveal Levertov's preference for representational as opposed to self-reflexive poetries.[27] From Duncan's perspective, this is to forego the power of the Logos—it is to fail as a poet. "Your decisions are so clearly not esthetic in character but . . . sentimental," he replies (Bertholf and Gelpi, *Letters* 687). But it would be an ad hominem fallacy to suggest that because of aggressive behavior Duncan's arguments for the autonomy of Poetry are invalidated. The episodes with Blaser and Levertov lead quickly to the question of what we want poetry to do. Is it supposed to console or to illustrate the correct political position on current issues? Do poets have to be nice guys? Or do they have to be skilled in the creative violence that smashes the rock of reality as it confronts us, so that something else might come to be?

The Via Imaginaria

Duncan invites the kind of commentary that has grown up around his war poems and his quarrels with old friends like Blaser and Levertov, not only because he conducted the latter in print, but because he thematizes war throughout his oeuvre. Yet the question that his work really raises is not whether poetry should or should not be tied to politics. There are political poetries and there are reflexive poetries and many in-betweens, all with legitimating discourses. But if we take Duncan on his own terms and assume with him that poetry is not the servant of reality, that its purpose is not to persuade or to console, we are still left with the Adornian question of the credibility of the vision. To repeat Kaufman, art that poses the potential for agency where there is none becomes a travesty. I began this book by suggesting in my introduction that the New American poets were the last generation *as a generation* to offer a prospective vision of the world rather than a critique of grim social actualities. For subsequent generations, the vision has been hard to maintain because of reduced personal agency in globalized, post-democratic societies. Anne Dewey, for example, argues that Duncan's generation experienced a "radical, often violent transformation of poetic and political subjectivity" ("Poetic Authority" 124) such that the public sphere would no longer be "structured by the agency of private individuals" (120). Yet Duncan's version of an alternative to the military-industrial complex is problematic even for the postwar decades because he often turns to the *pure* potentiality of language in the abstract, rather than the historically conditioned possibility that comes out of human limits (to go back to the Olson essay: this is what one can do; this is what one is doing). Pure potentiality is troubling if we are looking for "an actual earth of value": it is not so troubling if we read the poem as the human imagination of itself.

I think there is a more generous and fruitful way to read Duncan than for ethics or political allegories. His work is to drama as Olson's is to epic and Creeley's to lyric. If we read the poems as Duncan asks us to, as dramas in an ongoing world play, then the demand for authenticity or for ethical position-taking seems as absurd as it would if we were to ask it of an actor or playwright. We do not require Shakespeare to remove Iago or Macbeth from his dramas because the characters are evil, and we do not reproach actors for playing roles that, in real life, would be actionable or playwrights for making drama out of world-historical events like wars they have not experienced firsthand. They have, after all, our *permission* because we go to the theater to see what we have been, might be, could be, or unwittingly have become as well as what we think we are right now. Duncan's Poetry, like the theater, stages emotionally charged relationships between the Persons of the Poem, and like the theater, the broader the range and the finer the nuancing of the affections the better. Consider the emotional precision Duncan brings to a poem like "My Mother Would Be a Falconress," a poem about a son's rebellious love-hate relationship with his mother. And if the drama is Humanity, then Mae West and Hitler *do* have a place, as Duncan insists. Shakespeare is the patron saint of "The Venice Poem" because, as Duncan writes, "This stage . . . / is Truth— / never in living / but here, here, / [where] all felt things are, / permitted to speak" (49).

Certainly Poetry is Duncan's version of the postmodern commons. We meet not over what we know or how we identify ourselves socially but on a stage where *all* articulations of the species are permitted, evil and good, silly and profound. What Duncan asks us to consider as Poetry is a phenomenology of felt things rather than a representation of the *right* felt things. From this perspective, fantasy worlds are as valid an exploration as real ones because they equally instruct us in how humans fashion themselves. Olson's "Against Wisdom" *does* look restrictive from this point of view because Duncan's purpose is not to create a worldview that might suggest objective possibility (radical democracy, for example), but to explore the combinative capacity of the imagination to produce complex relations. Duncan's radicalism lies in his challenge to existing versions of what it meant to be human during an era when scientism and game theory were dominant in military and economic thinking,[28] and it remains a challenge to narrow definitions of the human in any era.

Reading Duncan's work as theater can also change the look of figure and ground. It is the actor's job to impersonate his character, often one larger than life. The fusion of the two is a measure of interpretive skill rather than a suspect ontology or questionable ethics. Duncan's creative interpretations of his sources (his derivations) or his personifications of Persons of the Poem such as the Master of Rime suggest the work of a grand and daring actor rather than appropriation—*if* the stage is the reference. In this craft, Duncan is an *adept:* a skilled actor and shamanic guide to the crypts and vaults of the Logos. In the theater, we do not ask for authenticity; actors do not usually step out of their roles to identify themselves, unless they be as Shakespeare's mechanicals who feel the need to explain to the ladies of the audience that the actor playing Lion is really Snug the joiner (A Midsummer Night's Dream V.i.219–26).

The price of dwelling in pure potentiality, however, is that the poet, like the stage actor, has limited agency in the historical world. He may be a skilled guide and free wayfarer of the inner life, but he may not be able to carry the freedom he has there into a plausible vision of the historical world. In "Close," a late poem from *Ground Work II,* Duncan says this of his loyalty to the "imaginal" and "irreal":

Wish   the daimon of this field   force
                    force before the gods came.

All the rest is archetype: Plato's in the Mind
            or Jung's   in psyche,   yes, glorious
                    imaginal   But this clime

is Fancy's . . .
. . . .

—You think I have some defense for it,   in it?
do not know the critical impossibility?

I make my realm this realm in the
            patently irreal—   History
            will disprove my existence.

The Book will not hold this poetry   yet
  all the vain song I've sung comes into it
                    spirit-bird cuckoo's   Song of Songs

one tear of vexation as if it were beautiful

falls into the elixir

one tear of infatuation follows
as if it were love

Let something we must all wonder about   ensue

one tear I cannot account for   fall

this: the flooding into the flooding

this: the gleam of the bowl in its not holding—(83–84)

In the land of Poetry, no defense is needed.

5

Jack Spicer

Castle of Skin and Glass

Introduction

As a student at Berkeley in the late 1940s, Jack Spicer participated in the creative commotion that was the Berkeley Renaissance, reading the moderns and trading poems with companions Robert Duncan and Robin Blaser.[1] But Spicer's position in this company and in relation to the Black Mountain poets was a contrary one.[2] Contra Duncan's symphonic structures and incarnational poetics Spicer pursued the personal lyric. Rather than Olson's chaosmicity and public voice, Spicer cultivated a Calvinist-inflected "Credo quia absurdum" (*CB* 180; *MV* 310[3]) and created around himself a private coterie. Closer to Creeley in poetics than to Duncan or Olson, Spicer nonetheless rejected Creeley's embrace of the generic word in favor of a universe "[e] xtended past what the words mean and below, God damn it, what the words are" (*CB* 182; *MV* 312). He also lacked the prospective optimism of his peers. As Peter Gizzi presents him, Spicer had a keen sense of immanent darknesses past and future, "as if he lived within the mechanistic and degraded future articulated in his poems, where computer stands in for God . . . silicon inhabits the heart . . . politics are informed by bombs . . . popular consciousness is preoccupied by outer space . . . the death of the author is an accepted trope of literary practice . . . and the social matrix of nation and community has collapsed into slums under the bosses of multinational self-interest" (Gizzi, *House* 173). It is my contention that Spicer's often dystopian vision derives from the most traditional of poetic aims: the saying of beauty and the reifying of emotion in a work of art. What makes Spicer an innovative poet and essential member of this company, however, is his recognition that this project had to be reinvented.

Robin Blaser opens his groundbreaking essay, "The Practice of Outside," with a little poem from Spicer's notebooks that catches Spicer's distinctive lyricism:

With fifteen cents and that I could get a
 subway ride in New York. My heart
Is completely broken. Only an enemy
Could pick up the pieces.
"Fragments of what," the man asked, "what?"
A disordered devotion towards the real
A death note. With fifteen cents and real
Estate I could ride a subway in New York. No
Poet starved. They died of it. (Spicer, *CB* 271)

This poem holds onto the difficult poetics that Spicer required of himself. He would build a poetry that "like a camera" (*ONS* 45; *MV* 26) would capture the real, and do this despite readings in linguistics that had left him radically skeptical of realist epistemology and public voice. If Spicer often seems to anticipate the poststructuralist theories that came into vogue after his death (and which were indebted to Ferdinand de Saussure), his writing is as contrary in spirit to the cool deconstructive play of the language-based philosophies as it is to Duncan's romancing of the Word. In *After Lorca,* Spicer famously writes of using words to "drag the real into the poem" (*CB* 25; *MV* 123), but he never lets go of the recognition that words and physical things are different orders of reality. When the human creature comes to itself in the languaged world, it loses the intimacy of preverbal sensation—what Jacques Lacan would call the real. Spicer's real, although closer in meaning to perceptual experience, suggests quite a different perspective on a similar recognition. Because experience as we come to know it is always already mediated by language and the mechanics of perception, it never adequately expresses what the individual must actually *undergo,* and more so than any of his company Spicer is a poet of undergoings. It is impossible, for instance, to make words communicate physical or emotional pain and pleasure in the same way that actual individuals, each of them unique, live these affects. As Creeley so ably demonstrates in "The Language," the words seem to have holes in them where living presences should be. Words are not feelings or things; at most the poet may trick the language into indexing a real it cannot really express.

In *One Night Stand,* a collection of early lyrics published posthumously, the eighteenth-century feel of Spicer is striking, although it is everywhere in the later work as well. "Dialogue between Intellect and Passion," for instance, reprises many such poetic dialogues that haunt the history of Christian, and particularly Puritan, poetry, but it also looks forward to Spicer's long struggle with language as a medium that fools the human animal into a longing for "specific witness" (Creeley's phrase) that, as an abstract symbolic order, it simply cannot deliver. The Enlightenment wish for perfect clarity, for a word that would exactly render an object or a sensual experience—a language that would deliver the real world—is at the bottom of Spicer's "devotion" to a real that is always withheld by the very medium that awakens the desire for it. Naming things *seems* to give them a clear and distinct form (I am thinking again of Bataille's *Theory of Religion*[4]), but for Spicer, as opposed to his eighteenth-century predecessors, clarity is a language-effect, purchased with the endistancing of the actual objects the poet is after. The thing recedes in its thingness the more the poet tries to name it. Paradoxically, the closer he or she tries to get to things as things, the *fuzzier* they become. Here is Spicer in "Fifteen False Propositions against God (X)":

. . . beauty
Will always become fuzzy
And love fuzzy
And the fact of death itself fuzzy
Like a big tree.
Let me chop down then one by one
Whatever is in the way of my eyesight
People, trees, even my own eyestalks.
Let me chop apart
With my bare hands
This blurred forest. (*CB* 91; *MV* 199)

The aim of this poem is highly traditional: it is to see and say the beauty of the world. But interfering with the poet's eyesight is the mechanism of vision—his "eyestalks." In chopping down this mediating mechanism—the only mechanism by which he can see anything at all—the poet chops down the "big tree" with the "blurred forest."

Now back to the "Dialogue" poem. The first stanza begins this way:

"Passion is alien to intellect
As hot black doves are alien to trees
On which they do not rest—
All are alone.
Of passion and intellect
Suspect

Neither bird nor tree
Of vicious privacy—
Nothing is intimate. . . ." (*ONS* 24; *MV* 15)

In this poem, the "hot black doves" are as other to the tree as passion is to intellect in medieval psychology. The birds "without rest" never get to light in the tree because birds and trees, like words and things, are different orders of reality. Each has its "vicious privacy" and "nothing is intimate" (*ONS* 24; *MV* 15). In the second stanza, however, the doves return at night in "swarms":

"They wait
Until the darkness make
Them dream-birds black
As needles and as ultimate.
As you branch blanketed in royalty
Each lacking claw, bird-real,
Will find its rest
Throughout your naked branches,
Make you feel
Birds in the bed
Locking their claws against
Your privacy." (*ONS* 24; *MV* 16)

If, in the daylight, the birds cannot land on the tree, in the dark, after reason has gone to sleep, the tree feels the claws of the birds digging into it. The images in this second stanza evoke bodily sensation, specifically pain (the sting of needles and claws). Locked against "your privacy" the claws not only grip the poet in his most vulnerable parts, but they also seem to drag personhood out of dumb nature as the tree turns into a second person "you." No matter, then, that words and physical things are disjunctive orders; we bear the claw marks of language in the flesh and we have no choice but to undergo the separateness for which we have been marked as a species. Words are the aliens that pull us out of our bed in the semiotic murmur of nature.

Spicer's attitude toward his Enlightenment predecessors is thus a mix of sympathy and irony. In "Lament for the Makers," Spicer calls on Alexander Pope in the language of Lewis Carroll:

Pope, Pope, Pope of the evening
Beautiful Pope. Help

Me as sheer ghost. I
Would like to write a poem as long as the hat of my nephew, as wide as is
spoiled by writing. (*CB* 110; *MV* 319)

The superimposition of these two poets, one a poet of "plain" speech and the other of nonsense (the reference is to Carroll's "Mock Turtle's Song," "*Soup of the evening, beautiful soup*" in *Alice's Adventures in Wonderland* [95, original emphasis]) shows what happens when language can no longer be conceived as a transparent window on the world. The self-evidentiality of commonsense perception—something as close and ordinary as a relative's hat—not only becomes utterly elusive, but also the evocation of it nonsensical. No less than Pope, Spicer would have *liked* to bind words to things, but once caught up in the skepticism reflexivity engenders, he discovers that the mirror he would hold up to nature is a funhouse mirror. The continual reversal of sense into nonsense this discovery triggers constitutes an instance of the "polar logic" of Spicer's work as Blaser discusses it in "The Practice of Outside."

I think Spicer glimpsed a real horror back of this crisis of faith in realist epistemology, and one that goes beyond the poststructuralist moment in which it was later thematized. I want to bring in Max Horkheimer and Theodor Adorno to help me describe it. Spicer, Blaser tells us, was not interested in philosophy beyond his early readings of Leibniz and Spinoza (Blaser, *Fire* 9), and I have no evidence that he read *The Dialectic of Enlightenment,* but this work, published in 1944, reacts to some of the same social and philosophical conundrums facing Spicer. The argument in the *Dialectic* is that Enlightenment rationalism, meant to liberate humanity from superstition, actually sublimates the old irrationalisms—magic, religion, and myth—and along with them the human will to power. (This view of reason is a very narrow one, but I think it a good fit for Spicer.) To follow the argument, magic and religion once veiled human efforts to control the natural world and other people, but far from being exposed and expelled by reason, the urge to dominate is reason's hidden motivator. By dismissing every aim except utility, the Enlightenment succeeded in instrumentalizing the world better than did magic, not just because the technology improved, but also because reason, unlike magic, recognizes no God, no cosmic Other, no wild *mana* apart from the unacknowledged human will. Horkheimer and Adorno see in de Sade a representative for the violence of rationalism because de Sade proposed that there is no reason intrinsic to reason itself not to instrumentalize whatever is not-me. And if de Sade is the unacknowledged spokesperson of the Enlightenment, the Nazis were its funhouse jokers, reaching for the Third Reich across the ash heaps of the uncounted dead. The will to power, Horkheimer and Adorno argue, is at the core of all civilizations and is the formative kernel of the subject itself. This is the impulse that constitutes

> . . . a denial of nature in man for the sake of domination over non-human nature and over other men. This very denial, the nucleus of all civilizing rationality, is the germ cell of a proliferating mythic irrationality: with the denial of nature in man not merely the *telos* of the outward control of nature but the *telos* of man's own life is distorted and befogged. As soon as man discards his awareness that he himself is nature, all the aims for which he keeps himself alive—social progress, the intensification of all his material and spiritual powers, even consciousness itself—are nullified and the enthronement of the means as an end, which under late capitalism is tantamount to open insanity, is already perceptible in the prehistory of subjectivity. Man's domination over himself, which grounds his selfhood, is almost always the destruction of the subject in whose service it is undertaken. (*Dialectic of Enlightenment* 54)

The extreme self-alienation of civilized humanity here described—and Olson's polemic against the estrangement from the familiar must come to mind again—ends in perversity. Horkheimer and Adorno write that a language purified of its so-called irrational content reverts to magical incantation:

> The more completely language is lost in the announcement, the more words are debased as substantial vehicles of meaning and become signs devoid of quality; the more purely and transparently words communicate what is intended, the more impenetrable they become. The demythologization of language, taken as an element of the whole process of enlightenment, is a relapse into magic. Word and essential content were distinct yet inseparable from one another. Concepts like melancholy and history, even life, were recognized in the word, which separated them out and preserved them. The absolute separation, which makes the moving accidental and its relation to the object arbitrary, puts an end to the superstitious fusion of word and thing. Anything in a determined literal sequence which goes beyond the correlation to the event is rejected as unclear and as verbal metaphysics. But the result is that the word, which can now be only a sign without any meaning, becomes so fixed to the thing that it is just a petrified formula. This affects language and the object alike. Instead of making the object *experiential*,

> the purified word treats it as an abstract instance, and everything else (now excluded by the demand for ruthless clarity from expression—itself now banished) fades away in reality. (*Dialectic of Enlightenment* 164, my emphasis)

Language becomes formula—and in quite another way structuralist renditions of language as a system of relations might qualify as such—and banishes lived experience to the dustbin of history, where it nonetheless continues to function all the more efficaciously as an alienated and dangerous, because unacknowledged, "outside." This is a theoretical way of describing the conditions under which a "practice of outside" becomes essential.

I have paraphrased and quoted these arguments from *The Dialectic of Enlightenment* because they get at the multiple levels of alienation at work in Spicer's poetry. Language may produce subjective experience, but read from a linguist's perspective as a system of signs in which personal pronouns are merely shifters, it also erases the particularity of its speakers. Spicer's work spins on the paradox that every experience brought to articulation by a languaged consciousness is also denied its uniqueness by the verbal *techne* that produced it. While this is a condition that would later find theoretical expression in Lacanian psychoanalysis and deconstruction, Horkheimer and Adorno's analysis suggests that this skepticism has encysted in it the will to power[5]—the will to appropriate the world as an object of knowledge. Spicer's reach for the real tropes on this will, but unlike the Enlightenment poets, he is acutely aware that the harder one looks, the fuzzier things get—that in fact conceptual clarity is incompatible with the temporal nature of things. Will then mutates to incurable desire and desire finds expression in the "magic" Spicer works to get the real into his poems. If "plain" speech fails to deliver the wished-for hats and lemons, Spicer will make words as opaque and nonsensical as incantations on magic's ancient premise that like calls to like, thing to thing; drain the word of meaning, *thingify* it, and perhaps then it can be used to conjure a real beyond itself. Magic, mysticism, and surrealism become strategies for indexing materialities that lurk beneath the concepts we use to parse the world. Writing both out of and *against* an extreme skepticism, Spicer makes potent theater of the absence of real presences in phonemes and graphemes, numbers and words. Symbols don't feel; people do.

That Spicer's poetry is one of ostension has been recognized early in the critical reception of his work. In the 1977 *boundary 2* Spicer special—the first significant academic response to his work—William Spanos writes: "The contemporary impulse to dis-cover or dis-close what a logocentric rhetoric or presence—a coercive naming, as it were—covers over or closes off and forgets, this impulse to reactivate the astonishment of original perception, reminds us, of course, of the antinomianism that, according to Roy Harvey Pearce, constitutes the forgotten origins of the American poetic tradition in poets like Walt Whitman" ("Jack Spicer's Poetry of Absence" 2). This comment raises questions about the degree to which antinomianism can be squared with deconstruction (antilogocentrism) since the former would seem to indicate an immanence beyond the words that deconstruction registers as theological. But Spicer's is an ironic immanence that recognizes the "outside" not as metaphysical presence but as temporal undergoing. Here is another version of figure and ground, played out between the individual and the symbolic order in which he or she has been interpellated. What I take from Spanos is an early recognition of Spicer's poetry as disclosive of what is absent in language as well as his sense that the Spicer poem is a reflexive gesture that points to itself pointing. In this same issue of *boundary 2*, Clayton Eshleman also remarks of Spicer's *After Lorca* that what remains after the poet has "lost his imagination" (Spicer's phrase from the poem "Juan Ramon Jimenez") are "pointed to 'real' things" ("The Lorca Working" 33), and Jed Rasula as well takes up the "sense of a finger pointing" in his reading of "Aquatic Park," from *After Lorca* (61). Michael Davidson, again in the *boundary 2* collection, identifies in Spicer's dictation an effort to "concretize an endlessly distanced voice" ("Incarnations of Jack Spicer" 130). Fast forward nearly thirty years to Daniel Katz's article of 2004, "Jack Spicer's *After Lorca:* Translation as Decomposition," and we find a section on *After Lorca* titled "Poetry as Pointing" (89).

What has to be distinguished about Spicer's "pointing," and especially because his work has been submitted to poststructuralist analyses,[6] is the empirical component there in the *devotion* to real things, however distorted they become in language, and in the *devotion* to a world the poet cannot not feel as beauty. And this devotion is *not* irony. In Spicer's ostensive gestures, all the love, pain, and longing that the human creature undergoes in the face of beauty presses against the surface of the words like a nose pressed against a candy shop window. And if such old-fashioned sentiment arouses derisive cackles in the skeptic?

So Bird and I sing
Outside your window
So Bird and I die
Outside your window.
This is the wonderful world of Dixieland
Deny

The bloody motherfucking Holy Ghost.
This is the end of the poem.
You can start laughing, you bastards. This is
The end of the poem. (*ONS* 80; *MV* 72)

My focus in this study will be on Spicer's ostensive strategies, all of which have as their aim the dragging of the real into the poem. A significant segment of Spicer commentary focuses on his theory of translation as correspondence in *After Lorca* and the poetics of dictation he discusses in the Vancouver lectures.[7] I want to turn to his treatment of mysticism and surrealism. Before I begin, however, I want to establish the *ur-game* back of these strategies. This is the duel—Spicer's ironized effort after the dualism of a referential language (word refers to thing) rather than the reflexive one of modern linguistics (word refers to word). Passion and intellect, flesh and words, the living and the dead are some of the combatants. Not only is the uniqueness of personal undergoing elided in the linguistic sign, but also the poet's voice is continually crowded by the dead voices that haunt the language and hang out in the cultural archive—that vie for attention with the living, and take away the poet's breath with an endless chorus of been-there's, done-that's. In "The Scrollwork on the Casket," an important early piece collected in *One Night Stand*, the battle between the dead and living is laid out in a dizzying farce. A "sweating author" tries to stuff a rigid corpse into his "casket of paragraphs" (*ONS* 36; *MV* 24). The corpse does not fit and the customers or readers complain that all caskets look alike anyway. "The customers are right," Spicer says. "The outside of the casket is made up mostly of the writer, his descriptions, his feelings, his fancies, his regrets—little or nothing about the corpse on the inside" (*ONS* 36; *MV* 24). Writing dialogue, the poet thinks, is more interesting because it shows "that there is space inside the casket" (*ONS* 36; *MV* 24). In the last four paragraphs of this vignette, the author and the corpse he is burying echo each other to the point where it is difficult to determine who is burying whom. The piece ends with the lines:

"I think I'm going to be sick," he said.
I think I am going to be sick. (*ONS* 37; *MV* 25)

"Scrollwork" is funny in a dark kind of way, but it has the edge of most of Spicer's jokes. Author and corpse vie for the outside, dominant position. But both positions—I am living and you are dead; I am the author and you are the object of my writing—turn out to be merely places in language. In this sense writer and corpse are both inside the casket, as Peter Gizzi intimates.[8]

And because the inside and outside of the casket are merely different rhetorical positions, the dualism implied by the opposition living-dead or inside-outside turns into a duel between opponents who duke it out from different corners of the same little language box. Dueling is thus an unwinnable game, but it has the virtue of dramatizing an "outside," that language cannot express. Dead people at least are indices of a singularity.

The Imaginary Elegies: Castle of Skin and Glass

At a talk titled "My Vocabulary Did This to Me," given at the Jack Spicer conference in San Francisco in 1987, Robin Blaser insisted on the depth in Spicer and pointed to his interest in the mystical writings of St. John of the Cross and St. Teresa of Avila (*Fire* 259). Blaser cited Michel de Certeau's essay in *Heterologies* (1986), titled "Mystic Speech," in his discussion of Spicer's dictation, and a look at this essay suggests why. First, de Certeau argues that European mysticism of the sixteenth and seventeenth centuries came out of social disenfranchisement and feelings of loss and powerlessness. Certain social classes and geographical enclaves had lost ground in the economic, social, and military shifts into modernity, and it is from these classes and regions that the major mystics came. St. Theresa belonged to an aristocratic class that had lost its wealth and power; St. John of the Cross also came from the fallen nobility. As de Certeau puts it, "The memory of past abundance survived in these conditions of impoverishment, but since the doors of social responsibility were closed, ambitions were redirected toward the open spaces of utopia, dream, and writing" (*Heterologies* 84). Second, the writings of St. Theresa and St. John oppose a tradition perceived as decadent, but claim the same universality as that of the tradition. In other words, the mystic speaks from a position that is supposedly more authentic than that of prevailing institutions and thus locates the true universal in the local. Third, the mystic space as de Certeau extrapolates it from the writings of the era bears a number of characteristics: it is an interior, imaginative space; it is experiential and therefore outside what counts officially as truth or knowledge; its texts are dictated, and this is the root of the claim to authenticity. In the mystic text, the "I" must empty itself of personal content so that the divine Other may speak through it; this is essential to the claim of authenticity and universality. And finally, the mystic speaks to an intimate circle of initiates who can be counted on to share his or her *Tao.* Experience is the only way of testing the mystic's claims. For the majority, who demand more conventional proofs, the mystic will appear to be foolish and the *Tao* too rigorous.

If we look at Spicer's work through de Certeau's spectacles for a moment, certain parallels between his situation and that of the mystic's stand out. Like the mystic de Certeau constructs, Spicer, by his choice of vocation, seems to have understood himself to have renounced the possibility of social agency. As he insists both in his poetry and his lectures, the poet has no political or social power. In this he disagreed publicly with Ginsberg ("I / don't see how you do it. One hundred thousand university students marching with you. Toward / A necessity which is not love but is a name" [*CB* 267; *MV* 426]). He also kept his distance from Olson, who he refers to in his last Vancouver lecture as an unofficial President Johnson of poetry (*House* 159). Blaser points out that Spicer came of a working-class family and that his father had been involved in the Wobblies, a union that had some political power for a time, but that was virtually broken by the end of World War II (*Fire* 253). But working-class, union culture, even if it had survived the war, was not exactly welcoming of homosexuals. In the mid-1940s, Spicer was attending anarchist (not union) meetings at the Workman's Circle in San Francisco, and it was through these meetings that he met Duncan.[9] I am suggesting that for Spicer, poetry and anarchism—the latter suggesting fluid, voluntary association rather than institutionalized sociality[10]—meant a turn inward and away from a public voice. Certainly, as Spicer emphasizes in his last Vancouver lecture, "Poetry and Politics" (*House*), he conceived of poetry as an intimate affair shareable among initiates rather than with a wider public. Everything about his writing and biography bears this out. In this last Vancouver lecture, he repeatedly refuses all queries from the audience directed toward claiming some public function for poetry. Pressed to say what poetry *does* do and who it might address, he simply replies that it carries messages from the outside that are quite useless for social or political ends (*House* 162), and of little interest to those other than poets (164). It seems over obvious to add that in the 1940s and '50s, homosexuality by itself was a guarantee of outsiderdom and powerlessness in the larger world, as the frigid reception of Robert Duncan's "An African Elegy" by the *Kenyon Review* under John Crowe Ransom's editorship had amply demonstrated.[11] During his brief writing life, Spicer famously held court in San Francisco bars like The Place or Gino and Carlos, for a small group of young, mostly homosexual men who were either fellow poets or pretty and artsy enough to find admission to the circle in advance of the poems they had not yet written. The social model, as Maria Damon has discussed, was that of the "George-kreis," a small, elite coterie centered on the German poet, Stefan George (*Dark End* 153). Ernst Kantorowicz, the medieval historian with whom Spicer, Blaser, and Duncan had all studied at Berkeley, had been a member and was the immediate inspiration.

As Spicer's social situation bears some resemblance to that of the disenfranchised mystic, so the strategies played out in the poems suggest an inverted mystic speech. In the Vancouver lectures, where he discusses the dictated poem, Spicer repeatedly emphasizes the importance of emptying out the self: the first stage of a dictated poetry is the accidental receiving of a poem as if it had come from outside; the second step, Spicer says, is to realize that the outside source cannot be tricked or commanded to come at will; and the third stage "is to try to keep all of yourself that is possible out of the poem" (*CB* 274–75; *House* 8). These steps set out the terms for a mystical space of enunciation from which the poet may receive "messages" other than the *merely* subjective. For Spicer, however, the "mere" of subjectivity is an effect of reflexivity, not of personal bias; what the poet thinks are *his* emotions and *his* experiences are rhetorical commonplaces. The point, then, is not to avoid the subjective, as in traditional mysticism, but to summon it as madly and extravagantly as possible. These lines from "A Fake Novel about the Life of Arthur Rimbaud" (*Heads of the Town*) demonstrate the problem:

"Dear X,
I love you more than anyone could ever do.
signed
Y" (*CB* 150; *MV* 282)

Any old "X" or "Y" might utter this most intimate of communications. So how does the poet convey what someone in love might actually be going through as opposed to what language can declare of love? Creeley's solution, as he proposes it in "The Language," was a performative one: put the words in a real mouth (see the Creeley essay for my commentary). Spicer's contrasting strategy is to "fool" the language into carrying messages from beyond its prison walls while at the same time holding onto the recognition that there is no thinkable beyond—that the poet is playing an impossible game that on one hand implies the otherworldliness of mysticism, and on the other madness or death, the only two kinds of exits the rational mind has been able to project as outside its own perceptual apparatus. To deliberately make for these exits, minus the mystic's religious faith, is to open a door into hell instead of heaven. The wax mountains of the poem "Arcadia for Dick Brown" are images of the absurd and Sisyphusian effort of such a poetry; hell is sliding back down the sentences that one has used to try to climb out of them (*ONS* 7). Spicer's mysticism thus differs in one crucial aspect from that of the religious mystic: the real to which he attends is not God but the actuality of flesh and feeling that "God" in the guise of the Word withholds from us.

In the first of the "Imaginary Elegies," Spicer sets up a duel between the eternal and the temporary.

When I praise the sun or any bronze god derived from it
Don't think I wouldn't rather praise the very tall blond boy
Who ate all of my potato-chips in the Red Lizard.
It's just that I won't see him when I open my eyes
And I will see the sun.
Things like the sun are always there when the eyes are open
Insistent as breath.
                    One can only worship
These cold eternals for their support of
What is absolutely temporary. (*ONS* 45; *MV* 26)

Using the poem as a device, the poet tries to catch the blond boy, but the poem is "blind like a camera" (*ONS* 45; *MV* 26), a mere word machine that may produce a snapshot but not the manner or movement or temporal dimensionality of the boy. Notice that the poem-as-camera is not interesting in itself; it is only what the poet can "catch" with it that holds his attention. So if the boy is not *in* the words, the words have to be made at least to announce his absence. "It is as if we conjure the dead," Spicer writes, "'I am little Eva, a Negro princess from sunny heaven.' / The voice sounds blond and tall. / 'I am Aunt Minnie' . . . / The voice sounds blond and tall" (*ONS* 46; *MV* 27). Here Spicer tries out the séance as a metaphor for poetry, and if I hear him rightly, this is his version of the performative solution to unique expression. The boy speaks through the dead voices (the well-used signs of a common language), but whatever he says is colored and torqued by his saying of it.

In the second elegy, "The moon is God's big yellow eye remembering / What we have lost or never thought" (*ONS* 47; *MV* 27). This eye of God is the virtual past—the past that in the differently oriented poetics of Olson and Duncan is the fertile ground of the future, the raw material of the cosmic *combinatoire.* In Spicer's poem, however, the eye suggests a knowing that is an effect of the Word-machine. The moon eye is an "old / Slow infinite exposure of / The negative that cannot happen" (*ONS* 47; *MV* 28). What is horrifying about this eye of God—and the eye plays off the camera lens of the first elegy—is that it includes and determines the actual before it happens. Like a photograph, whatever comes to be "developed" into perceivable form has to pass through the device: it has to be *exposed.* There is no way to bring the "negative" of the blond boy into the poem—his density as a temporal being—no relief from the *glare* of the Word. Given this impasse, Spicer turns to mysticism. In her *Interior Castle,* St. Teresa of Avila writes of the soul as a many-chambered inner castle in which God dwells at the center.[12] Spicer tropes on this castle as a device for enticing live boys into the poem. On the moon,

. . . the poet builds a castle
Made of dead skin and glass. Here marvelous machines
Stamp Chinese fortune cookies full of love.
Tarot cards
Make love to other Tarot cards. (*ONS* 48; *MV* 28)

The castle of skin and glass is a precise metaphor for Spicer's poetic practice. Dead skin is what a body sheds as it moves on. Glass, whether mirror or window, suggests the reflexivity of a medium that stands between the poet and the warm, live things he reaches for. Like a shed snakeskin, the mystic castle or poem is constructed of words and the leavings of presences (blond sounding "messages," perhaps) that move around somewhere beyond the words. Unlike the poem as camera, however, the castle offers a place for boys to hang out. Certainly, Spicer is aware of the absurdity of the strategy—that his castle is a dada device.

This is the sun-tormented castle which
Reflects the sun. Da dada da.
The castle sings.
Da. I don't remember what I lost. Dada.
The song. Da. The hippogriffs were singing.
Da dada. The boy. His horns
Were set with song. Dada.
I don't remember. Da. Forgotten.
Da. Dada. Hell. Old butterface
Who always eats her lovers. (*ONS* 48; *MV* 29)

Initially a powerfully subversive response to the humanist tradition in European art, dada is a recurrent phenomenon in the art world; read broadly, it is a gesture that moves to the edge of sense, wherever that edge may be at a given historical moment. Spicer's separation of the first syllable of the term creates a shorthand comment that works like an ideogram at this point in the poem. The syllable "da" gives us "there" in German, and it is to capture the immediacy of the "there" that the poet builds the mystic castle of the poem.[13] But "da" is also a baby syllable for "dad" and in this poem it is the Big Daddy in the sky who co-opts the "there"—the "I am"—of the infant's first cry. Only the Logos possesses the original "I Am"; every other "I am" has always already been spoken. Hence the poet's argument with "old butterface," the moon that bathes her poet-lovers with the reflected light of the sun. Dueling with her, the poet's "da" morphs into dada and a *negation* of memory as dada was a negation of European art traditions. In opposition to the God who remembers everything before it has happened, the poet tries to forget in order to make some space for the freshness of the "absolutely temporary": "Da. Forgotten. / Da. Dada. Hell" (*ONS* 48; *MV* 28–29). This amnesia, cultivated in order to short-circuit the mediate nature of memory and to trick the language into registering the real, again suggests an impossible stepping outside of the mechanisms of perception. As soon as the poet makes this move, the underworld (the madness of reason) appears in the poem:

Hell somehow exists in the distance
Between the remembered and the forgotten. (*ONS* 48; *MV* 29)

The elegy concludes with a host of "moon-children" crowding into the poet's moonlit room, like ghosts, "Flying, crawling, swimming, burning / Vacant with beauty" (*ONS* 48; *MV* 29). Beautiful images these are, sirens of the language that entice with pictures (snapshots) of things that are not at all what the poet is after.

In the third elegy, Spicer focuses on the sun, God's other eye. This eye "observes the goodness of the light it shines" and then devours its own light and goodness:

Cat feeds on mouse. God feeds on God. God's goodness is
A black and blinding cannibal with sunny teeth
That only eats itself. (*ONS* 49; *MV* 29)

Turning from the reflected light of the moon to the source of its light in the sun, the poet ends up with an imago that suggests the reflexivity of the Logos and perhaps the cosmos as process, of light feeding on light. This is Spicer's version of the *cannibal* cosmos, the enemy of poetry because it constantly devours its own beautiful things. (I will return to the cannibal cosmos in the Howe essay.) Spicer parries (this is a duel) with a twilight zone between the setting of the sun and the rising of the moon, an in-between state in which "the earth dances" and "most things happen" (*ONS* 49; *MV* 30). Somewhere between cognition and perception, between the mechanisms of language and the becomings of the universe, the poet imagines a place sheltered from the two eyes of God, where God is "blind as a gigantic bat" (*ONS* 50; *MV* 30), and the boys these elegies are meant to house are free to be only themselves. In the next sequence of images, however, the moment of imaginary peace turns into its opposite. The poet sees the boys asleep in the sun by a swimming pool. Red from the sun, they dream dreams of themselves dreaming. The poet wants to "splash them with twilight like a wet bat" and "unbind the dreamers," but the moment of tenderness twists into irony in the lines: "Poet, / Be like God" (*ONS* 50; *MV* 30). Even in sleep, the boys dream reflexively and hence are "sunburned." Like the claws of the bird-words that dig into the tree in the "Dialogue" poem, the sun marks the flesh of the creatures that come under its light. The poet, on the one hand, offers shelter in the poem, but in doing so, he subjects the boys to a "sunny" medium that burns them all the more. If, on the other hand, he makes himself "blind as a gigantic bat," he may save the boys from the light of his *knowing* them, but he has to forego the pleasure of their presences, which was the point of the poem in the first place. In other words, the poet fails whether he succeeds or not. This is the Orphic bind: the poet may look and lose, or rescue his beloved and not look at him.

In the fourth "Elegy," the dreaming boys have *aged* and so has the poet. In their 2008 edition of Spicer's collected poems (*My Vocabulary Did This to Me*), Peter Gizzi and Kevin Killian date "Elegies I to III" in the late 1940s, "Elegy IV" in 1955, and "Elegies V and VI" in 1959 (*MV* 441). Returning to the "Elegies after some years, Spicer finds the boys long gone. "Time does not finish a poem," Spicer writes, but it does finish off boys (*ONS* 51; *MV* 48). "What have I gone to bed with all these years?" he asks, and the answer is, "Only the shadows of the sun and moon" (*ONS* 51; *MV* 48). Instead of boys in his bed the poet finds "their creaking images," which turn out to be "Only myself" (*ONS* 51; *MV* 48). The castle of skin and glass returns in a cruel image at the end of the poem as a "giant funhouse" (a mockery of the poet's efforts) haunted by ghosts and seagulls (*MV* 49).

The imagery of "Elegy V" shifts toward the dictation that by the late 1950s had become one of Spicer's primary weapons in his duel with the language. In a tunnel now, riding a train, the poet is Prometheus, subjected to a "bird" that tears at his "live-r" (*MV* 230). Spicer's version of the mystic's role is held in that image. Emptying out the self, the poet invites messages from beyond (from the real), but these necessarily arrive in the shape of word-birds, feeding on his living flesh and parasitically using that energy to make themselves manifest. Notice that the effect of the assault is continual *pain,* continual sufferance. Spicer's spelling of the name, "Pro-me-thee-us" (*MV* 231) recalls the sacrificial elements of the myth. Prometheus steals the fire of heaven to benefit humanity; he is thus "pro" me, thee, and us. In a parallel gesture of sacrifice, Spicer submits to a Rimbaudian *dérèglement* of good sense in order to save the presences beneath the words. To go back to the Horkheimer and Adorno analysis, I sacrifice myself in order to forestall the sacrificing of myself. Language is one of the most powerful *technes* the human animal has at its disposal and its principal means of enduring beyond the moment. Spicer's very traditional gesture in the "Elegies" is to rescue beauty from age and certain death. Such has been the effort of poets since time immemorial. But putting boys into poems simply ensures death of another kind—the reduction of their vitality to the static image or generic word. The only way to drag vividness of life into language is to make the words somehow declare the nonidentity between the particular and its concept. The principle, again, is that of magic; like calls to like. To make words point instead of mean, the poet has to make them opaque and nonsensical. So he exposes his "live-r" to the word-birds that grow fat and heavy on it. (For a poet whose literal means of *dérèglement* was alcohol, the image is poignant.) Like the mystic, the poet goes through the rigors of personal sacrifice, but he does it to save the personal.

"And for what? One might ask. The sixth and final "Elegy" of the series begins with the word "Dignity," which immediately breaks into its syllables: "[D]ig is an obvious pun for / digging graves" and the "extra syllables" of "nity" "are unimportant" (*ONS* 53; *MV* 231), Spicer writes. Like madness and mysticism, graves mark the limit of experience; death is perhaps the most dramatic concept the poet could propose to index the difference between life and language. In this poem, that difference rides on the words like an "utterly alien cargo" (*ONS* 53; *MV* 231); a nonsensical surplus, "nity" is the cargo of singular personhood. In a last tightly compressed sequence of images, the nonsense, the mysticism, and the task of the poet come together:

Dig-
    nity
Or like that little window in Alice which she can't go through
    because she's 27 feet tall because she ate a bottle called
    Drink Me
Po-eatery, Po-eatery. The eaxtra slyllables is unimportant,
    because the poem said Drink Me. I'll find a substitute
For all your long-
Ing
And that little door with all those wheels in it
Be-
    leave in it
Like God. (*ONS* 54; *MV* 232)

The little garden in Lewis Carroll's nonsense epic, *Alice in Wonderland*, which Spicer references, puts another spin on the mystic castle of skin and glass. In

Carroll's book, Alice finds she cannot enter a marvelous garden paradise because she is too small to reach the handle of the garden gate. To grow taller, she drinks a magic potion, but then finds herself too big. Both ways she is excluded from the *paradiso* on the other side of a door that is never the right size. So it is that real persons are always too small (the particular as mere example is less than its concept) or too large (the particular as a complex route of occasions is more than its concept) to fit into the words. As Robin Blaser would write in *The Moth Poem*, "*the words don't fit you*," (*HF* 71, original emphasis). "Po-eatery" is the magic potion that is supposed to fit its subjects into a garden of verse—"a substitute / For all your long- / Ing," Spicer says. But instead, the poem turns into "Torture gardens and scenic railways"[14] (*CB* 51; *MV* 185), as Spicer would write that same year in *Billy the Kid* (1959). In "Elegy VI" the train metaphor works in two ways. On the one hand, we are the extra syllables the words carry, the "alien cargo"; on the other, the word-birds ride us, feeding on us livers.

Spicer's duel with language, like the mystic's dictated speech, rests on the assumption that undergoing is distinguishable from knowing. Love and death are easy enough to talk about, but talking is not the same as feeling. Love says *this* one, not *that* one; the two ones are nothing like each other, even though the "beloved," however we call him or her, is an empty signifier susceptible of infinite substitution. Somehow, the poem has to incorporate the "extra syllables" that accord dignity to the individual. Psychoanalysis dissolves love into desire; linguistics concerns itself with the structure and function of language ("Tarot cards / Make love to other Tarot cards" [*ONS* 48; *MV* 28]); and most philosophies are deeply invested in the analysis of concepts. In these too-bright, too-sunny discourses, there is no "outside," no "absolutely temporary," no real boys skulking around inside the poet's word castle. As Spicer writes in his last letter of the *After Lorca* series, "It was a game, I shout to myself. A game" (*MV* 153). These are *imaginary* elegies because the real they index is imaginary, cognitively speaking. But against this skepticism there is the irrefutable counterevidence of love and death and getting old. "Be- / leave," Spicer says.

After Lorca: The Surrealism of the Poet

Spicer's *After Lorca*, a series of poems and letters that address, translate, and rewrite the poems of Garcia Lorca, is famously about translation (Eshleman, "The Lorca Working" 1977; Chamberlain, "Ghostwriting the Text" 1985; Katz, "Jack Spicer's *After Lorca*" 2004). As in "The Scrollwork on the Casket," Spicer sets up the series as a duel between himself as a living poet and Lorca as a dead one. "It must be made clear at the start that these poems are not translations. In even the most literal of them Mr. Spicer seems to derive pleasure in inserting or substituting one or two words which completely change the mood and often the meaning of the poem as I had written it. More often he takes one of my poems and adjoins half of it to another half of his own, giving rather the effect of an unwilling centaur. (Modesty forbids me to speculate which end of the animal is mine)" (*CB* 11; *MV* 107). As Clayton Eshleman shows in his poem-by-poem commentary, Spicer's versions of Lorca include mistranslations that sometimes seem arbitrary, sometimes meaningful. But I would suggest that this dueling is largely spectacle and for the same reason as it is in "Scrollwork." Spicer's joke at the end of the introduction makes the point: "HERE LIES AN OFFICER AND A GENTLEMAN. . . . I wonder how they happened to be buried in the same grave?" (*CB* 12; *MV* 108). Both Spicer and Lorca occupy the same casket of paragraphs and verses, although being alive Spicer takes less kindly to it. The duel between them is merely a wrestling for who gets to temporarily occupy the subject rather than the object position—who gets to be on top. The real translation, the kind that occupies both poets, is the impossible translation of the real into language.[15] Tradition, Spicer says, "means generations of different poets in different countries patiently telling the same story, writing the same poem" (*CB* 15; *MV* 110–11). Here is the crucial passage on translation as correspondence: "Things do not connect; they correspond. That is what makes it possible for a poet to translate real objects, to bring them across language as easily as he can bring them across time. That tree you saw in Spain is a tree I could never have seen in California, that lemon has a different smell and a different taste, BUT the answer is this—every place and every time has a real object to correspond with your real object—that lemon may become this lemon, or it may even become this piece of seaweed, or this particular color of gray in this ocean. One does not need to imagine that lemon; one needs to discover it" (*CB* 34; *MV* 133). In this section of my commentary, I want to get at Spicerian correspondence by contrasting Spicer's version of the surreal with that of André Breton. The "surrealism of the poet," Blaser writes, is the "under-the-real which comes forward when the fixed-real dissolves" (Spicer, *CB* 323; Blaser, *Fire* 160).

In his 1934 essay, "What Is Surrealism?" André Breton identifies two phases of the surrealist movement. The first, in the 1920s, he says, was idealist because its practitioners privileged mind over the material world. The second phase of the movement was marked by a turn to dialectical materialism. Both phases, however, had as their aim the renovation of social life. Breton comments on how surrealism might accomplish this objective in an essay from 1947, "Rising Sign," on poetic analogy. He favors analogy over deductive logic because it can leap categories and reestablish "primordial" links among things (280). In this essay, he speaks of cosmogony reimagined. Poetic analogy differs from mysticism, he says, because it does not turn to the supernatural as a source of immanence but to the latent relations among empirical things—" 'absent' life," as he calls it (281): "The first duty of poets and artists is to re-establish analogy in all its prerogatives, taking care to uproot rearguard spiritualist thought, always carried along parasitically, which vitiates or paralyses its functioning" (282). Breton then adds "that thirty years ago Pierre Reverdy, first approaching the source of the image, was led to formulate this capital law: 'The greater and truer the distance between two juxtaposed realities, the stronger will be the image and the greater its emotive power and poetic reality' " (282). Analogy between two terms, however, should lead toward "health, pleasure, quietude, given thanks, consented usages" (282). The example Breton offers of these desirable analogies is a haiku: "Out of Buddhist kindness, Basho one day ingeniously changed a cruel haiku composed by his humorous disciple, Kikaku. The latter having written, 'A red dragonfly—tear off its wings—a pimento,' Basho substituted 'A pimento—add wings—a red dragonfly' " (283). Through such juxtapositions, surrealism, on the one hand, expands the synthetic powers of the imagination. Dada, on the other hand, as Breton deprecates it, is merely anarchic.

In these brief extracts I have taken from Breton's writings there are important points of overlap with Spicer's practice. They share, for instance, a sense of the immanence of a larger material life than that accommodated socially as "knowledge," and there is a surface similarity between the images that come out of Spicer's language games and those of Breton and other surrealists. Spicer's opening image of the "unwilling centaur" in *After Lorca* bears some resemblance, as a metatrope for the surrealist image, to "Your teeth are like a flock of sheep leaving the washpen" (282) or "Your tongue / The red fish in the aquarium / Of your mouth" from Apollinaire, both quoted in Breton (282–83). But it is the difference that is instructive. The "centaur" suggests a frozen dialectic, not a synthesis of disparates. The two terms retain their categorical differences rather than reconcile in a synthesis. The point is to force difference rather than synthesis into visibility—to point to what remains disjunct, "unwilling," and distinctly not liberated. As I have said in commenting on "Scrollwork," dualism gestures toward the duality the poet cannot bring to presence directly, between what can be articulated as knowing and what has to be experienced as undergoing. Yet there is no immediate social advantage to be achieved from such a demonstration. Although he can *sound* like a surrealist when he wishes to, Spicer's nod toward surrealism is a dadaist one.

Farcical as it is, Spicer's dueling implies a lack of faith in the socially transformative power of desire. While Breton writes that desire is surrealism's "sole act of faith" (*What Is Surrealism* 137), Spicer depicts desire as a sentence (pun intended) imposed on the human creature rather than a means of liberation; like Prometheus, the "liver" is condemned to suffer the beaks and claws of the word-birds. This view has serious implications for the role of art in society. I have noted Spicer's disapproval of Ginsberg's activism and the comments in the final Vancouver lecture, "Poetry and Politics," countering audience demands for some reassurance that poetry be publicly significant. As well, this turn away from a public poetry is an indirect response to Olson's mode of address to Gloucester's citizenry and to Duncan's gathering of a cultural archive that was to bring all persons into a common life. (Compare Spicer's showcasing of the private letter with Olson's public letters in the first volume of *Maximus.*) A needling of his peers over their projects, perhaps, but a serious challenge as well. Breton assumed, even in his second, materialist phase, that a change of consciousness can have a liberating effect on the actual world, and as otherwise different as they were, so did Ginsberg, Olson, and Duncan. As long as the poet or artist remains convinced of this, he or she can claim a crucial social role, ranging from the critique of false consciousness to the renovation of the subject or the refashioning of the *imago mundi.* Spicer's *sous*-realism (to honor the French preposition) is considerably darker and less socially ambitious; as such, it stands in relation to the work of his closest contemporaries as a crucial qualification, a devastating "but," and a reductio ad absurdum of the lyric's celebration of particular beauty.

In the "Imaginary Elegies," Spicer had written that "offering up your life to summon anything is a pretty silly thing" (*ONS* 52; *MV* 230), but in *After Lorca* he goes on to elaborate, nonetheless, a poetics of summoning. The "traditional" poet is the translator of real things; Spicer had got this far in the early "Elegies." In *After Lorca,* he folds in the idea of correspondences. Instead of worrying about the connotations of words, the prospective translator should recognize the emotional complex called up in the original and find a configuration of words in his own language that might evoke a similar kind of intensity. So Lorca's lemon is to become Spicer's seaweed. In *After Lorca,* words are famously "rope," which the poet uses to "drag the real into the poem" (*CB* 25; *MV* 123). Translation as correspondence thus suggests a formula something like this: word *x* (the rope) evokes thing *y* (the lemon) and emotion *z* in the original language; in the second language, word *a* (the rope) evokes thing *b* (the seaweed) and emotion *z* in the translator's language. The meeting ground is the affect engendered by the thing summoned, which the poet must be willing to experience in order to do the translation. Hence "the perfect poem has an infinitely small vocabulary" (*CB* 25; *MV* 123); it would be a gesture so minute, so much a pointing, and yet so precise in its figuration of whatever was under the words that the felt thing would be unmistakable. It follows that such a poetry requires intense commitment and is thus easiest to share among a small group of readers prepared to go all the way with the poem.[16]

I will look at two examples of Spicer's gesture toward the impossible poem, the poem with an "infinitely small vocabulary." What I want to show is a strategy in which Spicer negates concept and image in order to tease out an emotionally charged space below the words. "The Ballad of the Little Girl Who Invented the Universe" juxtaposes three highly charged and beautiful images: a jasmine flower, a little girl, and a bull. To get at the structure of the poem, I will quote it in full:

Jasmine flower and a bull with his throat slashed.
Infinite sidewalk. Map. Room. Harp. Sunrise.
A little girl pretends a bull made of jasmine
And the bull is a bloody twilight that bellows.

If the sky could be a little boy
The jasmines could take half the night to themselves
And the bull a blue bullring of his own
With his heart at the foot of a small column.

But the sky is an elephant
And the jasmines are water without blood
And the little girl is a bouquet of night flowers
Lost on a big dark sidewalk.

Between the jasmine and the bull
Or the hooks of the sleeping people of marble or
In the jasmine, clouds and an elephant—
The skeleton of a little girl turning. (*CB* 14; *MV* 110)

The poem opens as if setting a scene—the syntax suggesting stage directions—but the images quickly move beyond what can be easily pictured. The flower and the bull with his throat cut are easy enough and emotionally tensed to beauty and violence. But how to imagine an *infinite* sidewalk, and how to arrange map, room, harp, and sunrise? Each of these components of line two has an emotional charge. "Infinite sidewalk," for instance, rhymes affectively with the dead bull and flower of line one as melancholia, the sidewalk suggesting the loneliness of cities or the hardship of a long way to walk or maybe getting lost somewhere, as "map" might indicate. Yet no map covers the infinite, and the line loses itself in the (sublime) bafflement of the imagination, only to snap back with "map," "room," "harp," "sunrise." With few narrative connections, the possible combinations proliferate. Does "harp" go with the bull's death and suggest some kind of Sunday school afterlife? Or does "map" go with sidewalk as a way to get back to "room"? And what happens at sunrise? The poem does not answer. Instead, lines three and four move into a relation of pseudo-causality. The little girl "pretends" a bull of jasmine *and* the bull is a bloody twilight. The sequencing suggests that it is the little girl's imagination that brings the bull to presence, but her bull is made of jasmine, and the one that arrives is a "bloody twilight"—not at all, in other words, as she had pretended him. And how is it that the twilight comes to be a dying bull?

The second verse is structured like the proposition, if *x* then *y:* "If the sky could be a little boy," then "[t]he jasmines could take half the night to themselves," and the bull could have "a blue bull ring of his own." The third verse answers this hopeful imagining with a qualifying "but" and a series of predications that imply the impossibility of the sky ever becoming a little boy. Instead, the sky is an elephant, the jasmines are water, and the little girl is a bouquet of flowers lost on the sidewalk. There is no context for these assertions and therefore no way of scuttling for the relative safety of metaphor. The predications of verse three (*x* is a *y*) are simply presented as a state of affairs contrary to the hypothetical conditions of verse two that better favor little girls and bulls. Then, instead of resolving in an image or concept, the last verse reprises the principle images of jasmine, bull, and girl to exit with the "skeleton of a little girl turning." The "sleeping people of marble" contribute to the dreamlike quality of the whole sequence in which imaginative agency (the little girl's pretend) and cause-effect are both summoned and suspended.

If the poem parodies a propositional logic (if *x* then *y*, but *z*) that it annuls through the fantastic nature of the content, it offers nonetheless a powerful dream logic of condensation and displacement. In verse one, the bull has his throat slashed *and* he is made of flowers. In verse three, the little girl is made of flowers and the jasmines are "water without blood." In verse four, the little girl's skeleton turns, as if suspended by a hook. The hook, however, is linked to the "sleeping people of marble," although it cannot but conjure a meat hook in relation to the bull. If we begin to read the poem according to this associative logic rather than the propositional logic evoked by the syntax—this is where Breton's comments on analogy are instructive—the poem suddenly coheres as an emotional construct. The associations are traditional, underscoring Spicer's point that poets write the same poem about the same affective material: bull-animal vigor-death-melancholy-mourning; little girl-imagination-hope-love. And beauty is the lure. The emotional complex of the poem pits the heart's desire for love, life, and innocence ("If the sky could be a little boy") against the probabilities of violence, cruelty, and death ("But the sky is an elephant"). This structure coupled with the emotional charge of the images both invites desire and denies its fulfillment. By refusing closure to the emotions thus aroused, Spicer-Lorca achieves a kind of "translation"; he creates a "castle of skin and glass" that houses big, common emotions without attaching them to a specific narrative. Readers are thus thrown back on their own desires for beauty, their own needs for love, their own fears of suffering and death. These affective experiences will then *correspond* to those similarly undergone by the poet and whoever else is brave enough to risk the poem with him.

The difference between Spicer's strategy and that of the surrealism it resembles—marble sleepers with hooks, childish skeletons spinning between jasmine, clouds, and elephants—is that Spicer's poem opens up the sous-real below the image. In "Ballad," the concepts (the names for things) come undone in the series of interchangeable predicates attached to them: the sky is an elephant, the jasmines are water, the bull is dead, the bull is twilight, the girl is dead, and so on. In a surrealist poem, as Breton at least describes it, the startling juxtaposition of images leads to conceptual synthesis. If I add wings to a pimento and make it into a red dragonfly, I animate and liberate an inanimate thing—or I reverse the process in the "bad" haiku that takes the wings off a dragonfly to make a pimento. In each case, however, the resulting image can be expressed as an idea: the animation or brutalizing of the object. Similarly, if my tongue is a red fish in an aquarium, or my teeth are like sheep that have just had a bath, the concepts red mouth and white teeth are enhanced rather than negated by the image. In the Spicer poem, the concept is repetitively undercut with impossible images ("infinite sidewalk"), implausible predications ("the jasmines are water"), and the cancellation of the proposition, if *x*, then *y*.

My second example of Spicer's sous-realism is the Buster Keaton sequence in *After Lorca*. This sequence is written as a series of little dramas, remarkable for the radical disconnection they imply between emotion and event. The first of them, titled "Buster Keaton's Ride," opens with Keaton killing four children with a wooden dagger. "My poor children!" he says. The "stage directions," which become more fantastic and less like actual stage directions as the play proceeds, say that Keaton next "[counts] the corpses" and then "[g] rabs a bicycle and goes" (*CB* 17; *MV* 113). The following image is of a "Negro" eating a straw hat among "old rubber tires and cans of gasoline" (*CB* 17; *MV* 114). The only connection between these images is the cliché in each. Keaton's insincere exclamation over the children he has just murdered corresponds to an equally insincere and barely suppressed cliché: "poor old black Joe." Both sentiments blandly ignore the violent act that opens the scene and the brutal racism that created "old black Joes" in the first place. In this context, the crowing rooster of the opening line might remind us of the cock's crow that marks St. Peter's betrayal of Christ—a betrayal that, in the poem, takes the form of a denial of actuality just as the words of this sequence belie the actions of the characters and the emotions or feelings these acts might be expected to evoke.

The next sequence juxtaposes clichéd comments with actions to which they are not suited. "What a beautiful afternoon!" Keaton says, "I like riding a bicycle" (*CB* 18; *MV* 114). He then rides his bicycle into books, operas, and coal mines. In the same verse paragraph, "Adam and Eve run by, frightened as if they were carrying a vase full of water and, in passing, pet the bicycle of Buster Keaton" (*CB* 18; *MV* 114). This section of the sequence emphasizes category leaps such that two different orders of reality—a person riding a bicycle in three-dimensional space and a character in a book—occupy the same plane of reality. In fact, Spicer writes that Keaton's bicycle "has a single dimension" (*CB* 18; *MV* 114), an unimaginable collapse of all categories, even the two-dimensional. After a passage on Keaton's eyes and the lights of Philadelphia, the sequence then seems to turn toward a critique of the surrealism it evokes. An "American girl" enters and asks Keaton, "Do you carry a sword decked with myrtle leaves?" [. . .] "Do you have a ring with a poisoned stone?" (*CB* 19; *MV* 115). The sword circled with myrtle is a Tarot image; the poison ring references comic book stories or toys in cereal boxes. The questions thus seem to suggest card readings or comic book heroics, a comment, perhaps, on the relative facility of producing surrealist images—the formulaic quality of a "Singer machine" that encircles "big roses" or a bicycle running behind "two enormous gray butterflies" (*CB* 18, 19; *MV* 114, 115). The sequence ends with a young girl "with a wasp waist and high collar" falling off a bicycle (*CB* 20; *MV* 116). Miss Eleanor's dated clothing suggests a bygone era, perhaps one of greater decorum and chivalry than Spicer's mid-twentieth-century California, which would make Keaton's sexual play for the girl more transgressive. As he leans over her: "Darling Miss Eleanor, pardon me! (lower) Darling (lower still) Darling (lowest) Darling." And the final bracketed stage directions: "(The lights of Philadelphia flicker and go out in the faces of a thousand policemen)" (*CB* 20; *MV* 116). Keaton's two main acts in the sequence, the murder of the children and the sexual pass at "Miss Eleanor," are unconnected to the surrealist images that decorate the sequence and to Keaton's inane comments. The police, belatedly appearing in the last line, serve roughly the same role as did Breton in the surrealist movement: they are there to suppress unacceptable behaviors and feelings such as the tearing of wings off dragonflies. The whole sequence functions as a kind of spectacle that works to erase itself by emphasizing the disconnect between what is being said and what is taking place. When the parade of images is over, however, the pointed-to events are sex and violence. This is a dada-like response to surrealism that tears apart image and concept in order to point to the sous-real beneath the words—in this case the growling depths of Eros and Thanatos.

The second Keaton sequence, "Buster Keaton Rides Again: A Sequel," is subtitled "A Translation for The Big Cat Up There" and it turns on another dada-like duel with the surreal, this time involving elements of Catholicism. Keaton meets a talking pigeon—the Holy Ghost, perhaps?—who says, "I could love you if I were a dove" (*CB* 42; *MV* 143). He then converts to Catholicism and dances with the Virgin, while Alcohol, disguised as a cockroach, crawls up his leg. In this piece there is again a disconnect between what Keaton says and does, what he seems to feel and the emotions we would expect his actions to evoke. Before converting, for instance, he declares himself not a Catholic. The pigeon asks, "Don't you believe that God died?" and Keaton responds, crying, "No." He subsequently plays chess, is bitten by Alcohol, and witnesses the Virgin pray to herself. He throws a "bleeding pomegranate" from his heart (*CB* 44; *MV* 145). He declares "I love you," but it is not entirely clear whom he addresses. As in the first sequence, the actions and the affects are incongruent. Then there is the dada-like behavior of the Virgin, the literary critics, the policemen, and the chambermaids. All of these characters—never mind their behaviors for the moment—are icons of godliness, cleanliness, law and order, and university-approved, right thinking. This is a system that can afford to allow a few bohemians, a few Spanish dancers (read poets) for entertainment, decorated with little magazines up their butts as Spicer has it. But after a few drinks, Alcohol gets them all, and the order they represent falls apart. The announcer of a new world, Keaton also announces the death of Orpheus, a death that in myth marks the failure of poetry to rescue beauty from the underworld and precedes the dismemberment and scattering of the poet's body by the Bacchants. Twice the Virgin says to Keaton, "You have bumped the car" (*CB* 43, 44; *MV* 144, 145). Poetic *dérèglement* disrupts the orderly unfurling of cause and effect, of words congruent with deeds and thoughts with feelings. The poet-clown has "bumped" the rational universe in this poem, and what crawls out from below, along with the cockroach Alcohol, is the messiness of sex, death, and the will to power.

The Lorca poems, like the "Imaginary Elegies," are built to house the most common of experiences. Extravagant as they seem in imagery, the Keaton sequences deal with love, hate, sadness, lust, fear, and their accompanying cruelties, but they do so in a way that unhooks these affects from the rational structures that make them intelligible or therapeutically manageable ("I love you because . . . ," "I am sad because . . . ," "I murdered because . . ."). And because the emotions the poems encrypt are not bound to a concept, tamed by a narrative, or subordinated to a social project such as Breton's, they are wild and bellowing when Spicer turns them loose on the reader. The strategy is not to *say* the emotions but to make the poem *point* to them. This is a gesture that leaves the reader to do the undergoing. A Spicer poem is much easier to feel than to explain, and that is Spicer magic, his art of conjuring affects that are not *in* the words but above them in an aura of connotations and below them in the beating hearts of those who stumble in for a drink and end up staying for the night.

Heads of the Town Up to the Aether: The City as Ghost Town

If language expresses the suchness of its speakers poorly it is nonetheless the only medium they have, and they inhabit it as ghosts of their flesh and blood selves. In *The Heads of the Town Up to the Aether* Spicer reframes his pursuit of the real yet again, this time as a descent to the underworld that takes its imagery from Jean Cocteau's film, *Orpheus.* Set in the 1950s, the film redesigns the myth of Orpheus in ways that coincide uncannily with Spicer's lyrical push. Cocteau's Orpheus is a famous poet when the story begins, but he is losing his edge to younger singers. In the opening scene, after an altercation in a bar in which Death's leather-clad motorcycle minions run over a younger, hipper poet named Cegeste, Orpheus meets Death, personified as a beautiful and imperious Princess. With the body of Cegeste in her car, the Princess orders Orpheus along for the ride. Even though Orpheus is returned to the living, he quickly becomes fascinated by the Princess and by the "messages" he hears on the radio of the car that travels between the upper and lower worlds. He becomes a poet of dictation, in other words. In this film version of the myth, Eurydice is not the primary motive for Orpheus's descent to the underworld; rather it is the messages that Orpheus wants—the "poems" from the other side that come through the car radio—and it is the Princess he is in love with, more so, it seems, than Eurydice.

Spicer's *Heads* is divided into three sections, corresponding to a hell, purgatory, and heaven, Spicer says in the first Vancouver lecture (*House* 18); these sections are "Homage to Creeley," "A Fake Novel about the Life of Arthur Rimbaud," and "A Textbook of Poetry." "Homage" is further divided into poems and explanatory prose sections, such that each page is headed with a poem under which is an "explanation," partitioned from the poem by a line, although, as Susan Vanderborg has noticed, these paratexts both promise and frustrate explanation (*Paratextual Communities* 56). The "Homage" poems always point in two directions: they draw attention to language by making nonsense of it, and they poke and prod into life the emotional beasties on the other side of the words. In the film, mirrors are the doorways between the worlds of the living and dead. Heurtebise, Death's affable chauffeur, comes and goes with the help of magical gloves that turn the hard surface of mirrors into a permeable substance that can be passed through. Like the gloves, the nonsense of the poems is a magical device. The poem "Magic" exemplifies.

Strange, I had words for dinner
Stranger, I had words for dinner
Stranger, strange, do you believe me?

Honestly, I had your heart for supper
Honesty has had your heart for supper
Honesty honestly are your pain.

I burned the bones of it
And the letters of it
And the numbers of it
That go 1,2,3,4,5,6,7 . . . (*CB* 132; *MV* 264)

Even more obviously than words, numbers are incapable of registering living intensities, and yet they can powerfully impact real lives. For Spicer's generation, quantum physics was a privileged science because it had just unveiled the power of the atom. Yet where Olson drew inspiration from Heisenberg's Uncertainty Principle, Spicer's treatment of numbers is a reminder of the coldness of Einstein's formula $E = mc^2$, which says that life can be liquidated and untellable suffering inflicted without the slightest gain or loss on either side of the mathematical equation. Historically, the numbers that produced the atomic bomb reduced those strangers in Hiroshima and Nagasaki to bone or less ("I burned the bones of it"), but even in an exercise as simple as a child's counting ("1,2,3,4,5,6,7"), numbers are death-bearers because they carry the power of abstraction. That numbers can so affect us and we not them is, according to poetic logic, quite unfair. In this poem, the absurdity of burning or eating numbers and words suggests a shamanistic appropriation of their power. Ancient magic aimed at control through imitation. What Spicer does in "Magic" is similar: he reifies words and numbers (a kind of abracadabra gesture) so that what has devoured the real may itself be devoured. The "honesty" in this poem, however, requires that the poet acknowledge the limits of his device. Like a parlor magician, he makes something concrete out of something abstract (he pulls thingness out of thin air), but the more honest he is, the more he tries to reify and make visible the abstractions that shape us, the more compelling the illusion generated by these abstractions. The expository passage that is paired with this poem underscores the idea that magic does not really move consciousness closer to its outside. Spicer writes that "Orpheus was never really threatened by the Underworld during his visits there" (*CB* 132; *MV* 264). "In this poem," he says, "they present him with a diplomatic note" (*CB* 132). As long as one has a consciousness, one is still in the language box. "Honesty does not occur again in the poem," Spicer says, "the numbers do." This poem, like "Scrollwork," has a half-comic, half-nightmarish, Texas-chainsaw-massacre feel: every imagined escape leads the poet deeper into the madness of trying to use the mind to step outside the mind; every duel is contained in the box.

One of the ironies of "Magic" is that poetry *is* about number and number is everywhere in the syntax and the rhythm of poems. Number inhabits the body as rhythm (repetition and difference) where it literally bears on the living as time and death. Given this condition, and following Spicerian logic, biography is the most impossible of genres because it purports to treat of the uniqueness of a life. "Homage" is followed by "A Fake Novel about the Life of Arthur Rimbaud"—fake because a real biography would be impossible. In "Chapter III: Plato's Marmalade," however, Spicer *plays* with the idea of a sacred language that might literally hold onto someone's life.

> A is a blank piece of driftwood being busted. E is a carpenter whose pockets are filled with saws, and shadows, and needles. I is a pun. O is an Egyptian tapestry remembering the glories of an unknown alien. U is the reverse of W. They are not vowels.
>
> When he said it first, he created the world. (*CB* 163; *MV* 294)

The immediate source of this piece is Rimbaud's "Voyelles," (*Oeuvres* 86), although Spicer seems to combine it here with "Après le Déluge" (161), a poem about the world emerging in primordial freshness after a flood. That freshness of creation is the dream of every artist and poet. Spicer was familiar with Duncan's use of Kabbalah and the tradition of sacred languages. In the *Zohar,* where the letters of the Hebrew alphabet present themselves to God that he may create the world through them,[17] letters and things are perfectly aligned. For a poet who would like to put real boys and lemons into his poems, a sacred language is a limit concept. But as the title of the poem suggests—"Plato's Marmalade"—language is a sweet and sticky substance that one puts on top of something. In a sacred language, the word comes first and then the world, as Plato's Idea precedes its material actualization. Spicer's poem parodies this relationship between words and things by emphasizing the difference and distance between them. The link between "A" and a piece of driftwood is not at all apparent, and the arbitrariness of the connection points to the unmotivated nature of the linguistic sign rather than the coinherence of word and thing. As well, the fact that "I is a pun"—the facticity of puns—shows the sliding of the signifier over its signified. This is why Rimbaud has "a ready-made dead-letter officer" inside him (*CB* 164; *MV* 295) and why the dead-letter officer "grows in us like the river of years": "He writes poems, pitches baseballs, fails us whenever we have a nerve to need him" (*CB* 164; *MV* 296). Dead letters live our lives for us but refuse to carry our messages. As Derrida would later show, it is in the nature of the letter that it need never arrive.

But it is the difference between poet and philosopher that matters. The affective distance between Derridean indeterminacy and Spicer's "Credo quia absurdum" is beautifully modulated in "The Hunting of the Snark." In Spicer's version of this Lewis Carroll nonsense poem, snark hunters sit around a campfire and "sing songs of snark-hunting" in the company of "animals [that] distinguish us by our smells" (*CB* 165; *MV* 296). Smell is a chemical sense that can only be experienced in the presence of a living being. It is thus more evidence of a physicality that eludes language and that is also unarguably singular. In the animal world, scent is *the* operative signature. From the animal perspective, the words and songs of the snark hunters "disappear in the waiting fire" (*CB* 165; *MV* 296) because the fire is where the scent stops. The poem ends with the snark-hunters themselves "disappear[ing] into the clearing" (*CB* 165; *MV* 296). Through their songs and words, the hunters vanish from the animal world into a human space. This is the clearing that occurs when the human creature faces the world as *Dasein* rather than as an animal caught up in the flow of life. The poem dramatizes what Spicer has been saying about language all along: it "disappears" physical beings that are nonetheless uniquely present in the animal world. Carroll's poem ends with this verse:

In the midst of the word he was trying to say,
In the midst of his laughter and glee,
He had softly and suddenly vanished away—
For the snark *was* a Boojum, you see. (*Annotated Hunting of the Snark* 70, original emphasis)

The snark *is* a Boojum—that is, the duplicity and pain of the human animal that is always hunting itself, always caught between longed-for intimacy with the world and the equally longed-for clear knowing of it.

If we accept Spicer's description of *Heads,* then we might expect an ascent from the opacities of "Homage" to some relatively illuminating "explanations" in "A Textbook of Poetry." From a literalist perspective, this just does not happen. "Textbook" offers more of the sous-real. In poem 22, for instance, words are "postage stamps at best" that have to be canceled (*CB* 180; *MV* 310). More negation, more pointing. Yet "Textbook" includes Spicer's meditations on community and the common—his version of the City—and points toward a kind of communication through correspondence. When the sous-real presses its flesh against the sentence ("Where we are is in a sentence," Spicer writes [*CB* 175; *MV* 305]) it finds there a ghostly company. Ghosts Spicer defines "as an India-rubber eraser created to erase their own past" (*CB* 171; *MV* 301). The voices that hang out in the language, living or dead, are shades of themselves, decontextualized from historical specificity and the trajectory of their own memories. They "try to give us circuits to see them, to hear them," Spicer says (*MV* 300). The poet listens to their voices and records the messages they try to send through words, even while he struggles to be heard himself over their babble:

> The poet thinks continually of strategies, of how he can win out against the poem.
>
> Seeking experience for specific instances, drawing upon the pulp of the brain and the legs and the arms and the motion of the poet, making him see things that can be conveyed through their words. (*CB* 171; *MV* 301)

The strategy here suggests a kind of reverse incarnation. Instead of the word becoming flesh, the flesh tries to fit itself into words.[18] In words, the poet enters a ghost town.

Spicer describes the City in poem 14 of "Textbook" as "a collection of humans" who "sit together" and "form groups" (*CB* 175; *MV* 305). This description of the polis is loose enough to include the open spaces of Olson, Creeley, and Duncan. Whether as a series of interlocking multidimensional scapes (Olson), or Basic English (Creeley), or cultural archive (Duncan), the postmodern City as these poets built it is a fluid metropolis, open to anyone who wanders in. It is, as Spicer writes, simply a "collection of humans." But this is not the kind of community Spicer practiced. In a commentary on Spicer's community, Ross Clarkson turns to Jean-Luc Nancy's *Inoperative Community* to describe the kind of modern cityscape that is "too numerous" to know itself and which in fact need not know itself in order to share a geosocial space ("Jack Spicer's Ghosts" 200). Clarkson argues that in the absence of traditional communities in the urban collection of humans, Spicer creates a "community of absence"; like other modern and postmodern writers, he creates his own tradition, which does not depend on geography or immediate historical circumstance (200). I think Clarkson is right on this point, and right that other projectivists do the same. Rather than a metropolis, Spicer's ghost town is more like the "imagined community" that Anne Dewey describes (*Beyond Maximus*)—a group held together by shared identifications, aims, or symbols (6). It includes the poet's immediate company as well as his or her self-constructed genealogy of writers living and dead.

The weight of evidence and critical opinion (Davidson, "City Redefined," 1989; Damon, *Dark End of the Street,* 1993; Vanderborg, *Paratextual Communities,* 2001) rests here; Spicer's City is a small band of the like-minded, a congregation in the wilderness, perhaps. "The city redefined becomes a church," Spicer writes, "a movement of poetry. Not merely a system of belief but their beliefs and their hearts living together" (*CB* 176; *MV* 306). Augustine distinguishes between the earthly city that belongs to all men and the heavenly one that consists of the company of Christian believers (116). This second city—and the Puritan[19] effort after a Christian polis is the American example of it—consists of those who put their "beliefs and their hearts" together, as Spicer says. In the next lines of poem 15 in "Textbook," he writes: "They are angry at their differences—the dead and the living, the ghosts and the angels, the green parrot and the dog I have just invented. All things that use separate words. They want to inhabit the city" (*CB* 176; *MV* 306). Dogs, parrots, and angels reach for intimacy across their differences. The City of God, if such it be, suggests the overcoming of difference rather than a way to live with it. Vanderborg notices that while Olson envisioned a flexible public space inclusive of "multiple textual formulations of citizenship," Spicer militarizes his enclave (*Paratextual Communities* 56). So in *Heads of the Town,* Emerson's "Concord Hymn," becomes "Conquered Him" (*CB* 120; *MV* 252); the "goop is an international criminal organization / that talks to each other"

(*CB* 123; *MV* 255); and "Fort Wayne stands on the American fortress between California and reality" (*CB* 140; *MV* 272). These few examples could be multiplied from the poetry, the letters, and many stories in the Killian-Ellingham biography. At the end of poem 15, Spicer settles for "the city we create in our bartalk" as a "mixed and mirrored" image of the City and a "return from exile" (*CB* 176; *MV* 306). It is hardly an assemblage of "those who have nothing in common."[20] The bar may be a public house, but who gets to sit around the poet's table is a private matter.[21]

I read Spicer's apparent rejection of the human universe for coterie as a serious qualification of the Olson-Duncan project of a public poetry. Like these latter, Spicer recognizes the processive nature of the cannibal cosmos—the becoming of things, the mutual feeding of things on other things, the *derivation* of everything from something else, the network of interdependencies—although his is a linguist's version. But unlike his fellow poets, he does not suffer process gladly. Cosmicity, from Spicer's perspective, is a raw deal. In this, Spicer sets himself in symmetrical opposition to the whole Emersonian line of American poetry, including its postwar manifestations. I have stressed that composition by field and the process poetics it initiated allows the "I" projective size insofar as its acts make visible the larger ground of its being; the figure-on-a-ground is a consistent trope in the work of Olson and Creeley, and Duncan, too, when the latter is not too deeply inside an impersonation. Spicer takes up the obvious omission—the blind spot—in this poetics. Certainly he separates figure and ground, radically so; the whole point of performing the duel is to dramatize the difference. But Spicer's interest and attention rests entirely on the individual who must undergo his or her life in the singular and *not* as planetary becoming or linguistic indeterminacy or public persona. Pain, love, death, even the bodily odor of snark hunters—the "eaxtra slyllables"—can be pointed to as evidences of what has to be lived alone. "We are all alone," Spicer says, "and we do not need poetry to tell us how alone we are" (*CB* 181; *MV* 311). At the cosmic level, these affective elements of personhood simply disappear into the general becoming of the planetary Whole. Death does not exist at the level of the atom or of the phoneme or of the stars, however we may anthropomorphize. It only emerges as a corollary of perception—a perceived Other—through the human process of individuation. Death is an effect of individuation.

In a poem that plays on the difference between Eros and *caritas*, love as erotic pang and love as the pursuit of an impersonal good, Spicer writes: " 'If I speak in the tongue of men and angels . . .' / The sounding brass of my heart says / 'Love' " (*CB* 224; *MV* 381). This is a sly reversal of St. Paul's sermon on *caritas*. Clearly the poem favors the "sounding brass" of erotic love over the sacrificial *caritas* that Paul demands of Christians. Paul asks his interlocutors to make common cause with the largeness that sustains them: he calls it God; Spicer's peers call it cosmos. Yet the poet's heart says "love," even though its "metallurgical analysis . . . shows an alarming percentage of silicon" (*CB* 224; *MV* 381)—even though Eros is sure to end at the glue factory as this poem has it, old and worn out like a horse that has been used and abused. Love does not redeem the lover or rescue the beloved, however agile a duelist the poet may be. And this, from Spicer's perspective, is not fair: "No love deserves the death it has," he says in *Language* (*CB* 236; *MV* 393). Individuation places people in an untenable position, torn between the contrary desires for expression and a return to sustaining intimacy. At one extreme, Eros becomes Thanatos as desire for love twists into the desire to merge with the Other and lose individuality (things "are angry at their differences"); at the other, it seeks to absorb the world (the Ahab complex). There is "the death-plant in the skull," Spicer writes in *Language*—"Grows wings and grows enormous. / The herb of the whole system" (*CB* 222; *MV* 378). Neither option is a happy one from the perspective of the individual who has to suffer through love's inability to rescue beauty from distance and old age and death. The distinctiveness of Spicer's response to this sorry state of affairs is in his refusal of cosmicity as a way out. The clanging brass of the heart says that the sacrifice of personhood to the "triumph of life" or the loss of personal dignity to identities as interchangeable and common as bathroom graffiti, is simply sacrifice and without consolation or remedy.

Spicer's *devotion* (I return to that word) to the particular, the temporary, and the felt also means a different stance on creativity than that of Olson, Creeley, or Duncan. These latter look to formal innovation as expressive of the becoming of the chaosmos and the human potential to renew itself as a species. Complexity of form, as it emerges through the interaction of figure and ground, is a key value in their poetics because it maximizes the potential for new relations and hence for creative agency. This is the advance of the world as Whitehead expressed it. Where Olson and Creeley engage history polemically in order to insist on the new, Duncan embraces a tradition that is constantly under construction. His faith in the efficacy of language to hold and express the essence of human life, and his reliance on derivation for uniqueness of expression means that once a voice gets into the cultural archive it cannot die. Each time the voice is reanimated by readers or, say, derivative poets, it lives again. But as *After Lorca* says so plainly, Spicer does not construct tradition as a cultural archive of genres or rhetorical modes, nor does he find satisfaction in cosmic becoming. If tradition "means generations of different poets in different countries patiently telling the same story" (*CB* 15; *MV* 111), then nothing is ever really new.

Is it not right here, though, that Spicer's private face reverses into a public one? Emotions like love or sensations like pain[22] are as close to being universal and transhistorical as anything human can be, even though they have to be lived through uniquely. While the expression changes constantly, it is not the expression that matters to Spicer. To take the medium for the message is a misrecognition of the sous-real that the medium should point to, and *that* is where we connect through correspondence. Does this mean that Spicer refuses to make it new? refuses creative agency? Peter Gizzi writes that Spicer's California of 1965 "already showed signs of an American empire in decline—an empire that can be understood as 'ruins,' a beautiful failure that ghosts inhabit" (in *House* 201). He adds that "part of Spicer's commitment to the California scene and California landscape is possibly its status as a failure, a de-promised land, like a run-down farm out of which rise Oz-like imaginary communities" (in *House* 201–2). Certainly given the decline in America's superpower status and the incredibility of the myth of the promised land, Spicer seems prescient, but I think the point can be taken beyond social or political clairvoyance. Gizzi writes that "Spicer foresaw that 'futurity' is by nature degraded—what he called 'slums' " (in *House* 183), and I take it that the slum is built into Spicer's view of language as a kind of ghost town. (Cocteau's shabby underworld with its Kafkaesque interiors and bleak landscapes is particularly resonant.) Because Spicer dis-identifies with process both in language and in nature, the future does promise a place filled with the debris of past lives and a haunted language. But to read the future this way is to tie creative energy too tightly to form—to the already said—whereas the *life* of the future is latent in the sous-real where all is alive and kicking. That life will always require a fresh finger pointing.

Spicer's poetry is the strongest protest I know against the pain and paradox of being human. The gift of it is honesty, as immaculate as it is narrow ("Honesty has had your heart for supper" [*CB* 132; *MV* 264]). If the postwar project was to rebuild the City on a Hill, Spicer would show that the lyric poet better belongs outside the city walls, just where Plato left him. To Ginsberg, he writes: "At least we both know how shitty the world is. You wearing a beard as a mask to disguise it. I wearing my tired smile. I don't see how you do it. One hundred thousand university students marching with you. Toward / A necessity which is not love but is a name" (*CB* 267; *MV* 426). Robin Blaser's account of Spicer's last words add a final gesture to the oeuvre of a poet who wanted to get the real into his poems at all costs. This is the gesture that only someone else can recount because in it the poet dies. "My vocabulary did this to me," Blaser reports Spicer as saying. No poem could have made Spicer's point better. When the body dies, its words remain. That is a distinction Spicer had performed all his writing life. Temporal presence *is* the Holy Grail and as in Galahad's book (*The Holy Grail*), it is "as common as rats or seaweed" (*CB* 209; *MV* 354). What is most singular and most elusive is most common. That is what Spicer's poetry teaches, and death too.

6

Robin Blaser

The Practice of Outside

Robin Blaser's position in the Black Mountain–San Francisco constellation of poets is distinctive. In relation to Duncan, Spicer, and Olson, his closest kin in poetics, he is belated. *The Boston Poems,* a chapbook written between 1956 and 1959, is the earliest series he preserves,[1] and by the mid-1950s the other three had already produced substantial collections. In "The Fire," a first statement of poetics published in 1966, Blaser writes: "I come to poetry with a definite sense of foreignness. Spicer once said that I was the only person he had ever met who could speak quotation marks and these always appeared around the slang words I used" (*Fire* 7). And in the same essay: "I am thirty years old before I begin even tentatively to accept the title of poet. In San Francisco, I was tied to two other poets, Jack Spicer and Robert Duncan, who, it was my superstition, wrote my poems for me. When that notion became sentimental, I dropped it and became another poet" (*Fire* 9). In the process of becoming his own poet, however, Blaser paid careful attention to his two companions. He attended classes with them at Berkeley, notably Ernst Kantorowicz's lectures on Dante and medieval political philosophy. He went to Duncan's soirées on the moderns, reading Pound, Joyce, Lorca, and Mallarmé. He listened to poems read in kitchens before they were published, acted in Duncan's masques, and attended Spicer's circle on dictation.[2] Olson would become a correspondent during the Boston years (1956–58) and Creeley an admired companion in poetry. Yet while Blaser participated in the making of the New American poetry, he also produced some of his most important work during the decades that followed. The 1970s and '80s were the theoretical decades when the "isms" of philosophy-based literary criticism dominated discussions of literature, and poets like Olson fell out of favor. During these years, Blaser was reading Maurice Merleau-Ponty, Jacques Lacan, Michel Foucault, and Jacques Derrida among many others, and he has retained this interest in philosophy throughout his writing life, albeit from a poet's distance. His poetics essays are thus more attuned to the theoretical vocabularies of the times than those of the others. Blaser writes in "The Fire" that Spicer introduced him to Leibniz and Spinoza in 1945 but then "turned violently against [philosophy]" (*Fire* 9). Duncan wandered through Whitehead, as his Whitman essay shows, but he was more interested in theosophy and lore than in theoretical language. Creeley, as philosophically sophisticated as he was, did not engage the theoretical languages of the times as directly as does Blaser. Olson was deeply read in Whitehead, but his death in 1970 predates the turn to language in literary-philosophical discourses and the subsequent critique of speculative philosophies in the poststructuralist decades. And then Spicer died in 1965, Duncan in 1988. In contrast, Blaser's writing life spans multiple generations of writers and distinctive shifts of interest in poetry and poetics. He thus has a vantage point that allows him broad reflection on the directions poetry has taken from the early postmodern to the millennium.

Another biographical turn that distinguishes Blaser's position is his immigration to Canada in 1967. Blaser left Berkeley with an MA and MLS in 1955, worked at the Widener Library at Harvard, and then returned to San Francisco and a job in acquisitions at San Francisco State College (1962–65).[3] In 1967 he had a few chapbooks published, he was working on "The Fire" (*Fire* 3), and he had a new professorial position at Simon Fraser University in British Columbia to attend to. Although his work had been included in Donald Allen's *The New American Poetry* (1960), his exit from the United States at the inception of his career was tantamount to disappearance from the scene. In Canada, Blaser's arrival was poorly timed, despite the welcoming enthusiasm of young Vancouver writers interested in the new postmodern poetics that seemed to be traveling north from the States.[4] Elsewhere, however, the Canadian literary world was in the process of establishing itself in English departments with all the polemical energy of the hitherto repressed. The effect of these historical coincidences was to exclude Blaser from academic attention for decades, until the publication of the collected serial books, *The Holy Forest,* by Toronto's Coach House Press in 1993.[5] To Americans, he had become a Canadian; to Canadians, he was an American. Yet academic attitudes notwithstanding, Blaser formed a number of friendships with Canadian writers and poets. Louis Dudek, Nicole Brossard, George Bowering, bpNichol, Steve McCaffery, Michael Ondaatje, Sharon Thesen, Daphne Marlatt, Peter and Meredith Quartermain, and Erin Mouré, among others, became friends or literary companions or both. These various coincidences, influences, and relationships have placed Blaser in the position of being at once intimate with and outside of the major movements in Anglo-American and Canadian poetics and theory for the last fifty years. The poetic he has developed incorporates significant elements of Olson's, Spicer's, and Duncan's work, but finally, it is his own and it speaks eloquently to the contemporary possibilities of the New American line.

Two characteristics in particular distinguish Blaser's project: the historicization of the lyric and what Blaser calls his "companionablity." The particular kind of lyric voice Blaser claims for the poet is a carefully poised alternative to that of Olson (epic), Spicer and Creeley (lyric), and Duncan (drama). In "The Fire," he describes his version and Spicer's of the serial poem as a "story of persons, events, activities, images, which tell the tale of the spirit" (*Fire* 5), a "carmen perpetuum, a continuous *song* in which the fragmented subject matter is only apparently disconnected" (5, my emphasis). This comment has turned out to be a prescient and precise description of the structure of *The Holy Forest,* Blaser's lifelong serial poem. The *Forest* unfolds from one book to the next like a fugue; a theme announced in one poem or one series will return for elaboration in another, often in a different "key" or set of images. As the reference to song suggests, Blaser never abandons the lyric; rather, he modifies it to let in a wide range of historical and cultural content that is not traditional to the genre.

In *The Fire,* Blaser cites anthropologist Edith Cobb's comment that a child wants most of all "to make a world in which to find a place to discover a self" (*Fire* 6). "This ordering," Cobb says, "reverses the general position that self-exploration produces a knowledge of the world" (17–18). Blaser elaborates: "Edith Cobb in her interest in biological psychology moves to describe what she names a 'cosmic sense,' which in a separate essay, Margaret Mead describes as 'a human instinctual need for a perceptual relation to the universe.' This is the scientific basis for the proprioceptive process which Charles Olson speaks of. In this context, I am arguing not for my pretensions as a poet, but for what the poetry reflects, if it is entered. That the poet does the job of entering this world and continues through his life to record that entrance is a fact, not pretence—that it is personal, original, and singular is also fact" (*Fire* 6). A "personal, original, and singular" view of the wide world—that is lyric historicized. Consider the difference between Blaser's stance and that of Olson. Don Byrd has suggested that Olson's *Maximus Poems* unfold like a Whiteheadian actual entity.[6] To recall the three stages of the process, the entity first prehends its environs; it then synthesizes its prehensions, achieving "satisfaction" when it has maximized its potential. In the third stage, the organism passes on, although it may persist in one or more of its dimensions as a datum for other actual entities in the process of becoming. Translated into poetic method, this account of the creative advance means that the poet takes in and synthesizes his material, and then leaves the new *combinatoire* in the language where it becomes available cultural data for other syntheses. The method suggests two complementary perspectives: the multiplicity prehended by the poet is reduced to unity in the work, but the work, once completed, becomes only one of a multiplicity. The same can be said for Olson's voice as he shapes it through Maximus. Maximus contains the variousness of the world, and in this sense the voice is heroic, public, and allegorical—epic, in fact. But situated as a figure on a ground, Maximus is Minimus, just one voice among others. It is the *reader*, however, who has to extrapolate this reduction from Olson's poetics. In contrast, Blaser performs the reduction of the voice himself. Maximus often *seems* to be a lord of creation "astride the Cabot fault," although from time to time we can see him shrinking to the size of a violet.[7] Like Maximus, Blaser's "I" takes the world for a stage: in "Image-Nation 5," Blaser writes of "small poems read from / vast stages" (*HF* 150). Yet, however grand the vista or complex the subject matter, the voice that gathers and comments on the material is, as Blaser says above, always "personal, original, and singular." In *Pell Mell*, one of his finest serials, Blaser writes of "a large crowded reception in a private house" ("à cet ultime . . . ," *HF* 264); it is an apt description of *The Holy Forest.*

In "Particles," a piece first published in his own *Pacific Nation* journal in 1969, Blaser explicates his position on the personal and singular in the context of a discussion on poetry and politics. Unlike most writers who reach for a public poetry, Blaser suggests that what can be shared is particularity, not principles or "isms."

> Now, it is objected that the particularity of modern poetry, its concern with deeds, thoughts, place, make it private and irrelevant. This is not so much ignorance as it is disrespect for particularity. Which is to say that men share not their place, their time, and those invisible activities called emotions,—to which poets give permanence—, but only generality. That poem is about love, the man says. And it is forgotten that love does not exist, even in thought, without its particularity. I love one, and with the peculiar virtue words have of attaching sound to the name I give away, each man can grasp that love. Even if we are drawn into the love of god. Words are instruments. The sounds are so important; it is as if something outside oneself called. We loan our clothes to the World. We have clothed the world and god in our clothes. How particular the image is. This too is part of the activity of discourse. It is simply not true that we share only our generalities. (*Fire* 22)

This attachment to the particular (compare Spicer's "devotion to the real" *beneath* particular words) plays out in Blaser's poems as "companionability." The single voice cannot articulate itself alone. This recognition is left implicit in the work of Olson, Spicer, and Duncan; again, Blaser *performs* it. In "The Fire," he writes: "Because the personal stake in companionship becomes so great in the way I live, I am sometimes lost when a reader finds me uninteresting or too obscure, his interest too soon exhausted to come to any meeting" (*Fire* 3). "*Meeting*" then becomes method, enacted in the poems and essays through copious quotation. Sometimes citing from memory, sometimes more deliberately from texts, Blaser peoples his serials with other voices, often announcing them typographically with italics. The effect of this practice is to situate the poet's own "I" as one of a chorus, and this reduces the scale of the voice.

If we compare these two important qualities of Blaser's poetic voice (singularity and companionability) with Spicer's practice, more differences begin to appear. I have argued that Spicer's turn toward the singular and temporary actually indexes a common emotional space that others may recognize and experience in their own way. But Spicer had a more profound distrust of words than does Blaser, and his insistence on emotional authenticity, on the one hand, demands an intense level of participation from his readers. The poet builds a mystic house of poetry to trap the "absolutely temporary," but the reader then must enter that house and open him or herself to experiences parallel to those of the poet. The reader has to get "involved" in the lives of Arthur Rimbaud if he or she is to share in that life. The "city" created in "fuss and fury" and "bartalk" is thus necessarily small, personal, and intense—a few knights of the bartable willing to spend the night with the poet in the castle perilous of the poem. Blaser, on the other hand, is more the urbane host of the "crowded reception in a private house." The difference is partly temperamental, but it also comes from diverging conceptions of language.

In "The Fire," Blaser writes that "language is given to us and in the most insidious way it controls sight, sound and intellect, but it is also a medium which can be shaped" (*Fire* 16). Later, in response to the epistemological skepticism of the language-based philosophies, Blaser would argue a distinction between discourse, on one hand, and language as the "object of philosophers and linguists" on the other. Wlad Godzich is his ally here, in Godzich's foreword to Michel de Certeau's *Heterologies* ("Poetry and Positivisms," *Fire* 40). Considered as a linguistic object, and in the context of a demand for certainty or clarity or presence—those Enlightenment longings that inform Spicer's poetry—language seems to withhold the suchness of things through its indeterminacy and iterability. Understood as discourse, however, it offers a "record of the meeting" between self and world that holds the relational nature of experience ("Fire," *Fire* 4).[8] In "The Stadium of the Mirror," Blaser argues that "all experience is interiorized language" (*Fire* 31). It is possible, certainly, to deconstruct experience into its linguistic minims and grammatical elements, but in Blaser's view, this is a covert form of positivism when it is used to dismiss perceptual experience or reach for more truth, more certitude, or more authenticity than consciousness can manage. In the essays of the 1980s and '90s, "Poetry and Positivisms" (1989) and "The Recovery of the Public World" (1993), Blaser would direct a good measure of polemical energy against what he hears as a new form of positivism in language-based philosophies. But in "Stadium," he simply writes that "the Sublime, the Beautiful, the Terror are not exactly human (Arendt), and that is the reason the *Image-Nations* are not devoted to my *logic of desire*" (*Fire* 30, my emphasis). Spicer's "logic of desire" requires an impossible singularity: Blaser, like Creeley, accepts a mediated, context-dependent singularity. This means companionability.

Companionability might seem to throw Blaser into the Duncan camp, since it is Duncan who cultivated multiple personae and populated his poems from an enormous archive. But Blaser and Duncan differ in at least two important ways. First, Blaser quotes; Duncan impersonates. Quotation has the effect of drawing in heterogeneous voices, thus making the poem dialogic. In Duncan's performances, in contrast, the dominant voice is Duncan's, usually because the poet speaks in the place of the persons of the poem. Second, derivation implies a continuity between the source and the translation or performance or impersonation. This continuity, I have argued, is a point of contention in the quarrel with Blaser over the translation of Nerval's *Les chimères*. Where Duncan accuses Blaser of idiosyncrasy ("aim[ing] at signature or style" [*Audit/Poetry* 49]) instead of entering into the common ground of Poetry, Blaser's quotations suggest a Benjaminian relationship to the cultural archive. As Hannah Arendt writes in her "Introduction" to *Illuminations*, Walter Benjamin was a pearl diver of history, dredging up wonders from a past that had lost its authority to determine the present. For Duncan, the authority of tradition can be passed on through successive, heretical incarnations. When he speaks in the voice of Nerval or Southey or Donne, he speaks as keeper of the archive. He is its servant and master and can claim the weight of it. Blaser's voice, more like that of Creeley and Spicer in this regard, is resolutely singular.

Is there something Canadian about Blaser's difference? Certainly there are traditions that Canadians call Canadian. But to try to name them is to fall into a morass of conflicting perspectives that undo definitions as quickly as they can be made. The Canadian literary canon, like that of any other country, is constantly under revision. Once limited to collections of Anglophone or Francophone settler literature with British and French lineages, academic anthologies now include writings coming out of hitherto excluded communities (First Nations, African, Indian, Japanese, Chinese). If I turn to social instead of cultural definitions, again there is a slipperiness, such as that in seemingly perennial debates about the efficacy of multicultural policies, the future of federalism, or the relationship between Quebec and the rest of Canada. While it is possible to point to traditions that have been used to define Canadians against Americans (the parliamentary system, the social programs that are more "caring" than those of the States, the peace-keeping role of Canada internationally), these national myths are under review, as is the cliché of the polite, self-effacing Canadian. And as soon as we move from cliché to a more verifiable account of national difference, boundary making becomes very fraught. Blaser himself has resisted nationalist definitions of his work, explicitly so in the little essay titled "out of the velvet—the denim—the straw of my mind," published in 1999 in a special issue of *boundary 2*, where he denounces nationalism along with all the "isms" for reasons he had argued years earlier in "Particles": "isms" imply the repressiveness of *compulsory* like-mindedness. Yet perhaps it is safe to say at least that Blaser's immigration has given him not only a certain distance from the American poetry scene but also early access to such works as bpNichol's *Martyrology*, a long serial poem in which a small, lower-case "i" traverses a vast country from east to west, or to George Bowering's "just plain George" lyrics that Blaser recognizes in the title of his introductory essay to Bowering's *Particular Accidents: Selected Poems* (1980), "George Bowering's Plain Song." It is safe to say, too, that Blaser's historicized lyric and companionable practice have produced a poetic persona that is perhaps less insistent on itself than that of Blaser's closest American companions.

Broken Mirrors: The Early Serials

Blaser's early chapbook serials, *The Boston Poems, Cups, The Park, The Faerie Queene,* and *The Moth Poem,* along with "The Fire" essay, all written in the early to mid-1960s except for *The Boston Poems,* announce a cultural condition Blaser describes in "The Fire" through the myth of Orpheus: "One part of his story has to do with the power of death over love and the power of death over the dead," he says, but "the other part has to do with his death at the hands of the Bacchantes, when he is torn to pieces. . . . It is precisely in the image of the scattered body and mind of Orpheus that I place whatever I know about the poetic process—that scattering is a living reflection of the world" ("Fire," *Fire* 20). The self decentered, the world image shattered—this is a starting point for a poet ambitious enough to want to do for his times what Dante did for his.

"The Hunger of Sound" is an important early poem for Blaser because it establishes a view of language and poetic form that is foundational to the serial poems that follow. In the acquisition of language is a first deracination of the creature from nature's continuum, a first becoming-human.

The child says, "Draw me,"
and my hand trembles like a tree
first planted in chaos.
Hear the words sound a child's joy.
  What is uprooted.
Hear the wind howl at a world of exact proportions.
  A shape that was like him.
Hear the sound inhabit the mind,
bells in an orchard.
The words knock against chaos.

How measured a time that childhood,
joy and terror counted like marbles.
Beyond endurance, 10 fingers.
How measured the growth of the limbs upward.
Each word counted. The returning birds
or the new leaves counted. (*HF* 19)

Drawn into language from the primary sensorium, the child enters "a world of exact proportions" like a tree emerging from chaos. (Compare Olson's "The Ring of" where Venus rises out of the sea.) Physicality is logically prior to language, but language brings into focus a world of distinct things and thoughts where before there was a flow of sense experience. The wind does not *howl* around a shapely world nor the words *knock against chaos* until the child has been "drawn." The line, "A shape that was like him" holds the doubly implicated nature of humanity as a languaged animal: before language, there is the indefinite flow of life; after language there is form as opposed to what the languaged consciousness learns to call "chaos." "The Hunger of Sound" precedes Blaser's interest in Merleau-Ponty's phenomenology, but *The Primacy of Perception* (1964), *Signs* (1964), and *The Visible and the In-*

visible (1968) would become important sources for Blaser in the 1970s, especially when he was writing the first twelve *Image-Nations* and "The Stadium of the Mirror." What is of particular significance in Merleau-Ponty is the argument that human perception is chiasmatically entangled with nonhuman nature.[9] The relationship between words and chaos, self and world, visible and invisible, or inside and outside is that of complicated nonequivalence; the polarities are not ontologically distinct but neither do they collapse into each other. Neither strictly empirical nor strictly linguistic, they are transcendentally empirical. For Blaser, it would not be a large step from Merleau-Ponty's polarities to Deleuze's folds in the later serials.[10]

The second stanza of "Hunger" moves on to measure and emotion. Joy and terror, however invisible and uncountable, achieve duration and memorability in language. Like the child and the orchard, emotions are both linguistic and nonlinguistic phenomena; they are seated somewhere in the organism but they blossom in words. "Hunger of Sound" imagines a first meeting with the world in which the world and the child come into ever-sharper focus as they rise into worded, numerate consciousness: "each blossom counted and named." In this event, the body, the emotions, and the imagination take shape along with intellect. And the child's world, so freshly emergent, is paradigmatic of the poetic process, a play of "*sight, sound,* and *intellect*" (Louis Zukofsky's phrase, qtd in "Fire," *Fire* 3, original emphasis). As Blaser writes in "Stadium," "Form is alive, not a completion of the heart or of the mind" (*Fire* 27).

The serial poems of the 1960s extend the work Blaser began in Boston on the undoing of unreflective realism as well as the exploration of form as immanent to experience. In *Cups,* biographical elements from Berkeley and Blaser's childhood Idaho are juxtaposed with Dantean encounters with Amor, "offer[ing] with out-stretched hand / the heart to be devoured" (*HF* 33). Dante's rendezvous with Amor initiates the "vita nuova" that leads him to the wide world of *The Divine Comedy;* Blaser's meeting with Amor draws him into the service of a poetry devoted to love of the world. Love, I have suggested, is a mode of seeing the world in its "*beautifuls-uglies*" (*HF* 89, original emphasis). In committing to love, rather than Spicer's "logic of desire," Blaser *accepts* the aliveness and dynamism of form, which is also to say its transience. In his essay on Olson and Whitehead, he defines it as "a living sense of the relational" ("Violets," *Fire* 213). Love allows the other its being-thus, its withdrawal as an object of knowledge, and its death. This marks another difference from Spicer. In the late poems of *Language,* Spicer speaks of the "whorship of beauty"(*CB* 222; *MV* 378) because beauty always ultimately falls away to reveal the skull behind the face of the beloved.

Beauty is the shimmering, seductive surface of things (Nietzsche's beautiful illusion[11]) that leaves in its passing the ache of desire. From Spicer's perspective, the poet is condemned to desire; from Blaser's, the poet is committed to love. To love the world, however, is to open oneself to certain pain. "Cups 5" offers these lines:

The intensities
of these branches
of willow
open.

What is it
broke the skin?

How lovely
that jewel
of under the skin. (*HF* 35)

The image of the willow about to blossom suggests the immanence of form. But the "intensities" of the tree and the fact that the blossom must "break the skin" in order to manifest itself also suggest Orphic dismemberment. The poet has to let go his grasp on a world conceived as so many self-evident things arrayed in space and that letting go is painful because it means a decentering of the self and consequent loss of at-homeness. The willow blossom buds out of a branch, but it also seems to push up from the under the skin of the poet's hand. Amor, as he draws the poet toward the world, also betrays him (sends him to hell in Spicer's case) because the pursuit of the beautiful inevitably brings about a confrontation with mortality and loss. Blood on the hand ("The blood whose beauty crosses / the hand . . ." [*HF* 35]) recalls the stigmata of Christ, and like Christ, the poet gives himself up for love of the world, even though he knows that the world, in its finitude, will betray him.

Like *Cups, The Park* (1960) is full of small autobiographical vignettes taken from Idaho, and like *Cups,* the poems present a world order in ruins. This recognition is not simply a matter of discovering with Nietzsche that God is dead. Philosophical recognition of the "truth" about anthropomorphism does nothing to produce the kind of intimate perceptual relationship with the world that Blaser sees as a human need and (his) poetry's task. The aims of philosophy and poetry are thus to be distinguished. In this series, "True and false" are "two sparrows, / chittering" (*HF* 53). They "fall down the side of the building" and then, with "locked beaks," "fly up / in the nick of time" (*HF* 53). The image is comic, suggesting the aerial acrobatics of philosophies that always seem to save themselves somehow from the ending of philosophy they announce, but it also says that these poems cannot be read under the rubric of truth and falsehood. Like Olson, Creeley, and Spicer, Blaser focuses on undergoing the world rather than knowing it under whatever existing criteria count for knowledge. This is the same task Dante undertook when the pagan world order had collapsed—that of remaking a world image that could be intimately felt. The longing for worldliness comes through in this boyhood game Blaser records:

Bill took out the atlas and began to divide
the world between us General William Halley
England, the Americas, Russia he used his
own name, so I kept mine, but added Duc of
Orleans because I held France, China and Africa (*HF* 54)

As Blaser would write in "Particles," "We are after 'meaning and thing,' and the intensity of that activity is what is at stake" (*Fire* 24).

The search for "'meaning and thing'" with which Blaser begins in "Hunger of Sound," *Cups,* and *The Park* leads him repeatedly downward, as it did Spicer, to the experience of dismemberment, loss, and destabilization. In *The Faerie Queene* (1961), the poet imagines a sleeping Dionysus, lying against the cornerstone of a wall that "[breaks] into pieces of glass" (*HF* 61). In the next poem, the poet's mirror image "trembles / or floats as in water" and "The dismemberment happens / like rain against the sidewalk" (*HF* 62). Pieces of broken glass and broken mirror turn up again in "Charms" (1964–68), originally "The Holy Forest" section of *The Holy Forest.* In "Aphrodite of the Leaves" from this series,

in fragments
in some objects
the city is loved,
                    glass
cut into light (*HF* 125)

Again in "Bottom's Dream," from the same series, the poet finds

. . . the strewn pieces,
his pieces in the forest—there

recognized for what they are   glass
in this circumstance (*HF* 130)

And in "The Finder,"

I bend 'you' to my mouth
and suck 'your' breath away
only worlds caught

in the glinting lights of those
pieces of glass   found in the
forest   under a tree   crushed

and shining (*HF* 131–32)

This last example shows what happens to pronouns when "the world dies." The second person is in quotations because the poet does not know who "you" refers to. But if the loss of metaphysical certitude brings with it an instability of relations, including those between writer and reader, the fragments are full of wonder and beauty as well as loss. Later, in *Pell Mell* (1981–88), Blaser would remark dryly, "If there's one thing Harry learned / to love more than the sacred, it was / the sacred in ruins" (*HF* 295).

In addition to the broken mirrors and oddly complementary to them is the moth, another key image of the 1960s. *The Moth Poem* (1962–64) is an important serial in the establishing of Blaser's project, and in fact moths fly in and out of the poems as late as 2004.[12] Blaser's moth figures the questing mind and heart flying blind in the world. It is an image that responds to and gathers resonance in relation to Duncan's butterfly. *Roots and Branches* (1964) opens with Monarch butterflies arriving as "messengers of March," "tracing out of air unseen roots and branches of sense." The image is beautifully apt for Duncan's poetic practice since it catches in an image of one of the few migratory species of butterfly the poet's own wide-ranging flights among various "doctrines"—thus to restore the archive to living tradition as the butterfly "almost restore[s] / an imaginary tree of the living in all its doctrines / by fluttering about" (3). Of the same family as the diurnal butterfly, the moth is nonetheless a nocturnal insect, famously attracted to light, often to its own destruction. It is the blindness of moths that works as an element in Blaser's poetic practice: the idea is that the poet does not know where he is going, that he is attracted to light but without being able to name it in advance of the encounter. Two "Atlantis" poems of this series figure a lost world where "smokers // of poetry bathe among the ruins" (*HF* 77). Given, then, the ruin of the City, the poet, like the moth, must "[try] the way into corners" (*HF* 72). The unerring radar of the Monarch is a contrast to Blaser's preferred insect metaphor about giving up intellectual privilege in order to undergo a meeting with something other than the already thought.

Seeking nothing more than a homeplace, and attracted by warmth and light, Blaser's moth ends up in all manner of odd places—in pianos (*HF* 68), on mirrors (69), in electric blankets (74), flying toward floor lamps (76), or emerging, phoenixlike, from ashtrays (86). In a poem from 2003, written roughly forty years after *The Moth Poem,* Blaser says:

there's a way to walk blind
there's a way to talk blind
if you want to. (*HF* 492)

The Sacred Integrated: From *Les chimères* to *Image-Nations*

In retrospect, Blaser's affinity for Gérard de Nerval seems natural because both poets register metaphysical collapse as deprivation of worldliness rather than liberation. "El Desdichado"—"The Shadow" in Blaser's translation—begins like this:

I am the Darkness   the Widowed   the Unconsoled
the Prince of Aquitaine in his broken tower.
my only Star is dead   and my lustrous lute
carries a melancholy black sun (*HF* 97)

The poems go on to speak of the death of the gods—Greek, Egyptian, Christian—and the "cultural orphanhood"[13] that follows the collapse of each of those worlds. In "Christ among the Olives," Christ's vigil on the eve of the crucifixion is filled with visions of "dead worlds" (*HF* 105). Searching for "the eye of God," Christ finds the abyss—"a socket, / huge, black and bottomless" (*HF* 104). But *Chimères* does not rest on the death of God. In the succession of orders from pagan to Christian is the suggestion that the world image is renewable. The serial ends with the "Golden Poem," which begins the work of imagining the sacred again:

free of the dead,
what can be thought
seems to be yours in this world
where it *all coheres*

free to spend some powers,
but the universe is absent
from all your plans

take the ghost stirring
in an animal   each
flower, a piece of light
scattering love's mystery
asleep in metal   alive
the coherence takes power
over you
. . . .
often, a secret god exists
in the darkness
and like an eye born
with the lids closed,
a real ghost comes to be
under the surface of the stones (*HF* 108, original emphasis)

I draw attention to this poem because it is significant to Blaser's long meditation on the sacred, and it was also a particular point of contention in the quarrel between Blaser and Duncan over translation. I will recall Duncan's remarks first, ungenerous though they were, because they help to illuminate the importance of the poem to Blaser's oeuvre. In *Audit/Poetry,* where Duncan cites Nerval's original, Blaser's version, and his own translation, he reads this poem as referencing a "doctrine of neo-Pythagorean naturalism" (58) and takes particular exception to Blaser's translation of "âme" and "esprit" in Nerval's original as "ghost." The word "ghost," Duncan says, is etymologically tied to "ghastly" and "the kind of horror related to the sight of death of carnage" (59), and he adds: "In the world of Nerval's belief, the esoteric cult of the Kabbala, this effluvia of the decaying body, this corpse-gas, was particularly distinguished from the divine breath and the living spark" (59). In the same passage, Duncan notes that Blaser has taken the word "ghost" from Spicer and comments that "it is a serious criticism of Spicer's creation in poetry that he believed in ghosts and remained sceptic of and even antagonistic to life forces" (59). I have discussed some of the poetics behind the *Audit/Poetry* article in my study of Duncan, but the emphasis Duncan places on the "Golden Poem" sharpens the distinction between him and Blaser. Duncan understands tradition as a collectively created fiction and cultural archive of the orders of the imagination that may or may not bear on reality as it can be experienced. "Poetry" is a realm of permission where the imagination is to be given free play, and it is Duncan's care to preserve its orders—all of them—and especially the hermetic. Blaser, in contrast, is intent on the real—that which falls within the credible at a given historical moment. From his perspective, "ghost" is the better term because the supernaturalism that once animated the natural world has fallen out of belief and the gods have become ghosts of the culture. "Golden Poem" addresses a humanity that thinks itself "free of the dead" because it has cast off the supernaturalism of the old religions. But in Blaser's view, triumphant secularity is yet another anthropomorphism. Anthropomorphism does not end with religious projection (humanity projects itself as God); the positivist version of the universe as merely empirical is also anthropomorphic and equally a disguised reach for power (humanity projects itself as the only reality). This latter lays claim to the ownership of the real without due attention to the chiasmatic quality of perception that makes the real a process rather than a system and entangles human thought in a world that it does not fully possess. In both visions, the old and the new, "the universe is absent / from all your plans," Blaser writes (*HF* 108). Nerval and Duncan counter this vulgar secularity with pantheism, but for Blaser and Spicer, too, this is not a contemporary option. Nerval writes in his last stanza:

Souvent dans l'être obscure habite un Dieu caché,
Et, comme un oeil naissant couvert par ses paupières,
Un pur esprit s'accroît sous l'écorce des pierres. (*Oeuvres* 709)

Blaser translates "un pur esprit" as "a real ghost." "Pure spirit" would leave the pantheism of the poem intact as Duncan wanted to do, but Blaser's "ghost" suggests that secular humanity will be haunted by the gods it has thought to put aside, and the connotation is quite precisely that of the "ghastly." In a skeptical age, the affective content of perception may simply go underground, "sous l'écorce des pierres." Thus manhandled out of sight, the gods return in a maimed fashion; witness the current revival of politico-religious fundamentalisms on the global stage.

Les chimères brings forward the questions that drive Blaser's exploration of the sacred in the next serials. What happens to the affective content of religions when they fall out of belief? How might a poet account for the sacred without offending the intellect? The search for a generous reason that includes imagination is also the search for an image of the real, where "real" means the whole complex network of relationships between the human and nonhuman that make up what publicly counts for reality at a given historical moment. On *Astonishments,* a set of autobiographical audiocassettes that Blaser made in 1974, he describes the problem of the sacred this way:

> The word "soul" and the word "God," "ghost," a whole series of these, they're all broken words. They've fallen because they belong to a hierarchy of some kind, a world vision. The world vision fell, the words are still there and they float and haunt us, "ghost" in particular haunts us. [. . .] And one notices that the moment that the words dump out of their images, the hierarchy had the image of God as the old bearded daddy in the sky, a fully humanized figure, the soul with the very definite range of—well, there are even images attached to the nature of the soul. [. . .] As they fall down, the words all re-open and they re-open into their contents. One notices immediately that the moment that you know that the unknown is at the very edge of the known, and you can take the known to be you at whatever limit you're in at the moment—the unknown, that the moment you've hit that, you've also hit one of the contents that was inside the word "God." ("Excerpts" 294)

The *Image-Nation* poems, an ongoing series that traverses the other books, were begun at the same time as the Nerval translations (1963–64), and they pick up the task of tracking the scattered content of the sacred. In its deep structure, these poems suggest, the sacred is relational thought. As such, it is a function of consciousness, belonging neither to the empirical nor to the philosophical search for the really real. All religions establish a relationship with the nonhuman world, although most do it without awareness of their anthropomorphisms. In Blaser's view, this is the problem. In "The Stadium of the Mirror" he writes of "an anthropomorphism in tatters" (*Fire* 31). If we are not to absorb the world into the human image as "Golden Poem" implies (and like Olson's Ahab), then the universe must be at once distinguished from the human and related to it. The idea leads by a different route to Olson's distinction between figure and ground. Polarity is a first condition of the sacred secularized, and it is Blaser's way of restoring cosmicity to humanity. However, his particular contribution to what was really a generational task is not Olson's "familiar," Creeley's domestic, Duncan's archive, or Spicer's sous-real, but the direct attention he brings to the sacred.

"The Stadium of the Mirror," published with the first twelve *Image-Nations* in 1974, is an essay in which Blaser "read[s] the counsel of [his] own poems" retrospectively (*Fire* 26). Here he draws on Merleau-Ponty, Foucault, and Lacan, adapting them to his argument for a secularized sacred. Three tropes from these sources supplement one another and illuminate the first *Image-Nations:* the wild logos, the unthought, and the zero-phoneme. The wild logos comes from Merleau-Ponty's *The Visible and Invisible.* Merleau-Ponty had proposed a shift in the way that perception was to be conceptualized. Rather than suppose a perceiving subject and a perceived object and try to connect them epistemologically, he begins with the embeddedness of the human creature in the world and argues that the mind and the world fit because they were never separate. This means, however, that there is no stability of word or world because the perceived world cannot be grounded in either the subject (as psychology) or in the object (as science). If the chiasmus is primary there is neither transparency of representation (naive realism) nor disembodied textuality; there is only the Möbius twist of inner and outer. The wild logos is thus a logos that has lost its rootedness, and Blaser draws it into "Image-Nation 1" in the image of "white trees, rings around them, / [that] wander and roll . . ." (*HF* 89). The image recalls Orpheus's legendary ability to make trees and wild beasts follow him for his music, but it is also precise to Blaser's sense that word and world emerge coevally, as they do in "The Hunger of Sound," and are therefore essentially unstable; neither one can be used to ground the other in a permanence.

Blaser finds confirmation of this "polar logic" in Michel Foucault's discussion of the unthought in *The Order of Things.* Foucault winds up his study of epistemological history in this book with a penultimate chapter on the emergence of language as an object of knowledge and the effects of this reflexivity on consciousness. In this chapter (chapter 9, "Man and His Doubles"), which Blaser quotes in "Stadium" and later in "The Practice of Outside," Foucault says that reflexivity means a doubling of the thought with the unthought.[14] Thought loses its transparency and acquires a shadow as soon as it recognizes itself as situated; it becomes a figure on a ground. (The difference between this position and the deconstructive one that rivaled it is that Foucault describes the experience of experience while Derrida constructs scenes that show how experience is produced temporally, through differing and deferring.) In "Stadium," Blaser *chooses* to work with the experience of experience—"Poetry always has to do with consciousness" (*Fire* 29)—and this set him at odds with deconstructionists during the 1970s and '80s when many of the *Image-Nations* were written. This is not because Blaser's work directly challenges the deconstructive critique of "theologies of consciousness," but rather because it handles the "theologies" differently, not by deconstructing their truth claims but by exploring the deep perceptual ground of them. Blaser's alternative to irony, and it is one he shares with Olson, is to situate consciousness, rather than deconstruct its perceptual operations.

The third major theorist that Blaser references in "The Stadium of the Mirror" is Jacques Lacan. Anthony Wilden, Lacan's translator and commentator in *Speech and Language in Psychoanalysis,* was a colleague at Simon

Fraser University, and the citations in "Stadium" come from Wilden's volume. "The Stadium of the Mirror," Blaser says, is named after Lacan's "le stade de miroir," "translated for the metaphor" (*Fire* 32). Lacan argues that human subjectivity is formed through the acquisition of language and the subsequent foreclosure of unmediated, infantile sensation. What he calls the "mirror stage" is that moment in psychic development when the child recognizes itself in the mirror and erroneously identifies with its body image. In Lacan's view, this identification mistakes the unity of the body for psychic unity when in fact the psyche is structured like a language; it is not whole or self-present, but produced through substitutions and displacements that render the subject's *desire* for wholeness (possession of the [M]other) irreducible. Psychoanalysis devalues consciousness in a way parallel to that in which deconstruction devalues experience because it locates the real action in the unconscious, as deconstruction finds it in language. Blaser takes the same information and interprets it differently—not as a devaluation of consciousness but a positioning of it. The real, in Lacan's meaning of it, is lost to the psyche as soon as language enables an infant to distinguish between a me and not-me. For Blaser, this is another instance of the polarized relationship between consciousness and its Other, and he includes it in the poems as the zero-phoneme, or "Naught." As Anthony Wilden discusses this trope in his commentary on Lacan,[15] the zero is a mathematical concept that makes possible negative and imaginary numbers as well as the positive ones; it is the empty set that grounds all the others. A zero-phoneme performs a similar role for speech. It is the silence that is the unremarked ground of sound. In the Lacanian context, zero sits in the place of the real. Integrated into Blaser's poetics, it is a concept supplementing Foucault's unthought and a necessary marker of the finitude of the mind.

In "Image-Nation 2 (roaming," "Naught" is "the name of the bird who fell / from the hands of O-moon" (*HF* 90). Tumbled out of the sky, Naught suddenly appears as a traveling companion in the lines, "we, the apparatus, burned by a night / light, are traveling in company with the messenger" (90). "We," an "apparatus" through which the world achieves one form of visibility, are accompanied by a "messenger." At first, Blaser has "us" shadowed by "following angels" (90), but he lets the word fall out of the Christian world into the namelessness of "messenger," an etymological root of "angel." In "Stadium," he writes about Naught this way:

> In the poems I have asked you to read, Naught appears now and again in the sequence. He is the first drunkenness of the poems—always there at the point of the pencil. He is like a zero-phoneme—first in opposi-

> tion to all other phonemes—I can't hear—I can't see—then he is in opposition to the absence of phonemes (Jakobson via Wilden). In their original context, these poems are like squawking birds, events of the peril of the narration. Their devotion is to the unthought and the unknown as they are technical to my (our) experience. The method, which is the same thing as belief (Olson), composes a language before and at the end of our discourse, primary and penultimate. The ultimate language is absent,—that is to say, it is alive at the end of mine or yours. The ultimate of my languages or yours—or the culture's is missing. (*Fire* 35–36)

Hereafter, Naught becomes the "opposite and companion of any man's sudden form" (*Fire* 28), the irreducible Other that accompanies humanity when it begins to understand itself reflexively as a figure on a ground.

"Image-Nation 4 (old gold" offers another striking image of Naught, although Blaser does not use the word in this piece. The poem is set in Idaho in a cooled lava field called the Craters of the Moon. Now a state park, the field is composed of black volcanic rock solidified in waves that still look as if they were frozen in motion, and it includes an orchard, dead, but preserved upright in the lava. In the poem, a childhood game played with cinders spread to burn out references the volcanic energy of the craters:

a visit to the Longs
who run the pump house, stoke
its fires, spread the ashes

over a field to burn out
this is a surface of the moon
black and crusted   we ran

out on it, calling
"you're it," jumped, rang   with
laughter, the crust broke, his

bare feet slipped into the burning
coals beneath . . . (*HF* 92)

The image is of a crust that breaks into a bed of coals or volcanic fire, or later in the poem, "the / fire   of strawberries" (*HF* 92). What seems to be solid gives away to a heat and energy that makes strange the homeplace; suddenly there is fire, suddenly there is someone nameless, the "what's-his-name" who enters the poem in verse four. The poem then goes on to reach for a relationship with that strangeness through story. The crust must be Ella Cinders; agates are mud or pieces of frozen sunset; a moonstone is a piece of cheese. The poem calls up the childhood effort to accommodate strangeness; to recall Blaser's comments on Edith Cobb in "The Fire," the child wants to "make a world in which to find a place to discover a self" (*Fire* 6). Myth is a first response to Otherness.

So in the first run of the *Image-Nations, Image-Nations 1–12 & The Stadium of the Mirror* (1974), Blaser unravels the sacred back to raw experience. These are complex poems, and my commentary is only meant to sketch out Blaser's treatment of the sacred rather than the whole of what is there. I have selected "Image-Nations" 6, 7, 9, and 10 for brief remarks because in these pieces Blaser takes on some of the most traditional territories of the sacred, long considered untouchable by secular intellectuals: the sacraments, the question of a sacred language, the gods and their myths, and the soul. I call these revisionary meditations *de-constructions,* hyphenating to distinguish Blaser's orientation to perception from the textualist focus of post-structuralists.

"Image-Nation 6 (epithalamium" was a poem written for the wedding of friends, but the occasion quickly becomes an exploration of the deep ground of the sacraments:

in this abide   pulling the next branch
of the tree down to ring it   I have seen
that vision   over again   I had
married a tree   placing a ring on each
branch   to return again   another man
to pull down another branch   I would
have you see this tree   glistening
and her adornments

. . . .

I lean over the steering wheel to ask
this vision again   not to be mentally mine
but out there   to carry it
a gift to a wedding   for it came
15 years ago from reading a book
on the miracles of Mary in Egypt
  never found again   recurs daily
in marriage with the place

and hour   the two meet to see
from their stairways (*HF* 156)

Marriage with a tree, marriage "with the place / and hour"? Blaser moves back of church ceremony ("a gift to a wedding") to a wilder kind of sacrament. I find Derrida's essay "Faith and Knowledge" helpful in this context, although it comes well after the poem and there is no question of influence.[16] *Religio,* Derrida argues, holds the double sense of the "fiduciary" and the "unscathed." The former carries the sense of bond, promise, or testimonial, the "experience of *belief*"; the latter suggests the "experience of the unscathed, of *sacredness* or of *holiness*" ("Faith and Knowledge" 33, original emphasis). Etymologically, there is "*relegere,* what would seem to be the avowed formal and semantic filiation: bringing together in order to return and begin again; whence *religio,* scrupulous attention, respect, patience, even modesty, shame or piety—and, on the other hand . . . *religare,* [an] etymology 'invented by Christians' . . . and linking religion to the *link,* precisely to obligation, ligament, and hence to obligation, to debt" (36–37, original emphasis). In *religio* as *bond* is inherent a primordial sociality, a response-ability that initiates all human relations, including those of science and reason as well as religion. In *religio* as the *unscathed* is the duplicity of the sacrosanct and the sacrificed, or what Derrida goes on to thematize as autoimmunity. As a testimony or promise holds the possibility of deception, so the sacrosanct implies the possibility of violation. Autoimmunity is sacrifice to forestall sacrifice, or violence turned inward to protect whatever is held to be sacrosanct (place, identity, community). Blaser's "Image-Nation 6" presents the sacramental in its affective manifestations, as both celebration of the "*radiant world*" and mourning ("my sorrow") (*HF* 156, original emphasis). A conventional marriage ceremony says that two become one; primordially, however, "one"—really zero or nondifference—becomes two. With the emergence of difference, here suggested by the tree that comes and goes from visibility throughout the poem, "love's dream" becomes possible, but also death and mourning. *Religio* in its double potential is implicit in originary sociality. One is already two (to recall Wilden), and two demands response. And as Derrida's analysis suggests, the bond will be unstable, harboring both love and violence.

"Cups 9," preceding "Image-Nation 6" in presentation of this marriage to a tree, brings out this darker element of *religio.*

Upon that tree there was a ring.
HI   HO   HUM

The ring surrounded the darkest part.
HA HA HA
The ring imagined a marriage bout.
FIRE FIRE FIRE (*HF* 40)

This *Cups* version of the ceremony emphasizes the strangeness of the Other before it has been named and absorbed into the human universe. The "HI HO HUM" sounds like "FEE FI FO FUM," the words of the giant in the fairy tale, "Jack, the Giant Killer," and as everyone knows, fairy tales are always drenched in blood: human fear and cunning battle elemental forces and drives. The "FIRE" of the last line brings in the primal heat of the *holy* forest as the creative ground of such primordial encounters. In "Image-Nation 6," Blaser writes the dynamism of that ground in the daily repetition of the bond "with the place / and hour" (*HF* 156). Notice in this context the verb "abide" rather than the noun "abode." In organized religion or in everyday affairs, a bond is usually evoked to stabilize relationships and fend off the possibility of change or harm—to render safe and homely one's abode. "Image-Nation 6" leans toward this sense of the sacrament as a bond with the world that would hold it sacred and unscathed—"*a radiant world compelling / adoration*" (*HF* 156, original emphasis). But "Cups 9" hints at the sacrificial face of *religio*—sacrifice made in fear of sacrifice (compare Spicer's Promethean magic). I will return to the dark side in my discussion of Blaser's treatment of historical Christianity in *The Last Supper.*

"Image-Nation 7 (l'air" picks up the meditation on the sacred from a different angle, beginning with an inquiry into the nature of the abstract. Abstraction is a necessary if not sufficient condition for the instrumentalization of things. It is also contrarily tied to the human imagination of a sacred language through the Platonic-Judeo-Christian tradition that gives priority to the word over its material manifestation. Blaser searches out the abstract before it has settled into convention and institution:

Jeremy Prynne explaining
the abstract "it simply
means distance"
rain, rain dear Zeus
on their cornlands and
their pastures

the fearful noise and
the archaic smile

who is the physical
source of all things
gods and men included (*HF* 160, original emphasis)

These lines bring forward the fear of the Other that impels the human effort toward relationship through myth and magic.[17] What might once have begun as an effort to control large natural events through urgent solicitation of the gods turns to madness when it seeks to destroy whatever falls outside the human will: this is "a terror in the movement / of a man devouring / into his own shape" (*HF* 161). Humanity reshapes the world in its own image. Its most powerful tool is abstraction, realized largely through language and techno-science, whether the latter be a stick or a space shuttle. In this poem, Blaser moves backward again to imagine primordial encounters with the "fearful noise" and "archaic smile." This imaginative reach for the primordial, I think, is an effort to find astonishment and with it creative (sacred) ground. Abstraction may begin as distance—in fact the Freudian account of the origins of subjectivity in the Fort-Da game complements such a view—but it ends in anthropomorphisms that obscure the otherness of the Other. Blaser's repolarizing of self and world keeps the distance active and thus the possibility of relationship alive. The poem ends this way:

            the first
outward   is always
a distance

so   we hold it
in the middle
                        voice of
the companion   in the

air. (*HF* 163, original emphasis)

I think these lines imply a de-constructive view of what might constitute a sacred language. Traditionally such a language, whether it be Plato's forms or the letters of the Hebraic alphabet in the *Zohar* (Duncan again), is taken to hold the essence of things. It is a secret language of archetypes thought to hold creative power—even literal power in folk traditions such as that of the Jewish Golem. Blaser's "first / outward," however, is nothing other than the ordinary language we use everyday. What is sacred about it is just that which is intrinsic to every natural language—the power to create "betweens," like the invisible air between living things. The middle voice Blaser references in the above lines is a construct of Latin and Greek grammar between the active and passive voices, metaphorically significant to Blaser, as it was to Olson, because it suggests the coeval emergence of subject and object. In these lines, the middle voice hangs in the air as "distance" or "betweenness" as such. Language separates but it also provides the means to relate.[18] This is how the world comes to breathe, how it rises up into distinct form, parsed out, with space between things. There is nothing occult about language so conceived (Blaser's resistance to Duncan's love of the occult is palpable here); it is simply a human *techne* rooted in the primacy of the social. The etymology of "companionable" holds onto the only way that Blaser allows language to be considered "sacred": *com* means "with," and *pan* is related to "pain," "bread." To be born into the human world means to take things with bread—to take sociality as primary.

As "Image-Nation 7" de-constructs a sacred language, "Image-Nation 9 (half and half" explores the deep ground of myth through a parallel deconstruction of the gods.

there are shining masters
when I tell you what they
look like   some of it is
nearly false   their blue hair

but they are not ourselves   they
are the equivalents   of action   they
compose forms,   which we hear (*HF* 167)

No gods are named here because they have fallen out of their names, as it were. "They / compose forms," Blaser says, suggesting that the gods arise as the after-images of certain seminal events. And when the event has passed, what is left are the traces:

. . . a bone, a ball, a top
an apple, a mirror, a skein of wool (*HF* 168, original emphasis)

These toys closely match those that Hera used to lure the infant Dionysus to his death. In his *Orpheus and Greek Religion* (1935), W. K. C. Guthrie retells the story of her treachery. Jealous of Dionysus because he is the son of Zeus and Semele, Hera waits until Zeus is away and then entices the infant god out of safety with "a knuckle-bone, a ball, tops, apples, a mirror, a lump of wool" (121).[19] In Blaser's poem, these toys are left strewn as if the divine Child had just toddled off, and I take it that is the point. The sacred does not inhere in a particular form or object, but in the creative energy that brought the object forth.[20] Blaser's approach to myth—a radicalization of Olson's—is to de-construct and re-present it as some formative *meeting* prior to the settled narration of the gods and their deeds. Organized religions fetishize form rather than form-making power, but it is the latter that is the real site of the sacred. Dionysus's dismemberment, foreshadowed in the abandoned toys of the god, parallels the shattered mirrors of the early serials. This shattering of form, however disruptive of human identities, allows the world to emerge as creative process rather than ego-centered projection. The dismemberment of Dionysus is also the re-creation of the world. Here are the last lines of the poem:

rythmos (form's movement) to walk into "the
primordial always exists" face to face always outside
ourselves the astonishment is
that it is *kosmos*
playing out with one man entheos
they are
the *flowing boundary* taking birth *taking leave*
at the point of the heart a continual
division of halves. (*HF* 169, original emphasis)

In Heraclitus's cosmogony, the world comes about through the division of the four elements ("a continual / division of halves"). Fire is first and everlasting; it divides in half to make air; air then divides to make water; and water to make earth. Each element continues to divide into its contrary in such a way as to keep the balance between the four. Only the traces of this cosmogony remain in "Image-Nation 9," in the division of halves and the "*flowing boundary.*" What Blaser snatches from ancient cosmogony, however, is "form's movement," before it stiffens into a name, an image, a dogma, or a system. In "Stadium," Blaser situates his effort here with that of the moderns: "The movement back of the great poets is not to a tradition—a golden time or wisdom behind us that places thought in the past and kills it—but it is toward a reopening of words—toward the violence and dynamism of Language—the work of it is in Pound's return to Homer, Egypt, Na-Khi and in Olson's ultimate return to Pleistocene,—his curriculum. A beginning again with everything. This reopening of words lets us see their solidifications—the crystals FORMing in the work—(a crust, akin to *cruor*—blood, *Kyros*—icy-cold, a coagulation that is the 'external expression of a definite internal structure'" (*Fire* 31). Fire (creative energy) is the hidden trope in Blaser's *Holy Forest:* Heraclitean fire, volcanic fire, fire of the Holy Ghost, a forest fire—creative fires hot enough to melt the cold rock of reality.

Many years after "Image-Nation 9," in an essay first published in 1995 on Mary Butts's work, "Here Lies the Woodpecker Who Was Zeus," Blaser turns to Jane Harrison's *Themis* (1963) to discuss Butts's meditations on the archaic. Retrospectively, this essay speaks to the early *Image-Nations.* In Butts's book, *Armed with Madness* (1928), Zeus turns up in the form of a woodpecker, and Blaser tracks the image back to the wild *mana* of nature that Harrison finds at the origins of the god. *Mana* is a word for the potency of living things. Plants and animals have it, some more than others, and objects may have it too. *Mana* is the power to *be;* the more *mana,* the more vivid the creature or thing. *Mana* is to the sacred as the wild logos is to the Word. Both terms suggest a de-constructive release of the sacred from its iconic forms. If the sacred is taken away from the monopoly organized religions have held over it, then it is potentially always there in anyone's meetings with the world. One effort of Blaser's de-constructive work is to take the power of form making—the power to shape reality—away from established authorities. The wager of the *Image-Nations* is that the form the world will take is not entirely determined; it is open to chance and to the *mana* of the creatures that inhabit it. Hence Blaser's contention in the above lines that the "kosmos" plays out with one man.

In "Image-Nation 10 (marriage clothes" Blaser takes on another major topos of the sacred, this time the word *soul.* And "what a haughty standing along that is," he says (*HF* 170). The poem goes on to meditate on the history of the word, "trying to say what the soul is" (174).

they have said the word means breath   but that
is the meaning borrowed from *spiritus*   an
inhalation and exhalation of the world
          a steam   a vapour   or it means the
immortal part   given   it floats
in the language as the opposite   the *inseparable*
freedom   of a primal ambiguity (*HF* 170, original emphasis)

And a few pages later:

          . . . an Arapaho began
a list—the heart, the brain, the breath—

as well as a word meaning 'your body moulded
as a living man'

and Keokuk said there are fire shapes of the
'heart, flesh, life, names and family'
                                        and
the Navaho used a word which means
'that which stands within'   upright   a turquoise
image hidden in his breast
                                  the Snake people
say it looks like a hailstone (*HF* 174)

In Anglo-Saxon etymology, Blaser finds the word "*Saiwala,*"

            soul   blending with *awa,*
closely related to the word 'sea'
            the language, older and other
than I am
      prehistoric, sacred
geography   turns in the wind
uprooted
      the sea runs over the railbed (*HF* 175, original emphasis)

In these passages and many others, Blaser discovers "*the soul's profound duality*" (*HF* 170, original emphasis); it is something that wells up between the inside and outside of the human creature, a "primal ambiguity" that comes not only of being *in* the world but *of* it, chiasmatically. In the last passage I have quoted above, beginning with "*Saiwala,*" a prehistoric geography folds into the poet's own homeplace as in "Image-Nation 4." Uprooted from dogma, sacred places wander like the uprooted trees in "Image-Nation 1," sometimes right into the lives of the living.

The biography that comes into this passage from "Image-Nation 9" is buried in *Astonishments.* I will pause over the tapes for a moment because the relevant story shows how the personal and the cosmic fold together in Blaser's imagination, how the sacred wanders when it falls out of belief, and how the soul forms itself through "meetings." On the tapes, Blaser tells of a childhood in the Idaho desert, growing up alongside the railroad for which his grandmother, Sophia Nichols, worked as a telegrapher. Sophia's stories gave a young boy in a very austere environment his first imagination for a wider world—his first "outward." A late *Image-Nation* poem, "Image-Nation

25 (Oh pshaw," retells the story, and I cite from that source because the tapes are as yet unpublished:

> once the rains were so heavy the water rose up the opposite embankment, nearly reaching the railbed, and stayed for days—'a sea,' Sophia Nichols said, never having seen one, and it was wide and stretched along the tracks as far as I could see—we needed supplies from the commissary across there—Carnation condensed milk, I remember—and we plotted a way to cross that sea—the tin tub and a shingle, just the right size boat and paddle for me, we thought—round and round it went, being round, and drifted from shore meandering—she tossed me a broom, which luckily floated near enough to reach it—"see if you can touch bottom," she said—I could—"so push," she said—and I made it there circuitously, pulled my tub up on the beach, got the supplies, and returned—"circuitously Odyssean," she said, having spent hours those rainy days telling me stories of Odysseus, which were, she said, homeward journeys of the soul . . . (*HF* 383)

This story recalls "The Hunger of Sound" (the world emerging in childhood) and, again, the citation from Edith Cobb in "The Fire" (the child's search for a world in which to find a self), as well as with the lines from "Image-Nation 10" above. "Sacred geography" is hot geography, as Olson also knew, because form is alive there. In childhood, when the discovery of things is fresh, that liveness is a gift; later, the poet has to search it out by attending the doors of perception, as Blake would say. Blaser's story of a rain that brings the sea across the railway tracks in an Idaho desert is such an event and a formative one for a child who suddenly finds the archaic at his doorstep, not only as cultural history (Grandmother's stories of the *Odyssey*), but as the immanence of form in his own, close world.

To Put Together in Order: *Syntax* and *Pell Mell*

The problem with this picture of a hot world is that it seems counterintuitive to the determinism that most people feel themselves to be under. It is also contrary to philosophies and social sciences that emphasize the social constructedness of the individual. Blaser first addresses this skepticism in "Particles":

> The particularity of the poet is considered irrelevant, egotistical. And the future is seen, without a vision including the particular, to entail

> the modern superstitions—that we are given up to general, impersonal forces—" 'history,' 'necessity,' 'World-spirit,' 'laws of nature,' . . . society," or the will of the people. I use the passive with consideration, *we are given up to,* for, as verbs always do, the passive here denotes the intellectual condition of great parts of the world. For most men, if they recognize the interdependence of heart and mind on the world, know that there is no such thing as "the will of the people" or "Society" except as they describe the common denominators of biological necessity. Those generalities become the modern means of asserting political authority without regard to heart or mind. (*Fire* 21, original emphasis)

The radical, visionary democracy of "Particles" owes a debt to Hannah Arendt, which Blaser acknowledges at the beginning of the essay (*Fire* 13). I have written elsewhere[21] of Blaser's attention to Arendt, but to summarize, Blaser, like Arendt, distinguishes between social problems to be solved and political activity as a form of self-fashioning. Literature on Arendt is full of contention over this point. Arendt differs from most of her peers in her division of public life into social administration on one hand, and a political sphere that is creative and unpredictable on the other. In her argument for a public space given to creative self-fashioning, Blaser sees a point of intersection with the arts. In "The Recovery of the Public World," he extends the argument of "Particles" to make the Arendtian point that the real is "multi-dimensional" and "multi-logical" (*Fire* 65)—that it cannot be limited to questions of social need:

> The social has to do with large numbers of people: food, shelter, clothing, sanitation—in a word, necessity. To solve necessity, we draw together in reasoning, logic, and syntax—a discourse concerning these needs. This, it seems to me, is reality enough for social discourse to claim. Ideologies of social reality are built on this basis, and then in a little-understood and decadent Platonic fashion, whichever ideology is said to comprise reality. Only for the mass subjected to such ideology, out of which, as I've said, every man and woman drops repeatedly, even hourly, certainly daily. I am simplifying indeed but I have so stated this matter of social reality in order to insist that socio-economic reality, profound as it is, is not all of reality. At the risk of appearing impertinent, I mean to extend this limitation of the reality claims to the whole range of humanistic studies—sociologism, anthropologism, and psychologism—which tend to become closures of our thought of reality: for example, the utilitarian claim, along with its historical devel-

> opment in socialism, that reality, physical and cultural, is entirely determined by the social; or, for example, going the other way around, the apparent psychological defence of the individual, which defines the real by way of a self that becomes ahistorical, like the traditional soul, but otherless—and "therapeutically triumphant." This version of humanism collapses into itself, wordless, and leaves the large numbers of people who define it moiling. (*Fire* 66)

As this passage shows, Blaser defines the social in Arendtian terms as the realm of necessity, to be addressed with the best instrumental reason the civilization can muster. For the arts, however, he reserves a creative role that parallels what Arendt imagines for public life. What has to be added is that the essays and poems of the 1980s and '90s make clear that Blaser understands the public world to have disappeared beneath the "financial surface" of the times ("Recovery," *Fire* 82); public space in the Arendtian sense is not an actuality but rather a limit concept for a society that has lost its public life as it has lost its world image. In the poem "As If By Chance," from *Streams II* (1986–91) Blaser offers this breakdown of Reagan-era realpolitik:

the economy, which, at the upper level is called economics—that is, confused
science and confused theology prancing around together as usual, is
under the cultural, like oil or gas under the hood or roof, and
unpredictably disappearing from under us

and the political, which, by manipulation, is over the stunned *polis,* in order
to manage production, distribution, and consumption of wealth,
becomes political economy—thus, what is under becomes what is
over, and *vice versa,* to define realities without earth and sky which
are cultural habitudes (*HF* 347, original emphasis)

These lines suggest that when the production and distribution of wealth have taken over public life—when political economy is all there is—there is no public world and (I am extrapolating) diminished opportunity for the hot, creative world as well.

"Particles" and "The Recovery of the Public World" should be juxtaposed to "Mind Canaries" (1986), a catalog essay commissioned by the Vancouver Art Gallery for a large show by artist Christos Dikeakos, where Blaser poses the question of determination in another way, through a meditation on art and technology. This is an essay dense in citations from Octavio Paz's *Marcel Duchamp* and *The Bow and Lyre,* and I have called attention to it already in my introduction to these essays. From Paz, Blaser draws this key observation on technology: "Technology is neither an image nor a vision of the world: it is not an image because its aim is not to represent or reproduce reality; it is not a vision because it does not conceive the world as shape but as something more or less malleable to the human will" (qtd. in "Mind Canaries," *Fire* 237). Whether it is greeted as savior, demon, or unstoppable force, technology addresses the world as obstacle or problem rather than form. This way of seeing things permeates the social sciences and critical discourses as well. And if the social is a problem to be solved technologically or bureaucratically, then public life will be dominated by the statistical and the particularity of persons, places, and things will fall out of visibility there.

But if it is the artist's prerogative to present the world as image rather than material lump to be used for some immediate end (and what sort of end? who benefits?), what about the nonartist? Is it wildly utopian to imagine everyone addressing the world in the singular? *Syntax*, a serial written between 1979 and 1981, gets its name from its focus on particular syntaxes. The serial gets a push from a comment Olson once made to Blaser, recorded in a poem called "Diary, April 11, 1981":

Olson said, 'I'd trust you
anywhere with image, but
you've got no syntax' (1958) (*HF* 223)

This comment serves as a kind of shorthand rendition of the premise of *Syntax*. Blaser does not own the syntax of his poems to the degree that Olson does, and this series is very deliberately given over to the syntax of others. Certainly the variety of orders that can be inscribed in a language are subject to the broad rules of linguistic competency and conventions of usage—to this degree they are determined—but within those conventions and pushing them to evolve is an astonishing variousness. *Syntax* includes a series, called "The Truth Is Laughter," which is largely composed of found poems. One of the most striking comes from the writings of Joe Panipakuttuk, "originally written in Eskimo syllabics," Blaser's note says (*HF* 218). Panipakuttuk is describing his first sighting of musk oxen. At first, he says "*all I could see were huge rocks*" but at closer range

. . . I found out they were carrying
something on their backs   I thought
to myself they must be carrying
their little ones, but I soon learned

that this was part of the animal
when you see musk oxen for the first time
they have a huge back on them (*HF* 218, original emphasis)

Syntax multiplies these examples many times over, and not only in the "Truth Is Laughter" series. A poem called "The Mystic East," for instance, simply lists a number of place names from Newfoundland, including gems like "Jerry's Nose," "Blow-me-down," "Joe Batt's Arm," "Empty Basket," and "Sitdown Pond" (*HF* 228). The whole series demonstrates the wildness of language as it lives in the mouths of just about anyone.[22]

At the center of *Syntax* is a long poem called "Lake of Souls," subtitled "(reading notes." It collages a wide range of voices, thus contributing to the hubbub that makes up the book. Among these, for instance, are the Nicene Creed recited in Latin and French; a passage from *The Daily Cal,* a student newspaper at Berkeley from 1947; a poem from Blaser's student days (1947) titled "Song in Four Parts for Christ the Son"; fragments of poems from Oscar Wilde and William Blake; prose passages from René Girard's *Violence and the Sacred* (1977); Bernard-Henri Levy's *Barbarism with a Human Face* (1979); Geoffrey Hartman's *Beyond Formalism* (1970); Henry Corbin's *The Man of Light in Iranian Sufism* (1978); Thomas Merton's *The Behavior of Titans* (1961); and a long passage from Shelley's *Triumph of Life.* In addition to assembling this eclectic range of voices, the poem also furthers Blaser's thinking about the sacred. The citations from René Girard are particularly long, and they reprise Girard's argument that the sacred is an anthropomorphic rendition of forces that humanity cannot control—natural disasters, plagues, and most particularly its own violence (*HF* 234–35). When the "quality of transcendence" is lost, Girard says, there is no way to separate state-sanctioned violence from illegitimate forms, and the aggression latent in human sociality generalizes itself. This is an arguable position, particularly if it is taken to imply that a return to state-sanctioned religion might not be such a bad thing. The component of Girard's argument that interests Blaser, however, is the linking of the sacred to violence. Girard sees that the sacred has dropped out of belief in secular societies, and he reads that condition as dangerous. But cited in the context of *Syntax,* his study indirectly adds urgency to Blaser's *alternative* proposition—that we have to engage with particulars, rather than generalities; with form-making potential and process, rather than fetishized forms.

Against violence, *Syntax* poses the astonishment and personalness of fresh perception: "*when you see a musk oxen for the first time / they have a huge back on them*" (*HF* 218). "Tombstone" makes this point negatively; it is a poem that silently points to the destructiveness of *not* acknowledging the wonder of things that Joe Panipakuttuk so marvelously catches. The poem references the colonial history of British Columbia's west coast in its recording of a meeting at Burrard Inlet in 1782 between Captain James Cook and Squamish Chief George Capilano. Capilano also welcomed Captain George Vancouver to the territory and "*advised his people / to follow his example in welcoming / the adventurers*" (*HF* 212, original emphasis). The tombstone is an eloquent if mute testimony to the resulting destruction of one cultural syntax by another. "Tombstone" thus references an event of mythic proportion, a moment when reality was *forcibly* renegotiated. Much more frequently, however, Blaser emphasizes the alternative to this violent reordering of things; it lies in the possibility of honoring the singular, which is to say the fiduciary bond with the world. "Tombstone" has a contrary in a found poem by Opal Whiteley (from the autobiographical *Story of Opal*) that, in the sheer delight in idiosyncrasy, embodies the basic premise of *Syntax.*

after I did look looks at the clock, I did
look looks out the front window. There are
calf-tracks by our front window. These tracks
are there because when I went walking with
Elizabeth Barrett Browning on yesterday, I
had her wait at the front step while I did go
into the kitchen to get her some sugar-lumps.
She has a fondness for sweet things. I think
she will grow up to be a lovely cow. Her
mooings now are very musical, and there is
poetry in her tracks. She does make such
dainty ones. When they dry up in the lane, I
dig up her tracks, and I save them. (*HF* 240, Blaser's emphasis; *Story* 54)

In *Cosmopolitanism,* Kwame Anthony Appiah argues that irreconcilable differences between people of contrasting cultures and ethnicities need not be—perhaps *cannot* be—resolved through accords reached by principled argument. Rather, difference may be better handled by simply living with it. It is possible, he says, for homophobes to get used to the gay couple next door, or Christians to live on the same block as Muslims. Each has to encounter the stranger in his or her particularity rather than as the embodiment of a hated principle or practice. I think Blaser moves toward the same place in *Syntax;* wonder and curiosity, like that in the Panipakuttuk and Whiteley poems, are the countermeasures to violence.

The works that follow *Syntax*, "Poetry and Positivism" and *Pell Mell*, develop and defend Blaser's work on the sacred against the skepticism of the times. The essay and serial were written over the 1980s, at the height of poststructualist mania in North American universities. So in "Poetry and Positivisms" (1989), Blaser defends his antipositivist position. "I am not writing about the other world, but only about this one in which the relation to the complexity of the other is fundamental and should not be understood as the realm of the dead. This is a particularism—not ideology—in which the poet presumes, without letting go of an extraordinary sense of the materiality of language, 'a continuum between the linguistic and the psychological' (Godzich) depth and surfaces. [. . .] My insistence is that we take our poets seriously—their 'lived experience of the other' (Lévinas)—their sense that we cannot appropriate the other into a realm of knowledge" (*Fire* 40). Blaser goes on to name Edward Said in *The World, the Text and the Critic*, in order to quarrel with the idea that "the other and the sacred somehow are not secular" (*Fire* 40). Here, as in the earlier serials, Blaser's point is that in the rush to demystify consciousness, the "lived experience of the other" has been lost and with it the possibility of relational complexity. The historical record shows that human social relationships, like those with nature, tend toward exploitation or conquest. This is an enormous diminishment of possibility and a failure of the imagination.

Pell Mell is rich in de-constructive wonder and stout defenses of perceptual experiences that urge the power of the imagination to rearticulate the relations between things. A new poem on "The Soul," for instance, has the soul as "a slip of a thing, in and out"—the between of things again (*HF* 272). And there is a poem titled "belief" that takes up the idea, so often trotted out to justify war, that World War II "would / end things, especially strife, for / the peace of it" (*HF* 286). The poem exemplifies Blaser's suspicion that ideologies, both left and right, are too willing to engage in atrocities in the name of a utopian future. As early as "The Stadium of the Mirror," Blaser adopts Olson's definition of belief as *method*. Carried over to *Pell Mell* and Blaser's argument with poststructuralism, the idea that belief is method suggests that changing methods or interpretive strategies does nothing to dispel the unstable, perceptual component in thought—that is, it cannot rid the mind of "belief" with all its subjective connotations. The same idea comes up in "Utopia," where Blaser writes that "every anti-metaphysics / reverts into a metaphysics, / as Marx and men and women fucked their / physics" (*HF* 303). Blaser's de-constructive alternative to an antimetaphysics is relational thought. "Utopia" ends this way:

being is complexity—of reunions—
of act—of quality—
                    of the world
I have argued because, in the
complexity, 'we' could not argue it
together (*HF* 304, original emphasis)

The "good of the intellect" (Dante's phrase) is relational complexity, to be accomplished through attention to act and quality. This is the ethos of Blaser's poetics as opposed to that of those theoretical discourses that turn on the hermeneutics of suspicion. In "Image-Nation 18 (an apple" (*Pell Mell*), Blaser stands with Olson on this point:

Olson said, 'The MORAL IS FORM &
    nothing else and the MORAL ACT
    is the honest—"sincere" motion in
    the direction of FORM' (*HF* 250, original emphasis)

At the end of the poem, Blaser writes:

'Form, in fact, is now definable
as tensions'

'amo o' (*HF* 251)

Olson and Blaser converge significantly on the idea that the poet's reach for form is a "moral" act, not to be confused with traditional views about what constitutes good behavior. In "Among Afterthoughts on This Occasion," a concluding essay to the volume in which "The Recovery of the Public World" first appeared,[23] Blaser writes that "the arts do not often teach boys and girls to be good, but they do teach the undulating way toward meaning" (92). *Religio* practiced as "amo o" is love of the world in its suchness. It is a resistance to the human tendency to appropriate and reduce whatever it can and a refusal to accept the ironic, the technological, or the statistical perspectives as the only secular possibilities—all other orders of the imagination suggesting intellectual embarrassment or utopian fantasy. It is also implicitly a demand that a public art, like public space, account for its "particles," the particular ones right there to be responded to.

The Last Supper

Blaser's last major reworking of the sacred is his libretto, *The Last Supper* (2000). Coming after years of meditation on the secular sacred, this piece is a direct confrontation with historical Christianity. The opera was commissioned jointly by the Glyndebourne Opera in England, Deutsche Staatsoper in Berlin, and the Royal Festival Hall in London, and it has a score by British composer Sir Harrison Birtwistle. It opened at the Staatsoper in Berlin on 18 April 2000, and played again the following September at Glyndebourne. The richness of the interplay between score and libretto is beyond my scope here; Birtwistle's score has received some preliminary attention in Jonathan Cross's introductory compact disk, *The Last Supper Guide: An Introduction to the Story and Music,* recorded with Birtwistle, and a brief essay by Fiona Maddocks, "Birtwistle's Turning World," in the Glyndebourne "Programme." My purpose, however, is to focus on Blaser's treatment of the sacred in his libretto, so I will simply describe the opera briefly. The cast, in addition to Christ and the disciples, includes a character called Ghost, sung by a mezzo-soprano, and two female choruses of nine voices, a Chorus Mysticus and a prerecorded Chorus Resonus that was projected throughout the hall during performances. As well, a prerecorded chorus of nine female and nine male voices was used in three of the visions of the work. Ghost's role appears to combine that of the Holy Ghost, the human spirit, and the many ghosts of Christian history. Birtwistle chose a small orchestra of woodwinds, lower strings, percussion instruments, and accordion to create a darkly textured, dramatic soundscape, while the Latin, the only language of the choruses, adds to the allusive, haunted quality of the opera. In addition to the citations that Blaser includes in his libretto, the musical score for the piece draws on jazz, the medieval motet, and Bach's *St. John's Passion* among other sources. The music and poetry conjure both the historical and affective record of Christianity through a millennial revisitation of its inaugural event.

A prologue sung by the Chorus Mysticus and Ghost sets the tone of the libretto with some troubling first questions:

Chorus Mysticus: *Quis sit Deus?*
Quod est nomen eius?
Dixit Deus: *EGO SUM QUI SUM* (*LS* 5)

What is God? What is his name? God says: I am who I am. These questions and the enigmatic answer open up the metaphysical side of the religious history to be investigated because they imply that we do not know the name of the God that we have presumed dead. Blaser has Ghost sing: "*God is the being we are not.* / The origin of all possibility" (*LS* 6, original emphasis). This is God as fugitive content—spilled out of His name as Blaser had imagined years earlier in the passage from *Astonishments* I have quoted above. It puts the divine here with us in this world, in "an identical / region of being," rather than elsewhere (*LS* 6). This last phrase comes from Jean-Luc Nancy's meditations on the divine in *The Inoperative Community,* an important source for the *Supper* (*LS* 2). In a comment of particular relevance to the libretto, Nancy writes: "The gods prevent the supreme undecidedness of man; they close off his humanity, and prevent him from becoming unhinged, from measuring up to the incommensurable: in the end God sets the measure" (*Inoperative Community* 136). The significance of "being-unto-God" is magnified in the community that has no god, Nancy says. It becomes a society "burned at the stake by its Church, its Myth, or its Spirit." Without God, the community "thinks it is the devastating presence of God, because it is no longer placed facing him and his absolute remoteness" (143). The effect of asking the questions (*Quis sit Deus? Quod est nomen eius?*) is that we are invited to remember the posture of facing God; we are turned by these questions to face his withdrawal, and thus our own inadequacy to fill that deserted—desert—place.

Alongside this *affective* dimension of Christianity, Blaser places its historical record. Ghost and the Chorus Mysticus call up the "subterranean stream / of our history," which includes

. . . political and moral
despotism, body and reason
hated, genocidal impulses (*LS* 5)

The phrase "subterranean stream" comes from Hannah Arendt's 1950 preface to the first edition of her *The Origins of Totalitarianism.* Arendt concludes her preface this way: "We can no longer afford to take that which was good in the past and simply call it our heritage, to discard the bad and simply think of it as a dead load, which by itself time will bury in oblivion. The subterranean stream of Western history has finally come to the surface and usurped the dignity of our tradition. This is the reality in which we live. And this is why all efforts to escape from the grimness of the present into nostalgia for a still intact past, or into the anticipated oblivion of a better future, are vain" (*Origins* ix). Arendt's comments, made at midcentury, could serve as one introduction to the libretto, and the passage is a favorite of Blaser's, turning up in "Poetry and Positivisms" (*Fire* 52), "The Recovery of the Republic World" (*Fire* 64), "Preface to the Early Poems of Robert Duncan" (*Fire* 302), and

"Bach's Belief" (*Fire* 356). Sixty years after Arendt's *Origins of Totalitarianism,* the break-up of the old colonialism and the emergence of a new world order from economic and technological change have brought the "subterranean stream of Western history" to our attention as never before, along with a pressing need to rethink the groundwork of the Enlightenment.

These are the two major poles of the opera: the metaphysical, which is the affective, cosmological dimension of religion, and the historical, which is its political practice. Blaser holds them in dialogical tension throughout the libretto. I will take up the metaphysical first. Typically de-constructive, Blaser lets the question, "*Quis sit Deus*" do its work—he holds the question open. After the disciples have entered and introduced themselves they build a table for the Supper. When they are ready, they sing the Lord's Prayer, but the Prayer is interrupted by a solo voice (the disciple is unspecified in the libretto) with the lines:

Moses asked God: "Who shall I say sent me to them?"
God said: "Tell them I AM/I AM sent you to them." (*LS* 16)

This response complicates the familiar evocation of God's Name, Kingdom, and Will in the Prayer by posing Him as unpredictable. Suddenly the Prayer seems enigmatic and difficult, more meditation than supplication, as it throws us back to the question of God's quiddity and, inevitably, that of humanity as well. To similar effect, scenes from Isaiah's encounter with God also counterpoint this singing of the Lord's Prayer. These scenes, taken from Isaiah 6.1–13,[24] are set in the Jerusalem temple and give us a Yahweh who is both majestic and vengeful. This is the scene where Isaiah sees God flanked by seraphim and is afraid that, having looked, he must die. Instead, a seraph brings a coal from the altar and places it on the prophet's tongue in symbolic purification. Isaiah is then instructed to begin a ministry that God tells him will fail. The Israelites will "hear and hear" but not understand, and "see and see" but not perceive (Isa. 6.9). When Isaiah asks how long this must go on, he is told: "Until cities lie waste without inhabitants, and houses without men, and the land is utterly desolate" (Isa. 6.11). Transposed in Blaser's version of the prayer, the passages from Isaiah imply that the prayer has not been understood. Like the disciples, we hear, yet do not understand, the message of the "I AM" or the work it requires—a response and inquiry into the nature of the Other. A facing of the Other, to use Nancy's terms. Instead we take the Other "as a *threat* to be reduced" ("My Vocabulary," *Fire* 258, original emphasis), thus opening the door to an appropriation of the majesty and wrath of God

(Girard's explication of the sacred as human violence returns here) until "cities lie waste" through the human will to dominate and seek revenge.

This is the scene that Blaser sets for the entrance of Judas who comes in as the Lord's Prayer dies away. To agitated woodwinds, the eleven disciples fall to squabbling and name-calling (that human way of being-called) as they urge Judas to leave. Peter finally quiets them, saying that they "all want to understand this horror in [their] midst"; he suggests that they ask one question each (*LS* 19). The questions and answers that follow return to the "I AM," and the unnaming of the Other. But in the disciples' treatment of Judas, the historical practice of Christianity comes forward in their eagerness to punish and banish the betrayer. Just here, Blaser catches a doctrine in the process of reifying itself as dogma. But as Judas recounts his betrayal, the moment of closure begins to reopen. "My betrayal," Judas says, was

a terrifying—
a misapprehension—of the presence
and absence of God (*LS* 20)

The disciples hear and hear and see and see but do not understand. They pick up the word "betrayal" and again begin to agitate. In the midst of their ruckus, Judas is given an aria, drawn largely from Richard Crashaw, that is one of the most dramatically lyrical in the opera, "I looked upon his silver face and wept." The scene ends with a riddle. Thomas asks, "Who do you think Jesus is?" (*LS* 21), and Judas says,

We didn't know, did we? Even when he asked us.
We hoped for a Messiah, a David.
He was—he is—the answer to a riddle. (*LS* 22)

The riddle is "what can go in the face of the sun, / yet leave no shadow?" (*LS* 22). After the disciples guess wrongly, Christ appears among them and answers, "The Wind" (*LS* 23). The riddle suggests a parable in response to the disciples' reach after definitive answers about the nature of God, and it speaks to their self-righteous treatment of Judas. The implications of that grasping after knowledge and righteousness are made clear in the dramatic centerpiece of the opera, a scene that Birtwistle has ritualized as verse and refrain, where Christ washes the feet of the disciples. Peter is the first, establishing the pattern:

Christ: I have come to wash the dust
of centuries from you. One by one.
Now, Peter—you first.
Peter: What's this?
Christ: The shatters of that in which we trust.
All Twelve: Out of the dust.
Chorus Mysticus: *de pulvere.* (*LS* 27)

Christ's answers to the "What's this?" of the twelve form a catalog of the worst abuses of Christian practice: they are persecutions ancient and modern. The last to step up is Judas, and the irony of the disciples' reception of him comes home in Christ's response to his "What's this?" It is

the Irreparable: where I disclosed a religion
of love, they gave us bestiality and vileness. (*LS* 30)

The "irreparable" is Giorgio Agamben's word for the inevitable being-thus of being, and the barely concealed implication is that the demonizing of Judas throughout Christian history is a form of anti-Semitism, a hatred of others on the basis of an existential predicate—the "*existential given,*" as Blaser says in the poem, "Even on Sunday" (*HF* 372, original emphasis). In this poem from the *Exody* series (1993), he calls the persecution of others on the grounds of what they are said to be (women, Jews, blacks, intellectuals, primitives) a blasphemy, "so to revile existence" (*HF* 372).

Blaser's Christological corrective to the horrors of historical religious practices, implicit in the question that pulls from the word "God" the necessary suchness of being, is to hold the existential unharmed—that is, to practice *religio* as fiduciary responsibility and bond with the world. This is how the marriage ceremonies in "Cups 9" and "Image-Nation 6" come home in *The Last Supper: religio* has to be a practice rather than institution. No social or moral order can account for being in its full particularity. No imaginable collective naming can include all that has been, is, or will exist. Nor can any name ever approach the concrecity of the persons, places, things, or events it purports to call into language. The territory is not the map. And this means that institutionalized religion cannot substitute for the due care and attention of a *Tao.* Blaser suggests that human efforts to reify an earthly paradise quickly turn violent. In "Fousang," an important poem from *Pell Mell,* he writes that "the birds of paradise grow / feet and claws" (*HF* 254). Religious and secular thought alike betray themselves when they overreach their provisional versions of the real. This has been a repeated theme in Blaser's work.

To a similar end in the libretto, Christ asks the disciples who they think he is. In response they freeze in the attitude of Leonardo's *Last Supper* while Ghost sings a poem by A. M. Klein, "*Don't you hear Messiah coming in his tank, in his tank?*" (*LS* 35, original emphasis).

Blaser treats this oh-so-dangerous longing for an anthropomorphic God and an eternal kingdom in the here and now—let's call it the longing for safety, stability, and homeliness—with a mixture of understanding and horror. During the first of three visions that interrupt the disciples' progress toward the supper, scenes of the crucifixion are projected over a darkened stage, while the Chorus sings

O bone Jesu, exaudi me
et ne permittas me separari a te
[O Good Jesus, hear me
and do not allow me to be separated from You] (*LS* 23, original emphasis)

The pain of loss and fear of deprivation are chronic human realities, conditions of infancy and archaic mothers of myth and magic. They continue to inform the reach for permanent, safe states of being. But the "human grasp" after permanence, as Blaser says in "Image-Nation 7," is also its madness and terror.

The Last Supper is sharply focused on a struggle against the reification of the sacred. As St. Paul's ministry shows, the institutionalization of Christological love and passivity—its translation into the Roman world of realpolitik—begins to form itself in "thou shalt nots." Consider Paul's well-known instructions to the Romans: "What then? Are we to sin because we are not under the law but under grace? By no means! . . . For the wages of sin is death, but the free gift of God is eternal life in Christ Jesus our Lord" (Rom. 6.15, 23). In these verses, the transformation from inner light to external law takes place right under our eyes. Grace is a gift. This point of doctrine was in particular dispute during the Protestant Reformation, and it has given rise to numerous antinomian heresies, whose adherents claim themselves under grace rather than the laws of clerics and state powers. The fate of Anne Hutchinson is a good American example of the Puritan effort to hold to an orthodoxy against such heresies. But as Paul poses it here, grace becomes a token to be used in an exchange economy designed to regulate behavior. Sin *earns* the sinner a *wage* of death. But, asymmetrically, the *gift* of God is eternal life. "I am speaking in human terms because of your natural limitations," Paul says (Rom. 6.19). And here a host of associations come to mind—the claims of a long line of historical redeemers to be guiding the masses for their own good. These passages from Romans bring us to a contemporary dilemma: is there not a very practical recognition in Paul that few people have the leisure to make the effort to really do the meditative work required to face the Other? that most of us want institutional guidance? moral instruction? The "oughts" and "shoulds" usher in the military Messiah of the Klein poem. But if we take up the radical Christology implied in the libretto, we are asked to imagine a redeemed humanity that needs no institutionalized authority, just as in Blaser's earlier poems we are asked to imagine a public capable of taking up the considerable charge and inconvenience of a real democracy or individuals alert enough to see the world for themselves rather than through ready-made conceptions. These visionary forms of community disregard "natural limitation" as well as the potential for evil already there in the fiduciary bond.

The doubleness of human sociality, like a primordial wound (a spear in the side of Christ), cannot be made to heal over. Blaser's response to it comes out of a long-standing distrust of the human tendency to appropriate divinity for its own disastrous purposes. It is a tendency that haunts the history of Christianity, and Blaser encountered it as an issue in his student days at Berkeley under the tutelage of Ernst Kantorowicz. A scholar of medieval political theology, Kantorowicz was teaching the material that later became *The King's Two Bodies: A Study in Medieval Political Theology* (1957) when Blaser studied Dante with him (Blaser, "Excerpts from *Astonishments*" 295). In Kantorowicz's view, Dante resolved the question of the jurisdiction of Pope and Emperor by referring each to the perfections of his realm, the heavenly and the earthly respectively. Blaser recalls in *Astonishments* that he took from Kantorowicz the notion that Dante understood history as process and made the earthly paradise (not Heaven) a human rather than a divine responsibility ("Excerpts from *Astonishments*" 295–305). In the opera, Andrew asks Judas how he got out of hell, and Judas replies, "Hell is here" (*LS* 19). So also is the possibility of the Good. Christ says to his disciples:

Whether you believed in me or not,
I was there. I'm inside you.
I talked of sheep and lambs—of fishing—
of mustard seeds—this was before we entered the city—
to seek justice—a human skill—like love. (*LS* 36)

In this passage, Christ places himself both outside the polis and invisibly inside its inhabitants but not in the city as a public presence. Blaser too, time and again, divides the discourses as he does in "The Recovery of the Public World," assigning to poetry the guardianship of singularity and to the social sciences the statistical management of social life. Checks and balances, then, against a will to power for which there is no cure. Or to repeat Olson, "you do love or go down" (*CPr* 252). Yet, if the arrangement of our well-being here is our own business, if this poetic Christology gives us no more than a call to a best practice of *religio,* what is to be gained by proposing such a radical alterity as the sacred? How does a poetics that can only call or solicit rather than *oblige* make a claim on us?

The question itself reveals the lunge toward legitimacy—so common in critical discourses—as really a reach for the power to compel. But Blaser is honest about the fact that poetry does not, by itself, change the world. It *may* open hearts and minds to relational complexity, however, and complexity—that is the "good of the intellect"—is the poet's best argument against violence. The generation of the new millennium has inherited the insanity of the sacrifice of the earth and large segments of its living beings in order to bring about what? Present ease? Insurance against an unpredictable future? This is the unreason of reason. A poetics of the sacred inheres in an attitude or posture that has us turned to face the otherness of the Other. It is Greek hospitality to one who might be a god; or it is the self-limitation of God in the esoteric rabbinical tradition, a "contraction" (*tzimtzum*) that lets creation begin, as Gershom Scholem explains (*On the Kabbalah* 130); or it is an ordinary table that separates and relates those who sit around it.

I have titled this essay "The Practice of Outside" after Blaser's essay on Spicer because I think the phrase describes his own practice quite precisely. Always turned toward an outside—"god moves to the end / of our sentences" ("Image-Nation 5" 153)—Blaser's practice of the sacred takes him finally to a transformed consciousness and a new world image. I have said that the serial poems begin with the experience of "cultural orphanhood" and dismemberment, but they do not end there. In "Mappa Mundi" and the *Image-Nations* of the *Exody* series (1993), "the ashen boy—becomes—exodic" (*HF* 388). "Mappa Mundi" moves into a nomadology.

> Olson once said that he wished he could learn how to handle verticals from Boulez—horizontals being what we do everyday toward horizons—he had in mind the Second Piano Sonata, the *eruptive violence* of them—in conversation with Beethoven's *Hammerklavier*—a rage of rhythm—the rhythmic variations of the notes playing the as-

> tonishment of BACH's belief—counterpoints of monads becoming nomads—*of rhythm is image / of image is knowing / of knowing there is / a construct*—his dream
>
> of compossibility (*HF* 389, original emphasis)

The references to Olson, Boulez, and Bach look toward Blaser's essay, "Bach's Belief" (1995), of the same period, an essay in which Blaser reads the nomad through Gilles Deleuze's *The Fold* (1993). *Compossibility,* a Leibnizian term that carries over into Whitehead's cosmic vision, says that the whole of things moves toward its maximal horizon in God, a horizon always pushed to the future but nonetheless orienting the creative advance of things toward maximal satisfaction (the best possible world). Deleuze's modification of this vision is the nomadic one in which diverging series of linkages between things or flows (things *become* flows) form multiple worlds that do not have to fit together.[25] In "Bach's Belief," Bach and Boulez relate as monad to nomad in Boulez's *Second Sonata,* which is based on musical notes corresponding to the letters in Bach's name. Hence "monads become nomads" in a composition that Olson heard performed by David Tudor at Black Mountain College in 1951 and commented on: "*I hadn't heard anything as interesting as that since I once heard Bach*" ("Bach's Belief," *Fire* 350, original emphasis).

The nomad is an important trope for Blaser not only because it carries his crucial recognition that "form is alive," but also because it marks a transformation of the orphan and exile in Blaser's poetry. The nomad lurks in the poems as a possibility as early as "Image-Nation 5," for instance, when Blaser finds that what is left in the passing of things are

> traces the old Bedouin poets
> called them encampments of
> what was
> a movement (*HF* 151)

Twenty *Image-Nations* later, in "Image-Nation 25 (exody," Blaser draws on Hieronymus Bosch's *Garden of Earthly Delights* and Deleuze's *Fold* to follow the life of form into its labyrinthine possibilities. Bosch's *Garden* famously shows various species in the process of becoming-other or erotically joined in ways that look "as if Ovid's metamorphoses, without his cosmos, became delirium" (*HF* 394). And from *The Fold,* Blaser takes this passage: "*A labyrinth is said, etymologically, to be multiple because it contains many folds. The multiple is not only what has many parts but what is folded in many ways . . . A 'cryptographer' is needed, someone who can at once account for nature and decipher the soul, who can peer into the crannies of matter and read the soul*" (*HF* 396, original emphasis). The passage resonates with Blaser's poetic project—to "*account for nature and decipher the soul*"—but it is the final image of "Image-Nation 25" that is telling. Here Odysseus's circuit (the tale of a tub in the Idaho desert) gives way to the story of the Wandering Jew. The image comes from the leather back of an old rocking chair that used to sit in the boxcar by the railroad tracks that the Blaser family called home in Idaho. When the chair wore out, relatives cut out the back with the image and sent it to Blaser:

nevertheless, I rock there,
wandering Jew and nomad

I imagine mortality,
its unrest and proses

I imagine *evolutionary love,*

my thousand and one celebrations (*HF* 396, original emphasis)

In his "Author's Note" to the revised *Holy Forest,* Blaser writes: "The whole thing: just trying to be at home. That's the plot" (xxv). So the forest in which the poet was originally lost becomes itself a homeplace. The rocking chair and the wandering Jew combine in these lines to suggest that the exile has morphed into something else, that he has become at home in his wanderings. So the polarities, the fold, the rhizome are not simply tropes of a broken metaphysics; they constitute another kind of world image. In another poem from *Exody* titled "in the tree tops," humorously so for the poet of a holy *forest,* Blaser writes of that vision:

rarely a woman or man dies without having yet a few folds to
undo   but this happened   parallel to this *operation,* the
one or the other forms a *nucleus,* like a stone or a nut   the
inferior races, such as the white race, see the stone, nut, and
nucleus rather than the *unfolded fold*   the Mage sees, more-so,
the *unfolded fold*

the *unfolded fold* is important and onliest   what rests is
nothing but epiphenomenon (*HF* 376, original emphasis)

7

Susan Howe

A Special View of History

Introduction

Born in 1937, Susan Howe comes of a generation after that of Olson, and she is twelve years junior to Creeley and Blaser. As well, she turns to poetry in midlife after working in visual arts and theater, developing as a poet in the 1970s and '80s. In the considerable body of commentary now available on her work, she is usually grouped with American language writers because of her decentering of voice and her attention to the phonic and graphemic materialities of language. As well, she was a longtime participant in the poetics program at the State University of New York at Buffalo alongside Charles Bernstein. I do not deny the closeness of Howe to the language poets, nor her place in genealogies other than mine: Marjorie Perloff locates Howe in the line of Emily Dickinson, Hart Crane, and Samuel Beckett ("Collision" 528); Kaplan Harris reads her into a visual art genealogy that includes Kazimir Malevich, Marcel Duchamp, and Ad (Adolph Frederick) Reinhardt (442). Yet Howe is equally significant to my constellation of poets, not only because she pushes off from the trauma of the war as they do, but also because her treatment of the poetic field builds on and modifies that of Olson and his contemporaries. In the autobiographical essay that opens *Hinge Picture,* Howe writes her childhood as a confrontation with "Power and Progress" (*FS* 11), signposting her birth with the advent of the Nazi regime, the alliance between Germany and Italy, and the Spanish Civil War. Her earliest experiences included daily war news, a father anxiously awaited, and the bombing of Pearl Harbor. "From 1939 until 1946," she writes, "I saw signs of culture exploding into murder. Shots of children being herded into trucks by hideous helmeted conquerors" (*ET* 11): "This is my historical consciousness" (13). And then, in a much-quoted passage, she says that her project is to "tenderly lift from the dark side of history voices that are anonymous, slighted—inarticulate" (*ET* 14)

Howe brings this project of a poetry that includes history into the late twentieth-century world of speeded-up telecommunications, postmodern philosophies, gender awareness, and global consciousness. Her rendition of figure and ground thus comes at a moment when both were under empirical as well as theoretical revision. In her poems, figure gives place to the decentered consciousness, and the ground swarms with marginal voices and conflicting narratives. For Olson, figure relates to ground as one perspective of many in a complex, layered life-world; for Howe, figure gives way to "a route of evanescence"[1] and the strata'd landscape to incompatible worlds. Monad becomes nomad; beauty shakes, breaks, and shivers into the sublime.

Except the contrast is not so tidy. In the *Talisman* interview with Edward Foster (1990), as in her essay on Olson, "Where Should the Commander Be?" (1987), Howe acknowledges the importance of Olson as a predecessor and remarks on her enthusiasm for *Call Me Ishmael*, which, she says, "enthralled me when I first read it" (*Talisman* 158). In the same interview, she speaks of "space-time" rather than chronology (173), and this I take as an important point of intersection with Olson. Olson's layered spatiotemporalities are an important precedent for Howe's version of the field as a historical plenum of minor and muted voices. There are, however, some important differences between Howe and Olson in their respective constructions of history. Ishmael is Olson's first persona, and his relation to the past is that of the first person witness. The eyewitness, the one who has found out for himself and who now presents his " 'istorin," is key to Olson's presentation of history as present-pastness. It is the past as reconstructed in a particular, present tense perspective that interests him. There are two important consequences of this "special view." First, the past is wrested away from the totalizing claims of various official stories and returned to first person narration where it ceases to be authoritative and becomes instead a component of a present in the making. Second, this amounts to a claim that reality is always under construction and that it could and should be a democratic effort. Despite the projective size of Maximus in the middle volumes, I have argued, he is always only one of a multitude, and his view one of many. " 'Istorin" accommodates fallibilism. Yet a first person narrative also roots the story in the sensibility of the present; it is the survivor's view that we get in the persona of Ishmael and not the *alterity* of the past.

This is where Howe comes in. Her attention to the past as an unmasterable field of semiarticulated or not-yet-articulated historical vectors and potential relations marks a difference between her practice and that of Olson, even though the plenitude of this unstoried past is *implicit* in Olson's layered landscape. In her forays into Melville, Howe does *not* choose Ishmael as a point of entry, but Bartleby in *Melville's Marginalia* (1993) and Billy Budd in *Scattering as Behavior toward Risk* (1990). Bartleby falls silent before the Law, which he has been hired to copy. Billy has a stutter that prevents him from telling his story, to the point where he stands defenseless before the Law: he is unable to narrate—unable to articulate a *stance*—and thus unable to participate in the construction of reality in a way that can be heard and understood at the level of social institutions as these are represented by Captain Vere. I will come back to these characters and Howe's treatment of them. My point for the moment is that Howe draws out of Melville's characters something other than the eyewitness perspective; both Bartleby and Billy bring forward an alterity that cannot be articulated in the terms available under the prevailing social reality. Both subvert the Law—Law as psychosocial reality as well as judicial—by drawing it down on themselves. The inadequacy of the Law to deal justly with these characters reveals the limits of the Law and undoes its claim to universality and legitimacy. Moreover, this antinomian challenge suggested in Howe's treatment of Billy and Bartleby does more than just undermine the legitimacy of a given dominant order; *it brings to question the unavoidably perspectival nature of the real as such.* So, as Howe says on several occasions,[2] citing Olson, "the stutter is the plot" (*Talisman* 181). It is the plot of her poetry as well.

One way in which Howe stutters—one way in which she indexes alterity—is by scrivening like Bartleby. This is again a point of intersection and divergence with Olson. What Howe says of Emily Dickinson's work sounds much like a description of her own method: "Forcing, abbreviating, pushing, padding, subtracting, riddling, interrogating, re-writing, she pulled text from text" (*MED* 29). This is writing as active re-reading and hence reminiscent of Duncan's poetics of derivation as well as Olson's fascination with document. In Howe's case, however, the Bartleby factor dominates. While her readings of American literary history pull "text from text" she often begins the process by copying found scraps faithfully and pasting them into the poems or by following the textual trails of such scraps. Her attention to the holograph copies of Dickinson's poems, Shelley's notebooks, Melville's marginalia as reproduced in Wilson Walker Cowen's two-volume publication, or the genetic text of Billy Budd are cases in point, and these findings figure importantly in major poems. One could say the same about Olson—whole passages in some cases lifted from historical sources. But the difference is that Howe makes no effort to integrate the pasted scrap into a narrative. The scrap sits, like the enigmatic "x" that appears in some of her pieces (see *The Nonconformist's*

Memorial, page 96, for instance), like some mute testimony of an other time that is lost to writer and reader alike, or a speech impediment that delays the unfolding of a narrative. The artifacts that Howe imports, in other words, are often enigmatic. Like a bit of broken pottery, a scrap of metal dug up by some archaeologist, her *scraptures* drag the mystery of a lost or virtual context into the poem, and this other dimension then haunts the poem's scapes as something unthought. The *familiarity* of the ground to which Olson would return becomes *unheimlich* in Howe's poems.

This falling out of place—because that is the sensation Howe achieves with the decontextualized fragment—relates to her treatment of time. In an essay on *Pythagorean Silence* and Michel Serres's *The Parasite,* Gregory Dale Adamson draws attention to the similarity between Serres's discussion of time and Howe's writing of it. Building on Serres, Adamson distinguishes between a temporality realized as a succession of presents from one in which the "pure" form of time would coexist with the psychological present as the unrealized network of "relations and non-relations of the passage of social information," a kind of "ontological memory" as distinguished from individual memories (Adamson, "Serres Translates Howe" 117). This treatment of time parallels that of Deleuze, for whom the pure past is an a priori transcendental field in relation to the lifeworld. As Serres constructs it, the unrealized past registers as "noise" (Serres's term) in relation to consciousness because it lies outside of what the mind recognizes as information. In developing the idea of the parasite or noise in the system, Serres compares it to the discovery of irrational numbers that Pythagoras tried to repress. It was Pythagoras's pupil Hippasus who discovered that the hypotenuse of an isosceles triangle with legs of one unit each had to be described as the square root of two, an irrational number with a nonrepeating decimal to infinity. Pythagoras is said to have had Hippasus drowned rather than admit the validity of a mathematical discovery that would have jeopardized his worldview.

Howe's "Pythagorean silence" as unfolded in the serial poem of that title (1982) is analogous to noise in Serres's sense of it; more generally, noise is a metaphor in her poetry for the presence of something that a given order fails to recognize as meaningful, a blind spot in the present. Bartleby, Billy Budd, Stella Johnson, Cordelia, Hope Atherton, Mary Rowlandson, Mary Magdalene, James Clarence Mangan, and Juliette de Portalès are examples of noise. Where Olson works toward stance—and the *dynamism* of his method in which Whiteheadian "satisfaction" is taken away from consciousness has to be remembered—Howe allows the noise of the past to enter her text as an interruption of stance. Hence the absence of stabilizing perspectives and the courting of a pure past that in the infinity of its virtual relations suggests the disorientation of the Kantian sublime rather than the formal pleasure of the beautiful. In this imagined flooding of the present with the virtual past, landmarks of time and space loosen and drift. So in *Secret History of the Dividing Line,* for instance, the marks (any marks) are set wandering in lines like "mark mar ha forest 1 a boundary manic a land a / tract" (*FS* 89). In such a field, multiple and conflicting realities may cohabit, and I think this is the point. As Howe says to Foster, "the mystery is time. The undying Hittites and Babylonians may be waiting in another chronology completely. Who knows?" (*BM* 163).

The pure past as it haunts the present allows for incompatibility of the vectors in Howe's space-time field. This is another point of divergence between Olson and Howe on the special view of history, and if we are to understand what both can offer it is necessary to render the difference with some care. It is simply not accurate to say that Olson's chaosmos is closed while Howe's is open, or that Olson can be devoured through phenomenology and Howe through poststructuralism. These are oversimplifications. To repeat, Whiteheadian form, to which Olson's is tied, is dynamic; its completion is always deferred to the future. The primordial nature of God—God as the totality of what was, is, or might have been—as Olson points out in *The Special View,* is virtual. In effect, the primordial God registers in Olson's writings as the openness of the future. The human creature experiences this openness as process. But what Whitehead calls the "lure for feeling" is a *dream* of the fullness of time as *beauty;* this would be the world manifest so as to maximize the potential of each actual entity and thus the satisfaction of God. This is the gorgeousness of Olson's vision. The world is Venus rising out of the "genital wave," or it is Enyalion, "in the service of the law of proportions / of his own body" (Olson, *MP* 406). This Whiteheadian space-time field already opens upon incompossibilities that have the potential to shatter that formal beauty. This is a recognition latent in Olson, Creeley, Spicer, and Blaser, in different ways for each, but it is Howe who really takes on the implications of it and realizes most fully a nomadology. In his chapter on Whitehead and Leibniz in *The Fold,* Deleuze writes that Whitehead's cosmos differs from that of Leibniz in that the "monads" (read Whitehead's actual entities) are open to the ingression of others and hence to the possibility of diverging and unpredictable series of events.

> Now for Whitehead . . . a condition of opening causes all prehension to be already the prehension of another prehension, either to control it or to exclude it. Prehension is naturally open, open onto the world, without having to pass through a window. . . .

> For Leibniz, as we have seen, bifurcations and divergences of series are genuine borders between incompossible worlds, such that the monads that exist wholly include the compossible world that moves into existence. For Whitehead (and for many modern philosophers), on the contrary, bifurcations, divergences, incompossibilities, and discord belong to the same motley world that can no longer be included in expressive units, but only made or undone according to prehensive units and variable configurations or changing captures. In the same chaotic world divergent series are endlessly tracing bifurcating paths. It is a "chaosmos" of the type found in Joyce. . . . Even God desists from being a Being who compares worlds and chooses the richest compossible. He becomes Process, a process that at once affirms incompossibilities and passes through them. The play of the world has changed in a unique way, because now it has become the play that diverges. Beings are pushed apart, kept open through divergent series and incompossible totalities that pull them outside, instead of being closed upon the compossible and convergent world that they express from within. (Deleuze, *The Fold* 81)

In the final chapter of this book, Deleuze says that while Leibniz's monads suppose a world in which the multiple perspectives of the monads converge and harmonize "to the degree that the world is now made up of divergent series (the chaosmos) . . . the monad is now unable to contain the entire world as if in a closed circle that can be modified by projection." The monad "astraddle over several worlds, is kept half open as if by a pair of pliers" (*The Fold* 137).

It is possible to hear in Olson's breathlessness—the unfinished phrases that wander over the page, or the centrifugal energy in the various components of a poem like "The Kingfishers" (dream material, Mao's revolution, the "E" on the Delphic stone)—a chaosmos of diverging series. In a much more direct way, Blaser's chiasmus leads to this Deleuzean instability avant la lettre; recall the trees that "wander and roll" in "Image-Nation 1" (*HF* 89). But neither Olson nor Blaser confronts the contradictions of a nomadic field in the same way as does Howe. As soon as figure and ground become distinguishable—as soon as form comes to be articulated, even in as dynamic and *contained*[3] a way as Olson proposes—there is a dialectic and a repression of some un(re)cognized alterity. As Roland Barthes remarks, "we know, for example, that *the content of the word 'Order' always indicates repression*" (*Writing Degree Zero* 26, my emphasis). I think this is the challenge that Howe takes up—the challenge of a cannibal cosmos[4] in which things consume or repress other things in order to live and manifest themselves. In the *Talisman* interview, she says, "I don't want to be of Ahab's party. I want to find peace" (177). Juxtapose this remark to Rachel Blau DuPlessis' valuable insight, drawn from Howe's *My Emily Dickinson,* that the "impossible question posed in every crevice of this work is: How to make a culture that does not demand subjugation when 'Culture representing form and order will always demand sacrifice and subjugation of one group by another' " ("Whowe" 131). Olson's perspectivism does not bring peace, nor did Olson expect it to; Enyalion goes to *war* with a picture. Howe writes of *Call Me Ishmael* in the "Commander" essay that "real events that are Facts, are interconnected by ties and links to a deep inner theme of composition as *conflict*" (5). The Commander (the cogito, the sovereign self) may be deposed, but this only relativizes conflicting perspectives and diverging series; it does not prevent the war between them. Duncan's "order and strife" is a point of comparison as is Spicer's refusal of cosmicity as consolation for individual suffering and death.

So what can it mean to pursue peace in a sacrificial world? To think about this question, I want to move in a little closer on the difference between Howe's and Olson's rendition of figure and ground. In a poem titled "DECEMBER, 1960," Olson records selected events from settler-aboriginal conflicts in the seventeenth and eighteenth centuries on the coast of Gloucester. The longest single story of this poem comes from Richard Yorke's 1713 account of an encounter between Gloucester fishers and an unspecified group of "Indians" "dressed / in French clothing" (*Maximus* 197). After much discussion between the two parties, recorded in the narrative, the encounter turns hostile and five fishers are captured. The poem ends with Olson's marginal notes, identifying the men taken. For example:

III Josiah Ingersoll,
    prob. Samuel II's
    son, who m. Mary Stevens
        Dec. 30, 1712 (200)

I refer to this poem because it is a captivity narrative, although of a different kind than that which interests Howe. Yorke's story clearly fixes the perspective on the English position. The "Indians" are not identified by tribe or name, nor is the capture rendered in affective language. The bulk of the reportage is about who does what when, and the story, as Olson records it, ends at the point when the settlers have been captured. The first sections of "DECEMBER, 1960" focus on the coast as a contact zone between sea and land, fish and farm, settler and aboriginal ("a coast / is not the same /

as land" [*MP* 194]), but Olson lets the clash of cultures lie in the document with little fretting of the boundaries between them beyond the remarking of "imperial / European / nations / finding / future history / from Portuguese / fishing grounds" and the resulting "domestic / horror" (*MP* 197). Immediately after this poem is "Maximus letter # whatever" in which Olson retells the Algonquin legend of the man who carries his house on his head. Like Yorke's story, the legend is presented with no commentary. The two stories, Yorke's and the Algonquin tale, represent diverging perspectives unfurling in the same geographical space, but there is no mixing of these perspectives. If there is alchemy latent in the situation, it has to be performed by the reader. In Olson's chaosmos, the man who carries his house is a figure of containment and thus an example of the regrounded self. I take it this is the point: Olson allows conflicting perspectives to bump up against each other, but leaves them relatively intact. They thus retain a monadic feel, even though the collisions Olson records would logically imply some mutual trauma. In contrast, Howe focuses on the potential for transformation in the trauma.

Howe's "The Captivity and Restoration of Mrs. Mary Rowlandson" begins with a phrase from Roger Williams's *A Key into the Language of America* (1643): "Náwwatuck nôteshem," which Williams translates as "I came from farre." These words in a language that many readers will not understand strike the keynote of this piece. What comes from "farre" is allowed to interrupt the narrative. Howe's own account of Rowlandson's story is a collage of citations and speculations that jostle against one another. Drawing on Increase and Cotton Mather, Rowlandson's *Narrative,* John Winthrop's *Journal* and *Papers,* Anne Bradstreet's *Complete Works,* and Edward Johnson's *Wonder-Working Providence,* among other historical and contemporary accounts of early Puritan history, Howe traces the clash of European and indigenous cultures through religious, economic, and social confrontation. Where Howe's collage differs from that of Olson is in the detail and her focus on interruptions to the monadic perspectives of the various historical actors. So, for instance, Howe enormously expands description of the forces bearing on settler-aboriginal hostilities. On one side, there is the "harsh climate, a wilderness, tomahawks, powwows, quickhatch and wampumpeag" that terrify the immigrants, and on the other, a steady encroachment on land and pressure on food supplies that alarm and provoke the indigenous tribes (*BM* 90–91). What she is looking for in Rowlandson's narrative and in her other sources is the switch point where one point of view opens to another—where the monad is prized open by a diverging series. In the *Talisman* interview, Howe describes this point through the mathematician René Thom's definition of a singularity. In algebra, it is "the point where plus becomes minus"; "the singularity is the point where there is a sudden change to something completely else. It's a chaotic point. It's the point chaos enters cosmos, the instant articulation. Then there is a leap into something else" (173). Out of a *Narrative* bleached to orthodoxy—"[a]ll of the editions we have now depend on the text of a 'Second Addition Corrected and Amended'" (*BM* 97)—Howe pulls this image of Rowlandson in the company of her captors: "There she stands, blood about her mouth, savoring the taste of raw horse liver. God's seal of ratification spills from her lips or from her husband's pen" (*BM* 126). Rowlandson's "risky retrospective narrative will be safe only if she asserts the permanence of corporate Sovereignty," Howe writes. "Each time an errant perception skids loose, she controls her lapse by vehemently invoking biblical authority" (100). Of course it is the "errant perception" that is the main event for Howe.

But I am still on the trail of peace. In *Secret History of the Dividing Line* (1996), Howe has a poem on "the ancient town of SWORDS" that "derives its name from the Celtic word, *sord* meaning pure, originally applied to St Columbkille's well, which from time immemorial has been one of the principal sources of water supply to the town" (*FS* 92). The last verse of the poem goes like this: "According to ancient records, SWORDS was burnt by the Danes in 1012, 1016, 1030, 1138, 1150, and 1166 A.D.; and in 1185 it was taken and sacked by O'Malaghlin, King of Meath" (*FS* 92). This poem condenses the violent history of dividing lines, including that of European imperialism in the Americas: a desirable territory, claimed in the name of whatever purity (racial, ethnic, national, religious, or gendered), and then conflict around the ownership of it. It is to the point that the word "sord" in its sound and etymology links a valuable resource (the town of Swords and its well) with the concepts of both purity and violence. Over and over, in references to ancient, medieval, and modern history, Howe brings us to the aftermath of carnage in poems that are full of exiles and weeping women: "diadem dagger a voyage gibbet" (*Pythagorean Silence, ET* 84). The implication is that peace requires the permeability of boundaries and the re-thinking of borders. It requires a softening of stance.

This is where Howe's commentators have directed the bulk of their attention—on the liberating implications of Howe's challenge to dividing lines. Howe has generated strong critical interest, including the full-length studies of Rachel Tzvia Back (*Led by Language*, 2002) and Stephen Collis (*Through Words of Others*, 2006) as well as essays and book chapters by such distinguished scholars as Rachel Blau DuPlessis, Lynn Keller, Hank Lazer, Ming-Quian Ma, Peter Nicholls, Marjorie Perloff, Peter Quartermain, and John Taggart among many others. This body of scholarship has taken two related directions: a celebration of indeterminacy as liberation and a celebration of the feminist rescue of voices marginalized by history. So Quartermain reads *Scattering as Behavior toward Risk* as "throwing a halo of wilderness around *Billy Budd*" ("And the Without" 192) and Howe as tasking herself with "retrieving from erasure and marginality those (women) who have been written out" (194). Nicholls emphasizes the "unsettling" of the American wilderness in Howe's *My Emily Dickinson* (1985), *The Birth-mark* (1993), *The Nonconformist's Memorial* (1993), and *Singularities* (1996). The field of the poem, read as a homologue of social and political realities, is structured so that the "literal topography of 'borders' and 'margins' through which Howe maps early new England history is now elided with an equally literal topography of writing—the actual page, with its 'Cancelations, variants, insertions, erasures, marginal notes, stray marks and blanks'" ("Unsettling" 591). A passage Nicholls cites from *The Birth-mark* supports this reading. Howe writes that "the issue of editorial control [as exercised over the writings of Emily Dickinson, Thomas Shepherd, or Mary Rowlandson] is directly connected to the attempted erasure of antinomianism in our culture. Lawlessness, seen as negligence, is at first feminized and then restricted or banished" (*BM* 1).

This passage linking editorial control with political authority segues easily to the second component of Howe's poetics: the feminist rescue of forgotten or silenced voices (noise in the system) from the dustbin of history. DuPlessis hears a feminist appropriation of genre in *Secret History of the Dividing Line* and *Pythagorean Silence* ("Whowe" 129). Ma, in an essay on *The Non-Conformist's Memorial,* constructs Howe's project as the articulation of the inarticulate, to which end "Howe's poetic praxis pivots on a lyric consciousness upon which impinges a double mission of rescuing and breaking free: rescuing 'the stutter' that Howe hears in American literature 'as a sounding of uncertainty. What is silenced or not quite silenced' . . . and breaking free from a linguistic world in which, as Marjorie Perloff puts it in *The Dance of the Intellect,* 'the articulation of an individual language is all but prevented by the official discourses that bombard the consciousness from all sides'" (Ma, "Articulating" 469). So it is both the rescue of lost or damaged identities and the transformation of the concept of identity that are at issue. This is the critical line in which Hank Lazer reads Howe's "textual frontiers" (1996); Megan Williams *Melville's Marginalia* (1997); Ann Vickery *The Liberties* (1997); Susan Vanderborg Howe's palimpsests (2001), Rachel Back, the American and European history poems (2002); and Stephen Collis, Howe's anarcho-scholasticism (2006). Complicating rescue, however, is the "double mission" Ma notices, and this paradox has been well noted in a number of different readings. Lazer remarks on the "spirited fracturing" of Howe's texts, each one "a willed but also inevitable and necessary breaking apart" (*Op-*

posing Poetries 62). Vanderborg finds there the "restless contradictions" of Puritanism—a perennial defiance of authority and at the same time, an injunction to build a new City in the wilderness (*Paratextual Communities* 75). Collis remarks that the encloser and the antinomian are mutually constitutive personae of the poem (*Through Words of Others* 34): on one hand, the rescue of voice; on the other, the shattering of it. In the *Talisman* interview, Howe herself says: "I think a lot of my work is about breaking free: starting free and being captured and breaking free again and being captured again" (166). Might this rhythm in which freedom never quite overcomes capture and form never rests easy constitute a tragic vision?

Tragedy as human condition is certainly implicit in the project of trying to imagine an inclusivity that can accommodate diverging orders. In the lovely poem that pushes off from the 23rd Psalm in *Pythagorean Silence,* "Who is my shepherd / invisible" (*ET* 29), Howe writes:

The stress of meaning
dances

in an empty place with clowns
in crowns (*ET* 29)

So the postmodern clowns dance in the empty place of the sovereign. In that absence of authority, "Space steps into breath," widening out the monadic voice. This often subjectless voice "Broods infinity boundless" (*ET* 30), "Slipping / forever / between rupture and rapture" (31). Rupture implies separation, which inevitably yields some kind form; rapture suggests the ecstasy of primordial oneness and the dissolution of anything that might correspond to what Bataille calls the "clear and distinct" knowledge of things.[5] They are not compossible, these states; one cannot consciously step outside of consciousness. Only in the broodings of rapture does the incompossible seem thinkable and then not as experience but as a (romantic) imaginary,[6] an *idea* that can only present itself to experience as death—as the end of experience. Rupture moves the poem toward the articulation of marginalized voices and the consequent disruption of canonical histories; this is "writing as rescue" (Linda Rheinfeld's phrase). Rapture, in contrast, is erotic death-energy and it moves the poem toward silence. This Eros-Thanatos vector returns repeatedly in the poems as a whiteout: snowy landscapes or the white space of the page (the "WHITE FOOLSCAP" section of *The Liberties,* for instance) where the mind wipes out. DuPlessis notes that if Howe's texts were to be expressed as paintings they would be white canvases ("Whowe" 127).

This is Kaplan Harris's point as well, in his noting of Kazimir Malevich's significance to Howe (the famous *White Square on the White Background*, 1918) and that of her husband, David von Schlegell, whose *India Wharf Sculpture* (1972) "creates a large empty space at its center" ("Susan Howe's Art and Poetry" 464). Rapture is the contrary of formal beauty; it lures the poet toward a merge with his or her empirico-transcendental ground.

Pythagorean Silence explores the impossibility of peace without giving up the quest for it. The *silence* of Pythagoras references the practices of the original Pythagoreans,[7] but it also recalls the forced silence of Hippasus, a student of Pythagoras who discovered irrational numbers in the square root of two. The significance of irrational numbers to Howe's poem is that they articulate the concept of an infinite finitude. As a metaphor for the poem-space, the square root of two suggests the paradox of a chaosmos that is both infinite and numerable, in feeling-tone like Kant's mathematical sublime. Only such a *utopos* can answer the demand for radical inclusivity. For peace. Where else might all voices be heard, all achieve their full potential and none be sacrificed for another? Where else might noise in Serres's sense be rendered intelligible in the greater order of things? Puritan history takes as one of its founding moments John Winthrop's "A Modell of Christian Charity," the sermon Winthrop preached on board the *Arbella* in 1630 to a ragged band of colonists. He told them that the new settlement would be as a City on a Hill and a beacon to the world. Howe tropes on the City as a "Mystical gaiety" (*Pythagorean Silence, ET* 62), an "Open," "a vast / zero," "an idea an Ideal" (31). The "infinite city" of "irrational dimensions" (62) is an anti-image of the poet's search for peace because only such an unimaginable place could accommodate incompossible worlds in which no lion goes hungry and no lamb gets eaten. The Pound/Olson polis is *exemplary* and, in this respect, still in the Winthrop line of thinkable human communities. In Pound's *Pisan Cantos*, it is the fabled city of Dioce, "in the mind indestructible"[8] despite the failure of Italian fascism; in Olson's *Causal Mythology*, it is still the City on a Hill.[9] Howe's polis is unthinkable. The finite mind experiences such a concept as a whiteout and an overwhelming of the cogito to the point of death. If Olson's battle is to cut the Western male ego down to size, thus to check its ravenous devouring of things, perhaps Howe's is to prevent the decentered voice from disappearing entirely in the infinity of potential relations and incompossible trajectories that haunt her poems.[10] As Rachel Back notices, Howe teeters on the verge of disappearance into subjectless verbs, decontextuated noun phrases, and visual strategies in which lines are arranged at crisscrossing angles all over the page, often overwriting one another. In *Pythagorean Silence*, Howe writes, "Perspectives enter // and disappear" (*ET* 63); in *Thorow,* "The Adirondacks *occupied* me" (*S* 40, original emphasis).

Susan Howe's Melville

In her "Language Poetry and the Lyric Subject," Marjorie Perloff emphasizes the "dismissal of 'voice'" as a first tenet of language poetry (405), voice here to be understood as signaling "self-presence, and authenticity" (406). On this revision of the humanist subject and realist epistemology, she writes, language poets and poststructuralist philosophers converged in the late 1960s and '70s (407). However, Perloff goes on to critique what was then announced as the death of the subject, pointing out that Howe's stylistic signature (like that of other language poets) is "as unique and 'personal' as any we have in poetry today" (431). Perloff concludes that "what is different [twenty years after the initial polemics of language poetry] is not expressivity or subjectivity as such but the authority ascribed to the speaking voice" (432). This is the point from which I would like to begin a discussion of Howe's refiguring of figure and hence of figure and ground.

Howe writes the figure (voice, persona) as a finite infinitude. Figure emerges from "love's infolding"; the phrase positions agency in the selections one makes and the affinities one cultivates. The persona that emerges from interaction with the givens of the body and its environs is finite because it takes the form of a trajectory that cannot be undone (Giorgio Agamben's "irreparable"[11] comes to mind). This is Creeley's discovery too. Heraclitean time means that the steps a person takes are irrevocable. Every step into the future is simultaneously a self-creative act that brings foot and ground into being at the same moment. The path of the subject is utterly finite and unique. However, the component elements of the figure are common, infinitely combinable, and haunted by the pastness from which they come. Howe's visual poems illustrate this idea formally. On one hand, they are impossible to paraphrase. The complicated relations of sound and sense as well as the overwriting of one line by another are such that the poem cannot be gathered into a concept or reduced to a narrative. Like Bartleby, the poems neither confirm nor deny whatever exegetical tales writer or reader may spin about them. And like Billy Budd's stutter, each is *performatively* rather than conceptually distinctive. The stutter does not change the semantic content of Billy's words but does mark his particular way of saying them. Howe's poemscape has a very particular form that is unlike that of any of its materials. On the white space of the page, the poem must lie exactly this way and no other. So as Perloff says, Howe's signature is distinctive. At the same time, the potential of the words, phrases, sounds, and associations to combine into various meanings is virtually unlimited. And of course these materials are quite common, often drawn from publicly available sources.

Let me illustrate what this can mean for identity and voice with a detour through Howe's *Melville's Marginalia,* which features, among other figures, the Irish poet James Clarence Mangan and Melville's Bartleby. *Melville's Marginalia* draws Howe and her readers into a genealogy that quickly turns rhizomatic. In the prose passages that front the poem, Howe tells of finding Wilson Walker Cowen's two volumes of Melville's collected marginalia by chance in the Temple University Library (*NM* 89). This finding inspired a project in which Howe set out to track Melville's reading: "one way to write about a loved author," she says, is "to follow what trails he follows through words of others" (92). But Cowen's collection offers no easy trail because every annotated fragment leads to a different constellation of authors and so on out endlessly. Howe picks her way through this textual labyrinth with chance and affinity leading. "I began to write Melville's Marginalia by pulling a phrase, sometimes just a word or a name, at random from Cowen's alphabetically arranged Melville's Marginalia and letting that lead me by free association to each separate poem in the series" (105), she says. Affinity takes her to James Clarence Mangan, an enigmatic figure Howe reads as a prototype of Bartleby.

A Dubliner, Mangan is usually treated as a minor Irish poet best known for his rendition of nationalist Irish ballads and the melancholic life of the *poète maudit.* According to existing biographies, he was forced by family penury to work as a scrivener at a young age, first in a law office and then for the Irish Land Ordnance Survey. Later he would become an assistant cataloguer at Trinity College Library. He was a regular contributor of poetry and prose to various magazines, including the *Dublin University Magazine,* the *Dublin Penny Journal,* and *The Nation,* the latter an outlet for the nationalist Young Ireland Movement. The later years of his short life (1803–1853) seem to have been clouded by poverty and addiction, although whether to opium, alcohol, or both is not entirely clear. His early death has been attributed to poverty, alcoholism, and malnutrition. Although Mangan's poems appeared regularly in magazines, the only collection published during his lifetime was the *Anthologia Germanica* (1845), which included translations from Schiller, Goethe, and Heine. A collection published in 1859 by his editor John Mitchel includes the "Irish Anthology" as well as sections called "Apocrypha" and "Miscellaneous." D. J. O'Donoghue, a biographer and editor, published *Life and Writings* in 1897 and *Prose Writings* in 1904.[12]

Known in his time for the Irish poems, and constructed by Mitchel as a patriot and rebel, Mangan often presented himself in print as a polyglot translator. James Kilroy writes that he was fluent in German and that he tutored in that language. He was "reportedly educated" in Latin, French, and Italian (*James Clarence Mangan* 28), but this biographer finds it unlikely that he knew the other languages he pretended to translate, such as Welsh, Frisian, Bohemian, Danish, Arabic, Turkish, or Persian (Kilroy, *James Clarence Mangan* 28). His Irish poems were apparently composed from existing prose translations of the Gaelic. Two more points of note: Mangan's prose writings are notable for a kind of wild humor and inability to resist a pun however inappropriate, a point on which he has been compared to Poe. This point of style serves to render the tone of the poems more complex. The reader has to ask whether Mangan is serious or not, whether he is a bad poet or a skilled parodist. Second point: Mangan left an unfinished autobiography in which he mythologizes his life, thereby deepening the mystery surrounding him and blurring the lines between fact and fiction. In a particularly notorious passage he describes the family home as a hovel without doors or windows, one of "the dismalest domiciles . . . of any city in Europe" (*Autobiography* 19). He also claims to have been forced to share a bed with a leper when hospitalized as a youth (21). Kilroy, editor of this *Autobiography,* writes that "as a source of information on the poet's life, the *Autobiography* is of dubious reliability; none of Mangan's critics believes that hospital conditions in Dublin could be so primitive that he would have to share a bed with a leper. But the incident symbolizes his plight: the 'actual leprosy' is distinct from the poet's malady—less hideous but more destructive to his mental constitution" (Kilroy, *James Clarence Mangan* 7). Kilroy refers to Mangan's sense of injured genius, tied to a life of drudgery ill-suited to his temperament or abilities. In a remark that Howe quotes, James Meechan, another commentator, says of the hovel story: "[*This is purely imaginary; and when I told Mangan that I did not think it a faithful picture, he told me he dreamt it.*]" (qtd. in Howe, *Melville's Marginalia, NM* 97 original emphasis).

This thumbnail sketch indicates some of the difficulties in tracking a figure like Mangan. First, the multiple biographies lead to rumor in one direction and the history of Irish nationalism in another. Mangan's own account of himself is not only apocryphal but also trails off in midsentence after only a few chapters. David Lloyd's assessment of early biographical stories of Mangan, like Mitchel's introduction to the first collection of poems, is that Mangan was *constructed* by others as a type of Ireland by ignoring evidence to the contrary in his work. Commenting on Mitchel's depiction of Mangan as a rebel and Irish patriot, Lloyd writes that "the duality ascribed to Mangan, between his shabby outer life and inner and higher life of his spirit, 'one well known to the Muses, the other to the police' . . . is explicitly an image of an Ireland outwardly oppressed but secretly, spiritually, alive, 'for his history and fate were indeed a type and shadow of the land he loved so well'" (*Nationalism and Minor Literature* 32). Lloyd finds a similar pattern in Father C. P. Meehan's biographical accompaniment to *Poets and Poetry of Munster* (1884): "Here, however, Mangan's degradation is posed against his depiction as a gentle and amiable sinner striving to keep within the folds of the faith" (*Nationalism and Minor Literature* 32). Lloyd's thesis is that the Young Ireland Movement sought to achieve a national identity that would unite the Irish against the British through cultural contrivance because, as a colonized society, it lacked economic independence and historical continuity. Irish unity, however, was a piece of myth-making in a country that had already lost the Gaelic to English and its economic independence to the British Empire (*Nationalism and Minor Literature* 62). Mangan's sufferings, according to this reading, were typified as the sufferings of Ireland.

What Lloyd's study shows is that Mangan's biography is embedded in the history of his era and the interests of his biographers; if we pursue the figure, we end up with the ground and vice versa. Mangan's life is particularly well suited to show that the effect of genealogical investigation is to uncover a rhizome in Deleuze's sense of the term. From biographical events, the roots spread out to fictionalized accounts of family life, the interested memoirs of friends and editors, and from there inevitably to the Young Ireland Movement and the history of British-Irish relations. Mangan is the "Man in the Cloak"[13]; one of his sartorial eccentricities,[14] the cloak is also a metaphor for an identity that inhered *in* the various layers of his life and writing rather than *under* them. The harder we look for Mangan, the more we seek the authentic kernel of personality under the various narratives that form his "cloak," the more impenetrable the cloak seems to get. So it is with Howe's project of tracking Melville through his readings: the trail of the marginalia leads centrifugally away from Melville, so that "Melville" suddenly becomes the inflection or modalizing of a large territory.

In the context of British imperialism and Irish nationalism, the effort to establish Mangan as an Irish original is a reach for legitimacy. This circles me back to Perloff's comment that it is the "authority ascribed to the speaking voice" ("Language Poetry" 432) that is at issue in the decentered voice, not uniqueness of expression, which can be very well achieved without centering. Lloyd writes that Irish orientalists tried to find links between Gaelic and Persian or Arabic, which would place the Irish at the "remote origins of mankind" (*Nationalism and Minor Literature* 123). In a remark that Howe alludes to, Mangan responded to Charles Vallancy's research on the etymological ties between Irish and Oriental cultures with the comment that "according to Vallancy every Irishman is an Arab" (Lloyd, *Nationalism and Minor Literature* 123; Howe, *NM* 135). In matters of culture, the origin promises legitimacy. This is where Matthew Arnold comes in. Arnold's *Lectures and Essays* are heavily annotated in Cohen's *Marginalia,* meaning that he was a source for Melville. But the essays are of particular significance to Mangan studies because Arnold's was an evaluative criticism that had as its aim "to learn and propagate the best that is known and thought in the world, and thus to establish a current of fresh and true ideas" (Arnold, *Essays* 37). Arnold's push in "The Function of Criticism at the Present Time" is to argue for disinterested aesthetic judgment rather than judgment that pushes an extraliterary cause. By this criterion, Irish nationalist literature is minor and of merely local interest in relation to the major works of the British canon, which have universal significance. In his "On the Study of Celtic Literature," Arnold argues that the Celt complements the Anglo-Saxon as the female the male. The Celt is the sentimental, feminine member of the proposed union, unable to produce a sustained work of art and with no head for facts, whereas the Anglo-Saxon is the self-disciplined, entrepreneurial, energetic masculine type. The assimilation of the two races, Arnold thinks, would solve the difficulty of ruling Ireland and as well produce a synthesis that would return the race to its original wholeness in a common Indo-Aryan root. By Arnold's standards, Mangan is a dismissible poet; by the measure implied by Mangan's practice, Arnold's assumptions about art, authorship, and originality rest on an unexamined humanism that, in contemporary language rather than Arnold's, essentializes the British point of view.

Howe brings Arnold into proximity with Mangan in three visual poems. The first begins with the lines

So baneful
He could not storm the alphabet of art
bête x [Bestial ?]
and social weakness (*NM* 96)

Beneath these lines is a comment of Arnold's on a reviewer, which by extension could have applied to Mangan:

A style so bent on effect and the expense of soul
so far from classic truth and grace
must surely be said to have the note of
PROVINCIALITY (*NM* 96)

The implication is that the "he" of line two is too intellectually weak to make art. The word "bête" carries the French "stupid" as well as "beast," while "bestial," partitioned off in square brackets, hints of beastlike behaviors, perhaps immoral closeted practices that need to be enclosed. The reader may here insert Mangan's alcoholism or rumored opium addiction or the shame of his poverty. Stupidity, childlikeness, immorality—the imperial attitude that colonized peoples were more primitive than the colonizers and therefore in need of the paternalistic care accorded to children and animals—comes in here. Vertically, on the left-hand side of the poem, in capitals and separated from the poem by a line, is the word "NONCOMPATIBLES." The word resonates with an essay titled "Incompatibles" by Arnold in his Irish *Essays,* but here it suggests a "catastrophe of bifurcation"[15] between Arnold and Mangan.

With the Arnold references, Howe lets two incompatible aesthetics collide, one based on the humanist subject and the other on a dynamic, hybrid subject-function. This is where many have found in Howe a poetics of liberation from Arnoldian humanism. But there is something wrong with the picture. The rhizomelike subject-function anticipated in the figure of Mangan is incompossible with the margin-center paradigm that Mangan equally suggests. This, I think, is a central paradox of Howe's work, and it bears on the tragic tenor of it. Consider this poem from *Melville's Marginalia:*

Morality I will not thought
Along the glistening shore
we tramp to leave their print
Melville the source hunter
hawking corollaries for coal
foraging for fuel in copses
What a semi-barbarous ballad
Saw that the saw sawed thought
Skipping oblivion for forfeit
Wide universe no matter what
that their thought may go out
the margin s mile of welcome (*NM* 116)

The indeterminacy of the syntax and lack of punctuation in the first line leaves open the relationship among morality, will, and thought. The line might be read as "Morality I will, not thought," suggesting some decision for "morality" as opposed to whatever "thought" may bring up. Or it could be read as "Morality I will not," suggesting that the speaker would choose thought over morality or that morality means restraining the will ("I will not"). The first person singular balances indecisively between morality and thought. What is the morality of the margin? Its sheltering of disappeared and unrewarded poets like Mangan? Its potentiality for rescue? In this poem, it opens onto the sea and the "wide universe," bringing up thoughts of the *un*boundaried and sublime. But if the sublime was for Kant the confirmation of ethical freedom and human dignity, it has come to mean for the postmodern writer the failure of representation to adequately hold onto identities that melt into infinitized finitudes (the self as a network that can be traced outward endlessly).[16] The imagination balks at the indeterminacy of a figure like Mangan whose genealogy stretches across the globe (but is this not the case with everyone?). Confronted by a moving rhizome, the will and judgment may be stymied for action. In other words, the sublime registers as an aporia at the experiential level because it suspends practical agency. How is one to make a judgment or take action if every entity one encounters, and every position one might take, dissolves into endless, competing trajectories—routes of evanescence.

This is where Howe's margin-center paradigm cuts across the rhizome. Inclusivity is far easier to conceptualize than to actually imagine or to perform. Howe's foraging in Melville's foragings turns up Mangan's "The Saw-Mill," the "semi-barbarous ballad" of line seven. In this "mourne-ful ditty" of Mangan's, the speaker is lulled into a reverie by the buzz of a sawmill and imagines that the tree being sawed into planks speaks to him. The tree, whose life the saw has taken, is to become a coffin, foreshadowing of course the speaker's death. Here is a sample:

Anon the sound of the waters grew
  To a Mourne-ful ditty,
And the song of the tree that the saw sawed through,
Disturbed my spirit with pity,
                    Began to subdue
My spirit with tenderest pity!

. . . .

In a few days more, most Lonely One!
Shall I, as a narrow ark, veil
Thine eyes from the glare of the world and sun
'Mong the urns in yonder dark vale,
                    In the cold and dun
Recesses of yonder vale!

"For this grieve not! Thou knowest what thanks
  The Weary-souled and Meek owe
To Death!"—I woke, and heard four planks
  Fall down with a saddening echo.
                    I heard four planks
Fall down with a hollow echo. (Mangan, *Poems* 443–44)

In Arnold's terms, the poem is a disaster. The density of the internal rhyme, the strained conceit, the sentimentality of the tree's complaint, the awkward punning in verse two where the poet writes that he "saw the saw in the Sawmill" (443) combine to make the "semi-barbarous ballad" just the kind of versifying that earned Mangan his minor status. The poem stands as a prime example of "noise" in relation to the Arnoldian criteria of good taste and serious thought, and it is therefore a work of the margin.

Perhaps it is a masterpiece of the margin. The poem reminds us that the only "unboundedness" that consciousness can lay hold of is its own negation, its death. Mangan's sawmill poem works in much the same way as do Poe's internally rhymed ballads like "The Raven," "Leonore," or "The Bells." The assonance strains against the punctuation and syntax to blunt the meaning; try reading the first verse above out loud to hear the pull of the rhyme against the grammar. To my ear, the dominance of sound over sense gestures toward the dissolution of sense. Such a gesture is the closest language can come to imitating a state of nondifference on the other side of consciousness—the mind's Other—and in Mangan's poem that concept tilts toward the idea of insensibility and release from suffering rather than Kantian celebration of an intuited supersensible. In other words, Mangan understood, as did Poe, that death is the limit concept of experience. The thought of the sublime is here sawed off by the empirical interpellation of death between mind and concept and in a manner that parodies romantic deism. In the sawmill poem, nature speaks to the poet, and this, after all, is what the major romantic poets (Wordsworth, arguably Coleridge, Emerson, for example) had wanted to experience: a suturing of the wound of consciousness through integration into the One Divine Life. But the grotesquerie of a talking, weeping tree about to be sawed into planks makes a mockery of communication with nature and emphasizes the difference between humanity and the nonhuman world that it has instrumentalized to meet its needs. In a world of sawmills, a talking tree that complains of its death and threatens to become a "narrow ark" for its human interlocutor confronts us with the obvious fact that dreams of spiritual wholeness and peace have to account for the instrumentalizing of one life by another.

The sawing off of thought in Howe's line "Saw that the saw sawed thought" in the above cited poem underscores the idea that experience cannot accommodate the endless rhizome—that the world in its potentiality to mean and be exceeds our ability to gather it up. And as the sawmill poem implies, the passage from potential to actual may well be reductive and violent. Limit always intervenes to terminate our reception of the chaosmos. All the poet can do is to pick her way through a conflictual time-space field as it opens into the "wide universe." The way that Howe positions her speaker in the "margin s mile" suggests vulnerability: "we tramp" she says, which is to walk, to put the body out there without prosthetics (cars, airplanes, guns, tanks, email, fax, telephone, Internet) so that its smallness shows in relation to the unlimited distance there to be covered. To walk out into the open, unarmed, is perhaps the closest one can come to peace. This is the "impossible hope": "Who is my shepherd / invisible // and outside / shape (sheep) impossible hope // by the still waters" (*Pythagorean Silence, ET* 29).

The indeterminacy in Howe's poems is not simply about cognitive liberation. I have been using the Deleuzean rhizome as a trope more appropriate than those of deconstruction because it suggests proliferation rather than undecidability. But the rhizome does not undo the margin-center model in these poems; rather, it suggests proliferation of the model such that the world is composed of an uncountable number of margins and centers. This has two consequences. First, a multiplication of margins and centers establishes this relationship as both contingent and ubiquitous. It is not just the authoritativeness of official culture that is thus challenged, but also the power differential in any relationship. Consider the interplay of major and minor, dominant and subaltern, in just a few of the relationships represented by Mangan. In relation to Arnold and Shelley, Mangan is a marginal figure, both as a writer and as an Irishman up against British cultural and economic power. Yet as a self-described "Western" poet Mangan is, in relation to the "oriental" poets he pretends to translate, in the dominant position, at least from the Western perspective. Even if we accept that Mangan does indeed parody his position as a translator of "oriental" poems, parody still requires the framework of the margin-center; the parodist cannot step beyond that frame without making the same presumptions (the same cultural appropriations) that he wishes to parody. Distributed throughout the field, the margin-center model offers no innocent position. In a chaosmos where all life forms consume others in order to live, it is impossible to step out of this frame. This is what Mangan's sawmill poem brings out so clearly. Imagine, for a moment, the resolution of Irish-British inequities or the peaceable end of Western orientalizing. Imagine—and why not, because the margins and centers multiply faster than one can parody them—the pacification of gender views, which make their appearance in Howe's poem in the juxtaposition of Percy Shelley's Prometheus (*NM* 120) and Mary Shelley (*NM* 121), who we cannot help but associate with Frankenstein. Percy imagines peace; Mary imagines the will to power in her famous tale of scientific hubris. It is the unavoidability of this instrumentalizing will that Mangan's sawmill poem brings out. We use plants, animals, and other people; if we can see the contingency in these unequal relations we may well succeed in debunking the ideologies that clothe them, but we do not, by that gesture, abolish power differences.

This is where Bartleby comes in. Mangan is the prototype, Howe says, arguing that Melville could have come across him in the *United States Magazine and Literary Review,* which featured a section on "Some Irish Poets" in 1851, two years before writing "Bartleby" (*NM* 107). A thin nonentity, Bartleby installs himself at the center of economic and juridical power, scrivening in a conveyancing office on Wall Street. His astonishing gesture, in the face of power that is completely overwhelming in relation to his own, is to make himself into a creature of preferences rather than assumptions. Obviously outright opposition would have resulted in a confirmation of institutionalized power as effectively as full acquiescence. But Bartleby survives for a time because he inscribes himself at the most vulnerable point of the system. Capital requires predictability; it is based on the assumption that people will act in their "best interests," meaning that they will instrumentalize what they can of the world. This assumption does not hold with Bartleby, and it is relevant that he seems to die of starvation, although with Bartleby all assumptions are suspect. On this point, Mangan and Bartleby uncannily converge. Mangan's biographers tend to agree that he died of malnutrition or some combination of starvation and addiction. I am not suggesting that Mangan deliberately starved himself as his fictional counterpart seems to have done. But the potato famine in Ireland, during which time Mangan died, was exacerbated by British laissez-faire policies that modeled a reductive kind of economics incapable of calculating in empathy, chance, or self-sacrifice as bearing on human behavior. The link between the fictional Bartleby and the real-life Mangan on this point is that Bartleby's self-imposed starvation is readable as an extreme refusal of instrumentalization as such—the same kind of instrumentalization that in the form of economic aggression resulted in the horrors of the Irish famine.

It is worth recalling the extremes lurking in Melville: Olson begins his *Ishmael* with the citation of a true history of cannibalism that he reads as informing Melville's *Moby-Dick.* The story of Bartleby is the flip side: self-starvation rather than the consumption of anything. Bartleby's mild insistence on a preference not to participate in the "triumph of life," as Shelley was to word it, creates a noise in the system—a singularity—and this is why Melville's narrator is so hard put to fit his troublesome clerk into some kind of narrative that makes sense in terms of the order that he, the narrator, understands. When he is unable to draw from Bartleby any confirmation of the rightness of his assumptions he consigns him to the usual places designated by instrumental reason for whatever is inexplicable under its rubric: Bartleby is mad ("'a little deranged,' said I sadly" [Melville, *Selected Tales and Poems* 130]), or he belongs to some higher, spiritual realm (asleep with "kings and counselors" [Melville, *Selected Tales and Poems* 131]) that need not concern a practical man.

Giorgio Agamben's reading of "Bartleby" in *Potentialities*[17] brings out the significance of this story further, and I will trace his argument in this paragraph to better return to the paradox of the margin-center and rhizome models in Howe. Agamben hears Bartleby's "I would prefer not to" as a suspension of will that blocks the passage between absolute and actual potentiality. Absolute potentiality is that in which incompossible worlds may coexist; "ordered potentiality" is that in which compossible existents and relations may come to actuality (*Potentialities* 254–55). (I have discussed the difference as pure versus real potentiality in the Olson essay.) Bartleby, Agamben says, is a response to the question, "Under what conditions can something occur and (that is, at the same time) not occur, be true *no more than not true*?" (260–61). Agamben invokes Leibniz's "Palace of Destinies," an immense pyramid in the mind of God, the apex of which is the best of possible worlds, and the lower layers and base a chorus of lamentation "from everything that could have been otherwise but had to be sacrificed for the present world to be as it is. The best of all possible worlds projects an infinite shadow downward, which sinks lower and lower to the extreme universe—which even celestial beings cannot comprehend—in which nothing is compossible with anything else and nothing can take place" (266). This pyramid is Bartleby's space, Agamben says (the "Egyptian character of the masonry" in Bartleby's final resting place[18]), and it exercises a redemptive operation on the past: "The necessary truth of the tautology 'Sextus-will-go-to-Rome-or-will-not-go-to-Rome' retroactively acts on the past not to make it necessary, but rather to return it to its potential not to be" (267). This operation contrasts with Nietzsche's eternal return, which realigns the will with the past in order to restore agency in the face of determinism: the eternal return "transform[s] every 'thus it was' into a 'thus I willed it'" (267). This is analogous to Bartleby's task of copying the Law, Agamben says, and it still inscribes the "will to power" in the "will to will" (268). Copying thus remains tied to the elimination of incompossibles; it remains sacrificial. When Bartleby gives up copying, he suspends real in favor of absolute potentiality.

To return now to Howe, Agamben's reading can help us see that Bartleby is another trope in a series that includes the blank page, the white foolscap, the snow-covered landscape, or Pythagorean silence. He is the idea of peace in a cannibal cosmos and the logical extension of a figure like Mangan who shows the subject to be an endless series of vanishing perspectives. The other side of the story, however, is the sawmill and the violent reduction of the virtual as it passes into the actual. The cut tree makes a coffin, and suddenly in *Melville's Marginalia* we are adrift with Ishmael in a poem that begins "Coffin th sea" (*NM* 123). The truncated and overwritten words, and the crowded letters in this poem, like so much of Howe's visual work, give form to form itself as a diminishment of possibility in the passage to the actual. The saw cuts off the figure from the potentiality of its past to be or not-be, making its steps into actuality irrevocable and unique. Hence, in Olson's words, "the stain of form across all reality" (*SV* 49). Reflexive consciousness simply cannot be in the world as water in water; at best, it is condemned to figure and ground, and this polarity demands a facing-up to human complicity in the violence of becoming. One of Howe's achievements is to show that the margin-center model cannot be conceived as just a monumental binary, such that the minor or subaltern side of the paradigm can be automatically validated or that the center may be dispersed in a rhizomatic network. Instead, margin and center proliferate rhizomatically, so that all the strata of figure and ground are saturated with power inequities. All creatures, insofar as they exercise the will to live, participate in the cannibalism of the life process. The "stain of form" is blood. The complement to Bartleby is Billy Budd.

The Cannibal Cosmos

At the foundation of the Law is sacrifice (and here again, the dark face of religion). In *The Birth-mark,* citing Captain Vere in Melville's *Billy Budd,* Howe writes: "The heart here, sometimes the feminine in man, is as that piteous woman, and hard though it be, she must here be ruled out" (80). Billy, who "could be a virgin foundling" like Christ, is on the nether side of the Law: he is the Other against which the Law defines itself. On Christ, Howe writes: "We call him Authority Love and Faithfulness. We have little assurance. Brute force will beat the weaker part off. Noise for a time then down" (80). Radical Christology, manifest as antinomianism in Puritan New England, is incompatible with exoteric religions bent on controlling human behaviors through institutionalized morality. In this passage of *The Birth-mark,* Howe places

Thomas Paine's *Rights of Man* alongside Billy Budd, "Lamb of God . . . slain from the beginning," reminding us that Melville begins his narrative with the forced transfer of Billy from the Rights of Man to the Bellipotent, from the ideal to the actual: "Reason will trample on a force field of passionate enunciation" (81). There is a trail to be followed in Howe's writings that reproduces this gesture of ruling out "passionate enunciation." In "Turning," from *The Nonconformist's Memorial,* the disallowing of Mary Magdalene's testimony in the canonical Bible and the overwriting of apostolic uncertainty with canon law suggests the same foreclosure. In the *Eikon Basilike* from the same volume it is the King's death that signposts a shift in world orders, marking the ascendancy of merchant class Puritanism in Britain and the overturning of First Nations tribalism in the New England states. At each of these switch points, there is a momentary, deterritorializing breakdown of order before a quick and fierce reterritorialization. Howe directs her attention to that moment.

Scattering as Behavior toward Risk opens with a quotation from Deuteronomy, William Tyndale's version, that shows us an angry Old Testament Jehovah threatening his people with dispersal throughout the world in retaliation for worshipping false gods. Multiplicity is apparently to be punished by more multiplicity. Scattered, the Israelites lose the protection of organic statehood based on tribal sameness. In strange lands, they risk invisibility or persecution, as they become the Other to various national and ethnic orders. In the Old Testament context, scattering is punishment. The same might be said for Puritan New England, which banished dissenters like Anne Hutchinson to dangerous outlands. Scattering means increased vulnerability. The graphic of the coffin underneath the title of *Scattering* underlines the risk.

To take the stutter as the plot, Billy is all that the Law cannot hear or allow—its constitutive outside. It is to the point that at his execution, a sound like the "freshet-wave of a torrent" comes from the sea and from the sailors assembled to witness the punishment. And when the corpse is let slide, "a strange human murmur was heard, blended now with another inarticulate sound proceeding from certain larger seafowl" (Melville, *Selected Tales and Poems* 370). This semiarticulate murmur, partly inhuman, is quickly displaced by a military drumbeat that orders sound into signal. The "strange human murmur" that briefly makes its appearance at the scene of Billy's death—a brief surfacing of an inarticulate something—is thus quickly suppressed in order to direct behavior *against* risk, rather than toward it. Melville himself makes the connection between Vere's legalism and Puritan order. As Vere announces the events to his crew, "Their captain's announcement was listened to by the throng of standing sailors in a dumbness like that of a seated congregation of believers in hell listening to the clergyman's announcement of his Calvinistic text" (361). In the naval news report that follows the execution, these events are translated into a story intelligible under the Law: an officer is murdered by a sailor plotting mutiny.

In her opening piece, Howe takes a passage from the section of the tale in which Billy is poised for hanging. Here is Melville: "At the same moment it chanced that the vapory fleece hanging low in the East was shot through with a soft glory as of the fleece of the Lamb of God seen in mystical vision, and simultaneously therewith, watched by the wedged mass of upturned faces, Billy ascended; and, ascending, took the full rose of the dawn" (*Selected Tales and Poems* 367). And Howe:

"on a [p<suddenly . . . on a> was shot thro with a   dyed <dyed   a soft]"
(became the vision) (the rea) after Though   [though]That
Fa

But what is envy [but what is envy]
Is envy the bonfire inkling?

Shackles [(shackles)   ] as we were told the . . . [precincts] (*S* 63)

Ma and Quartermain both read this poem as mimetic, with the brackets shackling the "rea" as Billy's shackles bind him.[19] Outside the sets of brackets is the beginnings of a prepositional phrase, "on a" and then an "after." "Though" and "That" sound like the beginning of a qualification. The effect of the bracketed portions is to interrupt what looks like a narrative fragment with fragments of another narrative. Quartermain suggests ("And the Without," *Disjunctive Poetics* 185) that the third line, "Fa" could be read as a musical note or by sound association, any number of words such as "far," "father," or "fate"—the first syllable of a stuttered utterance, perhaps.

The middle two lines of the poem are taken from Melville's description of Claggart's spiritual state. A type of prelapsarian man, Billy's form is "heroic," Melville says (*Selected Tales and Poems* 323). In his heart is "the bonfire" that makes his handsome face luminous. Claggart is Billy's contrary. Like Milton's Satan on first sight of Adam and Eve, Claggart burns with envy and antipathy. Melville writes: "Now envy and antipathy, passions irreconcilable in reason, nevertheless in fact may spring conjoined like Chang and Eng in one birth. Is Envy then such a monster. . . . Something there is in it universally felt to be more shameful than even felonious crime" (323). Claggart suffers these emotions for the same reason as does Satan: "With no power to annul the elemental evil in him, though readily enough he could hide it; apprehending the good, but powerless to be it; a nature like Claggart's, surcharged with energy as such natures almost invariably are, what recourse is left to it but to recoil upon itself and, like the scorpion for which the Creator alone is responsible, act out to the end the part allotted to it" (Melville, *Selected Tales and Poems* 324). Howe's lines pull Claggart into juxtaposition with Billy at this moment of his execution. The line, "Is envy the bonfire inkling," is a collage from Melville, with the word "bonfire," in the passage I've cited above—a descriptor of Billy's good heart—here juxtaposed to the very different burning of Claggart's "envy." This drawing together of Billy and Claggart in a loose, scattered fashion serves to emphasize that both are outside the comprehensible in terms of the Law. The Law can no more punish Claggart's bad heart than it can recognize Billy's good one. Good and evil are not matters for the Law but for a higher court. This is Vere's view—that in times less perilous the case might be referred to the "Admiral." But of course Vere's court is the only one available in this world and the times are always perilous.

If I read Melville right, *Billy Budd* asks some pressing what-if questions. What if we assume with Spinoza that good and evil are perspectives? What if we further assume that no human order can peacefully resolve antithetical positions—that perspective as such is inevitable and just as inevitably bloody? What if the human heart is, as Vere implies, beyond the reach of institutionalized justice? And what if rebellion against those imperfect institutions for a good cause—the promise of the good ship *Rights of Man* on which Billy originally sailed—will produce more institutions that will prove to be equally limited in the justice they can provide and equally unable to accommodate the heart? Howe's repetition of the question, "But what is envy," I hear as insistence, and it is an important question to insist upon—rattling as it does the confines of the brackets and the confines of instrumental reason as well. Melville's point that envy and antipathy may be irrationally yoked is a significant one to make against the Enlightenment hope for rational, good government, not only in the wake of the French and American revolutions but right now as well. What is frightening about Claggart is not that he is bad, but that he may be constitutionally bad. If it is his nature to be antithetical to Billy, as venom is of the nature of the scorpion—if Claggart's way is just a *Tao* that is incompossible with Billy's—then we are brought to face a chaosmos that places each creature in the position of choosing to deny itself or destroy another. Human justice, from this perspective, is a sad compromise.

I think Melville pushes the reader into a corner with *Billy Budd;* either we accept the sacrificial nature of life with Vere, or we have to count on a transcendent world in the mind of God where incompossibles can coexist. Howe's poem is strewn with phrases that emphasize the "Violent order of a world"

(*S* 65) and its punishing, commercial ways. Consider this visual poem from *Scattering as Behavior toward Risk*:.

Loaded into a perfect commonwealth or some idea.

Bisket
Risk
Herring
Salmon
In common.

More imagined it. The best ordered commonwealth
VIZEADMIRALL
Ore Watchwords
That open
Would have no money no private property no markets.
the sayd
Utopian communism comes in pieces while the Narrative wanders.
aboord
Shrowds
Values in a discourse. Potentiality of sound to directly signal
To hull in the night
Meaning
wavering
Cape Rase overpast
wavering
any bruit
Saxon harmony sparrow that lamentation
or muttering
drawling
The overground level
and all that (I) sky
Always cutting out

They do not know what a syllable is

Wading in water
rigor of cold

(*S* 66)

Here Howe invokes “a perfect commonwealth,” referencing Thomas More’s *Utopia.*

More imagined it. The best ordered commonwealth
Would have no money no private property no markets. (*S* 66)

These lines are cut across by words suggesting commerce and war. “Bisket / Risk / Herring / Salmon” write over the words “best ordered.” At an opposing angle, cutting across the same reference to “The best ordered commonwealth,” are the words “VIZE ADMIRAL.” The word “vize” sounds like “vice.” In More’s *Utopia,* the inhabitants value modesty, simple living, economic equality, moderate work for all, and the abolition of property. More’s premise is that humanity can live peacefully if it can rid itself of the impulse to garner respect through competition and display. In *Utopia,* the Claggart factor is not inevitable; all of humanity is potentially compatible. Yet even if we could grant More this, his imagination of things exempts the human species from culpability in the use it makes of other life forms. More takes the human figure as the only measure; Howe cannot do this. She writes the word "brawling" on the vertical in this piece so that it collides with "harmony sparrow that lamentation." The phrase evokes the New Testament Christ's attention to every falling sparrow—a brutal contrast with "brawling." The reference to commerce ("Bisket / Risk / Herring / Salmon") reminds us that New England was first a fishing colony, built on venture capital rather than "Utopian communism." And of course with property comes the need to protect it, whether with fences or with "VIZE ADMIRAL[s]."[20] The next poem fittingly begins with the lines "The protection of sleep / The protection of sheep" (*S* 67).

All these institutions of the modern state—money, property, markets, fences, rules, and so on—are reterritorializations specifically aimed at reducing risk for those the state protects and favors. Scattering, like Billy Budd's stutter, is a best gesture toward an impossible pacification: "In the court of black earth / to be infinite" (*S* 67). Scattering increases the vulnerability of the subject to invasion and to becoming-other. If Ahab is about megalomania, Billy Budd is about sacrificial dissolution of the self. Bartleby suspends these two undesirable options, but then no one "lives [long] without dining" (Melville, *Selected Tales and Poems* 131). To allow every figure its fullness, every space-time field its range of potentialities, would require a radical Christology. The pyramid of incompossible worlds, to return to Agamben for a moment, exists in the mind of God. Only an infinite mind can hold the incompossibles in thought. Only a mind given over to love would want to.

A brief example from *The Birth-mark* will, I hope, bring this radical Christology into the realm of the mundane where it is a limit concept. In her introduction to *The Birth-mark,* Howe writes of growing up with F. O. Matthiessen and Perry Miller in the household as family friends. Matthiessen's omission of Emily Dickinson from his 1941 masterwork, *The American Renaissance,* of course exemplifies exactly the kind of blindness and deafness to voices outside his purview that Howe makes it her task to remedy. As a Harvard scholar and major academic intelligence, Matthiessen wrote from a position of power within his field, and he used it to shape the canon. One need not follow through Howe's painstaking tracking of Dickinson to pass judgment on Matthiessen; the skimpiest and most conventional of feminist critiques will do the job. But Howe does not evoke Matthiessen merely to castigate him or set up a straw man against which to validate her re-reading of classic American literature. Instead, she performs an excavation on Matthiessen that brings out a person more complex than his public face would suggest. A homosexual, Matthiessen "increasingly banished his homosexuality from his public and intellectual life," Howe says, and she reports that at Harvard his circle was aggressively heterosexual. But the private side of Matthiessen comes through in the letters he wrote to his life companion, Russell Cheney. They called each other "Rat" (Cheney) and "Devil" or "Deezie" (Matthiessen). "Dearest Rat . . . 'The splendid untrammeled freedom of love'—that's the essence of it all, right. . . . Our union has no name, no label; in the world it does not exist. It is simply the unpalpable, inexpressible fullness of our lives" (*BM* 13). And then there is this one, quoted like the above in *The Birth-mark:*

> Deezie, [Devil] on the back of your letter this morning was a shopping
> sugar list, and with a flood the actual scene of your life—
> cocoa your being alive there—was all through me. It sort
> cereal of took my breath it was so real—as though I'd
> eggs reached out and touched you
> bread
> salt
> pepper (14)

There is more. Matthiessen's youthful enthusiasm for Shelley and for Melville's marginalia. His carrying of Whitman in his pocket while a student at Cambridge. His suicide—"jumped from a window of the Manger Hotel during the night of March 31, 1950" (*BM* 17). Matthiessen does not long detain Howe. This section in *The Birth-mark* is short. But the effect of it is to complicate our view of this scholar because it forces us to suspend judgment for a moment. When we come back to that task, we may be feeling less certain, less righteous, less ready because Matthiessen has suddenly become more complex. Recall here the disciples' eagerness to punish Judas in Blaser's *Last Supper.*

In *The Liberties,* her poems about Shakespeare's Cordelia and the fictional/historical Stella (Esther Johnson) of Jonathan Swift, Howe evokes the moment in *King Lear* when Lear runs mad:

giggling in a whistling wind
        unbonneted he runs (*ET* 173)

This scene in a poem that restores opacity and dimension to Cordelia and Stella, as opposed to their flatness in canonical literature, offers a powerful image of authority deposed.[21] In the mad scene, Lear is "unbonneted" in every way. He has given up his crown; he has lost his power and his reason too. Only when he has reached this state does he begin, unwittingly, to articulate a different kind of justice. In the "courthouse" of Poor Tom's hovel, he pardons all: "None does offend, none I say." This is exactly the kind of higher court—the court of love, not justice—that is madness in relation to human law. And this, I submit, is the kind of *an-arche* that Bartleby waits for. Radical love, Christological love. In terms of any discourse other than mysticism, antinomianism, or poetry, it does not exist. This is the "irrational dimension" of the City that Howe brings to articulation.

Bartleby goes to the wall rather than give up such a radical *allowing.*

But what about the rest of us? What about Susan Howe? In a passage Howe quotes, Mangan writes:

The world is one vast caravanserai,
Where none may stay,
But where each guest writes on the wall this word,
O MIGHTY LORD! (*NM* 101, original emphasis)

The "caravanserai" holds in a trope the interrelatedness of all the world in one vast procession of life to which all must submit. But the caravan also picks up the trope of the nomadic poet who appears everywhere in Howe's work. In *Melville's Marginalia,* Mangan is a Cain, wandering "whithersoever," a "Pelican of the universe," Howe writes, and then the phrase, "love its own allegory" (*NM* 140). The biblical Cain, bloodied with fratricide, is condemned by God to wander forever; he can build cities, but not live in them. In comparison to Blaser's nomad who comes to feel at home in his wanderings, the poet-Cain is violently marked with the stain of form. I think the nexus of associations around Cain constitutes a poetic response to the problem of the postmodern sublime: the infinitizing of persons and things through linguistic indeterminacy, the consequent failure of representation and the diminishment of real agency. But if the rhizome and network are among the most common of postmodern tropes, it is not just because of converging trends in poststructuralist and postmodern philosophies. The coming of digital communications, the acceleration of transportation, the shrinking of the global village, the emergence of large trading blocks—these clichés of contemporary times—bring the pressure of incompossible aims, histories, and cultural claims to bear on persons and places with new intensity. If Howe's work is saturated with the histories of New England, Ireland, and Old Europe, it is also a formal analogue of the new techno-globe. In this accelerated landscape—

this landscape become verb—the poet who would find peace may end up like Mangan-Cain, without a City in which to dwell. And like Cain, a poet who has come to realize as intensely as does Howe the conflictual nature of the time-space field she inhabits can no longer save her innocence.[22] Hank Lazer has noticed the "personal autobiographical element to [Howe's] revisionist historiography" (*Opposing Poetries* 66), and autobiography places her squarely in the history of the colonizing of New England and the British occupation of Nigeria. As recounted in *Frame Structures* (1995), Howe comes from the more privileged of the middle class as the daughter of a Harvard law professor. If the Irish side is not so well positioned, then we have, as in the story of Mangan, another example of the persistence of the margin-center paradigm: the same person may be marginal from one perspective and more central from another. This paradigm, as Howe shows, is extremely flexible and durable if it is read as a model of power differences in all manner of relationships. In *Frame Structures*, for instance, Howe writes of an Irish grandfather and "younger son" (marginal position) who served the British army in Nigeria (central position) because "in the scheme of colonialism he didn't have many options" (*FS* 11). Margin-center contaminates everyone. If, in the high court of divine madness and Christological love, all are pardoned, in the lower court here on earth, all are guilty.

And so the poet wanders. In poem after poem, the mark of Cain appears on the narrator or the persons of the poem. *Hinge Picture* begins with Old Testament tribalism, where the Israelites "lived promiscuousl / y / in moveable tent / s" (*FS* 34). From there a parade of shadowy, half-articulated figures tramp through the rising and falling of empires: a "homeless tribe / a green-bellied sea" (*FS* 81) in *Cabbage Gardens;* "Rachel weeping for her children" in *Pythagorean Silence* (*ET* 21); a "Ragpicker heroine" in *The Defenestration of Prague* (*ET* 133); Hope Atherton in *Articulations of Sound Forms in Time* (*S*); a nameless walker, "Barefooted and bareheaded / extended in space" (49) in *Thorow* (*S*); Orpheus, Antigone, Tristan and Isolt in *Pierce-Arrow.* And in the last poem of *The Midnight,* Howe writes, "I am still moving" (173).

Pierce-Peirce: Evolutionary Love

Pierce-Arrow

The millennial vision of the world as a dynamic nexus of relations, complex beyond the imagination's capacity to grasp in an image, is itself a strong world image. Pierre Joris comments in his *Nomad Poetics* (2003) that the nomad is a way of inhabiting unmasterably complex geosocial space (39) as well as a view of the self as a manifold (44). During the 1970s and '80s while this picture was still forming in the work of postmodern philosophers and poets, it was generally conceived of as liberating the mind from whatever absolutisms it had managed to retain after modernism. I have argued that Howe's poetry was so received, as a liberation from the exaggerated reality claims of what was left of the humanist tradition. But the other side of the postmodern sublime is the medusa head: all writhing multiplicity, it paralyzes those mesmerized by it, trivializes individual and collective agency, undermines collective identifications and with them the possibility of community building. By the logic of the philosophies of becoming, any act, judgment, or identity will represent a reduction of the potential to mean of a given event, situation, or person. The sublime is *unlivable,* whether it is figured as linguistic indeterminacy or endless empirical becoming, because it is untrue to the actual reductiveness of consciousness and the either/or of the cannibal cosmos as it must be undergone; either lions go hungry or lambs must die. What went amiss in the theory decades was that cognitive liberation was handled as if it would translate into actuality. And when it expectably did not, running aground on historical events like globalization and the democratic deficit as well as perennially conflicting interests, the theory quickly went out of fashion. So the question is how to go on, how not to abandon the complexity of relation and the dynamism that the postmodern offered and yet cultivate a more pragmatic version of agency.

What this means for poetry now is that the postmodern sublime requires modification because it no longer convinces or inspires. The task at hand for the poet is always, ultimately, the Olsonian one of imagining "an actual earth of value," however circuitously. It was also Olson who said that "der weg stirb." In *Souls of the Labadie Tract* (2007), Howe says of her earlier work, "I believed in an American aesthetic of uncertainty" (16). Nowhere does she repudiate this aesthetic—nor do her three most recent books suggest it—but the verb is in the past tense. Her turn to American pragmatism in *Pierce-Arrow* (1999) offers, in my view, a way to go on. Certainly Charles Sanders Peirce qualifies as one of the maligned and underrated philosophers of history, and hence a candidate for rescue in "the margin s mile of welcome" (*NM* 116). But beyond her writing of the poem, Howe seems to have found Peirce's pragmaticism (Peirce's term) congenial. While teaching at SUNY, Buffalo, she offered courses in "Melville and Pragmatism" and "Poetry and Pragmatism," which she team taught with her husband, the pragmatist philosopher, Peter Hare. Pragmatism is congenial to Howe's work in a number of significant ways, and it provides philosophical support for a coming to terms with the twinned aporias of the postmodern sublime and the cannibal cosmos.

I will outline three areas in which I think Peirce's pragmaticism is companionable to Howe's practice before turning to *Pierce-Arrow* (1999) and the more recent books, *The Midnight* (2003) and *Souls of the Labadie Tract* (2007). Peirce is famously a philosopher of triads, which he arranges as firsts, seconds, and thirds. Firstness is cosmic virtuality and precedes any identifiable experience. "Airy-nothingness," Peirce calls it, but if I hear him rightly, this nothingness is the potential of the universe to cohere into somethingness. In contrast, secondness is the world felt as brute fact—as resistant and other but still uncognized. Thirdness is the realm of recognizable experiences and general laws; it weaves the universes together. This is the level at which human creativity manifests itself in the ongoing pursuit of knowledge. Peirce argues both the fallibilism of human knowing and its progress toward deeper truths. This is the basis of his rejection of nominalism. In his view, nominalism supposes some already formed reality (some thing-in-itself) that is inaccessible to the human mind. It thus blocks inquiry by supposing an ultimate unknowability. Peirce leaves room for the unknown but refuses its finality. Because the chaosmos is itself evolving, and because scientific inquiry constantly yields new truths, he finds an ongoing dialectic between the experience of things as given and the "abduction" (inferential reasoning) that can bring about new insights into the nature of things and new general rules. Peirce calls the free play of the mind engaged in abduction "interpretive musement."

Like Whitehead's metaphysics, Peirce's pragmatism is oriented to creativity at all levels of the chaosmos, from the natural world as it evolves through creative accident to "interpretive musement" in the arts and sciences. Emerging out of primordial indefiniteness, form is prospective. Whatever is, is there to be worked upon and superseded. Peirce treats substantives as processes that, through repetition, have become habits and that may, like habits, evolve (Hamner, *American Pragmatism* 108).[23] The realm of firstness—the potentiality of the chaosmos to produce relations and combinations—is in tension with "brute actuality" (the syntheses of the past, Deleuze would say), which reduces the potential as it passes into the actual. Thirdness weaves together the past actuality with its virtual dimension to open the future to new forms. In thirdness, Peirce presents the *disciplined* imagination as it encounters the limits of natural law, its own physiology, and its empirical circumstances. In Peirce's language, the purpose of inquiry is to overcome doubt and establish habit, which he glosses as clear knowledge, or "temporary warranted consensus" (Hamner, *American Pragmatism* 106). Pragmaticism thus encourages unending "interpretive musement" and deferral of ultimate conclusions as does the postmodern sublime, but it also offers a vocabulary for all the historical, genealogical, and personal pressures that bear on and limit actuality.

While allowing for the private play of the mind, Peirce locates agency in close attention to empirical circumstances and communal effort. "Warranted consensus" means that reality issues from communities of inquirers engaged in the various disciplines; "objectivity" means that the individual must put aside personal whim in order to participate in a discourse community.

From this epistemology and ontology, parallel in important ways to Deleuze's transcendental empiricism, comes Peirce's construction of the self, the second area of pragmaticism that I want to identify as of interest in relation to a reading of Howe. Peirce's psychology follows the triadic pattern of his ontology. Firstness is the uncognized feeling of being alive; secondness, the sense of opposition, duality, or exertion; and thirdness is purpose and desire, or what we recognize as conscious thought (Hamner, *American Pragmatism* 114). M. Gail Hamner, in explicating this element of pragmaticism, draws attention to Peirce's metaphor of a bottomless lake in which ideas and percepts are suspended at different depths: "Consciousness is of the same 'substance' as percepts (water) and ideas are percepts unified in the body of the lake. Percepts stem from a continual 'rain' of external experience (our sensory motor systems and the rules of logic guiding perceptual judgments). Although consciousness is of a single substance (water), real differences (ideas) exist at each level, and these affect the activity of and on the lake's surface (the present moment of consciousness)" (114). Hamner writes that the "metaphor of the bottomless lake suggests that the uniqueness of a person lies not in anything substantial, but in the particular relations or assemblages made among substances" (115). Mind and matter are thus polarities of a continuum rather than dualities (an idea that comes up variously in the poetics of all the poets I've assembled here). What Peirce calls "self-control"—the disciplined and purposive attention to some facet of communal inquiry—is the "combinatory engine," Hamner says.

Continuity or "synechism" is a key premise of Peirce's philosophy. It is not that the thinking mind holds the world but that a panpsychic chaosmos holds the thinking mind. "Thought" in this context is not limited to consciousness but suggests, rather, the primacy of "feeling," by which Peirce seems to have in mind the universal potential for relationship. Robert Corrington, in *An Introduction to C. S. Peirce,* comments on this point:

> Rejecting all forms of Cartesian dualism, whether in epistemology, philosophical anthropology, or metaphysics, Peirce developed a conception of the world as a vast intertwined network of signs and generals, punctuated by chance. This growing and internally connected universe moves from the bare continuity of potentiality and possibility to the

> attained continuity of innumerable sign systems. . . . The image here is not so much that of discrete meaning packets bumping into each other, so much as it is that of a growing vine that entwines itself around any organism in its vicinity. . . . Each sign system is like a climbing vine that hooks up with as much living semiotic matter as possible. (211–12)

Here is an image of the cosmic rhizome, with the self implicated in that becoming. As might be expected from Peirce's "synechism," the self is not so much an entity as a "vicinity" (Hamner's term). Synechism involves the theory of infinitesimals or quantities that are greater than zero but less than any imaginable number. The infinitesimals connect monadic points with one another in both time and space so that each entity or punctum has its halo or zone of vagueness where it interfaces with other entities. Corrington suggests that the infinitesimals are prespatial and ontologically unique in Peirce's system. They are "potentia" between nothingness and thirdness (*Introduction* 189). "We cannot find an infinitesimal," he writes, "if by 'find' is meant that we isolate it as an object of inquiry. However, we can feel the pulsations of infinitesimals whenever we see continua grow and, at the same time, allow for diversity" (189). In the "Arisbe" section of *Pierce-Arrow,* Howe writes: "If the present is connected to the past by a series of infinitesimal steps (The Law of Mind) a past cannot be wholly past" (16).

Peirce's vision of evolutionary love is the third area I want to identify as significant for Howe. Evolutionary love or "agapism" is Peirce's alternative to Darwin and to necessitarian views of evolution. Peirce's objection to Darwin is that the latter's account of evolution by chance and natural selection essentializes competition, flattering the minds of an era already disposed toward the "greed philosophy" (*Essential Peirce* 360)—the idea that "progress takes place by virtue of every individual's striving for himself with all his might and trampling his neighbor under foot whenever he gets a chance to do so" (357). It is not at all evident to Peirce, in other words, that self-interest promotes the general good (as market-oriented political economists claimed then and now), or that greed is the most fundamental human emotion. He similarly rejects necessitarianism, which he defines as the attribution of "all progress to an inward necessary principle, or other form of necessity" (359) because, in his view, the facts do not support it (360). Chance and effort, rather than mechanical necessity, collude in the evolution of things in Peirce's view. Although an individual cannot bring about change alone or arbitrarily by willing it, he or she can think and act in a way that maximizes the potentiality of the moment to produce order. This means alertness to the givens of experience and the discourse communities of the times.

Agapism maximizes the shapeliness of the chaosmos at the expense of individual whim.

Peirce bases evolutionary love on a metaphysics that makes the potential for relation and combination a primordial fact of existence. The principle of synechism, Corrington points out, means that "sympathy is not so much a chosen mental stance as it is an ontological structure" (*Introduction* 192) because everything is related to everything else. (The closest parallel idea in Whitehead is that every actual entity positively or negatively prehends every other one in the cosmos.) But whether we accept Peirce's effort to ground evolutionary love in ontology or not—this would mean retying fact and value—this element of his thinking reveals an important point of convergence with Whitehead and Deleuze. As well, "agapism" is congenial to poetry because it emphasizes creativity, cosmic complexity, and the disciplined imagination: the summum bonum of this ethos is the maximization of the development of the Open Whole. What Peirce shows is that this ethos cannot be twisted to mean the infinitization of *individual* wants (and unlimited demand for individual "freedom"), nor need it imply the blind sacrifice of same. The good life, lived in orientation to the Whole, is a creative one in which affectability and attention to the living possibilities of the moment are key capacities. In the context of Howe's work, agapism suggests one possible response to the cannibal cosmos: direct the inevitable sacrifices toward the intrication of the Whole, toward a condition that maximizes the chances of all entities to manifest themselves through participation in the creative advance. In *Poetry and Pragmatism,* Richard Poirier makes a similar point about Emerson and the Emersonian line in American thinking. Poirier points to Emerson's "Circles" as exemplary of this aspect of pragmatism. In "Circles," Emerson's metaphor of ripples spreading outward from a pebble cast in water suggests that each circle is a limit that is to be superseded in order to "refloat the world, to make it less stationary and more transitional, to make descriptions of it correspondingly looser, less technical and more uncertain" (Poirier, *Poetry and Pragmatism* 40), thus to maximize the possibility of new creation. Here Spicer's anti-Emersonian poetics need recalling for the contrast: his eros is a reminder that agape, however finessed, is still sacrificial.

I want to return now to Howe with these three ideas: creativity as a dialectic of the actual and virtual; complexity of the whole as the summum bonum; and the disciplined imagination as a response to the postmodern sublime. In a general way, these Peircean elements are characteristic of all of Howe's poetry. A nonresolving dialectic is evident in the typical alternation of prose and poetry, historical fact and textual indeterminacy and autobiography, as Howe holds these polarities in a rhythm of capture and release

(*Talisman* 166). Her rigorously focused attention to the subject matter of the poems shows a disciplined imagination at work, and the paradox that it illustrates is that the more Howe effaces herself in acts of attention, the more creative and complex her work becomes and the larger the territory she inflects as "Susan Howe." In the recovery of the unstoried past is the potential of the future *and* the possibility for personal development.

An important trope of pragmatism in *Pierce-Arrow* is the double arrow: one of the arrows never arrives; the other has always already reached its destination. In "Arisbe," the arrows come in through Zeno's paradoxes of motion: "Time (take Zeno's flying arrow) sets out in a past we place ourselves in. If the present is connected to the past by a series of infinitesimal steps (The Law of Mind) a past cannot be wholly past" (16). Zeno argued that because an arrow is coextensive with its space at any moment it does not actually move. This paradox depends on taking time as a series of isolated "nows," a view of temporality contrary to that of Peirce's theory of infinitesimals. The infinitesimals suggest that the arrow does indeed move, but that it may never arrive. As Howe's remark suggests, Peircean synechism draws the past into the present so that the past is always arriving. Thus the past is not simply a determinant of the present as brute fact (past syntheses); it is also the stuff of thirdness because it provides the material for new combination. In other words, the infinitesimals bring forward the combinatory complexity of the chaosmos. How, then, does it pass into actuality? How does the arrow arrive?

The question raises another, related paradox of Zeno's about Achilles and the tortoise. Achilles can never win a race with a tortoise if the creature has a head start because Achilles must pass through an infinite number of half distances before catching up (he must run half the distance before running the whole of it, and then half again and so on). Since no one can pass through an infinity of positions, it is impossible for Achilles to win. Modern calculus answers the paradox by saying that the time required to pass the tortoise is finite because the distance between halfway points decreases. This answer, however, begs the question of how an infinity of positions can be occupied by a finite creature. Another contemporary answer is that the paradox conflates two separate, incompatible processes: mathematical counting and physical gesture. I suggest that this dilemma parallels that which haunts the postmodern sublime: how to pluck agency out of indeterminacy. Peirce's response would be that pure potentiality belongs to the future. Cosmic virtuality as manifest in the infinitesimals, the plenum of history, or the realm of firstness is not available as actuality by definition. This is where the *disciplining* of the imagination comes in; the recognition that the universe and the self have a certain pure potentiality to become in no way frees the individual from brute fact or the pressure of history. Evolutionary love implies slow transformation through cooperative action. The parallel with the contemporary response to Zeno is that the infinitesimals are potentialities at a level of life not available as lived experience, just as atoms are not available to the eye. Recall in this context Donald Sherburne's distinction between real versus abstract potential (Olson essay). The postmodern sublime as a recognition of the enormous potential of sign systems to combine, or of content to overspill inherited forms of reality, is incompatible with human experience even though it may energize or even transform the life-world. To recall Olson's temporal scapes, change takes place at different speeds in the different strata of the world. Thinking is one of the fastest of these, wildly outpacing the body's lived time. While there is always the chance of an "eruption" of some kind, like an atomic bomb, a scientific discovery or a new technology, the rhythms of the strata are not transferable. The arrow that has to pass through an infinity of positions will never arrive in human time. To state the obvious: awareness of the indeterminacy of language or the complexity of individual genealogies in no way frees the individual from limit, although these recognitions *may* introduce subtle change over time to collective life.

The second kind of arrow in *Pierce-Arrow* is that of eros, not agape, and it always arrives. Love's arrow belongs to experience. This arrow passes through the heart, and Howe's poems are stained with mourning. In the "Arisbe" section, for instance, Hecuba is one of a long line of women in Howe's poems who mourn loss and exile. In the much longer section, "Leisure of the Theory Class," Howe draws the British Victorians into this drama. Among Peirce's coevals were George Meredith, Algernon Swinburne, and Thomas Peacock. Next to the heightened tone of the *Iliad* as referenced in "Arisbe," this section seems to strike a lighter note in calling on works such as Meredith's *Modern Love* (1862), Swinburne's "Triumph of Time" (1866) and *Tristram of Lyonesse* (1882), or Peacock's *Four Ages of Poetry* (1821), which trope on the theme of love and loss with a world-weary irony or, in the case of Peacock, a sense of belatedness. But I think this section is darker than it seems. Consider the back text. The title is a play on Thorstein Veblen's *Theory of the Leisure Class* (1899), a work that traces the development of the owning classes from tribal cultures into Veblen's own times. Veblen argues that two conditions are necessary to create a leisure class: the predatory habits of war and hunting and relatively easy subsistence to allow for some exemption from labor (25). Veblen hypothesizes that the economic activities of persons can be divided into those that exploit, either through war or the subjugation of nature and other persons, and those that constitute drudgery (27–28). This division of labor implicates gender as well (domestic servitude for women) (28).

All social value, he speculates, accrues to the exploiters. Honor, marked by the acquisition of wealth, signifies, at bottom, successful aggression (29). In another series of equations, Veblen suggests that wealth as the sign of honor is sought for the social approbation it confers (35); that is, property is desirable not primarily for its use value but because it is the basis of social esteem (37). Because esteem is tied to wealth, there is no truly radical challenge to this value system, he suggests; the exploited classes aspire to the positions of those that exploit them (the "habit of pecuniary emulation" [39]). Howe's title for the entire collection of poems, *Pierce-Arrow,* layers this back text of Veblen's with an ironic reference to the luxury automobile of that name, produced in Buffalo, New York, in the 1930s. Now an item for collectors, the car was once among the status symbols of the leisure class.

Veblen's theory of social honor suggests an oblique commentary on the cannibal cosmos, and it colors the literary types that Howe draws into this section. Her transposition of Veblen's title in her "The Leisure of the Theory Class" is a reminder that, in Veblen's schema, the intelligentsia of the Victorian bourgeoisie (and their contemporary counterparts in today's universities) were the inheritors of the priestly caste. The priests served the exploiters rather than the producers. Against this back text, Howe brings in *Modern Love,* Meredith's series about a couple who manipulate and betray each other. The collection references Meredith's own failed first marriage to Mary Ellen Nicolls, widowed daughter of Thomas Peacock. Tensions in the marriage came from Meredith's humble beginnings as the son of a tailor and his poverty in the years before his reputation was established, so the story references the class rivalries Veblen discusses. For a time, the couple was forced to live at the expense of Peacock, Meredith's father-in-law. Mary Ellen left the marriage in the company of Henry Wallis, an artist friend of the couple. Howe writes:

Husband and wife lived
apart (*Modern Love*) she
had wandered about for
some time after running
off with the artist who
painted Peacock's portrait (*PA* 34)

Meredith's comments on love in sonnet XXVI of *Modern Love* are rather more agonized. Love at first flies like an eagle, but once wounded he becomes a serpent. Of this latter unhappy state, fraught with suspicion and jealousy, Meredith writes:

I had the eagle in my bosom erst:
Henceforward with the serpent I am cursed.
I can interpret where the mouth is dumb.
Speak, and I see the side-lie of a truth.
Perchance my heart may pardon you this deed:
But be no coward:—you that made Love bleed,
You must bear all the venom of his tooth! (*Modern Love* 58)

And Howe:

Not look back oh I would
What shall we say person
to person I see the side-lie
We went side by side but
Side-lie this is my breast. (*PA* 35)

Meredith's poems thematize betrayal and loss; his biography layers this theme with class difference. Howe picks up the word "side-lie" from Meredith—the "side-lie" suggesting perhaps the lie that accompanies a truth half told or an evasive comment. What lies to the side of Howe's own series is that "Love's sail is black" (*PA* 54). This latter line comes in a poem about the writing of *Tristram,* presumably Swinburne's version. This story of many variations reinforces the theme of betrayal in Meredith's *Modern Love.* Tristram and Isolde are caught between duty to the social order of the day and their adulterous love for each other (Tristram serves King Mark; Isolde is Mark's Queen). The pair is ultimately betrayed by Iseult of the White Hands, Tristram's wife. Add to these allusions of love gone wrong those of the atrophy of life and love in Swinburne's "Triumph of Time": "Time swift to fasten and swift to sever / Hand from hand, as we stand by the sea" (82). Add as well the allusion to Peacock's *The Four Ages of Poetry,* a prose piece in which Peacock argues the decline of poetry in an age in which skepticism has supplanted emotional investment (Wordsworth is a "morbid dreamer," in Peacock's view [17]).

To put this tangle of references together, Howe's "The Leisure of the Theory Class" touches in Veblen what Peirce would call the "greed philosophy." The juxtaposition of it with material from the *Iliad* in "Arisbe" gestures toward the disheartening human record of war and competition that goes back 2,000 years and beyond. Collaged against these references is love as eros. Inherently unstable and often painful, vulnerable to chance and time, eros belongs to the world experienced as resistance or secondness. In the human record, eros dominates agape. Howe takes the thought home in her final section titled "Rückenfigur." This series of poems is given over to figures from myth and literature who have loved and lost: Tristram and Isolde, Orpheus and Eurydice, Antigone, and Prometheus, the latter torn by the "vulture passions" (*PA* 141). In an essay on *Pierce-Arrow* that features the "Rückenfigur" section, Peter Nicholls explains that this art-historical term refers to "staffage in painting which turns away from the viewer" ("'Pastness of Landscape'" 448). Often used in reference to the work of Kaspar David Friedrich, it is a device that makes the landscape seem "an interiorized self-portrait of the artist" with the effect of creating in the viewer "a curious sense of belatedness and estrangement" (449). The viewer of the painting sees what the figure in the painting has already internalized, but without access to the face of the latter. In Nicholls's analysis, taken from art historian Joseph Leo Koerner, the "Rückenfigur" suggests that "experience is constituted retrospectively, as always only a landscape of memory" (449). The "pastness of landscape" in Howe's phrasing (*PA* 133) would thus be a component of the existential given. The individual is *always* in a condition of loss, if not through betrayal or circumstance, then through time. If the experienced "landscape" is the past constructed in memory, then like Spicer's Alice, we are all in Wonderland, always too big or too small to get through the gate to the little garden we long for. In Peircean terms, the past brought into "interpretive musement" belongs to the future, not to present experience. The elegiac tone of *Pierce-Arrow* pays tribute to the longing of the individual who may look but not possess.

I have said that Peirce's pragmaticism refers personal loss to the future of the Open Whole, but not in a way that belittles suffering. Howe's poetry acknowledges the Peircean arrow that never arrives—that points toward the future—but mourns the arrow that passes through the heart. Like a rebus, the last lines of *Pierce-Arrow* hold the two kinds of arrow in proximity:

Lyricist come veil come lure
echo remnant sentence spar
never never form wherefor
Wait some recognition you
Lyric over us love unclothe
Never forever whoso move (144)

I read these lines backward, taking the last one first. Eros never rings twice. From the perspective of the individual, love's arrow means the continual fall out of potentiality into the actual until death terminates further possibilities. The "whoso move" of Howe's last line may be linked with either "never" or "forever," as in "never whoso move" or "forever whoso move." This rebus of a phrase brings never and forever together in the same textual space as "move," where "move" has both physical and emotional connotations: whoso(ever) never moves/may never be moved; whoso(ever) forever moves/may forever be moved. At the individual level, "never" and "forever" suggest absolute loss; at the cosmic level, these resonant words invite "interpretive musement" on the eternal return. There is no other way to move forward, nothing that moves us more, and nothing that never moves but change itself. ("What does not change / is the will to change," to recall Olson.) Beauty veils the sacrificial nature of the world, including the "pastness of landscape" ("echo remnant sentence spar"). This is the lyricist's veil, the veil of Maya, Nietzsche would say—the illusion of form in a chaosmos that is, in its deep structure, a becoming. It is typical of Howe to combine elegy, which attaches to the irreparability of life, with a determination to "dwell in possibility."

Epilogue: *The Midnight* and *Souls of the Labadie Tract*

I do not think that Howe's later books bring forward a new poetic, but they make more evident the rhythm of her work as it swings between capture and release. In *The Midnight* Howe defines "relational space" as that which is "alive with something from somewhere else" (58), and this is an apt description of poems that are all *form* from one point of view and all *content* from another. Range and indeterminacy of material pull against idiosyncrasy of inflection: however far the associational logic seems to run, the field of the poem always *takes place.* Containment is as significant an element as associational drift. Consider the fabric camlet, featured in a poem about an eighteenth-century New England bed hanging. Camlet is made of goat hair or, alternatively, camel hair and silk. It was produced in Brussels and England in the eighteenth century, but it was originally an Arabian fabric. (So was fustian, a weave with cotton warp and linen weft, so named for El-Fustat, a suburb of Cairo where it originated before becoming a fabric associated with coarse worker's clothing.) The reference to Arabia, buried in the history of the fabric, resurfaces in a later poem that includes the words, "Rookh" and "ARABY." "Rookh" brings in Lallah Rookh, a figure out of British orientalism of the nineteenth century. Francis John Wyburg's painting *Lallah Rookh and Her Persian Slave,* is typical of the exoticization of the Middle East in this tradition. As well, there is "Lalla Rookh: an oriental romance," a poem by Thomas Moore (1779–1852), in the same vein. A third association is that of a circus elephant that performed in the United States in the 1860s; this Lallah could stand on her head and walk a tightrope. The name thus evokes an orientalism that, in the context of Howe's oeuvre, recalls Mangan and Dublin as well as homegrown American exotica. The word "ARABY" reinforces these associations because it draws in James Joyce's short story of that title, a story about a young boy who wants to meet his sweetheart at a bazaar and is prevented from doing so by circumstances arising from his father's indifference to the request. In these associations, what seems to be near (a New England bed hanging made of camlet) turns out to be far (Arabia); and what seems to be far ("Araby") turns out to be near. The singular perspective apparently missing with the radical decentering of voice is there in the localizing of the self as vicinity. As Howe says in *The Midnight,* "I go in quest of my inheritance" (146).

I see the same rhythm in *Souls of the Labadie Tract.* In the "Personal Narrative" that introduces this collection, Howe writes:

> If I were to read aloud a passage from a poem of your choice, to an audience of judges in sympathy with surrounding library ture, [*sic*] and they were to experience its lexical inscape as an offshoot of Anglo-American modernism in typographical format, it might be possible to release our great great grandparents, beginning at the greatest distance from a common mouth, eternally belated, some coming home through dark ages, others nearer to early modern, multitudes of them meeting first to constitute certain main branches of etymologies, so all along there are new sources, some running directly contrary to others, and yet all meet at last, clothed in robes of glory, offering maps of languages, some with shining tones. (18–19)

This passage really gathers Howe's project. The rescue of the past (the "release [of] our great great grandparents") enriches the present with potentiality ("maps of languages, some with shining tones") that feeds the future ("robes of glory"). The more past that can be uncovered (the more disciplined the imagination), the more of a plenum it is as opposed to a few official narratives, the richer the possibilities for the future. This is evolutionary love in action: the disciplined imagination in the service of the chaosmos.

Souls of the Labadie Tract is composed of six sections: "*Errand,*" "Personal Narrative," "Souls of the Labadie Tract," another "*Errand,*" "118 Westerly Terrace," and "Fragment of the Wedding Dress of Sarah Pierpont Edwards" (original emphasis). The first "Errand" is that of Jonathan Edwards, the title referencing Perry Miller's recovery of the Puritan project in his *Errand into the Wilderness* (1964). What engages Howe, and provides a bridge between *The Midnight* and *Souls,* are Edwards's meditative notes to himself, characteristically pinned to his coat in the process of his walks. In *The Midnight,* Howe records the fact that Edwards wrote on the back of bills or other scraps of paper; here it is the notes he used to remind himself of ideas that came to him while traveling. It was Edwards's errand to settle the wilderness, but of course he is most interesting when the wilderness unsettles him. Edwards was fascinated by nature, and it shows in his *Images or Shadows of Divine Things. Images* brings out a side of Edwards other than the theologian or the orator of "Sinners in the Hands of an Angry God"; it shows a man capable of entrancement over the webwork of spiders (can they fly? how do they move from place to place?) to the point where spiders seem more interesting than whatever they were to be symbols of. Yet I think it is the structure of allegory that Howe lifts from Edwards—the "images and shadows" that hover around the things. This is "relational space" fraught with a "somewhere else."

"Errand" establishes a lineage that runs from Edwards through to Wallace Stevens and Howe herself and includes the Labadists, a pietist sect that settled in Maryland in the eighteenth century. The Labadie, as Howe explains in the prose preface to this section, were followers of Jean de Labadie, a renegade priest who started the sect in the seventeenth century. From 1684 to 1722, the Labadists inhabited a colony in Maryland consisting of 750 acres under the leadership of two of their elders, Jasper Daubers and Peter Shuyter. They called it New Bohemia. In Howe's words, "Labadists believed in, among other things, the necessity of inner illumination, diligence and contemplative reflection. Marriage was renounced. They held all property in common (including children) and supported themselves by manual labor and commerce" (*SLT* 24). The little poems that make up the sequence of "Souls," each one on its separate page, reference the emblem book, a popular genre in the sixteenth and seventeenth centuries and allegorical in structure like Edwards's *Images. Alciato's Book of Emblems,* published in 1531, consists of 212 Latin emblems or symbolical engravings with poems. Howe's version of the emblem book displaces the traditional, metaphysical circuit between material sign and spiritual meaning but keeps the double structure:

Anti-masque of five senses
arms and legs from Alciato
Naked emblemata for pack-

saddle with contiguous *volte-*
face in this sense ownerless (*SLT* 34)

This little poem deranges the image, seemingly leaving arms and legs akimbo while drawing attention to the "volte-/face." In a traditional emblem, the about-face or two-sidedness of it might have been the sensual image and the spiritual concept it was meant to illustrate. Here that relationship is overturned in another kind of "volte face" or "anti-masque." In this sense the poem is "ownerless" and the emblemata naked because they lack an anchoring concept. This is what happens to Edwards's mediations on nature as well when his very fine eye is drawn so deeply into the image that the guiding concept is shaken by the particularity of the thing seen. But Howe retains the double-sided structure of allegory in these poems to depict a relation between past and present. Here is the next poem in the series:

Door of surrender in the old
black letter picture in Alciat
I'd have gone in for you as I

am out and you're forever in
Oh—but of course of course (*SLT* 35).

This poem re-spatializes the up and down, the earth and sky of the metaphysical tradition, with a secular-horizontal "in" and "out," "then" and "now." It is the souls of the Labadie that Howe addresses in this series—the realm of the dead. In many of the poems they seem to speak to her directly and she to them. The series is uncharacteristically replete with personal pronouns (I, you, we), as if the poet were engaged in an intimate conversation with the dead—a séance. As if a door had swung open between past and present.

we're the past—we're too
close—to covet—you're
not to be afraid—breathe (*SLT* 39)

And another such "hinge picture":

Oh I see—I have to see
you fresh as those rough
streams are as power is (*SLT* 50)

In lines like these, who is speaking? Is it the Labadie? the poet? The Foucauldian answer that might have served several decades ago (language is speaking) is not wrong, but it does not hold the emotional intensity of this *conversation* with ghosts that is alive with presencings ("I have to see / you").

Verbal echoes so many ghost
poets I think of you as wild
and fugitive—"Stop awhile" (*SLT* 58)

Howe empties herself out so the dead can speak—"so many ghost / poets"—a strategy that reverses Spicer's dictation. Spicer's Orphic task is to rescue the beloved from a ghost-ridden medium—to force that medium to house and index the living. Howe welcomes the dead into the realm of the living because she accepts (as her poetry performs) the derivative nature of the singular. Through agape, she makes a kind of peace with the cannibal cosmos as Spicer never did. So she writes:

. . . beauty is what *is*
What is said and what this
it—it in itself insistent *is.* (*SLT* 97, original emphasis)

The "it in itself insistent," the beautiful and the sublime (form *and* its becoming-other) are brought together in proximate space. If ever a *utopos* could be precisely conceived it is here, in the finitude of the infinite and the infinite of the finite. Beauty "is what *is*"; "what is" is a *Tao.*

Nothing saves us from mourning, but evolutionary love urges "interpretive musement" on our future prospects. The last section of *Souls,* on the wedding dress of Sarah Edwards, is a visual series in which lines are skewed on the page, overwriting each other, and words are blanked out. The first poem in the series, placed opposite a visual reproduction of Sarah's dress, is another rebus. The words that are complete are "the past," "whose," "wing," "of," "becoming," "Soul," "winter," "walker," "snow," "lead," and "it" (*SLT* 113). The poem condenses the whole of Howe's project: her fascination with the past, the wings of poetry, the journey of the soul, the winter landscapes and whiteouts, and the walkers through those endless spaces. Then there are demiwords: "metam(orphosis)," "convi(ction) or convi(vial)?;" "ble," bleak? or blé, the germ of something?; [s]lant, as in a truth to be told; "tha," the demonstrative "that" or the comparative "than" or the beginning of "thank"; and "at," someplace to be, surely. Are these the sawed-off potentials of the past or the undone business of the future? They are, of course, in-between, and that is where everything happens.

Afterwords

These are difficult times for the arts. Globalization has meant an intensification of the divide between the political process and real (read private) decision making. The result is reduced agency for most of us and a crisis of credibility for the arts, whether the aim is to console, inspire, or critique. Visionary poiesis seems a travesty and ideology critique stalls on the disconnect between what one knows and what one can do about it. One lesson of the 1960s and the theory decades that followed is that market cultures absorb critique well, and they can survive the exposure of their ideological content. The six poets I have gathered here offer no consolation for this state of affairs, but there is much in their work that is prospective as method and measure. Measure says this is what we are doing; this is what we can do. It is the searching out of real versus pure potentiality through engagement of the affections and the embodiment of the intellect in its scapes. In making measure, projective verse is *initial* (Olson's "work of the morning"); it lays out emplacedness as a condition that is also a process and thus in need of constant revision. The territory shifts; the maps have to be redrawn. Here is a summary.

The Cartographic Method

(i) Document plus affect: these are the coordinates of Olson's map. Not self-expression, not pseudo-scientific objectivity, and not chronic skepticism over the fallibility of perception, but acute attention and response to that which is the case in as many dimensions as the poet can manage. So Olson responds to Heisenberg's Uncertainty Principle as negative capability: that is a personal take on a public fact that will stand up until the fact is superseded. "We are after 'meaning and thing,'" Blaser writes in "Particles," "and the intensity of that activity is what is at stake" (*Fire* 24).

(ii) Method is ethos. When the human actor behaves so as to articulate more, rather than less, of his or her ground, that actor increases the creative potential of the chaosmos. The assumption is that figure and ground emerge coevally, and it is a value of field poetics that the articulation be as complex as possible. In ecological language, this would mean an affirmation of diversity.

To summarize: it was Olson's achievement to redefine the scope of the poem as he had inherited it from Ezra Pound and William Carlos Williams. Building on Pound's Mediterranean and Chinese culture-scapes and Williams's localism, Olson proposed a new kind of geopoetics that would include history, geology, anthropology, the arts and sciences, technology (typewriter, car, television, atomic bomb), myth, dream, and memory. In this layered proto-Deleuzean field, inner and outer scapes would fold together. The articulation of the scapes is the business of *The Maximus Poems*—what Olson called repossessing the "familiar"—because it is a becoming-aware of the ground on which one stands. His polemic against Western metaphysics, Plato to Melville, comes of the conviction that humanity has so anthropomorphized its own material life and that of nature that it has mistaken the mental realm of concepts for reality as such. This, in the wake of Auschwitz, he judged to be dangerous. The "UNIVERSE OF DISCOURSE" (*CPr* 156) yields Ahabian man, humanity obsessed with shaping the world in its own image and enraged at the idea that the mind might not truly own itself—that it might somehow be akin to or have to deal with a resistance out there that it has not itself created. The whale has Ahab's leg. In Olson's view, Ahabian humanity is untenable, a burden to the earth and to itself. The species has to shrink, so to speak, so that its ground can reappear as something other than its own megalomaniacal projection. Hence Olson's interest in myth. There is no escaping the mind's forms, and certainly in *mythopoesis* the world is anthropomorphized, but in that humanized shape it is nonetheless greeted as something-other-than-me; it is given the respect due to an independent agent. Through the persona of Maximus, Olson situates humanity as a figure on that living, resistant ground. This is his proposed solution to the ravagings of instrumental reason and the self-insistence of the cogito (the Ahab complex): diminish and situate. Hence Stephen Fredman's useful insight that Olson is a poet of containment.[1]

(iii) Measure is an achievement of the embodied (contained) mind. Ethos, as measure, is not to be confused with conventional morality. Maximus is allegorical but he is not morally exemplary. He models human effort and fallibility rather than good behavior. To go back to "Maximus, from Dogtown I," Merry's behavior in fighting the bull is foolish and hubristic, but it gets into the poem because the act serves to make visible a certain dimension of the world called forth by that action. Merry draws out Mayauel, the goddess in her avenging aspect, and that is what matters. This was also Creeley's insight. Here again is a passage I have quoted above, in the Creeley essay: "I want to give witness not to the thought of myself—that specious concept of identity—but rather, to what I am as simple agency, a thing evidently alive by virtue of such activity. I want, as Charles Olson says, to come into the world. Measure, then, is my testament. What uses me is what I use and in that complex measure is the issue. I cannot cut down trees with my bare hand, which is measure of both tree and hand" (*CE* 488). This is how the poet achieves measure. Deleuze, channeling Spinoza, would call it extending one's clear zone, the zone of affectability. Or to work the idea through Whitehead, every actual entity has a relationship with every other one in the cosmos, but it does not actively engage in all of these. Most remain obscure and hence passively prehended because they are beyond the zone of active engagement. Extension of the zone means more awareness of what is there to be responded to and a better fit between cultures and species on a crowded planet. Does this mean that Merry would have acted differently if he had been more aware, more connected to his ground, more measured? This is a question that lands in the middle of current commentary on Spinoza; the idea that bad behaviors come about through inadequate ideas about the real relations between things raises questions about free will that would take me a long way from the poetics at hand.[2] Where Olson rests, I think, is in the idea that the more grounded the figure, the less *likely* he/she/they are to act reductively, although with "actual willful man" the bets are off. Ahab again exemplifies; the only way he can relate to the whale is to kill it, and that suggests a failure of the imagination. To repeat Robin Blaser's comment: "Our tradition sees the Other . . . as a *threat,* to be reduced" (*Fire* 258, original emphasis). This is where Olson begins after World War II in his essay "The Resistance": the reductiveness of the human mind and will, its tendency to instrumentalize, is the "intolerable way" to Auschwitz (*CPr* 174). But rather than lay down precepts designed to control such behaviors—that would be the business of philosophers, legislators, and politicians—the poet tries to expand the alternatives available to the imagination. The *scholar*-poet thus makes him or herself as aware and responsive to the variable measures of his or her world as possible, thus to maximize the options.

Correspondence: The Particular Is the Common

I began this series of essays by asking whether Charles Olson and Vincent Ferrini ever find a place to meet. The question was a way of highlighting the difficulty of specifying common ground or building a poetic practice when heterogeneity of population, variousness of cultural history, and social antagonisms mean that histories, traditions, and values are not shared. Projective poetics addresses this problem with multiple versions of correspondence. In "Particles," Blaser writes that "what we share is our particularity" (24); persons, places, things, events make up the common rather than universals like "the people."[3] Olson, Spicer, Blaser, and Howe each practice correspondence in different ways. For Olson, place is clearly the site of the common, but because place is dynamic and polyvalent, the articulation of it is an *activity* in which everyone has to engage. The idea is not to create a place *for* others but to allegorize the construction of place so that others may create their own: the more grounded I make myself, the more others can see in me a way (a *Tao*) through to their own situatedness. One way to read Olson's complaint about Ferrini is that the literary journal, *The Four Winds,* comes out of nowhere because its editor is speaking out of the "universe of discourse" rather than somewhere real where he might really be encountered. Hence Olson writes, "I begin to be damned to figure out where we can meet" (*MP* 27), because wherever he looks for Ferrini (Sterling's Drugs, the Library, Ferrini's own house) there is no Ferrini *there.*

Spicer's version of correspondence is a little trickier. In *After Lorca,* image "a" evokes an emotion in you that image "b" evokes in me. Lorca's lemon is Spicer's seaweed. But because it is the undergoing of the emotion Spicer wants to provoke in the reader, and because the consequent demand for commitment is high, Spicer insists that poetry is only of interest to a few poets.[4] If Lorca's lemon or my seaweed means nothing to you, then you are free to move on down to another seating arrangement at the bar.[5] Blaser, however, draws out the more public possibilities of Spicerian correspondence when he proposes an "image-nation" of "particles," each one corresponding to the others. The limit concept back of an essay like "Particles" or of Olson's epistolary appeals to the citizens of Gloucester is that of a fluid public space (radical democracy) that would take shape from whoever is there to shape it. Howe writes yet another variant of correspondence. Because image and voice are decentered, the trope of the particle does not quite work, but *trajectories* may correspond. What Howe's tracking of Emily Dickinson or James Clarence Mangan or Jonathan Swift's Stella or any of her other figures shows is that pursuit of another creates a historic trajectory or route that turns out to be a form of self-fashioning. As Howe tracks Emily Dickinson, for instance, she also fashions Susan Howe; as the reader tracks Susan Howe she similarly engages in creative autobiography. One path calls to another.

In these instances, correspondence may be established through place, emotion, image, or trajectory. What it implies for the world beyond the poem are the possibilities and pleasures of living with difference. I brought Appiah into my introduction and this seems like a good place to bring him back. What happens when groups of people or cultures with conflicting perspectives and histories try to inhabit the same space? Certainly paths collide and interfere with one another, as Howe so graphically demonstrates in her collages. But such serious differences, Appiah suggests, may not be resolvable through principle, because principle is precisely what cannot be agreed upon. Getting used to the other, as in living alongside and sharing affective experiences, may be the more workable method. This supposes, of course, some agreement on rule by law and secular government undefined by strong universals.[6] It also supposes at least a modicum of social justice; here is the contemporary sticking point and it is not one that poems can solve directly.

Creeley and Duncan demonstrate a variant route to the shareable. The poet provides a convening point to which others can bring their particular perspectives and experiences. For Creeley, the generic image (a house, a sunset) serves the same function as a well-known restaurant; it is a place for people to meet and share stories. I bring my version of a sunset to compare with yours. In the process of the telling, "sunset" is constantly extended in possibility and you and I get used to each other. There is an element of voluntarism here; I may not like sunsets, or, if I am blind, I will have never seen one. But the generic quality of the concept or event increases the chances that it can serve as a public gathering point. This again is a way of establishing community through shared particularities, but it has the advantage of acknowledging the need for an enabling device like the generic concept that can draw people together over some area of common interest or concern.

Duncan's strategy is similar but the level of abstraction is higher and the implications point toward his anarcho-pacificism rather than a pursuit of common places—this despite Duncan's emphasis on the communality of Poetry. The "grand collage" is the story of the species, so it literally includes all human possibilities. This mobilization of the species signifier is important to Duncan's insistence that there is no human behavior that can fall outside the designation "human." The tautology is a significant one and Duncan is passionate about it. Recall his vigorous defenses of "low" culture in *The H. D. Book* in passages like the one in which he insists that the burlesque dancer, Sally Rand, must have her place in the poem, or in "Man's Fulfillment in Order and Strife" where he argues that personages such as Hitler participate in the "demotic voice" of the species (*FC* 127). This gathering of all ways of being human under the species umbrella demands a facing up to ranges of behavior that it is easier to dismiss as aberration than to cope with as chronic, and I am not referring only to "bad" behaviors. For instance, the assumption of most social theory is that people will act in their own best interests if truly informed of them, but what about those for whom "best interests" does not mean material comfort or personal freedom? Or what about those who know their "best interests" and choose to act against them? What about mystics, saints, madmen, or nihilists? Or bringing this closer to home, what about people who prefer to identify-up socially rather than support initiatives that might actually better their conditions of life? Duncan opens a Pandora's box of possibilities with his use of the generically human to collect wildly diverging perspectives that make the human universe a good deal less predictable than theorists of either the right or left would like it to be—and, I have to add, correspondence even less of a sure thing. His "grand collage" is also a challenge to Olson's ethos. The idea that the well-grounded intellect that has tended its relations and extended its clear zone will issue in "a will of achievement" rather than "a will of power" (*SV* 45) supposes that all behaviors can be explained either through some version of self-interest or as lack of comprehension. If I behave badly with others or destructively to myself, then either I do not understand where my interests lie or my clear zone is not large enough; were I better informed (better educated?), I would act differently. Measure this view against Duncan's claim in *The New American Poetry* that he practices the art to exercise his faculties at large ("Pages" 407) or Spicer's remarks in "Poetry and Politics" that poetry is a socially useless activity (*House* 164). This latter remark leaves us to contemplate an activity engaged in for no apparent reason and, given the penury usually involved in being a poet, against the practitioner's best interests. Spicer's and Duncan's loosing of the passionate, unpredictable, and arational elements in human behavior suggests that what we think of as public, common, or communal is actually less open than it seems to be—that Howe's city of irrational dimensions is really the *only* kind of impossible space in which literally everyone might be included. This would imply the twenty-first-century task of re-articulating what is to count for public.

Cosmicity/Chaosmicity

(i) Does cosmicity mean that this-world problems get referred to other-world solutions? I think there is a difference between the romantic practice of cosmos and that of the projective poets. Here is a passage from Emerson's "Fate":

> One key, one solution to the mysteries of the human condition, one solution to the old knots of fate, freedom, foreknowledge, exists; the propounding, namely, of the double consciousness. A man must ride

> alternately on the horses of his private and his public nature, as the equestrians in the circus throw themselves nimbly from horse to horse, or plant one foot on the back of one and the other foot on the back of the other. So when a man is the victim of his fate, has sciatica in his loins and cramp in his mind; a club-foot and a club in his wit; a sour face and a selfish temper; a strut in his gait and a conceit in his affection; or is ground to powder by the vice of his race;—he is to rally on his relation to the Universe, which his ruin benefits. Leaving the daemon who suffers, he is to take sides with the Deity who secures universal benefit by his pain. (47)

Whether we read the "Universe" to mean an Idea in the mind of God or simply material becoming, what grates in this passage is that Emerson here refers suffering that must be undergone individually to a level of existence that is impossible to experience either because it transcends the human world or because it implies individual death (the "triumph of life"). In the projectivist version, cosmicity (read chaosmicity) means this-world complexity; it makes the ground appear, but it does not pacify or defer the antagonisms there. Nor does it equal depoliticized utopianism. In Olson's denunciations of absentee ownership (the corporate interests that were dismantling Gloucester's small fishing enterprises in his time); in Creeley's modeling of temporalities that are entirely contrary to that on which capital depends;[7] in Duncan's rebellious inclusion of the irreal and arational as factors in the human universe; in Spicer's resolute refusal to make poetry do any work; in Blaser's radical democratic view that public space is to be shaped by whoever is there to shape it; and in Howe's articulation of the marginalized and disappeared as well as her pursuit of peace, there is certainly an awareness of the antagonisms that polarize the social world. Yet the social is not a principle focus and for reasons basic to the "practice of outside." It is humanity as such that has to refigure itself as one species among others, and for ethical and creative reasons rather than epistemological ones. Here lies the source of Olson's hostility to the social sciences and Blaser's too:[8] psychology, sociology, and political science, on the one hand, center the world on the human. The "practice of outside," on the other hand, is a strategy that centers the human in the world. From the projective perspective, the root of "perjorocracy" is that secular humanity thinks its own immediate reality is the only one and acts accordingly. This megalomania is characteristic both of the species in its relation to nature and of the owning classes inside the *socius* in their relations with the dispossessed. What poetry can do is to suggest creative alternatives to megalomania by insisting on relational complexity.

(ii) Cosmicity as religion. Ah, the embarrassment of religion! But the deep ground of it is the primacy of relational thinking. Relationship is that which cannot not be undergone; it is the "lived experience of the Other" (Blaser, *Fire* 258). The experience of being inside something larger than the self is essential to perception; it is embedded in infancy and the process of coming into reflexive consciousness. This process begins when the world steps forward as something not-me. "And the figtree shouts at me and advances / Terrible and extended," Spicer writes (*CB* 22; *MV* 119). The scandal of institutionalized religions is their *méconnaisance* and appropriation of this primary experience and the subsequent loss of Otherness in anthropomorphic projection. That bloated image of the human (Ahab is God) is then used to legitimize human will and wish. Understandably, the religious element in these poetries I have gathered is an embarrassment to secular intellectuals. What does one do, for instance, with Olson's "I believe in religion not magic or science I believe in society / as religious both man and society as religious" (*MP* 422)? Or in Spicer's "Credo quia absurdum" (*CB* 180; *MV* 310) and his "God is a big white baseball" (*CB* 258; *MV* 416). Or in Blaser's lifelong refusal to stop talking about the sacred, despite the unpopularity of the topic? Or Howe's séances with the souls of the Labadie? Surely not Creeley, a colleague said to me hopefully when I tried to explain my project. But alas, there is "The Finger." If there is an unbeliever in the bunch I would put my money on Duncan because of his actor's detachment. But it has been an effort of these essays to suggest that disbelief in experience is not an option. In a comment that Blaser quotes repeatedly in *The Fire* essays, Geoffrey Hartman writes that "the secular is the sacred integrated, rather than degraded or displaced" (qtd. in "Among Afterthoughts" 90). Above all, cosmicity is about being placed; it is a corollary of human limit. That is the "religious" element in this poetry, and in my view it is worth going there, into a practice of outside, because that is where the affections can be retied to something larger than our immediate wants and wishes. The art of the Open Whole, I have argued, is a *techne* of the imagination by which we learn to extend ourselves outward. It is an art essential to the considered life and, I think, a pre-text for justice. It is what poetry can do.

Permissions

Charles Olson: Excerpts from the notebook, "Enniscorthy—June 1946–September 1946," Box 49. Charles Olson Research Collection. Archives and Special collections at the Thomas J. Dodd Research Center, University of Connecticut Libraries. Original material by Charles Olson from the Charles Olson Research Collection. © University of Connecticut Libraries. Reprinted by permission.

Robert Creeley: "Le Fou," "Juggler's Thought," "Wicker Basket," "To And," "The Paradox," "End of Day," "For WCW," and "A Piece" from Robert Creeley, *The Collected Poems of Robert Creeley, 1945–1975*. © 1982, 2006 by the Regents of the University of California. Published by the University of California Press. Reprinted by permission.

"For WCW" and "A Piece," United Kingdom and British Commonwealth © Marion Boyers Publishers, London. Reprinted by permission.

Jack Spicer: "Ballad of the Little Girl Who Invented the Universe" from *My Vocabulary Did This to Me.* © 2008 by Peter Gizzi and Jack Spicer, reprinted by permission of Wesleyan University Press. The notebook poem, "With fifteen cents and that . . . ," is reprinted with the permission of the literary estate of Jack Spicer.

Robin Blaser: The discussion of Robin Blaser's *The Last Supper* in chapter 6 was first published in "Spilling the Names of God: Robin Blaser's *The Last Supper*," in *Mosaic: A Journal for the Interdisciplinary Study of Literature* 36.3 (2003): 163–78. Reprinted with the permission of *Mosaic.*

Susan Howe: Susan Howe, page 66 from *Singularities.* © 1990 by Susan Howe and reprinted by permission of Wesleyan University Press.

Notes

Chapter 1

1. Olson kicks off "Human Universe" with a critique of Western culture dating from 450 BC (*CPr* 155)—quickly disposed of in three pages. And in "Letter 5, lerma march 8" from the *Mayan Letters* he critiques William Carlos Williams and Ezra Pound, his most immediate and important predecessors, as each contributing partially to a poiesis that is his to synthesize ("each of the above jobs are HALVES" [28]).

2. On 15 August 1971, the United States took the dollar off the Gold Exchange Standard. The value of the dollar had been pegged to the price of gold and all other currencies to the dollar. The floating of the currency facilitated trade in derivative financial products and this in turn contributed to a lifting off of the economy from industrial production. For a Marxist summary of post-1960s American economics, see David Harvey's *A Brief History of Neoliberalism* (2005). I have been helped in my understanding of the historical context of poetry-making in the 1970s by the conference presentations of Joshua Glover and Barrett Watten at the National Poetry Foundation Conference, "Poetry of the 1970s," 11–15 June 2008, at the University of Maine. Glover's paper was titled "The Sunday of the Seventies: The Saint of Negation," and Watten's "Late Capitalism and Language Writing in the 1970s."

3. AIM was formed in 1968 to address First Nations/Native American grievances—treaty violations, police brutality, and land claims among the most important of them. In 1973, members of the Lakota Nation at the Pine Ridge reservation invited AIM to assist them in addressing treaty issues, pollution on reservation territory, and corruption among tribal council members. The result was a seizure of the town of Wounded Knee, South Dakota, by armed AIM members and a consequent standoff against U.S. Marshals and FBI agents that lasted for seventy-one days. Following a negotiated disarmament, the U.S. Senate Subcommittee of Indian Affairs conducted hearings into the event. Both sides have claimed victories.

4. See Adrienne Rich's introduction to the second edition of her *Of Woman Born* (1986) for a retrospective on ways that the women's movement needed to adapt to accommodate women of color.

5. See Barrett Watten's "The Turn to Language and the 1960s," *Critical Inquiry* 29.2 (2002), for a contextualization of the language writing in the 1970s. This is a topic Watten has developed in multiple works. See also his "Radical Particularity, Critical Regionalism, and the Resistance to Globalization," a conference paper delivered at the Modernist Studies Conference, Long Beach, 1 November 2007, and posted online at Watten's home page.

6. See Lacan's account of the formation of the subject through interpellation into the symbolic order. In the essays of *Écrits,* Lacan discusses the role of language in the formation of the subject in "The Mirror Stage" (1–7); "The Function and Field of Language in Psychoanalysis" (30–113); "The Freudian thing, or the meaning of the return to Freud in psychoanalysis" (114–45); and "The agency of the letter in the unconscious" (146–78).

7. Bernstein's remarks in "Undone Business" are succinct on Olson's blindness to issues of sex and gender: "The problem is that for Olson 'maleness' is patriarchally assumed to be an 'all-inclusive' term for significant human experience by dint of an *unacknowledged* reduction of the nonmale to insignificance" (328, original emphasis).

8. In the context of his study of Olson in *Charles Olson's Maximus,* Don Byrd draws attention to Eric Havelock's discussion of Plato's view that "everything said by a mythologos or poet . . . is a 'going through of what has or is or will be'" (36).

Agamben's terms for the distinction between *knowing how* and *knowing that* are *experience* and *knowledge.* In *Infancy and History,* he writes: "The idea of experience as separate from knowledge has become so alien to us that we have forgotten that until the birth of modern science experience and science each had their own place. What is more, they were even connected to different subjects. The subject of experience was common sense, something existing in every individual . . . while the subject of science is the *nous* or active intellect, which is separate from experience, 'impassive' and 'divine'" (18).

9. Blaser does not use the terms *undergoing* and *knowing,* but he repeatedly argues that "reality, whatever we mean by the word, is . . . multi-dimensional and multi-logical" ("Recovery of the Public World," *Fire* 65). In the essay "Poetry and Positivisms," Blaser's argument against positivism makes my point in a different vocabulary (*Fire* 38–63).

10. The citations on Aztec philosophy come from the *Internet Encyclopedia of Philosophy.*

11. The relevant passage in the dialogue comes when Socrates questions Ion about Homer's knowledge of the different professions represented in the *Iliad.* He gets Ion to admit that Homer has no expertise in these areas and then asks Ion to pick out passages that would fall under a rhapsode's competence. Ion replies: "My answer, Socrates, is 'all of them'" (Plato, *Ion* 947). Latent in this response is Ion's sense that there is really a different kind of "knowing" at issue here than the technical kind by which Socrates mis-measures poetry.

12. The phrase "power to oblige" is Julia Kristeva's, from the essay "Thinking in Dark Times" (16).

13. I am referring to Plato's anecdote of the stick in the 10th Book of the *Republic:*

[Socrates]	And something looks crooked when seen in water and straight when seen out of it, while something else looks both concave and convex because our eyes are deceived by its colors, and every other sort of confusion is clearly present in our soul. And it is because they exploit this weakness in our nature that *trompe l'oeil* painting, conjuring, and other forms of trickery have powers that are little short of magical.
[Glaucon]	That's true.
[Socrates]	And don't measuring, counting, and weighing give us most welcome assistance in these cases, so that we aren't ruled by something's looking bigger, smaller, more numerous, or heavier, but by calculation, measurement, or weighing? (1207)

14. The phrase, "Map is *not* territory" (original emphasis), comes from Alfred Korzybski's *General Semantics Seminar 1937: Olivet College Lectures* (28). Spicer uses the phrase as the title of a poem in *Heads of the Town up to the Aether* (*CB* 122), and Blaser quotes Korzybski in "Poetry and Positivism" (*Fire* 38).

15. *Conatus* refers to the desire of the human creature to persist in its being and expand its active powers. See section VIII, "Spinoza's *Conatus* and the Ontology of Manner" in chapter 4 of Altieri's *Particulars of Rapture* (141–46).

16. Charles Bernstein writes that "the promise of *The Maximus Poems* is to create a collaged 'hyperspace,' [but that] such a transubstantiation remains largely theoretical—undone business" ("Undone Business" 333). This is a prescient and suggestive comment. In my view, Olson *did* lay the groundwork for a poetics of hyperspace.

17. Arjun Appadurai develops a language of "scapes" in his *Modernity at Large.* See chapter 2, "Disjuncture and Difference in the Global Cultural Economy" (27–65), but especially page 33 where Appadurai introduces the concept of the scapes. Scapes are transnational zones of energy and attention not necessarily embodied in the same way as is a landscape: they may include ethnoscapes and financescapes, for instance.

18. In particular, see "Poetry and Positivisms" and Blaser's discussion of Wlad Godzich's Foreword to Michel de Certeau's *Heterologies* (41–42).

19. Creeley mentions this work of Rot's in his essay "Inside Out: Notes on the Autobiographical Mode" in the *Collected Essays of Robert Creeley* (557).

Chapter 2

1. Paul Christensen draws a parallel between Olson's emphasis on perception and that of Maurice Merleau-Ponty in his *Call Him Ishmael;* William Spanos, in his 1980 essay on Olson in *Contemporary Literature,* defends Heidegger and Olson against the

Derridean push then afoot in universities. He argues, for instance, that interpretation of the oral in both writers as logocentrism is a misreading (46), and he points to similarities between Olson's reliance on the negative capability and the Heideggerian withdrawal of being from articulation (70).

2. *Sagetrieb* continued to publish many notable essays on Olson throughout the 1980s and '90s. Ralph Maud's newsletter, *The Minutes of the Charles Olson Society* (privately produced and circulated by Maud), has published scholarship and archival materials on Olson continuously since 1991. The State University of New York at Buffalo has an author's site for Olson at http://wings.buffalo.edu/epc/authors/olson with a link to the very useful OlsonNow Blog edited by Ammiel Alcalay and Michael Kelleher (http://olsonnowblogspot.com). My tour of the blog in January 2009 turned up a range of essays that investigate its "Olson now" theme, including multiple posts on an "OlsonNow" gathering of writers and scholars at MIT on 20 May 2006. The mini-conference was the third such aimed at discussing Olson's legacy, and blog posts include Benjamin Friedlander's address on Olson's legacy, "Charles Olson Now" (2006), John Hyland's description of the Boston event (2006), and a link to Nate Pritts's essay published in the online journal, *Jacket,* "Towards a Theory of Time in Olson" (2008), the latter a brief piece that indicates the importance of Henri Bergson's theory of time to Olson's work. Friedlander (editor with Donald Allen of the *Collected Prose of Charles Olson*) points to the archive Olson produced as a literary form of particular interest to writers in the age of the Internet.

My earlier trips to the blog over the course of this project have yielded essays on a variety of subjects, some of which are now available at SUNY Buffalo's electronic poetry center (http://epc.buffalo.edu). Anne Waldman ("Feminafesto: Olson") writes in finding a space for the feminine in Olson. Pierre Joris ("Where Is Olson Now?") offers a wide-ranging series of notes on contemporary possibilities in Olson including the similarity of his project to that of Deleuze. Don Byrd ("Cybernetics and Form") draws out the cybernetic potential in Olson and Duncan, and in a second essay, "Curriculum for the Conning of the New Polis (Olson Now!)," Byrd ponders the terms in which "an actual earth of value" might now be posed. Clayton Eshleman ("Notes on Charles Olson and the Archaic") offers an illuminating presentation of scholarship on the archaic elements in Olson's "La Chute." Alan Gilbert ("Charles Olson and Empire, or Charles Olson Flips the Wartime Script") compares Olson with the painter Philip Guston and investigates Olson's relationship with New Deal politics and the Popular Front in the 1940s. Jonathan Skinner's essay, "Charles Olson and the Question of Boundaries: The Poet-Scholar," ruminates on the relationship between poetry and scholarship and the conflicting demands of academic and poetic lives. These essays and more read Olson into the contemporary, but notice here that many of Olson's current readers are themselves writers or poet-scholars who look to Olson for inspiration and untapped formal possibilities. In the larger academic world, Olson's reputation is only now emerging from the penumbra of the theory decades.

3. Anne Dewey reads Olson as problematically attempting to discover the natural

ground for cultural forms (*Beyond Maximus* 54) and thus as mired in a latter-day romanticism. I begin from a different supposition through my reading of the Whiteheadian component in Olson's poetics; it is not that Olson begins from a subject-object dualism and then has to struggle to harmonize them, but that he begins with the continuity of the cosmos and then has to explain how subject and object evolve as polarized positions.

4. Bryant's thesis is arguable, I think, given Kant's work in *The Critique of Judgment* on aesthetic experience. Kant distinguishes between determinative judgment as an act of the understanding and reflective judgment as a play between the imagination and understanding. The former subsumes particulars under general categories; the latter derives unity from the play of particulars (purpose without purpose). Reflective judgment is that which constitutes an aesthetic experience; the unity of a work of art, for instance, is to be derived from that work and not from prior principles. This is not the place to open up this argument, but Bryant's construction of Kant as a philosopher who does not well handle particulars—useful as it is as a shorthand in my context—might be challenged through the third *Critique.*

5. In his essay, "Where Is Olson Now?" on the OlsonNow blog, Pierre Joris has this note: "(quick addendum: for me, however it is clear that the one thinker in Europe who without knowing Olson, expanded on Olsonian themes is Gilles Deleuze [w/Félix Guattari]—especially starting with the 1973—3 years after Olson's death—ANTI-OEDIPUS and then with A THOUSAND PLATEAUS, a book I am certain Olson would have delighted in. Note the 'nomad' theme that will come in later)." I discovered Joris's comment after settling on a Deleuzean explication of Olson's *Special View,* but it nonetheless precedes my reading.

6. At the beginning of *Process and Reality,* Whitehead locates the philosophy of organism in relation to cognate philosophies and remarks on his debt to Leibniz. "His monads are best conceived as generalizations of contemporary notions of mentality. The contemporary notions of physical bodies only enter into his philosophy subordinately and derivatively. The philosophy of organism endeavours to hold the balance more evenly" (*PR* 29, I.II.I). In his *Key to Whitehead's Process and Reality,* Donald Sherburne clarifies the relationship of the philosophy of organism to Leibniz's monadology: the former differs from the latter he says, in that Leibniz's monads are fixed whereas the actual entities are dynamic becomings. This is also how Deleuze reads Whitehead. In *The Fold,* he writes that because Leibniz's monads are closed, they admit, on the one hand, of only one world; Whitehead's actual entities, on the other hand, are open to one another and thus allow for "bifurcations, divergences, incompossibilities, and discord," resulting in a "motley world *that can no longer be included in expressive units,* but only made or undone according to prehensive units and variable configurations or changing captures" (81, original emphasis). If Leibniz proposes a cosmos, Whitehead offers a *chaosmos* (Deleuze's word) that is open and conflictual.

On Spinoza, Whitehead says that

> the philosophy of organism is closely allied to Spinoza's scheme of thought. But it differs by the abandonment of the subject-predicate forms of thought, so far as concerns the presupposition that this form is a direct embodiment of the most ultimate characterization of fact. The result is that the "substance-quality" concept is avoided; and that morphological description is replaced by description of dynamic process. Also Spinoza's "modes" now become the sheer actualities; so that, though analysis of them increases our understanding, it does not lead us to the discovery of any higher grade of reality. The coherence, which the system seeks to preserve, is the discovery that the process, or concrescence, of any one actual entity involves the other actual entities among its components. In this way the obvious solidarity of the world receives its explanation. (*PR* 10, I.I.II)

7. Bryant points out that Deleuze's "Copernican revolution" also implies that the difference between a critical philosophy that tries to account for how knowledge is produced and a speculative one that simply asserts some version of the real becomes difficult to distinguish (Bryant 175). What is it that allows Deleuze to make the claims he does? Where does the plane of consistence come from? Why the primacy of difference? How is it possible to move beyond human understanding without launching into dogmatic speculation or simple assertion? Levi Bryant tackles these questions in a chapter titled "Overcoming Speculative Dogmatism: Time and the Transcendental Field." He argues that Deleuze takes the Kantian critical turn all the way to a point "*where the unity of the subject is dissolved and critical thought becomes indiscernible from speculative thought*" (183, original emphasis). The arguments needed to ground this claim would take me far away from my topic—I refer the reader to Bryant's chapter for discussion—but I mention the point because Deleuze and certainly Whitehead before him are sometimes read as *merely* speculative philosophers. Olson has been accused similarly of simple assertion.

8. "Feed-back" in "The Kingfishers" specifically refers to Olson's reading of Norbert Wiener's *Cybernetics* (Maud, *What Does Not Change* 73). Don Byrd has picked up the cybernetic element in Olson in his essay "Cybernetics and Form," formerly on the OlsonNow blog, available online as of spring 2009 at http://epc.buffalo.edu/authors/Olson.

9. "The Moebius Strip," a relatively early poem, establishes Olson's familiarity with this figure. In this poem, human figures twist into each other or into landscape. For example:

A man within himself upon an empty ground.
his head lay heavy on a huge right hand
itself a leopard on
his left and angled shoulder.
His back a stave, his side a hole into the bosom of a sphere. (*CP* 55)

The images here anticipate Olson's contention in "Human Universe" and *The Special View of History* that humanity had best treat external reality as part of its own "process" (*CPr* 163).

10. I mean "scape" to be a flexible concept, resonant with Deleuze's strata, that can be adapted to describe various regions of the lifeworld. See note 17 of the Introduction, above, for the origin of the term in Arjun Appadurai's *Modernity at Large* (1996).

11. I have in mind Michael Kleinberg-Levin's discussion of evil in his *Gestures of Ethical Life: Reading Hölderin's Question of Measure after Heidegger.* In a meditation on the holocaust of World War II, Kleinberg-Levin suggests that radical evil comes about when finite beings lose their sense of measure. Confronted with the death of God, humanity may be tempted "to turn the fascination and horror of this groundlessness into a false grounding, a false measure, a totality that the finite will could appropriate for its own ends" (65). This definition of evil as a loss of ground I take as appropriate to Ahab.

12. This phrase comes from Robin Blaser's essay, "The Violets," a discussion of Olson and Whitehead centered on Olson's marginalia in Whitehead's *Process and Reality* (219).

13. Whitehead defines actual entities as both subjects and superjects; the entities are subjects for themselves and superjects for others: "An actual entity is to be conceived both as a subject presiding over its own immediacy of becoming, and a superject which is the atomic creature exercising its function of objective immortality. It has become a 'being'; and it belongs to the nature of every 'being' that it is a potential for every 'becoming'" (*PR* 71, II.I.III).

14. The model of the cone, as it draws together all three explications of the creative process (Whiteheadian, Hegelian, mythic) reveals Olson's debt to structuralism; the three tellings are homologues of one another. Paul Christensen, discussing Olson's structuralism in *Call Him Ishmael,* remarks that "at the heart of structuralist method lies the implicit assumption that consciousness is sensuous, organic, and . . . systematic" (42). Christensen points to Jung as a structuralist psychologist near to Olson (42). The structuralist geographer Carl Sauer was another important source. Sauer conceives of morphology as emerging from the "quasi-organic" unity of landscape or the potential of things to fit together into patterns. As well, it is *dynamic* and given to explication through homology of function. Olson's structuralism, like Sauer's, is genetic and dynamic.

15. On negative prehensions, Whitehead writes: "That there are two species of prehensions: (a) 'positive prehensions' which are termed 'feelings,' and (b) 'negative prehensions' which are said to 'eliminate from feeling.' Negative prehensions also have subjective forms. A negative prehension holds its datum as inoperative in the progressive concrescence of prehensions constituting the unity of the subject" (*PR* 35, I.II. II). In other words, what an organism negatively prehends, it excludes from its ontogenesis.

16. The "good" in Whitehead's system is that actualization of the world that maximizes its complexity and affectability. As Donald Sherburne clarifies, "God's own aim in the creative advance is to have a world emerge of such a sort that his own experience of that world will result in the greatest possible intensity in his own experience. He therefore . . . offers as a lure to each actual entity as it arises that subjective aim the completion of which, in that entity's own concrescence, would create the kind of ordered, complex world that, when prehended by God, would result in maximum intensity of satisfaction for him" (*Key* 227).

17. The phrase "nonreductive materialism" is used in *The Cambridge Dictionary of Philosophy* to describe philosophies that propose some irreducibility of mental phenomena to the physical processes from which they derive.

18. Stein comments that Jung does not give the archetypes a locus, either in the psyche or in a metaphysical entity (*Secret of the Black Chrysanthemum* 47).

19. I am presenting Olson's perspective here, not a scholarly comparison of Pound and Olson.

20. "Labour, life and language" is Michel Foucault's phrase, from *The Order of Things* (330).

21. In *Upheavals of Thought,* Martha Nussbaum offers many strong arguments for the centrality of the body to human possibility, and she reads our furious efforts to *overcome* the fragility and neediness of bodies as ultimately damaging to individuals and to the societies they create.

22. See George Hartley's exegesis of Žižek's politics in *The Abyss of Representation,* especially pages 264–73, for a much fuller treatment.

23. For example, Paul Christensen notes F. O. Matthiessen's reaction to *Call Me Ishmael:* "The professor chides his student, as he does others in this broad study, for having been hasty and sometimes plainly inaccurate in his hypotheses" (*Call Him Ishmael* 38). Or Thomas Bertonneau, discussing Olson's interest in the Maya, writes that contemporary scholarship reveals a violent, warrior culture ("Life in the Human Universe" 139), a "fact" that Olson apparently failed to register.

24. I am quoting from "The Truth Is Laughter 7," in Robin Blaser's *Syntax* (*HF* 210). Olson mentions the myth of Fenrir many times, but without naming the items that make up the magical thread. I take the list from Blaser.

Chapter 3

1. Eichmann was a traveling salesman before joining the military. Arendt records his "grief and sorrow" at never advancing beyond the rank of S.S. Obersturmbannführer (lieutenant colonel) (33–34).

2. In an essay on Creeley for the *boundary 2* collection (1978), Charles Altieri connects modernist poetics with "the presence or absence of a single privileged system of explanation giving meaning and purpose to particulars," while the postmoderns are more likely to adopt "multiple systems which all have equal explanatory power in appropriate circumstances" (521). In other words, no one discourse (psychology, poli-

tics, philosophy, for example) can establish exteriority in relations to the others. What Altieri identifies here as a modern-postmodern contention, I think, is an ongoing disagreement between theoretical perspectives that quilt the social field (understand the field as organized through a privileged set of signifiers like those of sexuality or social class) and those that do not (those that understand the field as a zone of competing antagonisms, none of which is privileged). Altieri's essay was published in 1978, but as I have argued in the preceding essay, there is a parallel tension between Deleuze and contemporary Freudo-Marxists like Žižek.

3. In a poem called "After," from the collection *Later* (1979), Creeley writes, "There is no world / except felt" (*CP* 104).

4. For a different treatment of recognition, see Robert Kern's "Composition as Recognition: Robert Creeley and Postmodern Poetics," in *boundary 2* (1978). Kern uses the term to distinguish a poetics of immanence from one of artifice. In the former, the poet *recognizes* an immanent order in the variousness of the experience; in the latter he or she understands order as that which is to be imposed on experience.

5. The speaker in Creeley's poems and the main characters in his prose are men. I have therefore chosen the masculine pronoun in places where I have used "the poet" or "the speaker" to indicate the voice of a Creeley poem.

6. Aloysius Bertrand's "Le Fou" is from a collection titled *Gaspard de la nuit*, Livre III. It is available online at http://cage.rug.ac.be/~dc/Literature/Gaspard/index.html.

7. In Deleuze's thinking, it is the pure past that functions like the zero in mathematics; it is a concept necessary to our understanding of time but not accessible experientially. In *Difference and Repetition*, Deleuze explains it this way: "The past does not cause one present to pass without calling forth another, but itself neither passes nor comes forth. For this reason the past, far from being a dimension of time, is the synthesis of all time of which the present and the future are only dimensions. We cannot say that it was. It no longer exists, it does not exist, but it insists, it consists, it *is*. It insists with the former present, it consists with the new or present present. It is the in-itself of time as the final ground of the passage of time. In this sense it forms a pure, general, *a priori* element of all time" (82). See also Levi Bryant's comments on this passage in *Difference and Givenness* (120–21).

Alternatively, in Lacanian language, the zero is a concept tied to the foreclosure of the unmediated "real" in the formation of the human subject. In the passage below, Anthony Wilden explains why, in Lacanian psychoanalysis, consciousness can never rid itself of its zero.

> . . . the subject's profoundest desire to be "One" again (to control the Other to whom he becomes subjected) is totally and absolutely irreducible. It is this desire for what is really annihilation (non-difference) that makes human beings human. And if we employ the insights of the mathematical metaphor, as Lacan does in the later works, we realize that this primordial "One" cannot be one at all, since one requires two. What it can be is zero, in the precise sense

> that, logically speaking, for mathematics the function of zero is to be the concept under which no object falls (all objects being defined as identical with themselves), because in order to "save the truth," zero is assigned to that concept "not identical with itself" (Frege). Zero makes a lack (but not a "nothing") visible. . . . (190–91)

8. For cosmos, read chaosmos. Throughout this essay and those to come I will use the older term where the new seems too awkward, but in all cases I refer to the Open Whole in the Deleuzean sense.

9. As I mentioned in my introduction to these essays, Freud associates religious feeling with preverbal infancy. The desire for "at-oneness," common to religious mysticism, he suggests is a residual memory. In the adult, the real fulfillment of this wish to be at-one uncovers the death drive because it implies annihilation of the ego that wishes to merge with the other (*Civilization and Its Discontents* 15–16).

10. I have in mind Bataille's *Theory of Religion* in which he distinguishes human self-consciousness from the "immanence and immediacy" of the animal who is in the world "like water in water" (23).

11. See Lyotard's much fuller description of capital as lack (inhibition, reserve) in *Libidinal Economy* (1993). Lyotard argues as well that credit money includes a speculative use that is mercantilist—which is to say that capital is not just a self-reproducing system of expenditure and return (lack in circulation) but also a "looting" through speculation (227).

12. See Jérôme Bindé's essay, "Toward an Ethics of the Future" (2000), for a discussion of the ways that contemporary commercial culture has appropriated the future of succeeding generations.

13. Gertrude Stein precedes Creeley as a writer acutely aware of perception as moment-to-moment difference in repetition. A likely source for Creeley's "insistence" is Stein's discussion of it in "Portraits and Repetition" (119).

In philosophy, Deleuze's analysis of temporal becoming is a helpful parallel, although more technical than the writings of either Stein or Creeley.

> A succession of instants does not constitute time any more than it causes it to disappear; it indicates only its constantly aborted moment of birth. Time is constituted only in the originary synthesis which operates on the repetition of instants. This synthesis contracts the successive independent instants into one another, thereby constituting the lived, or living, present. It is in this present that time is deployed. To it belong both the past and the future: the past in so far as the preceding instants are retained in the contraction; the future because its expectation is anticipated in this same contraction. The past and the future do not designate instants distinct from a supposed present instant, but rather the dimensions of the present itself in so far as it is a contraction of instants. (*Difference and Repetition* 71)

14. I realize that Emmanuel Lévinas is the philosopher of unmasterable Otherness and that he might well be expected to make an entrance in this context of Creeley's work on recognition. Lévinas's meditation on the face (*Totality and Infinity* 1969) might be usefully compared to Creeley's sense that others may be recognized by the incremental accumulation of meetings, but not absorbed as objects of knowledge. However, Lévinas's vocabulary does not easily lend itself to a Creeley exposition. If, as I have argued, Creeley is a poet of the *occasion*, if any given moment is a *coup de dès* that absolutely *decides* what is the case, then it would take some negotiating of terms to introduce Lévinas's saying of infinity to the mix. I leave this study for another occasion.

15. This is precisely the question of gonzo documentary filmmaker Michael Moore, who has made a career of bedeviling politicians and men of power by demanding that they stand publicly by their words and deeds.

16. See Žižek's analysis of the symptom in his chapter "From Symptom to Sinthome" in *The Sublime Object of Ideology*, particularly pages 78–79, where he argues "the Real of enjoyment" manifests in the symptom as "pre-symbolic Thing," illustrating his point with reference to the film *Alien* in which a "polyp-like parasite sticks on [John] Hurt's face" (79). Building on Lacan, Žižek argues that the real (preverbal at-oneness with the mother), foreclosed with initiation into the symbolic order, returns through the symbolic in fragmented, displaced form. What one enjoys in jouissance is a fragment of the mother's body, as it were. Hence the flip side of the "socio-symbolic Other is obcene [*sic*] enjoyment" (79). To make of jouissance a *spectacle*, as Creeley does in "Wicker Basket," ups the stakes in what is already a component of psychic life that bodes all manner of aggressions.

17. Creeley credits Sigfried Giedion, in *The Eternal Present* (vol. 1), for the distinction between the two kinds of abstraction (*RP* 30).

18. See my description of the Freudo-Marxian model vs. the Deleuzean in the Olson chapter, above.

19. I realize my comment directly contradicts Anne Dewey's very interesting argument in *Beyond Maximus*, for an Olson-Creeley shift from "harmonizing cultural with natural place to [a] view [of] culture as evolving by mechanisms different from those of nature" (74)—from latter-day romanticism toward a social poetry, in other words. As laid out in the Olson essay, my premises are different from Dewey's. I do not see in the projective poets a failed struggle to mend the nature-culture dichotomy (and a consequent turn to the social) but rather a refusal of dualism as a point of departure.

Chapter 4

1. For a discussion of Duncan's anarcho-pacifism, see Robert Bertholf's essay, "Decision at the Apogee: Robert Duncan's Anarchist Critique of Denise Levertov," and Ellen Tallman's "My Stories with Robert Duncan," both in the collection *Robert*

Duncan and Denise Levertov: The Poetry of Politics, the Politics of Poetry (2006), edited by Albert Gelpi and Bertholf.

2. For example, Ian Reid ("The Plural Text" 1979) explores the key myths of Eros and Orpheus, and Timothy Materer discusses alchemy as a trope of self-fashioning in Duncan's work ("Robert Duncan and the Mercurial Self" 1990). Nathaniel Mackey writes about "Uroboros: Dante and A Seventeenth Century Suite" (*Scales of the Marvelous* 1979); Jayne Walker discusses Duncan's Stein imitations ("Exercises in Disorder"); and Don Byrd the relationship between Duncan's poetics and that of Olson ("The Question of Wisdom as Such" 1979). Then there are commentaries like Steven Carter's "Robert Duncan and Erwin Schrödinger: Esthetics of the Wave Function" (1990) or Stephen Collis's "'The Frayed Trope of Rome': Poetic Architecture in Robert Duncan, Ronald Johnson, and Lisa Robertson" (2002), an essay that draws comparisons between Duncan and much younger poets. More recently, Albert Gelpi's collection of essays on the Duncan-Levertov letters (see note 1 above) has foregrounded the fraught discussion of poetry and politics that has grown up around the correspondence.

3. Michael André Bernstein writes that "the tradition Duncan continues never existed before him, and its creation increasingly begins to seem like the central poem of his imagination, the ground-work from which all of the other texts ultimately derive" ("Robert Duncan: Talent and the Individual Tradition" 180).

4. In "Prophetic Frustrations," an essay in the Bertholf-Gelpi collection, Peter O'Leary takes up the implications of Kabbalistic creation narrative in Duncan's poetry through the work of Moshe Idel's *Absorbing Perfections.* In a passage that is analogous to my point about the Neoplatonic relationship between figure and ground, Idel writes: "Knowledge of the inner aspects of the Torah is conditioned on the attainment of the highest intellectual faculty, the prophetic intellect, which is seen as tantamount to prophetic experience. Understanding the secrets is a function of blurring the gap between God as intellect and the human intellect: the latter acquires a divine, holy intellect, which is the sine qua non for fathoming the secrets of the Torah" (qtd. in O'Leary, "Prophetic Frustrations" 138).

5. This paragraph from Gershom Scholem's *On the Kabbalah and Its Symbolism,* explains the terms "*en-sof*" and "*sefiroth.*"

> Most if not all Kabbalistic speculation and doctrine is concerned with the realm of the divine emanations of *sefiroth,* in which God's creative power unfolds. . . . Insofar as God reveals himself, He does so through the creative power of the *sefiroth.* The God of whom religion speaks is always conceived under one or more of these aspects of His Being, which the Kabbalists identified with stages in the process of divine emanation. This Kabbalistic world of the *sefiroth* encompasses what philosophers and theologians called the world of the divine attributes. But to the mystics it was divine life itself, insofar as it moves toward Creation. The hidden dynamic of this life fascinated the Kabbalists, who found it reflected in every realm of Creation. But this life as such is not separate from, or subordinate to, the Godhead, rather, it is the revelation of the

> hidden root, concerning which, since it is never manifested, not even in symbols, nothing can be said, and which the Kabbalists called *en-sof*, the infinite. But this hidden root and the divine emanations are one. (*On the Kabbalah and Its Symbolism* 35)

6. The Florentine Academy consisted of a circle of scholars devoted to the study of Plato and the reconciliation of Platonism with Christianity and the Kabbalah. It was established in 1462 when Marsilio Ficino was given a villa at Coreggio under the patronage of the Medicis. Cosimo Medici had become interested in Platonism through the lectures of George Gesmistus Plethon in 1438 and inspired Ficino to turn his studies in that direction. Also associated with the Academy were Lorenzo Medici, who ruled in Florence from 1469 to 1492, and Giovanni Pico della Mirandola as well as many followers of Ficino and Pico.

7. Here is Plato's ladder of love, from *The Symposium:* "This is the right way of approaching or being initiated into the mysteries of love, to begin with examples of beauty in this world, and using them as steps to ascend continually with that absolute beauty as one's aim, from one instance of physical beauty to two and from two to all, then from physical beauty to moral beauty, and from moral beauty to the beauty of knowledge, until from knowledge of various kinds one arrives at the supreme knowledge whose sole object is that absolute beauty, and knows at last what absolute beauty is" (94). This passage from *The Symposium* is key to the Neoplatonism back of the courtly love tradition in the Renaissance. See for instance Baldassare Castiglione's *The Book of the Courtier* (ca. 1504), especially p. 337.

8. See Scholem's discussion of the *Sefer Yezirah,* or "Book of Creation," in his *Kabbalah* (23–24). On the *Zohar,* or "Book of Splendors," Scholem considers it to be the layered work of multiple authors, among them Moses de Leon, a Spanish Kabbalist (d. 1305) (Scholem, *Zohar* 12). He dates the work from late thirteenth century Spain, around 1280 (16). The *Zohar* belongs to the same body of Kabbalistic writings on cosmogony as the *Sefer Yezirah.*

9. For a discussion of the structure of the poem as deriving from the sonata—exposition, development, recapitulation—see Robert Bertholf's essay, "Robert Duncan's 'The Venice Poem' and Symphonic Form," in the online journal *Jacket* (2005). Bertholf's reading also brings forward the personal dimension of the poem in a failed love affair.

10. This phrase is from Bertholf's essay, cited above. Bertholf is quoting Duncan's notes from an unpublished annotated copy of "The Venice Poem" dating from 1950. Here is Bertholf on the personal and symbolic references of the sapphire: "The 'boy's eye' refers to Landis Everson . . . a poet from Berkeley who has striking blue eyes. In his eye, 'He,' fictive Duncan, finds a 'central sapphire.' The sapphire and blue reoccur through 'The Venice Poem' as 'the suspended star-sapphire . . . and stands for,' Duncan notes, 'sapphire of intellect, the passionate intellect, maleness.' So the central passion of male sexual drive is at the center of the poem, and 'He' read that out in Landis Everson's eyes" ("Robert Duncan's 'The Venice Poem' and Symphonic Form" 3).

11. The passage in Stravinsky's *Poetics of Music* comes in the context of his remarks on the sounds of nature such as those of a brook or bird's song: "These natural sounds suggest music to us, but are not yet themselves music. . . . They are promises of music; it takes a human being to keep them: a human being who is sensitive to nature's many voices, of course, but who in addition feels the need of putting them in order and who is gifted for that task with a very special aptitude. In his hands all that I have considered as not being music will become music" (23).

12. For a different perspective on the role of violence in Duncan's poetics, see Michael Davidson's "Marginality at the Margins: Robert Duncan's Textual Politics," in *Ghostlier Demarcations* (1997) (171–95). Davidson threads the violent imagery in many of the poems through Duncan's sexualized relationship with his source texts. He reads Duncan's blurring of boundaries between his own voice and that of others as the assembling of marginalized voices into community (194–95).

13. Duncan retells the story of the castration of Uranus in several passages from "Two Chapters" in *The H. D. Book,* emphasizing the relationship between a divine trinity, variously figured, and the male genitals. "After the Titanic Kronos cut[s] away the genitals of the Father Uranus, the Great Sky, and casts them away behind him upon the raging sea (that may be the sea of the act itself) '*they were swept away over the main a long time: and a white foam spread around them from the immortal flesh, and in it grew a maiden*'—Aphrodite—and with her, Eros and Himeros. A transformation has taken place. In this Greek figure the Father's parts, the essential 'Father,' reappear in three persons: the goddess Aphrodite or Beauty where his penis was, and the attendant gods, Eros and Himeros, where his testicles were" (69–70, original emphasis). And here is a passage on the Mother in which her violation enables male creativity: "Hidden, the Eros is the very vitality in the stone. Revealed, he is shown as an idea, a youth flying up from the head of a titanic Mother or Matter awakening or come alive in the ground, the Earth-goddess Ge or Gaia. This Earth is also the artist's content, the ground of potential ideas in which he works. In the figure shown by Jane Harrison on page 639 of the *Prolegomena,* attendant upon the work are two satyrs with pickaxes, breakers of the ground; the giant female head uprises; and from the aroused head two *erotes* spring—the primal Eros and Himeros."

14. Adorno has theorized the relationship between concept and thing in his *Negative Dialectics,* where he suggests that the *adequation* of concept to thing requires repression of the historicity of the thing so named. Adorno writes: "But no matter how hard we try for linguistic expression of such a history congealed in things, the words we use will remain concepts. Their precision substitutes for the thing itself, without quite bringing its selfhood to mind; there is a gap between words and the things they conjure" (*Negative Dialectics* 53). In this gap between word and thing there is potential for a dialectical refreshment of the world. For a recent political interpretation of this nonidentity between the particular and universal, see George Hartley's chapter, "Can the Symptom Speak," in *The Abyss of Representation* (2003) (235–94), particularly the section titled "The Politics of the Universal" (266–68).

15. See Ekbert Faas's chapter, "The Shaman Poet," in his biography, *Young Robert Duncan* (79–92).

16. Duncan's translation of *Les chimères* is included in *Audit/Poetry* (1966) and in *Bending the Bow;* Blaser's *Chimères* is available in *The Holy Forest* (2006) (97–108).

17. The symbology of alchemy is inconsistent and deliberately difficult because the alchemists wished to conceal the process from the uninitiated. The four stages are as follows, although these are sometimes condensed into three: separation of the elements, union of opposites (usually male and female principles), death of the product of the union, and rebirth or production of the philosopher's stone. The symbols Duncan lifts from the poem seem to apply to the third and fourth stages. After the death of the child (night of the tomb) comes the washing of the ashes (consolation) and spiritual vigil (Holy Mountain). The final stage is the rebirth or production of the philosopher's stone, sometimes associated with the sea. See Jung's *Psychology and Alchemy* for a detailed description of the process (231–32).

18. Iakchos is a variant of Iacchus, an epithet of Dionysus associated with the Eleusian mysteries (the fertility cult of Demeter and Persephone, ca. 1500 BC). Iacchus, considered to be the son of Zeus and Demeter was a torchbearer of the Eleusian procession and was sometimes taken to be the Child of the goddess. The rites were secret because initiates were thought to be united with the god and awarded divine privileges in the afterlife. The "Romance of the Rose" refers to the French *Le Roman de la Rose,* a medieval Neoplatonic allegory about the art of love in which the titular "Rose" is both a woman and a symbol of Woman. *Le Roman* was written in two stages by two different authors. Guillaume de Lorris (ca. 1230) is credited with the first 4,058 lines; Jean de Meun (ca. 1275) with another 17,724 lines. Lorris's lines are sometimes considered to be more idealized than Meun's. These references would take Duncan into the Neoplatonic circle of love.

19. The Lusignan family rose to prominence in tenth-century France, in Poitou near Lusignan. By the twelfth century, members of the family controlled the kingdoms of Jerusalem and Cyprus. As crusaders, they established ties with the Hethumid rulers of the Kingdom of Cilicia (a kingdom founded in the eleventh century by Armenian refugees in what is now Turkey), which they inherited through marriage in the fourteenth century. The family dynasty eventually died out with the Ottoman conquest of their middle-eastern kingdoms.

The Gontaut-Birons take their name from Chateau de Biron, a family seat from the twelfth century when it was briefly seized by the Cathars in 1211 and retaken the next year by Simon IV de Montfort. Charles de Gontaut (1562–1602), son of Armand de Gontaut (1524–1592), was created duc de Biron. Both father and son were Marshals of France. Armand, baron de Biron, distinguished himself in several battles during the religious wars between Catholics and Huguenots of the sixteenth century (1562–98). He fought on the royal side.

20. As Blaser was writing *Les chimères* in the early 1960s, the old Duncan-Spicer-Blaser circle was disintegrating. Duncan and Spicer were not speaking; Blaser was

often caught in the middle of rivalries that were both poetic and personal. See Andrew Mossin's "In the Shadow of Nerval" (1997) for an account of the *Chimères* quarrel.

21. See also Marjorie Perloff's "Poetry, Politics, and the 'Other Conscience': Robert Duncan's Letters to Denise Levertov" for a comparable defense of Duncan's demand that Levertov consider the formal possibilities in her poems—those that reach beyond the immediate message (38).

22. Martha Nussbaum's remarks on Proust resonate remarkably with Duncan's making of art out of personal pain. In the context of her Proust discussion, Nussbaum writes that "the raw material of self-knowledge and artistic expression is pain. But to use this pain as raw material for a work of universal communicative power and formal beauty is a profound delight and a consolation" (*Upheavals* 517). The price of this intellectual joy, however, may turn out to be a punishment of the actual life—that is, a dismissal of real relationships with all the attendant cruelties that dismissal can entail.

23. Paul Lacey comments in his "The Vision of the Burning Babe: Southwell, Levertov, Duncan" that "it is important to recognize what is happening here. Levertov sends a *poem* to a friend and reader she trusts, expecting it to be read *as* a poem, but Duncan responds to it only as *a psychological document* recording a danger to her poetry" (162).

24. At www.polarization.com/eyes/eyes/html.

25. For a different reading of "The Burning Babe," see Paul Lacey's "The Vision of the Burning Babe" cited above. Lacey sees in Levertov's version of the poem a "vision [that] alters the poet's view of the outer world," whereas in Duncan's poem the scene "forces him to *insight*" (175).

26. Anne Dewey's reading of "Passages 30: STAGE DIRECTIONS" bears interestingly on this scene from "The Burning Babe." Dewey comments that the retelling of Medusa's story in the "Passages" poem replaces "the embodied person's vision . . . by confusedly impersonal, disembodied viewers (camera and unidentified cameraman, wound, medusa's severed head, staring mouths)." Instead of a reciprocal gaze of recognition between individuals, "focus on the horrific wound and voraciously 'yawning' mouth replaces the compassionate, familiar human gaze with a dizzying abyss, an appetite out of control" ("Poetic Authority and the Public Sphere of Politics" 122). In the context of Dewey's argument about the difficulty of retaining a sense of individual agency in a postliberal democracy like the United States at midcentury, this Medusa scene suggests "the destruction of private integrity and the resultant inchoate welter of agency and affect exposed in the absence of conventional political agents" (122). I suggest that the staring eyes of the napalm victim in "The Burning Babe" has a similar effect. That gaze turns the spectator to stone because there is no adequate way of returning it.

27. See Albert Gelpi's essay, "Poetic Language and Language Poetry: Levertov, Duncan, Creeley," for a discussion of Duncan's poetry as reflexive and Levertov's as referential (181).

28. Cold War game theory took as a supposition that human nature is essentially

selfish. It was developed by John von Neumann and Oskar Morgenstern in 1944 in a book called *Theory of Games and Economic Behavior* and was used to shape economic policies and nuclear strategies. John F. Nash is also credited with developing game theory; in 1994 he shared the Nobel Prize in economics with Reinhard Selten and John Harsanyi for this work. Nash's story is featured in the film *A Beautiful Mind* (1999), a screen adaptation of Sylvia Nasar's biography, and in a BBC documentary called *The Trap* (2007). The latter hypothesizes that game theory was partially responsible for dismantling ideas of citizenship and public good in favor of the self-serving consumer. On a Princeton University Web page devoted to Nash, *A Beautiful Mind* is characterized as highly fictional. This Web site recommends to the curious *The Essential John Nash* (2002), edited by Harold W. Kuhn and Sylvia Nasar.

Chapter 5

1. Michael Davidson's *San Francisco Renaissance* (1989) and Kevin Killian and Lew Ellingham's biography of Spicer, *Poet, Be Like God* (1998) (1–33), offer rich commentary on the Berkeley Renaissance. As well, Ekbert Faas has a chapter on Berkeley in *Young Robert Duncan* (1983), a biography of Duncan's early years (203–22), and Robin Blaser describes the period in an interview with Miriam Nichols in *Even on Sunday: Essays, Readings, and Archival Materials on the Poetry and Poetics of Robin Blaser* (2002) (349–92).

2. Spicer's closest touchstone was Duncan, and the contrariety shows in Spicer's insistence on a linguist's construction of language—a perspective diametrically opposite to that of Duncan who tropes on the Kabbalistic tradition of a sacred, living language. Duncan fully identifies with the life *of* language; Spicer with the life *under* the language. For Spicer's relationship to Olson and Creeley, see Ellingham and Killian's biography. The Black Mountain connection was not direct, as was that among Duncan, Spicer, and Blaser, nor was it particularly friendly. For instance, Ellingham and Killian record an incident between Spicer and Olson that ended badly, with Olson remarking on an occasion when Spicer had laid out Tarot cards, "Your poetry is bullshit, just like your rituals, just like your cards" (88). What I mean by contrariety in this context is, in relation to Olson, Spicer's determined privacy as opposed to Olson's public persona. Spicer is closer to Creeley in his struggle to get experience into the language, but Spicer built a poetics around the distrust and negation of words rather than an effort to renovate them through strategies such as Basic English.

3. *My Vocabulary Did This to Me,* a new edition of Spicer's collected poems released in 2008, edited by Peter Gizzi and Kevin Killian, is now circulating. For ease of reference, I will include page numbers from both the first edition, *The Collected Books of Jack Spicer* (*CB*) edited by Robin Blaser, and *My Vocabulary* (*MV*) wherever there is a crossover.

4. I have in mind particularly chapters 1 and 2 of *Theory of Religion* (1992), in which Bataille talks about the forming of clear and distinct ideas through the devel-

opment of tools and the use of the language. Animals, in contrast to the human, are in the world "like water in water" (25).

5. See also *The Sublime Object of Ideology* (1989) where Žižek writes that "the position from which the deconstructivist can always make sure of the fact that 'there is no metalanguage'; that no utterance can say precisely what it intended to say; that the process of enunciation always subverts the utterance; is *the position of metalanguage* in its purest, most radical form" (154–55). I think a similar argument could be made against Žižek when he moves into the ongoing negation of all imaginable social conditions or psychic states. The point in all examples is, as Horkheimer and Adorno argue, that the more ruthlessly pure the skepticism, the more it encrypts a will to power.

6. See Stuart and Scoggan in "Orientation of the Parasols" in the *boundary 2* special issue on Spicer (1977). This is a very long deconstructive essay that argues that Spicer constructs truth and presence as missing or misplaced, thus repressing the trajectory of the signifier.

7. On Spicerian translation, see Clayton Eshleman ("The Lorca Working"), Lori Chamberlain ("Ghostwriting the Text"), and Daniel Katz ("Jack Spicer's *After Lorca*"). On dictation, most of Spicer's readers include some commentary on it. In particular, see Robin Blaser's "The Practice of Outside" (*Collected Books of Jack Spicer* 1975; *Fire* 2006). Peter Gizzi's extended Afterword in *The House That Jack Built* (1998) offers a very important overview of Spicer's work.

8. Commenting on "The Scrollwork on the Casket," Gizzi writes that the piece "has the hallucinatory quality of a crime, although it is hard to distinguish between perpetrator and victim" (in *House* 181). He goes on to say that "the confusion is due partly to the notion that the poet is already posthumous in the act of composition, so there is no way of knowing if by nailing the dead into place he or she has merely been drawn into the underworld in order to be trapped there" (181). I would say that as soon as the living author opens his mouth he is already in the prison house of language.

9. See Ellen Tallman's "My Stories with Robert Duncan" for a description of the Anarcho Pacifist Libertarian Circle where she first met Duncan, Spicer, and Blaser (63).

10. Ellen Tallman records this definition of anarchism from notes taken at the Circle:

Anarchism
A revolution without authority
That destroys power wielding institutions
And replaces them by voluntary
Cooperative institutions. ("My Stories" 64)

11. Ekbert Faas recounts John Crowe Ransom's rejection of "An African Elegy" following the publication of Duncan's essay "The Homosexual in Society" (*Young Robert Duncan* 149–54).

12. St. Teresa describes the soul "as resembling a castle, formed of a single diamond or a very transparent crystal, and containing many rooms" (*Interior Castle* 4). The aim of the devout is to traverse the seven mansions that lead to the center where God dwells. Each step involves its disciplines of purification and devotion. Commenting on the transparency of the castle, in his *Teresa of Avila*, Archbishop Rowan Williams writes that "although this is primarily meant to excite our wonder at the beauty of the soul, there is [. . .] a kind of subtext which indicates a less benign element in this language. The castle is made of diamond or glass: thus we can see through it. We can see enough to know that God is there. Yet there are many chambers; and if their walls are transparent, we cannot know very securely how many separate us from the deceptively visible centre" (*Teresa of Avila* 114). The image here is precise to Spicer's treatment of the poem as a castle in which we can "see" the boys but are separated from them by the deceptively transparent labyrinths of language.

13. I have in mind the "Fort! Da!" game Freud describes in *Beyond the Pleasure Principle* (1959), as well as Heidegger's Dasein—being-in-the-world. "Fort! Da!" is about the acquisition of language. As a toddler, Freud's nephew would throw objects away from himself, uttering an "o-o-o-o," which Freud and the child's mother interpreted as "Fort." The child would then retrieve the objects, uttering "Da" (*Beyond the Pleasure Principle* 33). Jacques Lacan would later make much of this game as evidencing the acquisition of language through a learning of presence and absence. For commentary on Lacan and "Fort! Da!" (scattered throughout the text) see Anthony Wilden's *Speech and Language in Psychoanalysis* (1968). I have no evidence that Spicer was familiar with Freud's "Fort! Da!" nor that he read Heidegger.

14. Michael Snediker's engaging analysis of *Billy the Kid* in *Queer Optimism* (2009) complements my reading of the "Elegies," although our vocabularies differ quite sharply. Snediker treats the poem as a hideout for Billy, at once "shelter and threat" (145). It is a shelter because it saves him from the "posse" and certain death; it is a threat because it references capture. Similarly, the "Elegies" shelter the boys from exposure to the two eyes of God, but by reducing them to snapshots the poem also kills them. The poet *wants* to entice the boys to his "castle of skin and glass," and yet knows that if he does he will "be like God"—equally reductive in pinning them down with a gaze. Snediker suggests that Spicer's seriality, as it plays out in Billy's many identities and aliases (in and out of the poem), saves the singular from reduction through the "multiplicities emerging from personality" (167). In his terms, the *fake* is a key to nonreductive singularity. In my terms, serial identities suggest a mimesis of temporality.

15. Ross Clarkson makes this point in a slightly different way in his "Jack Spicer's Ghosts and the Immemorial Community." Clarkson notes that "in Spicer's sense of tradition, language does not establish a correspondence of words to things so much as it does a cross-temporal correspondence of poets, translators, and readers" (203). A few lines later, he writes that "this silent poem [a poem with an infinitely small vocabulary] is an image of language effacing itself before the experience of the object" (203).

16. Davidson argues that conversation within a small community was essential to Spicer's poetics—that "poetry is created in dialogue and argumentation, and in this sense contrasts with the Symbolist based poetry of the New Critics who upheld the autonomy of the single poem and the authority of the creative imagination" ("The City Redefined," *Acts* 80). I think this element of Spicer's methodology is particularly evident in his rivalry with Duncan. Not only did he quarrel with Duncan personally, but he also constructed a poetics built on exactly what Duncan leaves out: the incommunicable singularity of undergoing something.

17. See my comments in the Duncan essay above on Duncan's use of the Kabbalah, particularly the cosmogony of the *Zohar.*

18. Discussing Spicer's dictation, Michael Davidson argues that the embodiment of the message from "outside" in language is a kind of incarnation ("Incarnations" 109). I find it more useful to think of the relationship between the real and the word as a deliberate dis-incarnation. Language seems to offer up the world to human cognition; Spicer suggests that it only offers a ghostly abstraction or shade of actual life.

19. Blaser notes Spicer's attention to Calvin ("Practice of Outside," *Fire* 151); Davidson remarks on Spicer's antinomianism ("Incarnations" 105) and "Calvin's absolutely endistanced God" (109).

20. The phrase "the community of those who have nothing in common" is the title of a book by Alphonso Lingis.

21. In "The City Redefined," Michael Davidson describes Spicer's Berkeley community as a "circle of sectarian adepts, close in shared sexual and intellectual affinities. They were students of literature and history at UC Berkeley, researching the lore of the Middle Ages and reviving, in postwar California, the "spirit of romance" within their own mystic brotherhood. They self-consciously modeled themselves on the Stefan George circle in Germany, of which their teacher, Ernst Kantorowicz, had been a member" ("The City Redefined," *Acts* 80). As cited in the text, Maria Damon has also discussed the resemblance of the Spicer circle to the "George-kreis" in her *Dark End of the Street* (1993) (153).

Spicer's detective novel, *The Tower of Babel* (posthumously published in 1994) portrays a number of bar scenes that resonate with the Spicer circle Ellingham and Killian describe in *Poet, Be Like God.* Ralston, Spicer's protagonist in *Tower,* is always attentive to who is sitting at the table and who joins. In several scenes, he expresses his distaste for the conversation or the company by moving from the communal table to the bar or ordering single glasses of ale for himself instead of beer for everyone.

22. In *Billy the Kid,* Spicer plays with the incommunicability of pain.

What I mean is
I
Will tell you about the pain
It was a long pain
About as wide as a curtain
But long
As the great outdoors (*CB* 80; *MV* 187)

Chapter 6

1. On *Astonishments,* a series of autobiographical audiotapes made in 1974, Blaser recalls destroying his early writings after an instructor at Northwestern criticized them as derivative of Whitman. Mrs. Arpan turns up in "A Literalist," from *The Moth Poem,* as "the wife of a sailor" (*HF* 67). Of poems written at Berkeley, the only one extant of which I am aware is "Song in Four Parts for Christ the Son," quoted in "Lake of Souls" from *Syntax* (*HF* 231–33). This is not to say what awaits discovery in Blaser's papers, housed in the Contemporary Literature Collection at Simon Fraser University since 2008.

2. See Kevin Killian and Lew Ellingham's biography of Jack Spicer, *Poet, Be Like God,* for a description of Spicer's circle and the Sunday poetry sessions. The chapter titled "The Hell of Personal Relations" (140–79) deals with this phase of Spicer's writing life. In particular, see Stan Persky's firsthand account of a Sunday session, quoted on page 172.

3. For a chronology of Blaser's life, see *The Fire* (401–10).

4. Under the mentorship of Warren and Ellen Tallman, both teaching at the University of British Columbia in the early 1960s, a number of young Canadian poets were exposed to the New American poetry scene. The Vancouver Festival of the Arts (1962) and the Vancouver Poetry Conference (1963), both held at the University of British Columbia, were largely organized by the Tallmans, and these events brought Olson, Duncan, Creeley, Levertov, Ginsberg, and many more to Vancouver. As well, the Tallmans facilitated many smaller readings, including one for Spicer, Blaser, and Stan Persky in 1965. These cross border visits gave a push to what later became an important strand in Canadian postmodernism. *TISH,* a seminal little magazine, came out of Warren Tallman's class and a Duncan visit to Vancouver in 1962 (see Frank Davey's Introduction to *TISH 1–19* for the story [7–11]). Of the poets associated with *TISH*—Frank Davey (editor), George Bowering, Jamie Reid, Fred Wah, and David Dawson—Davey, Bowering, and Wah have since gone on to long and distinguished university careers that have contributed substantially to shaping contemporary Canadian writing.

5. Critical attention to Blaser's oeuvre began to pick up after the publication of the first edition of *The Holy Forest,* edited by Stan Persky and Michael Ondaatje (Coach House Press, 1993). A conference on his work held in 1995 at the Emily Carr College of Art and Design in Vancouver attracted a wide range of distinguished scholars and issued in a collection of essays, *The Recovery of the Public World* (1999), edited by Charles Watts and Edward Byrne. Another collection of essays and archival materials, *Even on Sunday,* which I edited, came out in 2002. Ondaatje's introduction to Blaser on the occasion of the conference confirms my own impressions of Blaser's reception in Canada. As Ondaatje said then, "it has taken us a long time to welcome him in Canada" ("Introduction," *Recovery* 454).

Of the essays in these collections, I have found Steve McCaffery's "Blaser's Deleuzean Folds" from *Recovery* and Peter Middleton's "An Elegy for Theory" from *Even on Sunday* to be particularly apposite and helpful to my own work on Blaser.

6. See Don Byrd's description of the Whiteheadian structure of *The Maximus Poems* in *Charles Olson's Maximus* (168–69). Blaser quotes from this passage in his own essay on Olson and Whitehead, "The Violets" (*Fire* 215–16).

7. In "The Violets: Charles Olson and Alfred North Whitehead," Blaser draws attention to just this trope of Olson's. The title of the essay comes from a Black Mountain College lecture from 1956 in which Olson says that important thinkers like Whitehead come out like violets when they are needed ("The Violets," *Fire* 202).

8. Peter Middleton draws attention to Blaser's definition of discourse as performative—"the use of language each of us agrees to" ("An Elegy for Theory" 202). He comments that "this neatly modulates certain waves of poststructuralism which have too readily repeated Saussure's thesis that 'language is a system of differences' as if it were a natural law rather than heuristic method" (202).

9. Merleau-Ponty's chapter, "The Intertwining—The Chiasm," in *The Visible and the Invisible* is a particularly important source for Blaser (131–55): "What there is then are not things first identical with themselves, which would then offer themselves to the seer, nor is there a seer who is first empty and who, afterward, would open himself to them—but something to which we could not be closer than by palpating it with our look, things we could not dream of seeing 'all naked' because the gaze itself envelops them, clothes them with its own flesh" (131).

10. See Steve McCaffery's translation of polarity into Deleuzean language ("Blaser's Deleuzean Folds" [378]) and his remarks on *The Holy Forest* as both a "monadography" and a "nomadography" (381). McCaffery points out that in "The Practice of Outside," Blaser takes the "fold" from Blake, rather than Leibniz-Deleuze (379). The Deleuzean fold comes later in the poems of *Exody* (1993), the last serial of the first edition of *The Holy Forest.*

11. See the opening pages of *The Birth of Tragedy* in which Nietzsche associates Apollo with image and Dionysus with music; the one with form, the other with process. Apollo creates the illusion that life is beauty; Dionysus shatters that illusion in wild becomings that are at once ecstatic and brutally destructive of individuals.

12. The poem beginning with the phrase "no body," from OH! (2004), has a green moth flutter in (*HF* 501).

13. The phrase "*cultural orphanhood*" comes from the Preface to *Syntax.* Blaser writes that "*Syntax* felt odd when I wrote and published it in 1983. The *cultural orphanhood* that has hunted me since childhood came to the surface" (*HF* 203).

14. See "Man and His Doubles" in *The Order of Things,* particularly pages 351–58 on the "unthought."

15. See note 7 from the Creeley essay for Wilden's explication of the Lacanian zero.

16. I am aware that I may be read as contradicting myself by first distinguishing Blaser's poetry from the poststructuralist project and then glossing a Blaser poem on the sacramental with citations from Derrida. This after identifying Blaser's project as moving toward that of Deleuze, Derrida's rival. Yet "Faith and Knowledge" is about reopening the word "religion" and this is a point of intersection with Blaser. As I sug-

gest in my comments on Blaser's use of Merleau-Ponty, Foucault, and Lacan, Blaser does not dismiss poststructuralism or Lacanian psychoanalysis; rather, he adapts these critical methods to serve his own orientation to perceptual experience. In the early *Image-Nations,* Blaser focuses on the creative moment in which both self and world emerge: this is the sacred in its primordial form. Derrida's focus is elsewhere; "Faith and Knowledge," is about the undecidability of *religio* in its double root as the unscathed (the sacrosanct) and the fiduciary (bond, trust, promise). It is Derrida's particular art to hold the concept in *suspension;* it is Blaser's to track the dynamics of form as it is emergent.

17. In "Particles," Blaser devotes a generous paragraph to quarrelling with Ernst Fischer, a Marxist art critic and author of *The Necessity of Art: A Marxist Approach,* over the latter's remarks on myth and magic. Fischer argues that archaic art serves a cultic function—"power over nature, an enemy, a sexual partner, power over reality, power to strengthen the human collective" (qtd. in "Particles" 14). Blaser objects that "magic is a kind of knowledge, not power. . . . Knowledge involves discipline and seeing. Fischer gives us relations but no participation" (*Fire* 14). Blaser would thus contest my linking of magic to archaic efforts to control nature or other people.

18. I am adapting the phrase "separate and relate" from Hannah Arendt's *The Human Condition.* In its original context, it is a descriptor of public space. It comes from this passage, which Blaser quotes in "The Recovery of the Public World": "To live together in the world means essentially that a world of things is between those who have it in common, as a table is located between those who sit around it; the world, like every in-between relates and separates men at the same time" ("Recovery," *Fire* 78; *Human Condition* 48). Arendt's "in-between" is a key concept, freely adapted, throughout Blaser's oeuvre.

19. For a discussion of the symbolism of the toys, see Guthrie (*Orpheus and Greek Religion* 121–26).

20. Rudolf Otto's description of the uncanny is close to Blaser's sense that the gods emerge from primordial astonishments: "It first begins to stir in the feeling of 'something uncanny,' 'eerie,' or 'weird.' It is the feeling which, emerging in the mind of primeval man, forms the starting-point for the entire religious development in history. 'Daemons' and 'gods' alike spring from this root, and all the products of 'mythological apperception' or 'fantasy' are nothing but different modes in which it has been objectified" (*Idea of the Holy* 14–15). I cannot comment on the accuracy of Otto's claim as religious history, nor do I think Blaser's *Image-Nations* are to be read as such. Blaser engages the affective content of *religio;* he does not offer a thesis on the origin of religions.

21. See my essay "Introduction: Reading Robin Blaser" in *Even on Sunday,* especially pages 49–58.

22. Obviously, *Syntax* (1981) predates widespread use of the Internet and sites like YouTube. But to what extent this new global medium reopens public space to real variousness seems to me a vexed question that would have to include a study of the disconnect between popular expression and executive power in North American de-

mocracies (the democratic deficit); the genealogy of grassroots organizations like moveon.org out of Net culture; the use of the Web by mainstream media; and the difference between what Arendt and Blaser mean by public space and the great quantities of idle chatter to be found on the Web. These questions are beyond my scope on this occasion.

23. "The Recovery of the Public World" and "Among Afterthoughts on This Occasion" were first published in *Reflections on Cultural Policy: Past, Present, and Future,* a collection Blaser edited with Evan Alderson and Harold Coward.

24. All citations from the bible are taken from *The Oxford Annotated Bible,* edited by Herbert May and Grace Metzger (1962).

25. Deleuze discusses the nomad in his "1227: Treatise on Nomadology—The War Machine" in *A Thousand Plateaus* (1987, with Guattari) (351–423) and in the last chapter of *The Fold* (1993). The nomads are "things-flows" (*Plateaus* 361) without the horizonal orientation still available in Whitehead's chaosmos, and Olson's too. Whitehead's God is a "lure for feeling" toward a universe of maximum complexity; Deleuze imagines relational complexity raised to another level, such that incompossible worlds coexist in virtuality. For a discussion of the mutation of monad to nomad in the context of Blaser's oeuvre, see Steve McCaffery's "Blaser's Deleuzean Folds," as referenced above in note 10, especially the section titled "From Monad to Nomad" (380–82).

Chapter 7

1. I am quoting Emily Dickinson's hummingbird poem #1463, "A Route of Evanescence" (*Complete Poems* 619).

2. In the *Talisman* interview, Howe associates the stutter with the feminine and finds it in Olson's syntax and silences despite what she hears as his masculinist treatment of female figures (180–81). Howe comes back to the stutter in the interview with Lynn Keller. Keller asks whether Howe has found a "kind of permission" in the French theorists (Walter Benjamin, Julia Kristeva, Emmanuel Lévinas, Maurice Blanchot, Jacques Derrida, Michel Foucault), as she had in Olson. Howe replies: "It's different. Foreign, because usually they are French, and they seem to know so much. The thing I like about Olson is what I've talked about as the stutter in American literature, the hesitation, and you won't find any of that there. French theorists do *not* stutter. They don't help my poetry, but they help my essays" (Keller, "An Interview" 30, original emphasis).

3. See Stephen Fredman's important commentary on Olson in *The Grounding of American Poetry* (1993). Fredman argues that Olson, like Thoreau, proposes an ethos of containment: "When we practice attention and care toward the limits that define us, we become productive people. . . . One exercises containment not by measuring oneself against an external standard but rather by learning to recognize and utilize oneself more and more fully. By recognizing and respecting our limits, we come to know ourselves as what we always were" (38).

4. I am indebted to Don Byrd, in *Charles Olson's Maximus,* for the idea that

Olson recognized that cannibalism is a generalized condition of life in a processive cosmos (15).

5. I am again referring to Bataille on animal versus human consciousness in *Theory of Religion*. The animal is in the world "like water in water" (25): the human, in its construction of the object as tool, establishes a distance from the thing that allows a clear articulation of it as thing, as object lifted out of the continuum of life (27–30).

6. I have in mind Wordsworth's deism in which man and nature are reconciled in the One Life.

7. In addition to his mathematical and philosophical achievements, Pythagoras (ca. 570 to 490 BC) was at the center of a religious cult known for its asceticism and religious discipline. Aspiring disciples had to maintain silence for five years (*Stanford Encyclopedia of Philosophy*).

8. The line is from the first "Pisan Canto" (LXXIV):

I believe in the resurrection of Italy   quia impossibile est
4 times to the song of Gassir
        now in the mind indestructible (*Cantos* 462)

9. Olson turns to Winthrop's "City on a Hill" in *Causal Mythology*, citing John F. Kennedy's citation of Winthrop:

> I mean the city of earth, which as far as I know on this continent arose in Massachusetts, and was, as you all know, quoted by . . . in fact the only time I found Mr. Kennedy interesting, verbally was when he made his appearance, just after his successful election, before the General Court of Massachusetts. I don't know how many of you would have known that he, immediately after his victory, came to, appeared, and made a speech before the General Court of Massachusetts and quoted that remarkable phrase of Winthrop's: "that this colony shall shine like a city on a hill." I may garble it, but some of you that know the speech may remember it. That's the one time I was moved by Mr. Kennedy. (*Causal Mythology* 19)

10. Back interprets this "surrender to a place of 'soft origin'" differently than I do, as a kind of immortality. Discussing *Articulations of Sound Forms in Time*, she writes: "The life force of the forest resides in the rejection of singularity, the suspension of 'cold intellect' (34), . . . the surrender to a place of 'soft origin' where words make their own connections. . . . 'Dear Unconscious scatter syntax / scythe mower surrender hereafter,' writes Howe, linking the liberation of language from syntax with a type of immortality, a triumph over death as it appears in the guise of the scythe mower" (47). To derive immortality from such a "surrender," figure and ground would have to be coextensive, and this cannot take place as a conscious experience.

11. The term "irreparable" comes from an appendix in Giorgio Agamben's *The Coming Community*: "The Irreparable is that things are just as they are, in this or

that mode, consigned without remedy to their way of being. States of things are irreparable, whatever they may be: sad or happy, atrocious or blessed. How you are, how the world is—this is the Irreparable" (89). See also Blaser's essay, "The Irreparable" (*Fire* 98–110), which is a meditation on Agamben's concept. Irreparability is an important point of intersection between Blaser and Howe.

12. More recent attention to Mangan has come from a brief biography by James Kilroy in 1970; a life and writings by Henry J. Donaghy (*James Clarence Mangan*, 1974); David Lloyd's *Nationalism and Minor Literature* (1987), a new historical assessment of Mangan and source for Howe; and Brendan Clifford's *The Dubliner: The Lives, Times, and Writings of James Clarence Mangan* (1988). Postdating Howe's poem are Ellen Shannon-Mangan's *James Clarence Mangan: A Biography* (1996); *The Collected Works of James Clarence Mangan*, edited by Jacques Chuto (ca. 2002); and a *Selected Writings* edited by Sean Ryder (2004).

13. The phrase "The Man in the Cloak" comes from Balzac's "Melmonth Reconcilié," translated by Mangan. Ellen Shannon-Mangan cites the phrase in her biography: "I am *now The Man in the Cloak*. In other words, I am henceforth a being of mystery—none must see me as I really am" (qtd. in Shannon-Mangan, *James Clarence Mangan* 196, original emphasis).

14. Ellen Shannon-Mangan records this account of Mangan's appearance:

> People took note of the poet's blue broadcloth cloak not because it was unusual but because such a garment was intended for evening wear, and Mangan, as well as wearing it winter and summer, also seems to have worn it night and day. Another friend described him as garbed in a brownish coat and pantaloons that were obviously too large for him, although such trousers, like the cloak, were also in style at the time. Sometimes he wore a soldier's fatigue cap, but his hat, often described as high and peaked, was of a style popular with artists during the earlier years of the century. Thus his costume was not particularly eccentric piece by piece, but put together the various articles of clothing probably looked very odd indeed. He apparently continued to wear the same thing, year in and year out, so his appearance became increasingly peculiar. (*James Clarence Mangan* 163)

This description follows that in O'Donoghue's *Life*, although O'Donoghue includes an account of Mangan's "huge pair of green spectacles" and the padding in his clothing, apparently to compensate for a narrow chest and shoulders (qtd. in Shannon-Mangan, *James Clarence Mangan* 195).

15. The phrase, "catastrophe of bifurcation" is Howe's, from the *Talisman* interview, taken from René Thom's *Mathematical Models of Morphogenesis* (in *BM* 173–74). Howe uses the term in the following passage: "That poem [the *Eikon Basilike*] for me is . . . a catastrophe of bifurcation. That's the perfect description" (*BM* 174).

16. See George Hartley's *The Abyss of Representation* for an analysis of the postmodern sublime as a failure of representation and threat to agency.

17. I am indebted to Will Montgomery for drawing my attention to Agamben's reading of "Bartleby" in his essay on Howe's *Melville's Marginalia* ("'Lyric for Crossing Over': Time and Telepathy in Susan Howe's *Melville's Marginalia*" (2004).

18. The pyramid Agamben references comes at the end of Melville's story, when Bartleby has been incarcerated in the "Tombs": "The yard was entirely quiet. It was not accessible to the common prisoners. The surrounding walls, of amazing thickness, kept off all sounds behind them. The Egyptian character of the masonry weighed upon me with its gloom. But a soft imprisoned turf grew under foot. The heart of the eternal pyramids, it seemed, wherein, by some strange magic, through the clefts, grass-seed, dropped by birds, had sprung" (Melville, *Selected Tales and Poems* 130).

19. See Ma's "Susan Howe and the Revision of History," section 2 (723–35) and Peter Quartermain's "And the Without: An Interpretive Essay on Susan Howe" (1989), especially pages 183–92 where Quartermain offers a detailed reading of the first poem of *Scattering.* In both readings, the visual elements of the poem are taken as dramatizations of the meaning.

20. For a different reading of this poem, see Ma's "Poetry as History Revised: Susan Howe's 'Scattering as Behavior toward Risk'" (731–33). Ma reads the poem as a liberating attack on "the best ordered commonwealth," which he understands as patriarchal and repressive.

21. See Rachel Blau DuPlessis' reading of this Lear scene in her essay, "'Whowe': On Susan Howe," in *The Pink Guitar.*

22. Nicky Marsh reproaches Howe with "a desire, at times, to dismiss her own subjective presence. This desire to unleash the indeterminacy of language, to relinquish herself into her text," Marsh says, "prevents her, at times, from acknowledging the full implications of her own cultural positioning" ("'Out of My Texts I Am Not What I Play'" 8). In my view, Howe refuses innocence as well as victimhood.

23. See my discussion of Deleuzean habit in the Olson essay of this collection. Deleuze's account of habit bears a resemblance to Peirce's discussion of how substance forms itself from difference and repetition.

Afterwords

1. See Stephen Fredman's Olson chapter in *The Grounding of American Poetry: Charles Olson and the Emersonian Tradition.*

2. I have in mind Žižek's quarrel with Spinoza in *Organs without Bodies,* particularly the chapter, "Is It Possible Not to Love Spinoza" (33–41). Because Spinoza attributes "bad" behaviors to inadequate knowledge of the cosmos, effectively turning "ought" into "is," Žižek argues, through Kant, that Spinoza's ethics limit freedom: "from the Kantian perspective, Spinoza's position appears as a nightmarish vision of subjects reduced to marionettes" (41).

3. It is clear in "Particles" that Blaser has in mind strong rather than weak universals. The difference is that strong universals are wedded to local contexts, whereas weak ones are empty concepts that can be used in multiple contexts. So a universal

like "the people" becomes strong when "the people" is a code phrase for the will of a few. Blaser draws an example from Spain's fascist period under Francisco Franco, but he also attacks leftist political writers who speak of historical forces or trends rather than particular persons and events.

4. Responding to an audience member after his "Poetry and Politics" lecture, Spicer says:

> I just don't believe that there is an audience for poems. [. . .] it seems to me that you're lucky if you get two or three people within a five-year period who understand any of your poems. So it seems to me that the only reason for writing poetry is because poetry is sort of forced through the poet and is just there, like Mallory's great thing on Everest. [. . .]
>
> What I'm trying to say is that I don't really think that a poet can have any effect whatsoever on society. (*House* 162)

5. The success of the second edition of Spicer's collected poems, *My Vocabulary Did This to Me* (2008) suggests that a great many more readers than he might have imagined are capable of "corresponding" with Jack Spicer. In my view, this is consistent with the principle of correspondence as Spicer lays it out in *After Lorca.* As I have argued in the Spicer essay, the emotions encrypted in the poems are very common, but this does not alter Spicer's point that his is not a poetry aimed at renovation of the public sphere. It takes a Blaser to draw out the political implications of corresponding "particles."

6. See note 3 above. In *Cosmopolitanism,* Kwame Anthony Appiah calls "thin" those concepts like "right and wrong, good and bad" that are common to everyone, and "thick" those concepts that are particular to a given society (47). Conflicts arise when a given group attributes "thick" content to a "thin" universal: *my* definition of "justice," for instance, is the only one.

7. Capital depends on manipulating the future into predictability as much as possible; it is a political economy that does everything possible to appropriate the future for present ends. As I have discussed, Creeley practices a temporality that is aimed at the opposite effect. His attention to the moment is an effort to *un*determine the future. Olson's and Howe's focus on history could be analyzed in a parallel way: the more historical territory uncovered, the more directions open up for the future.

8. Olson in *Special View:* "There are two estrangements, the permanent one, from that which is slipping by in the grass without moving a leaf of grass's top; but this other one, the contingent, of touch on all side—of the company of the living, that they are distracted and dispersed. It is a lie of discourse to split this latter problem into the individual and society. No ancient man could be so logical and sociological, and a post-modern man is, to his waste and grief" (25). In "The Recovery of the Public World," Blaser also rejects the totalizing claims of the social sciences—social or psychological determinism, for instance. This kind of humanism, he says, is worldless because it acknowledges no Other (*Fire* 66).

Works Cited

Adamson, Gregory Dale. "Serres Translates Howe." *SubStance* 26.2, Issue 83: An Ecology of Knowledge: Michel Serres: A Special Issue (1997): 110-24.

Adorno, Theodor W. *Negative Dialectics.* Trans. E. B. Ashton. New York, London: Continuum, 2004.

Agamben, Giorgio. *The Coming Community.* Trans. Michael Hardt. Minneapolis: U of Minnesota P, 1993.

———. *Infancy and History: Essays on the Destruction of Experience.* New York: Verso, 1993.

———. *Potentialities: Collected Essays in Philosophy.* Ed. and trans. Daniel Heller-Roazen. Stanford: Stanford UP, 1999.

Ahmad, Aijaz. *In Theory: Classes, Nations, Literatures.* New York: Verso, 1992.

Alciatus, Andreas. *The Latin Emblems.* Ed. Peter M. Daly. 1985. Toronto: U of Toronto P, 1988.

Alderson, Evan, Robin Blaser, and Harold Coward. *Reflections on Cultural Policy: Past, Present, and Future.* Waterloo: Wilfrid Laurier UP for the Calgary Institute for the Humanities, 1993.

Allen, Donald. *The New American Poetry.* New York: Grove, 1960.

Alpers, Paul. *What Is Pastoral?* Chicago: U of Chicago P, 1996.

Altieri, Charles. *The Particulars of Rapture: An Aesthetics of the Affects.* Ithaca: Cornell UP, 2003.

———. "Placing Creeley's Recent Work: A Poetics of Conjecture." *Robert Creeley: A Gathering.* Ed. William Spanos. *boundary 2* 6.3; 7.1 (1978): 513–44.

———. "Some Problems about Agency in the Theories of Radical Poetries." *The Recovery of the Public World.* Eds. Charles Watts and Edward Byrne. Vancouver: Talonbooks, 1999. 411–27.

André, Michael. "With Michael André." *Tales Out of School.* By Robert Creeley. Ann Arbor: U of Michigan P, 1993. 101–21.

Appadurai, Arjun. *Modernity at Large.* Public Worlds, Vol. 1. Minneapolis: U of Minnesota P, 1996.

Appiah, Anthony Kwame. *Cosmopolitanism: Ethics in a World of Strangers.* New York: Norton, 2006.

Apuleius. *The Transformation of Lucius, otherwise known as The Golden Ass.* Trans. Robert Graves. New York: Farrar, 1951.

Arendt, Hannah. *Eichmann in Jerusalem: A Report on the Banality of Evil.* Rev. ed. Viking Press, 1963. Rev. ed. 1965. Rpt. Harmondsworth, Penguin, 1983.

———. *The Human Condition.* Chicago: U of Chicago P, 1958. Garden City: Doubleday, 1959.

———. "Introduction." *Illuminations.* By Walter Benjamin. Trans. Harry Zohn, ed. Hannah Arendt. 1969. Rpt. New York: Schocken, 1978. 1–55.

———. *The Origins of Totalitarianism.* 1948. Rpt. New York: Harcourt, 1976.

Arnold, Matthew. "The Function of Criticism at the Present Time." *Essays in Criticism,* First Series. London: Macmillan, 1907. 1–41.

———. "The Incompatibles." *English Literature and Irish Politics.* Ed. R. H. Super. Ann Arbor: U of Michigan P, 1973. 238–85.

———. "On the Study of Celtic Literature." *Lectures and Essays in Criticism.* Ed. R. H. Super. Ann Arbor: U of Michigan P, 1962. 291–386.

Audit/Poetry: Featuring Robert Duncan. 4.3 (1967).

Augustine, Saint, Bishop of Hippo. *The City of God.* Trans. Gerald G. Walsh et al. Ed. Vernon J. Bourke. New York: Doubleday, 1958.

Back, Rachel Tzvia. *Led by Language: The Poetry and Poetics of Susan Howe.* Tuscaloosa: U of Alabama P, 2002.

Barthes, Roland. *Writing Degree Zero.* Trans. Annette Lavers and Colin Smith. 1968. Rpt. New York: Hill and Wang, 1980.

Bataille, Georges. *Theory of Religion.* Trans. Robert Hurley. New York: Zone, 1992.

Bernstein, Charles. "Hearing 'Here': Robert Creeley's Poetics of Duration." *Sagetrieb* 1.3 (1982): 87–95.

———. "Undone Business." *Content's Dream: Essays 1975–1984.* Los Angeles: Sun and Moon, 1986. 321–39.

Bernstein, Michael André. "Robert Duncan: Talent and the Individual Tradition." *Sagetrieb* 4.2–3 (1985): 177–90.

Bertholf, Robert. "Decision at the Apogee: Robert Duncan's Anarchist Critique of Denise Levertov." *Robert Duncan and Denise Levertov: The Poetry of Politics, the Politics of Poetry.* Eds. Albert Gelpi and Robert J. Bertholf. Stanford: Stanford UP, 2006. 1–17.

———. "Robert Duncan's 'The Venice Poem' and Symphonic Form." *Jacket* 28 (October 2005). *Jacket.* Web. 30 June 2009.

Bertholf, Robert and Albert Gelpi, eds. *The Letters of Denise Levertov and Robert Duncan.* Stanford: Stanford UP, 2004.

Bertonneau, Thomas F. "Life in the Human Universe: Charles Olson's (Post) Modernism in Context (An Anthopoetics)." *Sagetrieb* 13.3 (1994): 117–52.

Bertrand, Aloysius. "Le Fou." *Gaspard de la nuit: Fantaisies.* Livre III. *Gaspard de la nuit.* Web. 18 June 2009.

Bhabha, Homi K. *The Location of Culture.* London: Routledge, 1994.

Billitteri, Carla. *Language and the Renewal of Society in Whitman, Laura (Riding) Jackson, and Charles Olson.* New York: Palgrave Macmillan, 2009.

Bindé, Jérôme. "Toward an Ethics of the Future." *Globalization.* Millennial Quartet, Vol. 2. Ed. Arjun Appadurai. *Public Culture* 12.1 (2000): 51–72.

Blake, William. "Infant Joy." *Songs of Innocence. The Complete Poems.* 3rd ed. Ed. W. H. Stevenson. Edinburgh: Pearson Longman, 2007. 60–61.

Blaser, Robin. *Astonishments.* With Angela Bowering, Dwight Gardner, Martina Kuharic, Daphne Marlatt, and Warren Tallman. Audiocassettes. Simon Fraser University, Burnaby, Contemporary Literature Collection, 1974.

———. "Excerpts from *Astonishments.*" *Even on Sunday: Essays, Readings, and Archival Materials on the Poetry and Poetics of Robin Blaser.* Ed. Miriam Nichols. Orono: National Poetry Foundation, 2002. 275–347.

———. *The Fire: Collected Essays.* Ed. Miriam Nichols. Berkeley: U of California P, 2006.

———. *The Holy Forest.* Eds. Stan Persky and Michael Ondaatje. Toronto: Coach House, 1993.

———. *The Holy Forest: Collected Poems.* Rev. ed. Ed. Miriam Nichols. Berkeley: U of California P, 2006.

———. "Interview." With Miriam Nichols. *Even on Sunday: Essays, Readings, and Archival Materials on the Poetry and Poetics of Robin Blaser.* Orono: National Poetry Foundation, 2002. 349–92.

———. *The Last Supper.* London: Boosey and Hawkes, 2000.

Bové, Paul. *Destructive Poetics: Heidegger and Modern American Poetry.* New York: Columbia UP, 1980.

Bradstreet, Anne. *The Works of Anne Bradstreet.* Ed. Jeannine Hensley. Foreword Adrienne Rich. 1967. Rpt. Cambridge: Belknap P of Harvard UP, 1981.

Bram, Shahar. *Charles Olson and Alfred North Whitehead.* Lewisburg: Bucknell UP, 2004.

Breton, André. *What Is Surrealism? Selected Writings.* Ed. Franklin Rosemont. New York: Monad, 1978.

Bryant, Levi R. *Difference and Givenness: Deleuze's Transcendental Empiricism and the Ontology of Immanence.* Evanston: Northwestern UP, 2008.

Buchanan, Ian. *Deleuzism: A Metacommentary.* Durham: Duke UP, 2000.

Butterick, George. *A Guide to the Maximus Poems of Charles Olson.* 1978. Rpt. Berkeley: U of California P, 1980.

———. "Seraphic Predator: A First Reading of Robert Duncan's *Ground Work.*" *Sagetrieb* 4.2–3 (1985): 273–83.

Butts, Mary. *Armed with Madness.* London: Wishart, 1928. Rpt. London: Penguin, 2001.

Byrd, Don. *Charles Olson's Maximus.* Urbana: U of Illinois P, 1980.

———. "Curriculum for the Conning of the New Polis (Olson Now!)." OlsonNow Blog. Eds. Ammiel Alcalay and Michael Kelleher. Web. 30 June 2009.

———. "Cybernetics and Form." OlsonNow Blog. Eds. Ammiel Alcalay and Michael Kelleher. Web. 30 June 2009.
———. "The Question of Wisdom as Such." *Scales of the Marvelous.* Eds. Robert J. Bertholf and Ian W. Reid. New York: New Directions, 1979. 38–55.
Cambridge Dictionary of Philosophy. Ed. Robert Audi. New York: Cambridge UP, 1995.
Carroll, Lewis. *Alice's Adventures in Wonderland and Through the Looking Glass.* Oxford: Oxford UP, 1971.
———. *The Annotated Hunting of the Snark.* Ed. Martin Gardner. New York: Norton, 2006.
Carter, Steven. "Robert Duncan and Erwin Schrödinger: Esthetics of the Wave Function." *Studies in Humanities* 17.1 (1990): 36–48.
Castiglione, Baldesar. *The Book of the Courtier.* Trans. Charles S. Singleton. New York: Doubleday/Anchor, 1959.
Certeau, Michel de. *Heterologies: Discourse on the Other.* Trans. Brian Massumi. Theory and History of Literature, Vol. 17. Minneapolis: U of Minnesota P, 1986.
Chamberlain, Lori. "Ghostwriting the Text: Translation and the Poetics of Jack Spicer." *Contemporary Literature* 26.4 (1985): 426–22.
Charters, Ann. *Olson/Melville: A Study in Affinity.* Berkeley: Oyez, 1968.
Christensen, Paul. *Call Him Ishmael.* Austin: U of Texas P, 1975.
———. "Robert Creeley and Me." *Northwest Review* 38.2 (2000): 102–13.
Clark, Tom. *Charles Olson.* New York: Norton, 1991.
Clark, Tom, ed. *Robert Creeley and the Genius of the American Common Place.* New York: New Directions, 1993.
Clarkson, Ross. "Jack Spicer's Ghosts and the Immemorial Community." *Mosaic* 34.4 (2001): 199–211.
Clifford, Brendan. *The Lives, Times, and Writings of James Clarence Mangan.* Belfast: Athol, 1988.
Cobb, Edith. "The Ecology of Imagination in Childhood." *Daedelus* 3 (Summer 1959): 537–48.
Cohn, Jack R., and Thomas J. O'Donnell. "An Interview with Robert Duncan." *Contemporary Literature* 21.4 (1980): 513–48.
———. " 'The Poetry of Unevenness': An Interview with Robert Duncan." *Cadences* 3.2 (1985): 91–111.
Collis, Stephen. " 'The Frayed Trope of Rome': Poetic Architecture in Robert Duncan, Ronald Johnson, and Lisa Robertson." *Mosaic* (December 2002): 143–62.
———. *Through Words of Others: Susan Howe and Anarcho-Scholasticism.* Victoria: English Literary Studies Editions, 2006.
Corbin, Henry. *The Man of Light in Iranian Sufism.* Trans. Nancy Pearson. Boulder: Shambhala, 1978. New York: distributed by Random House, 1978.
Corman, Cid. " 'For Love' Of." *Robert Creeley's Life and Work.* Ed. John Wilson. Ann Arbor: U of Michigan P, 1987. 103–22.

Corrington, Robert. *An Introduction to C. S. Peirce.* Lanham: Rowman and Littlefield, 1993.
Cowen, Wilson Walker. *Melville's Marginalia.* New York: Garland P, 1987.
Creeley, Robert. *The Collected Essays of Robert Creeley.* Berkeley: U of California P, 1989.
———. *The Collected Poems of Robert Creeley, 1945–1975.* 1982. Rpt. Berkeley: U of California P, 2007.
———. *The Collected Poems of Robert Creeley, 1975–2005.* Berkeley: U of California P, 2006.
———. *The Collected Prose of Robert Creeley.* New York: Marion Boyars, 1984.
———. *A Day Book.* New York: Scribner's, 1972.
———. *The Finger.* Los Angeles: Black Sparrow P, 1968.
———. *For Love: Poems 1950–1960.* New York: Scribner's, 1962.
———. "Introduction to *Whitman: Selected by Robert Creeley.*" *Collected Essays of Robert Creeley.* Berkeley: U of California P, 1989. 3–12.
———. *Pieces.* New York: Scribner's, 1969.
———. *Tales Out of School: Selected Interviews.* Ann Arbor: U of Michigan P, 1993.
———. *Was That a Real Poem and Other Essays.* Ed. Donald Allen. Bolinas: Four Seasons, 1979.
———. *Words.* New York: Scribner's, 1967.
Cross, Jonathan. *The Last Supper Guide: An Introduction to the Story and Music, with Harrison Birtwistle.* Glyndebourne Productions, 2000.
Damon, Maria. *The Dark End of the Street: Margins in American Vanguard Poetry.* Minneapolis: U of Minnesota P, 1993.
Davey, Frank. "Introduction." *TISH 1–19.* Ed Frank Davey. Vancouver: Talonbooks, 1975. 7–11.
Davidson, Michael. "A Book of First Things: *The Opening of the Field.*" *Scales of the Marvelous.* Eds. Robert Bertholf and Ian Reid. New York: New Directions, 1979. 56–84.
———. "Cave of Resemblances, Cave of Rimes: Tradition and Repetition in Robert Duncan." *Ironwood* 22 (1983): 33–65. Also in *The San Francisco Renaissance: Poetics and Community at Mid-Century.* Cambridge: Cambridge UP, 1989. 125–49.
———. " 'The City Redefined': Community and Dialogue in Jack Spicer." *Acts* 6 (1987): 80–84. Rev. version in *The San Francisco Renaissance: Poetics and Community at Mid-Century.* Cambridge: Cambridge UP, 1989. 150–71.
———. *Ghostlier Demarcations: Modern Poetry and the Material World.* Berkeley: U of California P, 1997.
———. "Incarnations of Jack Spicer: Heads of the Town up to the Aether." *boundary 2* 6.1 (1977): 103–34
———. *The San Francisco Renaissance: Poetics and Community at Mid-Century.* Cambridge: Cambridge UP, 1989.
Deleuze, Gilles. *Difference and Repetition.* Trans. Paul Patton. London: Athlone, 1994. New York: Columbia UP, 1994.

———. *Empiricism and Subjectivity: An Essay on David Hume's Theory of Human Nature.* Trans. Constantin Boundas. New York: Columbia UP, 2001.

———. *The Fold: Leibniz and the Baroque.* Trans. Tom Conley. Minneapolis: U of Minnesota P, 1993.

———. *Spinoza: Practical Philosophy.* Trans. Robert Hurley. San Francisco: City Lights, 1988.

Deleuze, Gilles and Félix Guattari. *A Thousand Plateaus: Capitalism and Schizophrenia.* Trans. Brian Massumi. Minneapolis: U of Minnesota P, 1987.

Derrida, Jacques. "Faith and Knowledge: The Two Sources of 'Religion' at the Limits of Reason Alone." *Religion.* Eds. Jacques Derrida and Gianni Vattimo. Stanford: Stanford UP, 1996. 1–78.

———. *The Gift of Death.* Trans. David Wills. Chicago: U of Chicago P, 1995.

Dewey, Anne. *Beyond Maximus: The Constitution of Public Voice in Black Mountain Poetry.* Stanford: Stanford UP, 2007.

———. "Poetic Authority and the Public Sphere of Politics." *Robert Duncan and Denise Levertov: The Poetry of Politics, the Politics of Poetry.* Eds. Albert Gelpi and Robert J. Bertholf. Stanford: Stanford UP, 2006. 109–25.

Dickinson, Emily. *The Complete Poems of Emily Dickinson.* Ed. Thomas H. Johnson. Boston: Little, 1960.

Diehl, Paul. "The Literal Activity of Robert Creeley." *Robert Creeley: A Gathering.* Ed. William Spanos. *boundary 2* 6.3; 7.1 (1978): 335–46.

Donaghy, Henry J. *James Clarence Mangan.* New York: Twayne, 1974.

Duncan, Robert. *Bending the Bow.* New York: New Directions, 1968.

———. *Caesar's Gate.* Berkeley: Sand Dollar, 1972.

———. *Fictive Certainties: Essays.* New York: New Directions, 1985.

———. *Ground Work: Before the War.* New York: New Directions, 1984.

———. *Ground Work II: In the Dark.* New York: New Directions, 1987.

———. *The H. D. Book,* Part I: Chapter 1. *Coyote's Journal* 5–6 (1966): 8–31.

———. *The H. D. Book,* Part I: Chapter 2. *Coyote's Journal* 8 (1967): 27–35.

———. *The H. D. Book,* Part I: "Beginnings," Chapter 5: "Occult Matters." *Stony Brook* 1/2 (Fall 1968): 4–20.

———. *The H. D. Book,* Part II: Chapter 5. *Credences II* 1.2 (1975): 50–94.

———. *The H. D. Book,* Part II: "Nights and Days," Chapter 9. *Chicago Review* 30.3 (1979): 37–88.

———. *The H. D. Book:* "Rites of Participation." *Caterpillar* 1 (1967): 6–29.

———. "Letters on Poetry and Poetics." *Ironwood* 22.9 (1983): 95–135.

———. *The Opening of the Field.* New York: New Directions, 1960.

———. "Pages from a Notebook: Statements on Poetics." *The New American Poetry.* Ed. Donald M. Allen. New York: Grove, 1960. 400–407.

———. *Roots and Branches.* New York: New Directions, 1964.

———. "Two Chapters from *H. D.*" *TriQuarterly* 12 (Spring 1968): 67–98.

———. "The Venice Poem." *Poems 1948–1949.* Berkeley: Berkeley Miscellany Editions, 1949. 21–52.

———. *The Years as Catches.* Berkeley: Oyez, 1966.

DuPlessis, Rachel Blau. "'Whowe': On Susan Howe." *The Pink Guitar: Writing as Feminist Practice.* London: Routledge, 1990. 123–39.

Edelberg, Cynthia Dubin. "Creeley's Orphan Lines: The Rhythmic Character of the Sequences." *Sagetrieb* 1.3 (1982): 143–62.

———. "In London." *Robert Creeley's Life and Work: A Sense of Increment.* Ed. John Wilson. Ann Arbor: U of Michigan P, 1987. 275–300.

Edwards, Jonathan. *Images or Shadows of Divine Things.* Ed. Perry Miller. 1948. Rpt. Westport: Greenwood, 1977.

———. "Sinners in the Hands of an Angry God." *The Sermons of Jonathan Edwards: A Reader.* Eds. Wilson H. Kimnach, Kenneth P. Minkema, and Douglas A. Sweeney. New Haven: Yale UP, 1999. 49–65.

Eliot, T.S., *The Waste Land and Other Poems.* London: Faber and Faber, 1972.

———. "Tradition and the Individual Talent." *Selected Essays.* 1932. London: Faber, 1986. 13–22.

Ellingham, Lew, and Kevin Killian. *Poet, Be Like God: Jack Spicer and the San Francisco Renaissance.* Hanover: UP of New England, 1998.

Elliott, David L. "An Interview with Robert Creeley." *Sagetrieb* 10.1–2 (1991): 45–65.

Emerson, Ralph Waldo. "Circles." *Essays.* 1st Series. New York: AMS, 1968. 301–22.

———. "Fate." *The Conduct of Life.* New York: AMS, 1968. 4–49.

Entwistle, Alice. "'For W. C. W.,' 'Yet Complexly': Creeley and Williams." *Journal of the English Association* 50 (Summer 2001): 126–48.

———. "Robert Creeley and Robert Duncan: A World of Contradiction." *Journal of American Studies* 32 (1998): 263–79.

Eshleman, Clayton. "The Lorca Working." *boundary 2* 6.1 (1977): 31–50.

———. "Note on Charles Olson and the Archaic." OlsonNow Blog. Eds. Ammiel Alcalay and Michael Kelleher. Web. 30 June 2009.

Faas, Ekbert. *Young Robert Duncan: Portrait of the Poet as Homosexual in Society.* Santa Barbara: Black Sparrow, 1983.

Felstiner, John. "The Hasid and the Kabbalist." *Robert Duncan and Denise Levertov: The Poetry of Politics, the Politics of Poetry.* Eds. Albert Gelpi and Robert J. Bertholf. Stanford: Stanford UP, 2006. 81–89.

Ferrini, Henry, and Ken Riaf. *Polis Is This.* DVD. Ferrini Productions, 2007.

Fischer, Ernst. *The Necessity of Art: A Marxist Approach.* Trans. Anna Bostock. 1963. Harmondsworth: Penguin, 1964.

Ford, Arthur L. *Robert Creeley.* Boston: Twayne, 1978.

Foucault, Michel. *The Order of Things: An Archaeology of the Human Sciences.* Trans. of *Les mots et les choses.* Paris: Gallimard, 1966. 1970. Rpt. London: Routledge, 2005.

Fredman, Stephen. *The Grounding of American Poetry: Charles Olson and the Emersonian Tradition.* Cambridge: Cambridge UP, 1993.

Freud, Sigmund. *Beyond the Pleasure Principle.* Trans. James Strachey. 1959. Rpt. New York: Bantam, 1972.

——. *Civilization and Its Discontents.* Trans. and ed. James Strachey. New York: Norton, 1961.

——. *Future of an Illusion.* Trans. James Strachey. New York: Norton, 1961.

Friedlander, Benjamin. "Charles Olson Now." OlsonNow Blog. Eds. Ammiel Alcalay and Michael Kelleher. Web. 20 May 2006. Web. 16 January 2009.

Gelpi, Albert, and Robert Bertholf, eds. *Robert Duncan and Denise Levertov: The Poetry of Politics, the Politics of Poetry.* Stanford: Stanford UP, 2006.

Giedion, Sigfried. *The Eternal Present: A Contribution on Constancy and Change.* Bollingen Series, Vol. 1, 35.6.1. New York: Bollingen, 1962.

Gilbert, Alan. "Charles Olson and Empire, or Charles Olson Flips the Wartime Script." OlsonNow Blog. Eds. Ammiel Alcalay and Michael Kelleher. Web. 30 June 2009.

Girard, René. *Violence and the Sacred.* Trans. Patrick Gregory. Baltimore: Johns Hopkins UP, 1977.

Gizzi, Peter. "Afterword: Jack Spicer and the Practice of Reading." *The House That Jack Built: The Collected Lectures of Jack Spicer.* Hanover: UP of New England, 1998. 171–225.

——, ed. *The House That Jack Built: The Collected Lectures of Jack Spicer.* Hanover: UP of New England, 1998.

Glover, Joshua. "The Sunday of the Seventies: The Saint of Negation." Conference presentation. Poetry of the 70s. Orono, Maine, University of Orono, 13 June 2008.

Godzich, Wlad. "Foreword." *Heterologies: Discourse on the Other.* By Michel de Certeau. Trans. Brian Massumi. Minneapolis: U of Minnesota P, 1986. vii–xxi.

Grenier, Robert. "A Packet for Robert Creeley." *Robert Creeley: A Gathering.* Ed. William Spanos. *boundary 2* 6.3; 7.1 (1978): 421–41.

Guthrie, W. K. C. *Orpheus and Greek Religion: A Study of the Orphic Movement.* London: Methuen, 1935.

Haas, Robert. "Creeley: His Metric." *Robert Creeley's Life and Work.* Ed. John Wilson. Ann Arbor: U of Michigan P, 1987. 391–400.

Halden-Sullivan, Judith. *The Topology of Being: The Poetics of Charles Olson.* New York: Peter Lang, 1991.

Hamner, M. Gail. *American Pragmatism: A Religious Genealogy.* Oxford: Oxford UP, 2003.

Harris, Kaplan. "Susan Howe's Art and Poetry, 1968–1974." *Contemporary Literature* 27.3 (2006): 440–71.

Harrison, Jane. *Themis: A Study of the Social Origins of Greek Religion.* 1963. London: Merlin, 1977.

Hartley, George. *The Abyss of Representation.* Durham: Duke UP, 2003.

Hartman, Geoffrey. *Beyond Formalism.* New Haven: Yale UP, 1970.

Havelock, Eric A. *Preface to Plato.* Cambridge: Belknap P of Harvard UP, 1963.

Harvey, David. *A Brief History of Neoliberalism.* Oxford: Oxford UP, 2005.

Hejinian, Lyn. "The Person and Description." *The Language of Inquiry.* Berkeley: U of California P, 2000. 199–208.

Horkheimer, Max, and Theodor W. Adorno. *The Dialectic of Enlightenment.* Trans. John Cumming. New York: Herder, 1972.

Howe, Susan. *Articulations of Sound Forms in Time. Singularities.* Middletown: Wesleyan UP, 1990. 1–38.

———. *A Bibliography of the King's Book, or, Eikon Basilike. The Nonconformist's Memorial.* New York: New Directions, 1993. 45–82.

———. *The Birth-mark: Unsettling the Wilderness in American History.* Middletown: Wesleyan UP, 1993.

———. *Cabbage Gardens. Frame Structures: Early Poems 1974–1979.* New York: New Directions, 1996. 57–72.

———. *Defenestration of Prague. The Europe of Trusts.* Los Angeles: Sun and Moon, 1990. 85–146.

———. *Hinge Picture. Frame Structures: Early Poems 1974–1979.* New York: New Directions, 1996. 31–56.

———. "An Interview with Susan Howe." Conducted by Lynn Keller. *Contemporary Literature* 36.1 (1995): 1–34.

———. *The Liberties. The Europe of Trusts.* Los Angeles: Sun and Moon, 1990. 147–217.

———. *Melville's Marginalia. The Nonconformist's Memorial.* New York: New Directions, 1993. 83–150.

———. *The Midnight.* New York: New Directions, 2003.

———. *My Emily Dickinson.* Berkeley: North Atlantic, 1985.

———. *The Nonconformist's Memorial.* New York: New Directions, 1993.

———. *Pierce-Arrow.* New York: New Directions, 1999.

———. *Pythagorean Silence. The Europe of Trusts.* Los Angeles: Sun and Moon, 1990. 15–84.

———. *Scattering as Behavior toward Risk. Singularities.* Middletown: Wesleyan UP, 1990. 61–70.

———. *Secret History of the Dividing Line. Frame Structures: Early Poems 1974–1979.* New York: New Directions, 1996. 87–121.

———. *Souls of the Labadie Tract.* New York: New Directions, 2007.

———. *Talisman* Interview with Edward Foster. *Talisman* 4 (Spring 1990). Rpt. in *The Birth-Mark.* Middletown: Wesleyan UP, 1993. 155–81.

———. *Thorow. Singularities.* Middletown: Wesleyan UP, 1990. 39–59.

———. "Where Should the Commander Be?" *Writing* 19 (1987): 3–20.

Hyland, John. "An Account of OlsonNow in Boston." OlsonNow Blog. Eds. Ammiel Alcalay and Michael Kelleher. 2006. Web. 30 June 2009.

Idel, Moshe. *Absorbing Perfections: Kabbalah and Interpretations.* New Haven: Yale UP, 2002.

Internet Encyclopedia of Philosophy. EIP. Web. 8 July 2007.

Jacobi, Jolande. *The Psychology of C. G. Jung.* Trans. Ralph Manheim. New Haven: Yale UP, 1968.

Johnson, Edward. *Wonder-Working Providence of Sion's Saviour in New-England (1654) and Good News from New England (1648)*. Delmar: Scholar's Facsimiles and Reprints, 1974.

Joris, Pierre. *Nomad Poetics*. Middletown: Wesleyan UP, 2003.

———. "Where Is Olson Now?" OlsonNow Blog. Eds. Ammiel Alcalay and Michael Kelleher. Web. 30 June 2009.

Joyce, James. "Araby." *The Dubliners*. Ed. Jeri Johnson. Oxford: Oxford UP, 2000. 19–24.

Jung, C. G. *Psychology and Alchemy*. 2nd ed. Bollingen Series, XX. *The Collected Works of C. G. Jung*. Vol. 12. Trans. R. F. C. Hull. Eds. Herbert Read et al. 1953. Rpt. 1968. Rpt. Princeton: Princeton UP, 1970.

Kant, Immanuel. *Critique of Judgement*. Trans. James Creed Meredith. Oxford: Oxford UP, 2007.

———. *Critique of Pure Reason*. Trans. and ed. Marcus Weigelt. London: Penguin, 2007.

Kantorowicz, Ernst. *The King's Two Bodies: A Study in Medieval Political Theology*. 1957. Rpt. Princeton: Princeton UP, 1981.

Kapur, Ratna. "Dark Times for Liberal Intellectual Thought." *Profession* (2006): 22–32.

Katz, Daniel. "Jack Spicer's *After Lorca:* Translation as Decomposition." *Textual Practice* 18.1 (2004): 83–103.

Kaufman, Robert. "Poetry's Ethics? Theodor W. Adorno and Robert Duncan on Aesthetic Illusion and Sociopolitical Delusion." *New German Critique* 97, 33.1 (2006): 73–118.

Keelan, Claudia. "Revising the Parade: In Question of Witness." *Denver Quarterly* 31.3 (1997): 82–87.

Keller, Lynn. "An Interview with Susan Howe." *Contemporary Literature* 36.1 (1995): 1–34.

Kenner, Hugh. "Robert Creeley's Continuum." *Robert Creeley's Life and Work*. Ed. John Wilson. Ann Arbor: U of Michigan P, 1987. 410–14.

Kern, Robert. "Composition as Recognition: Robert Creeley and Postmodern Poetics." *Robert Creeley: A Gathering*. Ed. William Spanos. *boundary 2* 6.3; 7.1 (1978): 211–30.

Kilroy, James. *James Clarence Mangan*. Lewisburg: Bucknell UP, 1970.

Kleinberg-Levin, David Michael. *Gestures of Ethical Life: Reading Hölderin's Question of Measure after Heidegger*. Stanford: Stanford UP, 2005.

Korzybski, Alfred. *General Semantics Seminar 1937: Olivet College Lectures*. 3rd ed. Ed. Homer J. Moore, Jr. New York: Institute of General Semantics, 2002.

Kristeva, Julia. "Thinking in Dark Times." *Profession* (2006): 13–21.

Lacan, Jacques. *Écrits*. Trans. Alan Sheridan. New York: Norton, 1977.

———. *Speech and Language in Psychoanalysis*. Trans. and ed. Anthony Wilden. 1968. Rpt. Baltimore: Johns Hopkins UP, 1981.

Lacey, Paul A. "The Vision of the Burning Babe: Southwell, Levertov, Duncan."

Robert Duncan and Denise Levertov: The Poetry of Politics, the Politics of Poetry. Eds. Albert Gelpi and Robert J. Bertholf. Stanford: Stanford UP, 2006. 161–79.

Lazer, Hank. *Lyric and Spirit: Selected Essays 1996–2008.* Richmond: Omnidawn, 2008.

———. *Opposing Poetries: Volume Two: Readings.* Evanston: Northwestern UP, 1996.

Leibniz, Gottfried Wilhelm. *The Monadology and Other Philosophical Essays.* Trans. Paul Schrecker and Anne Martin Schrecker. Indianpolis: Bobbs-Merrill, 1965.

———. *Philosophical Texts.* Trans. and ed. Richard Francks and R. S. Woolhouse. Oxford: Oxford UP, 1998.

Levertov, Denise. *To Stay Alive.* 1965. New York: New Directions, 1971.

Lévinas, Emmanuel. *Totality and Infinity: An Essay on Exteriority.* Trans. Alphonso Lingis. Pittsburgh: Duquesne UP, 1969.

Lévy, Bernard-Henri. *Barbarism with a Human Face.* Trans. George Holoch. New York: Harper, 1979.

Lewis, Wyndham, ed. *BLAST 1 (June 20, 1914).* London: John Lane, 1914. Toronto: Bell and Cockburn, 1914.

Lingis, Alphonso. *The Community of Those Who Have Nothing in Common.* Bloomington: Indiana UP, 1994.

Lloyd, David. *Nationalism and Minor Literature: James Clarence Mangan and the Emergence of Irish Cultural Nationalism.* Berkeley: U of California P, 1987.

Lyotard, Jean-François. *Libidinal Economy.* Trans. Iain Hamilton Grant. Bloomington: Indiana UP, 1993.

Ma, Ming-Quian. "Articulating the Inarticulate: Singularities and the Counter-Method in Susan Howe." *Contemporary Literature* 36.3 (1995): 466–89.

———. "Poetry as History Revised: Susan Howe's 'Scattering as Behavior toward Risk.'" *American Literary History* 6.4 (1994): 716–37.

MacAdams, Lewis. "With Lewis MacAdams." *Tales Out of School.* By Robert Creeley. Ann Arbor: U of Michigan P, 1993. 71–100.

Mackey, Nathaniel. *Paracritical Hinge: Essays, Talks, Notes, Interviews.* Madison: U of Wisconsin P, 2005.

———. "Uroboros: Dante and A Seventeenth Century Suite." *Scales of the Marvelous.* Eds. Robert J. Bertholf and Ian W. Reid. New York: New Directions, 1979. 181–97.

Maddocks, Fiona. "Birtwistle's Turning World." *Glyndebourne Touring Opera Programme.* Edenbridge: Westerham, 2000. 39–40.

Mallarmé, Stéphane. *Vers et prose.* Paris: Garnier-Flammarion, 1977.

Mangan, James Clarence. *Anthologia Germanica.* 2 vols. Dublin: Currey, 1845.

———. *Autobiography.* Ed. James Kilroy. Dublin: Dolmen, 1968.

———. *The Collected Works of James Clarence Mangan.* Ed. Jacques Chuto. Dublin: Irish Academic P, 2002.

———. "The Saw-Mill." *Poems.* New York: Rennie, Shea and Lindsay, 1859. 443–44.

Marinetti, Filippo T. *Critical Writings.* Trans. Doug Thompson. Ed. Günter Berghaus. New York: Farrar, 2006.

Marsh, Nicky. "'Out of My Texts I Am Not What I Play': Politics and Self in the Poetry of Susan Howe." *College Literature* 24.3 (1997): 124–37. *BNET Arts Publications.* Web. 10 July 2006.

Materer, Timothy. "Robert Duncan and the Mercurial Self." *Sagetrieb* 9.1–2 (1990): 7–24.

Matthiessen, F.O. *American Renaissance: Art and Expression in the Age of Emerson and Whitman.* London: Oxford UP, 1941.

Maud, Ralph. *Charles Olson at the Harbour: A Biography by Ralph Maud.* Vancouver: Talonbooks, 2007.

———. *Charles Olson's Reading: A Biography.* Carbondale: Southern Illinois UP, 1996.

———, ed. *Minutes of the Charles Olson Society.* Vancouver.

———, ed. *Selected Letters: Charles Olson.* Berkeley: U of California P, 2000.

———. *What Does Not Change.* Madison: Fairleigh Dickinson UP, 1997.

Maud, Ralph and Sharon Thesen, eds. *Charles Olson and Frances Boldereff: A Modern Correspondence.* Middletown: Wesleyan UP, 1999.

McCaffery, Steve. "Blaser's Deleuzean Folds." *The Recovery of the Public World.* Eds. Charles Watts and Edward Byrne. Vancouver: Talonbooks, 1999. 373–92.

McGuire, Jerry. "No Boundaries: Robert Creeley as Post-Modern Man." *Sagetrieb* 1.3 (1982): 97–118.

McIntyre, Wendy. "The Logos of Robert Duncan." *Maps* 6 (1974): 81–97.

———. "Psyche, Christ, and the Poem." *Ironwood* 22 (1983): 9–22.

Meachem, Clive. "Creeley's Company." *Sagetrieb* 18.1 (1999): 131–48.

Meehan, C.P. [Untitled autobiographical fragment on James Clarence Mangan]. *The Poets and Poetry of Munster: A Selection of Irish Songs by the Poets of the Eighteenth Century.* Introduced by John P. Dalton. Dublin: J. Duffy, 1925

Melville, Herman. *Moby-Dick.* Introduction by Edward Said. New York: Vintage, 1991.

———. *Selected Tales and Poems.* Ed. Richard Chase. New York: Holt, 1950.

Meredith, George. *Modern Love and Poems of the English Roadside, with Poems and Ballads.* London: Chapman and Hall, 1862.

Merleau-Ponty, Maurice. *The Primacy of Perception and Other Essays on Phenomenological Psychology, the Philosophy of Art, History, and Politics.* Ed. James M. Edie. Evanston: Northwestern UP, 1964.

———. *Signs.* Trans. Richard C. McCleary. Evanston: Northwestern UP, 1964.

———. *The Visible and the Invisible.* Ed. Claude Lefort. Trans. Alphonso Lingis. Evanston: Northwestern UP, 1968.

Merton, Thomas. *The Behavior of Titans.* New York: New Directions, 1961.

Mesch, Harold. "Robert Creeley's Epistemopathic Path." *Sagetrieb* 1.3 (1982): 57–85.

Michelson, Peter. "A Materialist Critique of Robert Duncan's Grand Collage." *boundary 2* 8.2 (1980): 21–44.

Middleton, Peter. "An Elegy for Theory: Robin Blaser's Essay 'The Practice of Outside.'" *Even on Sunday: Essays, Readings, and Archival Materials on the Poetry and Poetics of Robin Blaser.* Orono: National Poetry Foundation, 2002. 179–206.

Miller, Brett. "Chelsea 8: Political Poetry at Midcentury." *Robert Duncan and Denise*

Levertov: The Poetry of Politics, the Politics of Poetry. Eds. Albert Gelpi and Robert J. Bertholf. Stanford: Stanford UP, 2006. 93–108.

Miller, Perry. *Errand into the Wilderness.* 1956. Rpt. Cambridge: Belknap P of Harvard UP, 1964.

Mitchel, John. "James Clarence Mangan: His Life, Poetry, and Death." *Poems.* By James Clarence Mangan. Ed. John Mitchel. New York: Haverty, 1894. 7–31.

Montgomery, Will. " 'Lyric for Crossing Over': Time and Telepathy in Susan Howe's *Melville's Marginalia.*" *Paragraph* 27.3 (2004): 32–48.

Moore, Thomas. *Lalla Rookh: An Oriental Romance.* 6th ed. London: Printed for Lonman, Hurst, Rees, Orme and Brown, 1817.

Moramarco, Fred. "Pieces of a Mirror: Robert Creeley's Later Poetry." *Robert Creeley's Life and Work.* Ed. John Wilson. Ann Arbor: U of Michigan P, 1987. 335–44.

More, Thomas, Sir. *Utopia.* Trans. Clarence H. Miller. New Haven: Yale UP, 2001.

Mossin, Andrew. "In the Shadow of Nerval: Robert Duncan, Robin Blaser, and the Poetics of (Mis)Translation." *Contemporary Literature* 38.4 (1997): 671–704.

Nancy, Jean-Luc. *The Inoperative Community.* Trans. Peter Connor, Lisa Garbus, Michael Holland, and Simona Sawhney. Ed. Peter Connor. 1991. Theory and History of Literature, Vol. 76. Minneapolis: U of Minnesota P, 2001.

Nash, John. *The Essential John Nash.* Eds. Harold W. Kuhn and Sylvia Nasar. Princeton: Princeton UP, 2002.

Nerval, Gérard de. *Les chimères. Oeuvres.* Tome 1. Édition de H. Lemaitre. Paris: Garnier Frères, 1966. 693–709.

Neumann, Eric. *The Great Mother.* Trans. Ralph Manheim. Bollingen Series XLVII. 1963. Rpt. Princeton: Princeton UP, 1991.

Neumann, John von, and Oskar Morgenstern. *Theory of Games and Economic Behavior.* Princeton: Princeton UP, 1953.

Nichol, bp. *The Martyrology.* Toronto: Coach House, 1972.

Nicholls, Peter. " 'The Pastness of Landscape': Susan Howe's Pierce-Arrow." *Contemporary Literature* 43.3 (2002): 441–60.

———. "Unsettling the Wilderness: Susan Howe and American History." *Contemporary Literature* 37.4 (1996): 586–601.

Nichols, Miriam, ed. *Even on Sunday: Essays, Readings, and Archival Materials on the Poetry and Poetics of Robin Blaser.* Orono: National Poetry Foundation, 2002.

———. "Introduction: Reading Robin Blaser." *Even on Sunday: Essays, Readings, and Archival Materials on the Poetry and Poetics of Robin Blaser.* Orono: National Poetry Foundation, 2002. 25–77.

Nietzsche, Friedrich. *The Birth of Tragedy and the Genealogy of Morals.* Trans. Francis Golffing. New York: Anchor/Doubleday, 1956.

Nussbaum, Martha. *Upheavals of Thought: The Intelligence of Emotions.* Cambridge: Cambridge UP, 2001.

O'Donoghue, D. J. *The Life and Writings of James Clarence Mangan.* Edinburgh: Geddes; Chicago: Fitzpatrick, 1897.

———. "Preface." *Poems of James Clarence Mangan.* Dublin: O'Donoghue, 1903. xi–xxvi.

———. *The Prose Writings of James Clarence Mangan, 1803–1849.* New York: AMS Press, 1978.

O'Leary, Peter. "Prophetic Frustrations: Robert Duncan's Tribunals." *Robert Duncan and Denise Levertov: The Poetry of Politics, the Politics of Poetry.* Eds. Albert Gelpi and Robert J. Bertholf. Stanford: Stanford UP, 2006. 126–47.

Olson, Charles. *Call Me Ishmael.* San Francisco: City Lights, 1947.

———. *Causal Mythology.* San Francisco: Four Seasons, 1969.

———. *Charles Olson and Ezra Pound: An Encounter at St. Elizabeths.* Ed. Catherine Seelye. New York: Grossman, 1975; New York: Paragon House, 1991.

———. *Charles Olson and Frances Boldereff: A Modern Correspondence.* Ed. Ralph Maud and Sharon Thesen. Middletown: Wesleyan UP, 1999.

———. *The Collected Poems of Charles Olson, Excluding the Maximus Poems.* Ed. George Butterick. Berkeley, U of California P, 1987.

———. *Collected Prose.* Eds. Donald Allen and Benjamin Friedlander. Berkeley: U of California P, 1997.

———. "Enniscorthy—June 1946–September 1946." Box 49. Charles Olson Research Collection. Archives and Special Collections at the Thomas J. Dodd Research Center, University of Connecticut Libraries.

———. *The Mayan Letters.* Ed. Robert Creeley. London: Jonathan Cape, 1968.

———. *The Maximus Poems.* Ed. George Butterick. Berkeley: U of California P, 1983.

———. *Muthologos: The Collected Lectures and Interviews.* Vols. I and II. Ed. George Butterick. Bolinas: Four Seasons, 1978.

———. "Poetry and Truth." *Muthologos,* Vol. II. Ed. George Butterick. Bolinas: Four Seasons, 1978. 7–54.

———. *Selected Letters.* Ed. Ralph Maud. Berkeley: U of California P, 2000.

———. *The Special View of History.* Ed. Ann Charters. Berkeley: Oyez, 1970.

Ondaatje, Michael. "Introduction to Robin Blaser's 'Hello!'" *Recovery of the Public World.* Eds. Charles Watts and Edward Byrne. Vancouver: Talonbooks, 1999. 454.

Oppen, George. "The Mind's Own Place." *Selected Poems.* Ed. Robert Creeley. New York: New Directions, 2003. 173–82.

Otto, Rudolf. *The Idea of the Holy.* 2nd ed. Trans. John W. Harvey. 1950. London: Oxford UP, 1957.

Ovid. *Metamorphosis.* Trans. David Raeburn. London, New York, Toronto: Penguin, 2004.

Oxford Annotated Bible. Ed. Herbert G. May and Grace M. Metzger. New York: Oxford UP, 1962.

Paine, Thomas. *The Rights of Man.* 1915. London: Dent, 1969.

Paul, Sherman. *Olson's Push: Origin, Black Mountain, and Recent American Poetry.* Baton Rouge: Louisiana State UP, 1978.

Paz, Octavio. *The Bow and the Lyre.* Trans. Ruth L. C. Simms. Austin: U of Texas P, 1973.

———. *Marcel Duchamp: Appearance Stripped Bare.* Trans. Rachel Phillips and Donald Gardner. New York: Viking, 1978.

Peacock, Thomas Love. *The Four Ages of Poetry. The Four Ages of Poetry, Shelley's Defense of Poetry, Browning's Essay on Shelley.* Ed. H. F. B. Brett-Smith. Boston: Houghton, 1921. 1–19.

Pearce, Roy Harvey. *The Continuity of American Poetry.* Princeton: Princeton UP, 1961.

Peirce, Charles Sanders. *The Essential Peirce: Selected Philosophical Writings.* Vol. 1 (1867–1893). Eds. Nathan House and Christian Kloesel. Bloomington: Indiana UP, 1992.

Perloff, Marjorie. "'Collision or Collusion with History': The Narrative Lyric of Susan Howe." *Contemporary Literature* 30.4 (1989): 518–33.

———. "Language Poetry and the Lyric Subject: Ron Silliman's Albany, Susan Howe's Buffalo." *Critical Inquiry* 25 (Spring 1999): 405–34.

———. "Poetry, Politics, and the 'Other Conscience': Robert Duncan's Letters to Denise Levertov." *PN Review* 112, 23.2 (1966): 33–38.

Peters, Robert. "The House That Jack Built Has an Atwater Kent in the Living Room or Jack Spicer's Romanticism Didn't Come Easy." *Manroot* 10 (Fall 1974–Winter 1975): 181–91.

Pico della Mirandola, Giovanni. *On the Dignity of Man.* Trans. Charles Glenn Wallis. Indianapolis: Bobbs-Merrill, 1965.

Plato. *The Ion.* Trans. Paul Woodruff. *Plato: Complete Works.* Ed. John M. Cooper. Indianapolis: Hackett, 1997. 937–49.

———. *The Republic.* Trans. G. M. A. Grube, rev. C. D. C. Reeve. *Plato: Complete Works.* Ed. John M. Cooper. Indianapolis: Hackett, 1997. 971–1223.

———. *The Symposium.* Trans. Walter Hamilton. 1951. Rpt. Harmondsworth: Penguin, 1983.

Poirier, Richard. *Poetry and Pragmatism.* Cambridge: Harvard UP, 1992.

Pound, Ezra. *The Cantos of Ezra Pound.* 1970. Rpt. New York: New Directions, 1996.

Pritts, Nate. "Towards a Theory of Time in Olson." *Jacket* 35 (2008). *Jacket.* Web. 16 January 2009.

Quartermain, Peter. "And the Without: An Interpretive Essay on Susan Howe." *Difficulties* 3.2 (1989): 71–83. Rpt. in *Disjunctive Poetics: From Gertrude Stein and Louis Zukofsky to Susan Howe.* New York: Cambridge UP, 1992. 182–94.

———. "Robert Creeley: What Counts." *Robert Creeley: A Gathering.* Ed. William Spanos. *boundary 2* 6.3; 7.1 (1978): 329–334.

Rasula, Jed. "Spicer's Orpheus and the Emancipation of the Pronouns." *boundary 2* 6.1 (1977): 51–102.

Reid, Ian. "The Plural Text: 'Passages.'" *Scales of the Marvelous.* Eds. Robert J. Bertholf and Ian W. Reid. New York: New Directions, 1979. 161–80.

Rich, Adrienne. *Of Woman Born: Motherhood as Experience and Institution.* New York: Norton, 1986.

Richards, I. A. *Basic English and Its Uses.* New York: Norton, 1943.

Rifkin, Libbie. *Career Moves: Olson, Creeley, Zukofsky, Berrigan, and the American Avant-Garde.* Madison: U of Wisconsin P, 2000.

Riley, Peter. "The Narratives of The Holy Grail." *boundary 2* 6.1 (1977): 163–90.

Rimbaud, Arthur. *Oeuvres complètes.* Ed. Louis Forestier. Paris: Laffont, 2004.

Ross, Andrew. *The Failure of Modernism: Symptoms of American Poetry.* New York: Columbia UP, 1986.

Rowlandson, Mary White. *Soveraignty* [*sic*] *and Goodness of God: A Narative* [*sic*] *of the Captivity, Sufferings, and Removes of Mrs. Mary Rowlandson.* Boston: Printed and sold by Nathaniel Coverly in Black-Horse Lane: North-End. 1770.

Ryder, Sean. *James Clarence Mangan: Selected Writings.* Dublin: University College Dublin P, 2004.

Said, Edward. *The World, the Text, and the Critic.* Cambridge: Harvard UP, 1983.

Sauer, Carl O. *The Morphology of Landscape.* 1925. Rpt. Berkeley: U of California P, 1938.

Scholem, Gershom. *Kabbalah.* Jerusalem: Keter, 1974. Rpt. New York: New American Library, 1978.

———. *On the Kabbalah and Its Symbolism.* Trans. Ralph Manheim. New York: Schocken, 1965.

———, ed. *Zohar: The Book of Splendor.* 1963. Rpt. New York: Schocken, 1983.

Sedgwick, Eve Kosofsky. *Touching Feeling: Affect, Pedagogy, Performativity.* Durham: Duke UP, 2003.

Shakespeare, William. *A Midsummer Night's Dream. The Riverside Shakespeare.* Ed. G. Blakemore Evans. Boston: Houghton, 1974. 222–49.

Shannon-Mangan, Ellen. *James Clarence Mangan: A Biography.* Dublin: Irish Academic P, 1996.

Shelley, Percy Bysshe. "The Triumph of Life." *Poetical Works.* Ed. Thomas Hutchinson. 1905. London: Oxford UP, 1948. 507–20.

Sherburne, Donald, ed. *A Key to Whitehead's Process and Reality.* New York: Macmillan, 1966.

Shurin, Aaron. "The People's P**K: A Dialectical Tale." *Robert Duncan and Denise Levertov: The Poetry of Politics, the Politics of Poetry.* Eds. Albert Gelpi and Robert J. Bertholf. Stanford: Stanford UP, 2006. 71–80.

Silliman, Ron. "Language, Realism, Poetry." *In the American Tree.* Ed. Ron Silliman. 1986. Rpt. Orono: National Poetry Foundation, 2002. xvii–xxiii.

———. "My Vocabulary Did This to Me." *Acts* 6 (1987): 67–71.

Skinner, Jonathan. "Charles Olson and the Question of Boundaries: The Poet-Scholar." OlsonNow Blog. Eds. Ammiel Alcalay and Michael Kelleher. Web. 16 March 2007.

Snediker, Michael. *Queer Optimism: Lyric Personhood and Other Felicitous Persuasions.* Minneapolis: U of Minnesota P, 2009.

Southwell, Robert. "The Burning Babe." *The Poems of Robert Southwell.* Eds. James H. McDonald and Nancy Pollard Brown. London: Oxford UP, 1967. 15–16.

Spanos, William W. "Charles Olson and Negative Capability: A Phenomenological Interpretation." *Contemporary Literature* 21.1 (1980): 38–80.

———. "Jack Spicer's Poetry of Absence: An Introduction." *boundary 2* 6.1 (1977): 1–2.

———. "With Bill Spanos." *Tales Out of School: Selected Interviews.* By Robert Creeley. Ann Arbor: U of Michigan P, 1993. 122–92.

Spicer, Jack. *The Collected Books of Jack Spicer.* Ed. Robin Blaser. 1975. Rpt. Los Angeles: Black Sparrow, 1980.

———. *The House That Jack Built: The Collected Lectures of Jack Spicer.* Ed. Peter Gizzi. Hanover: UP of New England, 1998.

———. *My Vocabulary Did This to Me: The Collected Poetry of Jack Spicer.* Eds. Peter Gizzi and Kevin Killian. Middletown: Wesleyan UP, 2008.

———. *One Night Stand and Other Poems.* Ed. Donald Allen. San Francisco: Grey Fox, 1980.

———. *The Tower of Babel.* Ed. Lew Ellingham and Kevin Killian. Hoboken: Talisman House, 1994.

Spinoza, Baruch. *Ethics.* Ed. and trans. G. H. R. Parkinson. Oxford: Oxford UP, 2000.

Stein, Charles. *The Secret of the Black Chrysanthemum.* 1979. Rpt. Barrytown: Station Hill, 1987.

Stein, Gertrude. "Portraits and Repetition." *Look at Me Now and Here I Am: Writings and Lectures 1909–45.* Ed. Patricia Meyerowitz. N.P: Peter Owen, 1967. Rpt. Harmondsworth: Penguin, 1971.

———. *Tender Buttons: Objects, Food, Rooms.* New York: Claire Marie, 1914. Rpt. Los Angeles: Sun and Moon, 1990.

Stevens, Wallace. *Collected Poetry and Prose.* New York: Library of America, 1997.

Stravinsky, Igor. *Poetics of Music.* Trans. Arthur Knodel and Ingolf Dahl. 1942. Rpt. Cambridge: Harvard UP, 1977.

Stuart, Colin, and John Scoggan. "The Orientation of the Parasols: Saussure, Derrida, and Spicer." *boundary 2* 6.1 (1977): 191–257.

Swinburne, Algernon. *Tristram of Lyonesse. Major Poems and Selected Prose.* Eds. Jerome McGann and Charles L. Sligh. New Haven: Yale UP, 2004. 206–312.

———. "The Triumph of Time." *Major Poems and Selected Prose.* Ed. Jerome McGann and Charles L. Sligh. New Haven: Yale UP, 2004. 82–91.

Taggart, John. "Play and Poetry of Susan Howe." *Songs of Degrees: Essays on Contemporary Poetry and Poetics.* Tuscaloosa: U of Alabama P, 1994. 114–22.

Tallman, Ellen. "My Stories with Robert Duncan." *Robert Duncan and Denise Levertov: The Poetry of Politics, the Politics of Poetry.* Eds. Albert Gelpi and Robert J. Bertholf. Stanford: Stanford UP, 2006. 63–70.

Tallman, Warren. *Three Essays on Creeley.* Toronto: Coach House, 1973.

Teresa of Avila, Saint. *The Interior Castle, or, The Mansions.* 4th ed. Trans. from the Autograph of Saint Teresa of Jesus by a Benedictine of Stanbrook. Rev. and annotated by the Very Rev. Prior Zimmerman, O.C.D. London: Thomas Baker, 1930.

Thiong'o, Ngugi Wa. "For Peace, Justice, and Culture: The Intellectual in the Twenty-First Century." *Profession* (2006): 33–39.

Thompson, John. "From 'An Alphabet of Poets.'" *Robert Creeley's Life and Work: A Sense of Increment.* Ed. John Wilson. Ann Arbor: U of Michigan P, 1987. 153–56.

Vanderborg, Susan. *Paratextual Communities: American Avant-Garde Poetry since 1950*. Carbondale: Southern Illinois UP, 2001.

Veblen, Thorstein. *The Theory of the Leisure Class*. Intro. C. Wright Mills. New Brunswick: Transaction, 1992.

Vickery, Ann. "The Quiet Rupture: Susan Howe's *The Liberties* and the Feminine Marginalia of Literary History." *Southerly: A Review of Australian Literature* 57.1 (1997): 91–102.

Von Hallberg, Robert. *Charles Olson: The Scholar's Art*. Cambridge: Harvard UP, 1978.

Wagner, Linda. "Creeley's Late Poems: Contexts." *Robert Creeley's Life and Work*. Ed. John Wilson. Ann Arbor: U of Michigan P, 1987. 310–20.

———. "With Linda Wagner." *Tales Out of School: Selected Interviews*. By Robert Creeley. Ann Arbor: U of Michigan P, 1993. 22–70.

Waite, Arthur Edgar. *The Pictorial Key to the Tarot*. New York: Harper, 1971.

Waldman, Anne. "Feminafesto: Olson." OlsonNow Blog. Eds. Ammiel Alcalay and Michael Kelleher. Web. 1 July 2009.

Walker, Jayne. L. "Exercises in Disorder: Duncan's Imitations of Gertrude Stein." *Scales of the Marvelous*. Eds. Robert J. Bertholf and Ian W. Reid. New York: New Directions, 1979.

Watten, Barrett. "Late Capitalism and Language Writing." Conference presentation. Poetry of the 70s. Orono, Maine, University of Orono, 13 June 2008.

———. "Radical Particularity, Critical Regionalism, and the Resistance to Globalization." *Barrett Watten Home Page, Department of English, Wayne State University*. Web. 18 June 2008.

———. "The Turn to Language and the 1960s." *Critical Inquiry* 29.2 (2002): 139–83.

Watts, Charles, and Edward Byrne, eds. *The Recovery of the Public World*. Vancouver: Talonbooks, 1999.

Weston, Jesse. *From Ritual to Romance*. Cambridge: Cambridge UP, 1920.

Whitehead, Alfred North. *Process and Reality*. New York: Macmillan, 1929.

Whiteley, Opal. *The Story of Opal: The Journal of an Understanding Heart*. Boston: Atlantic Monthly P, 1920.

Whitman, Walt. *Whitman: Selected by Robert Creeley*. Harmondsworth: Penguin, 1973.

Wiener, Norbert. *Cybernetics: Or, Control and Communication in the Animal and the Machine*. Cambridge: Technology P, 1948.

Wilden, Anthony. "Lacan and the Discourse of the Other." *Speech and Language in Psychoanalysis*. By Jacques Lacan. Trans. Anthony Wilden. 1968. Rpt. Baltimore: Johns Hopkins UP, 1981. 159–311.

Williams, Megan. "Howe Not to Erase(her) [*sic*]: A Poetics of Posterity in Howe's *Melville's Marginalia*." *Contemporary Literature* 38.1 (1997): 106–32.

Williams, Roger. *A Key into the Language of America*. London: Gregory Dexter, 1643.

Williams, Rowan, Archbishop. *Teresa of Avila*. 1991. London: Continuum, 2002.

Wilson, John, ed. *Robert Creeley's Life and Work: A Sense of Increment*. Ann Arbor: U of Michigan P, 1987.

Wind, Edgar. *Pagan Mysteries in the Renaissance.* Rev. ed. New York: Norton, 1968.

Winthrop, John. *Journal: "History of New England": 1630–1649.* 2 vols. Ed. James Kendall Hosmer, LL.D. New York: Scribner's, 1908.

———. "A Modell of Christian Charity." Excerpted in *Life and Letters of John Winthrop.* By Robert C. Winthrop. Boston: Ticknor and Fields, 1867. 18–20.

———. *Winthrop Papers.* 5 vols. Boston: Massachusetts Historical Society, 1929–47.

Wollheim, Richard. *On the Emotions.* New Haven: Yale UP, 1999.

Žižek, Slavoj. *Organs without Bodies.* London: Routledge, 2004.

———. *The Sublime Object of Ideology.* New York: Verso, 1989.

Index